T0226194

IFIP Advances in Information and Communication Technology 484

Editor-in-Chief

IFIP – The International Federation for Information Processing

IFIP was founded in 1960 under the auspices of UNESCO, following the first World Computer Congress held in Paris the previous year. A federation for societies working in information processing, IFIP's aim is two-fold: to support information processing in the countries of its members and to encourage technology transfer to developing nations. As its mission statement clearly states:

IFIP is the global non-profit federation of societies of ICT professionals that aims at achieving a worldwide professional and socially responsible development and application of information and communication technologies.

IFIP is a non-profit-making organization, run almost solely by 2500 volunteers. It operates through a number of technical committees and working groups, which organize events and publications. IFIP's events range from large international open conferences to working conferences and local seminars.

The flagship event is the IFIP World Computer Congress, at which both invited and contributed papers are presented. Contributed papers are rigorously refereed and the rejection rate is high.

As with the Congress, participation in the open conferences is open to all and papers may be invited or submitted. Again, submitted papers are stringently refereed.

The working conferences are structured differently. They are usually run by a working group and attendance is generally smaller and occasionally by invitation only. Their purpose is to create an atmosphere conducive to innovation and development. Refereeing is also rigorous and papers are subjected to extensive group discussion.

Publications arising from IFIP events vary. The papers presented at the IFIP World Computer Congress and at open conferences are published as conference proceedings, while the results of the working conferences are often published as collections of selected and edited papers.

IFIP distinguishes three types of institutional membership: Country Representative Members, Members at Large, and Associate Members. The type of organization that can apply for membership is a wide variety and includes national or international societies of individual computer scientists/ICT professionals, associations or federations of such societies, government institutions/government related organizations, national or international research institutes or consortia, universities, academies of sciences, companies, national or international associations or federations of companies.

More information about this series at http://www.springer.com/series/6102

Gilbert Peterson · Sujeet Shenoi (Eds.)

Advances in Digital Forensics XII

12th IFIP WG 11.9 International Conference,
New Delhi, January 4–6, 2016
Revised Selected Papers

 Springer

Editors
Gilbert Peterson
Department of Electrical and Computer
  Engineering
Air Force Institute of Technology
Wright-Patterson AFB, Ohio
USA

Sujeet Shenoi
Tandy School of Computer Science
University of Tulsa
Tulsa, Oklahoma
USA

ISSN 1868-4238   ISSN 1868-422X (electronic)
IFIP Advances in Information and Communication Technology
ISBN 978-3-319-83483-2   ISBN 978-3-319-46279-0 (eBook)
DOI 10.1007/978-3-319-46279-0

Printed on acid-free paper

This Springer imprint is published by Springer Nature
The registered company is Springer International Publishing AG Switzerland

Contents

PART VI   IMAGE FORENSICS

PART VII   FORENSIC TECHNIQUES

PART VIII   FORENSIC TOOLS

Contributing Authors

Oluwapelumi Aboluwarin is a Software Engineer with Nexmo, London, United Kingdom. His research interests include natural language processing, text mining and conversational user interfaces.

Sudhir Aggarwal is a Professor of Computer Science at Florida State University, Tallahassee, Florida. His research interests include password cracking, information security and building software tools and systems for digital forensics.

Irfan Ahmed is an Assistant Professor of Computer Science at the University of New Orleans, New Orleans, Louisiana. His research interests are in the areas of malware detection and analysis, digital forensics, industrial control systems security and Internet of Things security.

Ahmed Almarzooqi is a Ph.D. student in Digital Forensics at De Montfort University, Leicester, United Kingdom. His research interests include digital forensics and information security.

Panagiotis Andriotis is a Research Associate in the Information Security Research Group, Department of Computer Science, University College London, London, United Kingdom. His research interests include digital forensics, text mining, content analysis, systems security and human aspects of security, privacy and trust.

Sara Baghbanzadeh is a Software Engineer with Gnowit, Ottawa, Canada. Her research interests include web crawling and session reconstruction for rich Internet applications.

Andres Barreto is a Software Developer for Archon Information Systems, New Orleans, Louisiana. His research interests include digital forensics and building scalable and usable web applications.

Nicole Beebe is an Associate Professor of Cyber Security at the University of Texas at San Antonio, San Antonio, Texas. Her research interests include digital forensics, cyber security and advanced analytics.

Gregor Bochmann is a Professor of Computer Science at the University of Ottawa, Ottawa, Canada. His research interests include software engineering for distributed applications, peer-to-peer systems and rich Internet applications.

Mikhaila Burgess is an Associate Professor of Digital Forensics at Noroff University College, Kristiansand, Norway. Her research interests include digital forensics, information security, data management and big data.

Raymond Chan is a Ph.D. student in Computer Science at the University of Hong Kong, Hong Kong, China. His research interests include digital forensics and critical infrastructure protection.

Vivien Chan is a Research Project Manager at the University of Hong Kong, Hong Kong, China. Her research interests include cyber criminal profiling and digital forensics.

Kam-Pui Chow is an Associate Professor of Computer Science at the University of Hong Kong, Hong Kong, China. His research interests include information security, digital forensics, live system forensics and digital surveillance.

Swasti Bhushan Deb is a Senior Project Manager at the Kolkata Cyber Laboratory, Data Security Council of India, Kolkata, India. His research interests include cyber crime detection, and computer and mobile device forensics.

Muhammad Faheem is a Post-Doctoral Researcher in the Department of Computer Science at the University of Ottawa, Ottawa, Canada. His research interests include information retrieval, web archiving, knowledge representation logics and rich Internet applications.

Jayaprakash Govindaraj is a Senior Technology Architect at Infosys, Bangalore, India; and a Ph.D. student in Computer Science and Engineering at Indraprastha Institute of Information Technology, New Delhi, India. His research interests include mobile device security, digital forensics, web application security, Internet of Things security and security in emerging technologies.

Gaurav Gupta is a Scientist D in the Department of Electronics and Information Technology, Ministry of Information Technology, New Delhi, India. His research interests include digitized document fraud detection, mobile device forensics and cloud forensics.

Salman Hooshmand is a Ph.D. candidate in Computer Science at the University of Ottawa, Ottawa, Canada. His research interests include software engineering and rich Internet applications modeling and testing.

Andrew Jones is a Professor of Cyber Security and Digital Forensics and Director of the Cyber Security Centre at the University of Hertfordshire, Hatfield, United Kingdom. His research interests include digital forensics, information security and risk management.

Guy-Vincent Jourdan is a Professor of Computer Science at the University of Ottawa, Ottawa, Canada. His research interests include distributed systems modeling and analysis, formal system testing, rich Internet applications and software security.

Umit Karabiyik is an Assistant Professor of Computer Science at Sam Houston State University, Huntsville, Texas. His research interests include digital forensics, cyber security, computer and network security, and expert systems.

Rajesh Kumar is an Assistant Professor of Forensic Science at the Institute of Forensic Science, Aurangabad, India. His research interests include computational forensics, multimedia forensics, image processing and pattern recognition.

Michael Kwan is an Honorary Associate Professor of Computer Science at the University of Hong Kong, Hong Kong, China. His research interests include digital forensics and cyber investigations.

Changwei Liu is a Researcher in the Department of Computer Science at George Mason University, Fairfax, Virginia. Her research interests include cyber security and network forensics.

Huiming Liu is an M.S. student in Computer Science at Tsinghua University, Beijing, China. His research interests include network and mobile device security.

Lishu Liu is a Machine Learning Engineer at RetailMeNot, Austin, Texas. Her research interests involve the application of machine learning algorithms to locate, extract and present relevant information from massive data sets.

Wei Liu is an M.S. student in Computer Science at Tsinghua University, Beijing, China. His research interests include network and mobile device security.

Seyed Mirtaheri is a Research Assistant in the Department of Computer Science at the University of Ottawa, Ottawa, Canada. His research interests include parallel processing, distributed systems, web crawling and rich Internet applications.

Martin Olivier is a Professor of Computer Science at the University of Pretoria, Pretoria, South Africa. His research focuses on digital forensics – in particular the science of digital forensics and database forensics.

Iosif Viorel Onut is a Principal R&D Strategist at the Center for Advanced Studies, IBM Canada Lab, Ottawa, Canada; and an Adjunct Professor of Computer Science at the University of Ottawa, Ottawa, Canada. His research interests include software security, rich Internet applications and information security.

Sriram Raghavan is a Forensic Data Scientist with Telstra in Melbourne, Australia; and a Visitor in the Department of Computing at the University of Melbourne, Melbourne, Australia. His research interests include the development of quantitative metrics for cyber security and the mathematical foundations of security incident analysis.

S.V. Raghavan is the Chief Architect of India's National Knowledge Network in New Delhi, India; and a retired Professor of Computer Science and Engineering at the Indian Institute of Technology Madras, Chennai, India. His research interests include the design of scalable, large-scale secure networks.

Huw Read is an Associate Professor of Digital Forensics and Director of the Center for Advanced Computing and Digital Forensics at Norwich University, Northfield, Vermont. His research interests include digital forensics and computer security.

Vassil Roussev is a Professor of Computer Science at the University of New Orleans, New Orleans, Louisiana. His research interests include digital forensics, cyber security, distributed systems and human-computer interaction.

Ravi Saharan is an Assistant Professor of Computer Science and Engineering at the Central University of Rajasthan, Ajmer, India. His research interests include algorithms, computer graphics, image processing and steganography.

Bhupendra Singh is a Ph.D. student in Computer Science and Engineering at the Defence Institute of Advanced Technology, Pune, India. His research interests include digital forensics, file system analysis and user activity analysis on Windows systems.

Anoop Singhal is a Senior Computer Scientist in the Computer Security Division at the National Institute of Standards and Technology, Gaithersburg, Maryland. His research interests include network security, network forensics, web services security and data mining systems.

Gaurav Somani is an Assistant Professor of Computer Science and Engineering at the Central University of Rajasthan, Ajmer, India. His research interests include distributed systems, computer networks, cloud computing and digital forensics.

Minghe Sun is a Professor of Management Science and Statistics at the University of Texas at San Antonio, San Antonio, Texas. His research interests include mathematical programming and related areas for classification and solving hard optimization problems.

Iain Sutherland is a Professor of Digital Forensics at Noroff University College, Kristiansand, Norway. His research interests include digital forensics and data recovery.

Atsuhiro Takasu is a Professor in the Digital Content and Media Services Research Division at the National Institute of Informatics, Tokyo, Japan. His research interests include symbol sequence and time series analysis based on statistical models and their application to information integration.

Songpon Teerakanok is an M.S. student in Information Science and Engineering at Ritsumeikan University, Shiga, Japan. His research interests include cryptography, location-based services, privacy and digital forensics.

Elizabeth Thomas is a Consultant at Coalfire Systems, Manchester, United Kingdom. Her research interests include digital forensics and payment card systems.

Theo Tryfonas is a Senior Lecturer in Systems Engineering at the University of Bristol, Bristol, United Kingdom. His research interests are in the areas of smart cities, cyber security, systems engineering and technologies for sustainable development.

Tetsutaro Uehara is a Professor of Information Science and Engineering at Ritsumeikan University, Shiga, Japan. His research interests include digital forensics, cyber security and information system management.

Robin Verma is a Ph.D. student in Computer Science and Engineering at Indraprastha Institute of Information Technology, New Delhi, India. His research interests include digital forensics, privacy-enhancing technologies and mobile device forensics.

Duminda Wijesekera is a Professor of Computer Science at George Mason University, Fairfax, Virginia. His research interests include systems security, digital forensics and transportation systems.

Konstantinos Xynos is the Computer Security Course Leader at the University of South Wales, Pontypridd, United Kingdom. His research interests include computer security, computer forensics, network security and reverse engineering.

Haiyu Yang is an M.S. student in Thermal Engineering and a visiting graduate student in the Network and Information Security Laboratory at Tsinghua University, Beijing, China. His research interests include mobile device forensics and systems security.

Jianwei Zhuge is an Associate Professor of Computer Science in the Institute for Network Science and Cyberspace at Tsinghua University, Beijing, China. His research interests include Internet threat detection, malware analysis, and software vulnerability analysis and mitigation.

Preface

Digital forensics deals with the acquisition, preservation, examination, analysis and presentation of electronic evidence. Networked computing, wireless communications and portable electronic devices have expanded the role of digital forensics beyond traditional computer crime investigations. Practically every type of crime now involves some aspect of digital evidence; digital forensics provides the techniques and tools to articulate this evidence in legal proceedings. Digital forensics also has myriad intelligence applications; furthermore, it has a vital role in information assurance – investigations of security breaches yield valuable information that can be used to design more secure and resilient systems.

This book, *Advances in Digital Forensics XII*, is the twelfth volume in the annual series produced by the IFIP Working Group 11.9 on Digital Forensics, an international community of scientists, engineers and practitioners dedicated to advancing the state of the art of research and practice in digital forensics. The book presents original research results and innovative applications in digital forensics. Also, it highlights some of the major technical and legal issues related to digital evidence and electronic crime investigations.

This volume contains twenty revised and edited chapters based on papers presented at the Twelfth IFIP WG 11.9 International Conference on Digital Forensics, held in New Delhi, India on January 4-6, 2016. The papers were refereed by members of IFIP Working Group 11.9 and other internationally-recognized experts in digital forensics. The post-conference manuscripts submitted by the authors were rewritten to accommodate the suggestions provided by the conference attendees. They were subsequently revised by the editors to produce the final chapters published in this volume.

The chapters are organized into eight sections: Themes and Issues, Mobile Device Forensics, Network Forensics, Cloud Forensics, Social Media Forensics, Image Forensics, Forensic Techniques, and Forensic Tools. The coverage of topics highlights the richness and vitality of the discipline, and offers promising avenues for future research in digital forensics.

This book is the result of the combined efforts of several individuals. In particular, we thank Gaurav Gupta, Robin Verma and Jayaprakash Govindaraj for their tireless work on behalf of IFIP Working Group 11.9. We also acknowledge the support provided by the Department of Electronics and Information Technology, Ministry of Communications and Information Technology, Government of India; U.S. National Science Foundation; U.S. National Security Agency; and U.S. Secret Service.

GILBERT PETERSON AND SUJEET SHENOI

I

THEMES AND ISSUES

Chapter 1

ON A SCIENTIFIC THEORY
OF DIGITAL FORENSICS

Martin Olivier

Abstract   A suitable theory to serve as scientific grounds for a digital forensic science is still elusive. Such a theory needs to satisfy the demands imposed by science and justify the facts derived as evidence using the theory. A number of grounding theories have been proposed. This chapter revisits three prominent theories, those of Gladyshev, Carrier and Cohen, and: (i) determines the requirements they suggest for a digital forensics theory; (ii) analyzes their primary differences; and (iii) assesses them using the norms that exist for science. This enables us to sketch the outlines of a new theory that better reflects the scientific requirements and the intended application of forensic science in a digital context.

Keywords: Forensic science, digital evidence, digital forensic science, theory

1.   Introduction

Forensic science is, quite literally, a science intended for use in the forum – the place in society where matters of law are debated. The role of forensic science is to contribute to the debate by providing answers to issues relevant to the debate, where the veracity of the answers stems from the use of science.

Exactly what constitutes science is a question that has occupied (reflective) scientists and philosophers for over a century. The problem of distinguishing between the scientific and non-scientific is often referred to as the "demarcation problem." Although much insight has been gained about the demarcation of science, the problem is far from settled. Gratzer [9], for example, recounts a number of instances where theories that were not scientific were for periods deemed to be scientific. He is not interested in cases where scientists actively attempted

© IFIP International Federation for Information Processing 2016
Published by Springer International Publishing AG 2016. All Rights Reserved
G. Peterson and S. Shenoi (Eds.): Advances in Digital Forensics XII, IFIP AICT 484, pp. 3–24, 2016.
DOI: 10.1007/978-3-319-46279-0_1

to deceive others by, for example, fabricating data. He is also not interested in "tales of scientific lunacy." He studies cases that may be referred to as "pathological science." He is fascinated by "the way that false theories and imagined phenomena sometimes spread through the scientific community. ... Sometimes such a perversion of the scientific method results from external ... pressures, but at other times it is a spontaneous eruption" [9].

Where Gratzer looks at aberrations in the broad scientific enterprise, Turvey [22] uses much stronger language when he speaks about forensic fraud that thrives in the "science cultures" of forensic examiners. Examiners are often not scientists, but they are put in a position where they act as scientists. Even when examiners are scientists, Turvey shows convincingly that the culture of law enforcement is that of a "noble cause" – one that brings criminals to justice. In contrast, the scientist is one who ought to value scientific truth above all else. Yet, many (if not most) forensic examiners are employed by law enforcement agencies. This juxtaposes two cultures that differ in their primary virtues. Foucault [5], for example, claims that, in order to understand the penal system, one has to determine whether "the insertion in legal practice of a whole corpus of 'scientific' knowledge, is not the effect of a transformation of the way in which the body itself is invested by power relations."

This latter question resonates in the questions posed by Harding [10] about whose science and whose knowledge is valued and pursued. In her critique, she distinguishes between "bad science" and "science-as-usual." Her critique of bad science overlaps with Turvey's critique and contains some elements of Gratzer's accounts. Her critique of science-as-usual is primarily based on the power structures in which the science is situated and the impossibility of the situated knowledge to be value neutral.

The questions that have been raised about the scientificness of digital forensics as a forensic discipline are primarily about demarcation. The underlying questions are about the scientific method used in digital forensics. Some responses have dealt with characteristics of digital forensic techniques; in general, the characteristics that have been mentioned are necessary, but not sufficient to declare that digital forensics is a science. Some answers have taken the form of suggesting a foundation for digital forensics that could make digital forensics scientific.

This chapter revisits the line of thought that seeks a theory for digital forensics that may serve as a scientific foundation for the discipline. In its quest to find such a theory, it attempts to stay within the boundaries of what would be considered scientific by science at large. It recognizes that scientific facts may be useful to solve a crime that has (possibly) been committed. However, it attempts to focus on science as an arbiter of fact (within the limits of science), rather than science used in the pursuit of a criminal. In simple terms, it explores the possibility that digital forensics can consider some claim c and express scientifically-justifiable support for or rejection of the claim — if (and only if) scientific grounds exist to reach such a conclusion. Such proven claims (c or $\bar{c}$) may, if relevant, be accepted by a court of law.

In order to justify this course of action, the next section recounts the underlying logic employed by society in its use of scientific evidence. This is followed by a discussion of prominent attempts to formulate a foundational theory for digital forensic science. The intention to canvass these earlier theories is twofold. On one hand, the theories shed light on what scholars in the field have deemed to be important in a theory. On the other hand, it is possible to critique the theories based on the role of digital evidence that is elucidated in the initial sections of this chapter. Finally, the chapter identifies the characteristics that underpin a theory of digital forensic science.

2.   Rationale for Scientific Evidence in Society

Science cannot prove the superiority of scientific knowledge over other forms of knowledge. However, the superiority of scientific knowledge is deeply ingrained in the fabric of many modern societies.

As a society, we (subjectively) value scientific claims; we rely on scientific claims about the safety and efficacy of our medicines; we are willing to board aircraft under the assumption that science assures us that the planes will indeed fly; and we will allow driverless cars to share our roads once we believe their safety has been demonstrated scientifically. We know that science is not infallible, but we generally experience an increase in the knowledge and understanding of our world and our technology and are willing to increasingly rely on science. In our narrower circle, as digital forensic practitioners and researchers, we are, after all, the readers and authors of scientific literature and are unlikely to devote our lives to an enterprise in which we do not believe. It is only natural that we want to have facts at our disposal when decisions in legal matters are made. And when such facts are not obvious, we prefer scientific proof of allegations above any other means of knowing, whenever possible. Our reliance on science is not shared globally – in some legal systems, religious insights are deemed more valuable than scientific ones. To the scientific mind, the grounds of beliefs of others seem particularly unreliable when used as proof – beliefs that are often built on a metaphysical foundation that does not allow objective scrutiny.

Accepted scientific theories are expressed as concise laws, such as the iconic $E = mc^2$. Sometimes these laws are conditional – they apply in a physical vacuum or where no external force has an effect on the body of interest. Once the preconditions are met, it is possible to apply science in even more specific terms: a feather dropped in a vacuum from the top of the Leaning Tower of Pisa will reach the ground in a time that can be calculated with extreme precision. These are the types of facts that, we hope, science will put on the table in our courts of law: this specific revolver fired the round that was found in the body of the victim; the fingerprints of the suspect match those found at the crime scene; Jack is the father of Jill. In the end, the scientist has to testify about some claim c. We prefer to hear a resounding yes, c is true; or a resounding no, c is false. In reality, the scientist will say that c is true or false – to some degree of certainty. We also realize that a scientist sometimes may not be in a position to confirm or deny c – tests are not always conclusive or even always possible. However, when tests purport to be conclusive, they must be reliable.

As a society, we have formed (absolute) rules to deal with uncertainty. In the current context, the rule that a suspect is innocent until proven guilty is a mechanism that deals decisively with uncertainty.

However, much of life is cloaked in uncertainty and no fixed rules exist to deal with the uncertainty. When a crime is committed, law enforcement may have much more uncertainty than certainty at its disposal. There may be leads, suspects, hunches and many metaphysical opinions may be expressed. A few facts may be available and some of them may be scientifically provable. However, in these uncertain conditions, it is often unclear whether such facts will turn out to be relevant – and one of the defining characteristics of evidence is relevance.

It is in this nebulous world of uncertainty that a detective investigates a crime (without even being certain that a crime was committed). Facts – even scientifically-proven facts – may help the detective plot a course through the leads, facts and opinions in a process known as an investigation. The detective is a puzzle solver, but not in the sense that Kuhn [12] uses to describe the activities of the (normal) scientist. The detective formulates theories about what happened, but these theories are very different from the theories formulated in science; the detective's theories correspond to something like the general theory of relativity only in name. The detective may formulate hypotheses about what happened, but the hypotheses again only have a family resemblance to the hypotheses that are formulated (and formally tested) in a scientific endeavor. At the end of the investigation, the detective turns all the uncovered evidence over to a prosecutor, who decides whether a *bona fide* (or, more cynically, a winnable) case can be made against certain parties. If so, the matter is referred to a court, where facts become the currency presented to the presiding officer or jury. It is up to the court to decide whether or not the case has been proven. It is in this forum where the claims of the forensic scientist are offered as facts. These same facts may have played a role during the investigation – just like other leads, claims and hunches. However, it is in this forum where the evidence is proffered as scientific facts. It is in this forum where the claims may impact the life of the suspect (or of the scientist) for years to come.

The disentanglement of investigation and examination is important, not only because they are two inherently different activities that superficially mimic one another, but also because many of the problems in current forensic practice stem from investigative methods that drifted to the forensic laboratories without ever establishing scientific grounds – a problem highlighted by the seminal U.S. National Academies' report on forensic science [13].

From the narrative above, it is clear that a scientific theory of digital forensics needs to: (i) consider the domain of digital forensics; (ii) reflect on the nature of claims that may be offered as scientific fact; and (iii) reflect on the certainty with which the claims can be offered as facts. This is the journey that is followed in the remainder of this chapter. During the journey, it is important to also reflect on what others who previously attempted similar journeys said. From their journeys, we learn about the expectations of such journeys. We also learn about the pitfalls that prevent their theories from being the ultimate blueprint of digital forensic science. It is also prudent to be aware that the journey – like those that have gone before – is bound to be found lacking in many respects. However, we hope that one more foray into the world of digital forensic science will shine more light on a topic that is likely to remain murky and foggy for some time to come.

3. Domain of Digital Forensic Science

Digital forensics is often seen as an activity with the purpose of extracting evidence from all things digital for use in judicial proceedings. One consequence of this informal definition is that, taken to its logical conclusion, digital forensics encompasses almost every form of scientific (and much non-scientific) evidence. Almost every piece of laboratory equipment runs some software that processes values from a range of sensors and presents the results of a test or measurement in a visual form to the scientist (or technician or even novice) who interprets it. This would put digital forensics in a peculiar relationship with other forensic

Table 1.   Technical specifications of a DNA analysis system [7].

Name	Description
Data Output Files	`.bmp`, .fsa and `.cmf` formats
. . .	. . .
Internal Memory	80 GB solid-state drive
External Connections	USB 2.0
	GPS (USB 2.0; L1 frequency reception; sensitivity $> -150\,\text{dBm}$)
	Wi-Fi 802.11
	Ethernet (RJ45 10/100/1,000 Mb data rates)
	SVGA, DVI
Security	Multiple encryption systems for stored data
	WPA2 encryption
	Strong passwords; secure logging of all accesses to local database
System Clock	Clock synchronizes with GPS signal

sciences. As an example, consider the relationship between a forensic biologist and a digital forensic specialist. The brochure of a DNA analysis system states [7]:

> "The instrument's Expert System software analyzes the data after run completion and provides real-time feedback on the usability of the STR profiles for database searching."

Table 1 lists some of the specifications of the device. The quotation and selected specifications leave no doubt that the instrument is a digital computer. If the definition of digital forensics as provided in the opening sentence of this section is accurate, it follows that evidence about the output of this device should be in the domain of digital forensics. In this manner, digital forensics becomes the universal forensics because very few instruments do not operate in a digital fashion at their core.

As noted in Table 1, the DNA test instrument produces files in the `.bmp`, `.fsa` and `.cmf` formats. Identification and classification are core forensic competencies [11]. The average digital forensic practitioner will probably be willing to identify and/or classify a `.bmp` file. However, it is quite possible that the average digital forensic practitioner has never encountered the other two file types and the question then becomes: Which forensic branch is able to express an opinion when the tampering of such a file is alleged?

However, we should be cautious when introducing the notion of tampering: digital forensics has, for a long time, been preoccupied with identifying tampering and information hiding and, in general, trying to outsmart the really clever hacker. The average computer user is arguably equally able to store secret information in, say, the slack space of an ext4 volume as he/she is to modify the code in the DNA analysis instrument. This does not mean that either is impossible. This also does not mean that a capability to detect such interference with normal system operation is unimportant. Instead, the consequence is that most digital information is an accurate representation of what it purports to be (subject to the well-known volatile nature of data where a file date is, for example, inadvertently modified by someone who opens the file to read it and then saves it when closing it).

Hence, we contend that digital forensics should, in the first place, focus on digital evidence that has not (maliciously) been tampered with (beyond what average users are able to do, such as deleting files). However, this assumption of correct data does not diminish the need to identify inaccurate data – it just means that there is a gap in our work on the scientific extraction of evidence from normal data.

As noted elsewhere, the forensic scientist should be able to testify to facts, which are usually formulated as claims or propositions. When initially faced with a claim, the forensic scientist considers it as a hypothesis (in a general sense), tests it, decides whether to reject or accept it (with due regard to the inherent problem of accepting a statistical hypothesis) and then testifies to the finding based on the result of the test.

The question then is: What facts can the digital forensic scientist testify to? The assumption that the facts may relate to all things digital is clearly problematic. We suggest that postconditions of computations may form this foundation.

This chapter explores a system that is simple, but powerful enough to form a foundation for digital forensics. Note that the intention is not to describe forensic methods or a real-world approach to conducting digital forensics.

3.1 Foundational Concepts

At the core, the digital forensic scientist examines digital artifacts that are acted upon by computational processes.

Definition 1. *A digital artifact is a sequence of bits that has (or represents) meaning. The meaning is often (but not always) determined by context.*

As an example of contextual meaning, consider the first few bytes of a file. They often indicate the type of the file. These bytes are the file signature or magic number. In other contexts, the same bytes may have no meaning (or a different meaning). In our definition, a sequence of bytes that function as a signature is a digital artifact.

A file is arguably a more obvious example of a digital artifact. The file technically is a file because it exists on a digital medium where metadata links its various blocks together, names it and details its other attributes.

Corollary 1. *A digital artifact may contain or consist of other digital artifacts.*

Corollary 2. *A combination of digital artifacts may constitute a digital artifact.*

One interpretation of this corollary is that the sum of the parts may be more that the parts on their own; however, no grounds for this interpretation are provided at this time.

Corollary 3. *The component parts of a digital artifact often provide details that help an examiner to classify (or even individualize) the artifact.*

The definition and corollaries enable one to denote (or name) artifacts, as well as to refer to the attributes of artifacts. A file f may, for example, have a name. The claim that

$$\text{name}(f) = \texttt{example.txt}$$

may be confirmed or refuted through examination.

Definition 2. *Processing (or computing) may create, modify or destroy digital artifacts. Stated differently, a computational action α may have one or more effects. It may be useful to indicate that such an action pertains to a specific artifact, although this will not always be practical.*

As an example, consider the editing of file f. An example of an action that causes a change to f is saving (or writing) the file:

$$w(f) \rightsquigarrow f'$$

In addition, writing may cause a backup file to be created (or updated):

$$w(f) \rightsquigarrow \exists f^{\sim} \text{ where } f^{\sim} = f$$

Other consequences of the write operation are that the file date is updated (or that the modification date and time of the "new" file f' is set to the time and date of the write operation). The update also impacts the containing disk:

$$w(f) \rightsquigarrow d' \text{ where } f\mathsf{E}d$$

where E is used to indicate an element of the structure – in this case, the disk d. Such a structure may sometimes be equivalent to a set; however, a disk allows multiple instances of the same file and, hence, more closely resembles a bag. Note that ∈ is used to indicate bag membership.

This chapter does not intend to introduce new notation. Many specification languages, such as Z, already have a rich notation in which postconditions can be specified.

Note that a computation often has a wide array of effects (manifested as postconditions) on the system. The algorithm used by software transforms its input into output, with (often) some logical relation between the input and the output. In some cases, details of the implementation may be left to the developer and, thus, specific software may leave its fingerprints in the output; different software suites may, for example, encode pictures slightly differently. Depending on the software, the input, output or both may remain in the system as artifacts. Software may leave other traces of its operation such as entries in a log file. All these characteristics are potentially postconditions of the computation.

It is not always useful (or even possible) to consider all the postconditions of a computation. The use of postconditions with the greatest discriminatory power and highest resilience are (obviously) the ones to focus on, but certainty also derives from redundancy. A sufficient number of postconditions need to be verified before a conclusion can be reached. It is not obvious what would constitute a sufficient number; this problem is part of ongoing work [18] and is not considered further in this discussion. It is worth noting that DNA evidence faces a similar problem, albeit in the realm of natural phenomena. The human genome is incredibly complex but, in general, of little forensic value. The major variations that tie genetic material to individuals occur in a small portion of genetic material. DNA evidence achieves its success by focusing on a very small set of loci that show enough variation in a given population to discriminate between individuals, if enough of the loci are used for comparison.

4.   Achieving Scientific Status

We now turn our attention to the manner in which a truth claim can be justified in a scientific manner. This is the question that lies at the core of the seminal work on the scientific bases of digital forensic science. The best known answers are arguably the following (risking some oversimplification for the sake of brevity):

- **Gladyshev** [8]: Find a path through a finite state automaton that fits all known facts and terminates in the current state of the finite state automaton; such a path is known as an explanation.

- **Carrier** [3]: Formulate and test a hypothesis or a sequence of hypotheses.

- **Cohen** [4]: Establish the physics of information as a new science and use the facts in this science to find consistencies or inconsistencies to support or refute a claim.

In addition to these proposals, one has to consider digital forensic practice as, for example, embodied in the best known forensic tools. These tools typically extract data from devices and enable forensic examiners to inspect or observe data. In addition, the relationships between data can be rendered in a variety of ways (for example, using a visual representation). This enables the examiner to observe relationships, patterns and other potentially interesting characteristics of the data being examined.

In fact, observation is one of the key elements of all three theories, as well as of digital forensic practice. However, the perspectives of the theories with regard to observation differ and, therefore, require deeper exploration.

The three theories use automata theory as a foundational concept, albeit in different roles. The fundamentally different uses of automata theory also require exploration.

The theories (and practice) disagree about what they deem to be the primary artifacts of a digital examination. Cohen starts with a "bag of bits" and identifies the larger units of meaning in the bits. Carrier distinguishes between primitive and complex artifacts; complex artifacts are of primary interest, but one examines them with a hypothesis (or assumption) that the primitive artifacts that constitute them are sound (or can be shown to be sound – or not).

4.1   Observation

An important difference between the three theories is the relationship between (scientific) theory and observation.

Carrier and Cohen say that digital evidence is latent – that it cannot be observed by the naked eye. This is arguably consistent with the view of vendors of digital forensic tools and does not contradict Gladyshev's statements. Carrier, for example, states that "[t]he investigator cannot directly observe the state of a hard disk sector or bytes in memory. He can only directly observe the state of output devices." He immediately follows this remark about the nature of digital evidence by postulating that, "[t]herefore, all statements about digital states and events are hypotheses that must be tested to some degree."

The requirement to observe, inspect or measure a feature of a (digital) object is a common activity in most scientific enterprises. In forensic science, in particular, these activities commonly occur in forensic laboratories. Examples include measuring the alcohol level of a blood sample, observing the presence of Y chromosomes in genetic material or inspecting blood spatter patterns. When evidence is latent, some instrument is, by definition, required for observation or measurement.

The question whether mere observations can be the foundation of a science is an old one. The logical positivists were already deeply divided about the role of observation (or protocol sentences [14]) in science, with the non-verifiability of personal observations at the core of the controversy. Much of the controversy can be traced back to Wittgenstein's *Tractatus Logico-Philosophicus* [23].

The outcome of this controversy was an almost unanimous rejection of observation as a building block in science. Bunge [1], in his comprehensive review of the philosophy of science, mentions parts of this controversy in passing; the role of observation is not a point of debate in his exposition. French [6] uses an apt analogy to illustrate the inability to generalize from observation to theory by reflecting on what and how a botanist would observe in a forest:

> *"Is she just going to parachute into the jungle, unbiased and without presuppositions and simply start observing, left, right and center? And observing what? All the plants, all the trees, all the strange animals and insects? No, of course not. She will know what she is looking for, what counts and what doesn't, what conditions are relevant, etc.; she may even have some theory in mind, some set of hypotheses that is being tested. Of course, serendipitous observations happen, new plants or animals are discovered, for example, but a botanist observing without bias in the field would be overwhelmed."*

Carrier attempts to avoid direct observation (and measurement); the formulation of hypotheses and the subsequent testing of the hypotheses form the core of his claim that his work contributes to the discourse of the science of digital forensics. However, a large number of his hypotheses deal with situations where direct observations or measurements appear to be natural and the use of hypotheses artificial. An example is a scientist who observes the disk capacity on the label of the disk. The scientist then formulates a hypothesis that the disk capacity is indicated by the label (possibly after finding the relevant documentation of the device and determining the specifications from the manual). A tool may then be used to confirm the capacity. The debate about observation arguably explains this approach. However, simply measuring the capacity of the device appears to be a much simpler approach to achieve the same result.

Carrier, in fact, points out that "[m]ost forensic science disciplines have theories that are published, generally accepted, and testable." However, while Carrier's work emulates this process, it does not lead to theories that are tested, generally accepted and published. His process leads to contextualized theories – that are, in general, not published and do not become theories that are generally known – and, therefore, are not theories that would be generally accepted.

Philosophers who study measurement encounter problems similar to those who reflect on observation [20]: measurement is not theory-free, yet measurement (for example when testing hypotheses) helps create theories. This mutual influence of measurement and theory questions the very foundations of scientific theories. However, Carrier's approach is not one that is intended to shape scientific theories. When Carrier formulates a hypothesis about disk capacity, his intention is to determine the capacity of the disk. Measurement would have had the same value as a hypothesis-based approach.

Cohen reminds us that digital evidence, by its very nature, is latent: all observation occurs via instrumentation. Observation in this context is very similar to measurement. Observation is, as noted, not theory independent; however, because observation only provides information about the case at hand – rather than impact a general theory – the problem of circularity is avoided. The claims of the proponents of protocol sentences apply; the critiques of opponents are avoided. An attempt to introduce hypothesis testing where observation or measurement suffice does not improve the scientific validity of digital forensics.

It is also worth noting that, unlike Carrier, both Gladyshev and Cohen appear to accept observation (through instrumentation).

4.2   Automata Theory

All three theories discussed here use automata theory as one of the tenets on which claims of being scientific are based. From this one may infer that justifiable facts about computational processes are deemed important by all three theories. This extends the domain beyond the examination of digital artifacts – which seems to be the primary focus of commercial digital forensic tools, where artifacts such as pictures and other documents may yield partial indications of the events that occurred during processing.

All three theories use finite state machines. Given that Turing machines define computability, the use of much less powerful finite state machines is somewhat surprising.

Cohen initially discusses finite state machines, but later correctly notes that a finite state machine with an unlimited tape added to it becomes a Turing machine. This happens before the core of his theory is presented. He notes that complexity and computability are based on Turing machines and derives a number of insights that are key to his theory of the physics of information. While both finite state machines and Turing machines are important concepts in Cohen's theory (and complexity, an important part in the theory itself), automata theory *per se* is not a core element of the theory.

Carrier employs an interesting variation of finite state machines. Instead of using the finite number of states that characterize a finite state machine, he suggests that the states between transitions are variable – that they play the role of memory that can change over time. In addition, the finite state machines may change from transition to transition, given the fact that a computer system changes as disks are mounted and unmounted. If an infinite number of finite state machines are available to substitute one another, the resulting device may well be Turing-complete. However, finite state machines play a minor role in Carrier's eventual theory and we, therefore, do not explore the computing power of these machines.

In contrast to the other two theories, finite state machines form the basis of Gladyshev's theory. The finite state machines do not directly model computations in the sense that a finite state machine is a representation of a program being examined. Instead, the states of the finite state machine are key indicators of important parts of the system state. While it may, in theory, be possible to consider the entire state of a system, the (theoretical) costs are prohibitive. A system with n bits of storage has 2^n possible states, ignoring the fact that additional storage may be added. In addition, the transitions between the states would be hard to determine; although, it is clearly not Gladyshev's intention to follow such an approach. Unfortunately, even when Gladyshev uses simple examples to illustrate his theory, the number of states quickly becomes unmanageable and raises the question if such an approach is practical.

Carrier remarks that his theory is not intended to be used in all its details for investigations in practice; just like a Turing machine is a very useful model of a real computer, but programming a Turing machine is unwieldy at best. The question then is whether an impractical theory of digital forensic science sheds useful insights on such science; if it does, it clearly has merit. Unfortunately, Gladyshev does not explore the nature of such (abstract) insights that may be gained from his model – and state explosion limits its practical use. Some questions may also be raised about how one would determine the parts of the global machine state that should be included in the states modeled in the finite state machine – in particular, where multiple programs may have an impact on the state. However, this is an interesting problem for future research rather than a critique of Gladyshev's model.

Gladyshev's model presents an intriguing mechanism to test hypotheses. His model assumes that the current state of the finite state machine is known and that some intermediate states may be known. A trace of a path through the finite state machine states that covers all the known intermediate states and terminates at the current state explains the observations (or knowledge of intermediate and current states). Clearly, at least one explanation has to exist, else the observed evidence (or model of the states) cannot be correct. To test a hypothesis about whether an intermediate state of interest was reached, it is inserted as evidence and a search for explanations is initiated. The hypothesis is refuted when no explanations are found.

Unfortunately, this method of hypothesis testing also raises concerns about practical use of the theory. The time frame in which evidence was observed and the time frame in which the hypothesized state occurred has to be specified (with a finite degree of deviation allowed). This makes it impossible to ask and answer whether a given state may ever have been reached. Again, the practical implications of this aspect of the model are not quite clear. It is possible that this choice was required to prevent the complexity of computing the explanations from reaching intractable levels.

4.3   Bits, Bytes or Files?

A third area raised by the three theories is the notion of layers. Cohen asserts that the examiner starts with "a bag of bits" and infers the meaning at a higher layer (e.g., these bits are a JPEG file) using criteria he details.

Carrier distinguishes between (low level) primitive categories and (high level) complex categories. He suggests that investigations are usually performed at the complex level, with the primitive level serving as a theoretical backdrop on which the complex level rests. If necessary, remarks about complex categories can be mapped to primitive categories and examined at the primitive level. However, the important thing is the knowledge that this is possible, rather than an operational practice that is sometimes (or even ever) done.

Gladyshev notes that programs can be mapped to finite state machines (as discussed above), and proceeds to work at the lower level, without exploring the relationships between layers any further.

All three theories acknowledge the existence of layers. It may be argued that two layers do not adequately allow the creation of abstractions in the digital domain. A database built on a filesystem is a new reality, with the filesystem providing primitive support [15]. A dedicated application on a computer may use a database as a primitive, but leave no clue to the user of the system that a database is running in the background.

Other branches of forensic science are also confronted by such layers. A DNA forensic scientist and a forensic pathologist both work with human tissue, but at very different layers. Both know that tissue consists of atoms that, in turn, consist of sub-atomic particles. However, the existence of these sub-atomic particles does not directly impact the work of either scientist. Cohen observes that the division of digital artifacts cannot proceed beyond the bit-level – in contrast to the physical example above. From this, Cohen derives valuable insights for his physics of information. However, this does not detract from the fact that physical and digital artifacts may both be examined at different levels.

In this regard, Carrier's position is most closely aligned with other forensic disciplines: while particles of an artifact may shed some light on its working (and may be important to understand the operation of the higher layer artifact), the artifacts that confront the forensic examiner should be the starting point of an examination. The question whether a file f was digitally signed by some user u is best addressed using notions of files, signatures, public/private keys and the algorithm(s) that could have been used given the known keys. Determining the truth of such a claim involves processing bytes (or even bits), but the terms listed are those that are used to formulate and answer the question.

Stated differently, the question posed to a digital forensic scientist determines the level at which an examination occurs. Analysis at a deeper level is only needed if a specific reason for the deeper analysis exists. The reasons may include anomalies found during processing or a separate request to express an opinion on the integrity of an artifact.

To defend the claim made in the previous paragraph, consider that an artifact may exist independently or exist embedded in some context. Copying a file from one medium to another does not change the content of the file. (The usual chain of integrity may be confirmed by computing cryptographic hashes of the original and copy, and comparing the hashes – a standard practice in digital forensics.) However, copying the file from one medium to the other may significantly change the order of the sectors that the file occupies on the medium, may change the number of sectors per cluster and, hence, the total number of sectors occupied by the file, may change the content of the slack space in the final cluster, and so on. Whether or not these changes are important depends on the nature of the question to be answered. If there is no reason to doubt that the artifact to be examined is, indeed, a file, it may be examined as a file instead of as a sequence of clusters of sectors existing on some medium.

4.4   Investigations, Examinations and Analyses

The distinction between investigative and probative work was highlighted earlier in this chapter. This distinction is also present in the three theories being discussed.

Carrier sees the terms investigation and forensics as equivalent: "Digital investigations, or digital forensics, are conducted ... " Carrier also states that some definitions of digital forensics "consider only data that can be entered into a legal system while others consider all data that may be useful during an investigation, even if they are not court admissible." He continues by pointing out that laws of evidence differ from one jurisdiction to another and concludes that "the set of objects with legal value is a subset of the objects with investigative value."

We have argued elsewhere [17] that facts are useful during an investigation; facts are useful as evidence; however, facts are only one of the elements of an investigation – experience, hunches, tip-offs and the gut feel of the experienced detective are often just as useful, if not more useful – to investigating an incident than the mere facts. The detective follows leads and identifies possible sources of further evidence, possibly identifying and excluding suspects. When a suspect, for example, has a convincing alibi, the attention shifts to other suspects. While one may talk about the detective's theory or hypothesis, the meanings of these words are very different from what a scientist means when using the same words (see, e.g., the critique of Carrier's use of the term hypothesis [21]).

In the context of investigative psychology, Canter and Youngs [2] describe an investigation as a decision making problem, where the investigator is continually confronted by choices between alternatives to explore deeper next. Suspect profiling is one way in which investigative psychology helps in this regard: if it is known that the act being investigated is most often committed by someone who meets certain personal criteria (age, gender, employment status, relationship status, ethnic origin, and so on), then the investigation can be expedited by focusing on the suspects who match the profile. If the science underlying such profiling is sound, it will, indeed, expedite most investigations because it will more often than not point the investigator in the right direction. However, such profiling does not constitute evidence.

When investigating a case based on a profile, an investigator may uncover facts that do constitute evidence. For example, the investigator may prioritize obtaining a DNA sample from a suspect who matches the predicted profile. If the sample from the suspect matches the DNA found at a crime scene, a fact has been established that not only guides the subsequent actions of the investigator, but that may also have probative value in a legal context. Note that both claims (the profiling and the DNA match) are factual and grounded in science. However, only one of them would be considered evidence, even in a colloquial sense.

Carrier attempts to avoid the issue of admissibility to work with "a general theory of evidence [...] which can be restricted to satisfy the rules of evidence in a specific legal system." This statement is made after the observation that the definitions of digital forensics differ in their emphasis on an investigative process and obtaining evidence for use in legal proceedings. It is clear that evidence is a subset of the useful inputs to an investigation; it is not clear that, if all the elements of an investigation without probative value are removed, then one would be left with a non-empty set of elements with probative value. Phrased in simpler terms, if a theory describes an investigative process, it does not follow that the theory inherently says something about evidence. This is elucidated below using an example taken from Carrier.

It is, however, important to briefly reflect on the importance of this issue before proceeding. During the establishment of the NIST Forensic Science Standards Board, digital forensics was not included as a forensic science because doubts were expressed about the status of digital forensics as a science. One of the key documents in this debate was "Digital and Multimedia Evidence (Digital Forensics) as a Forensic Science Discipline" published by the Scientific Working Group on Digital Evidence [19] "to assist the reader in understanding that digital forensics is a forensic science and to address confusion about the dual nature of the application of digital forensic techniques as both a forensic science and as an investigatory tool." The document suggests that digital forensics is a science when (or because) it uses scientific methods. When used in a digital investigation, "identification and recovery" are the primary activities that (as may be seen from its final paragraph) do not necessarily have to be scientific – this is in line with our discussion thus far. Whether or not the document convinces the reader that digital forensics is a science is not important for our purposes at this stage. The distinction between forensic science, on the one hand, and investigations, on the other, is indeed important.

An additional claim in the document – that forensic science may be useful for investigations – is (as noted already) obvious (assuming that this is what is meant by the claim that "the output of digital forensics can easily be used as direct input in digital investigations"). However, the claim that "[i]nformation can easily flow from digital investigations into digital forensics, [if it is] subjected to the rigorous process demanded by the scientific method and rules of evidence" is, at best, confusing. If forensic facts are proven during an investigation, they do not have to "flow into digital forensics" – they are then already proven forensic facts. Any investigation may lead to questions that can be answered by scientific tests; a digital investigation may lead to questions about the digital realm that may be answered in a scientific manner. If the notion that information may "flow from digital investigations into digital forensics" indicates that an investigation may raise questions that may be answered by scientific methods, then the nature of these questions arguably defines digital forensic science. We contend that this is not easy and that the word flow is only justifiable if claims such as information from murder investigations can easily flow into forensic pathology or into DNA forensics can be made in a meaningful manner.

In a telling example, Carrier illustrates his use of hypotheses where contraband in the form of pictures is suspected. His initial hypothesis is that the contraband is in the form of JPG images – an act of prioritization based on prevalence; in other words, a form of profiling that in most cases increases the likelihood of successfully locating evidence early in the investigation. However, when this hypothesis has to be rejected if no incriminating JPG files are found, then the outcome of the investigation is not affected. The search simply moves to less frequently used options to search for evidence; ultimately, the search involves carving files from the disk. In the end, whether the hypotheses are accepted or rejected has no impact on the nature of the evidence. It is only after the search space is exhausted that the conclusion is that no evidence was found. This matches many aspects of investigations from the investigative psychology perspective: profiling usually accelerates evidence discovery (and may even help solve cases that would otherwise not be solved). However, the fact that the evidence matched a more or less likely profile is of little evidentiary use in itself.

5.   Discussion

The preceding discussion suggests that a grounding theory for digital forensic science needs to address four areas of concern:

1. **Observation and Measurement:** Observation is already theory laden. Neither observation nor measurement can form the essence of a grounding theory. A theory is a prerequisite for observation and measurement. The discussion suggests that the effects of computations may form a suitable theory that could guide observation and measurement. Such effects are well known in computer science, where they are typically encountered in the form of postconditions.

2. **Automata Theory:** While automata theory appears to be a natural fit for digital forensic science applications, its use in digital forensic science theories has not resulted in the successful development of a digital forensic science. It seems too far removed from computational processes to model computations in real or ideal examinations. The insight by Cohen that computational complexity based on automata theory can help determine if examinations should be conducted deserves to be developed further. Other work [16], which indicates that probabilistic algorithms may enable the examiner to quantify error rates, also needs to be developed further. Hence, it is suggested that computability theory may be more useful than automata theory as an ingredient of an overarching digital forensic science theory.

3. **Artifacts:** The insight (in Carrier's words) that complex objects exist out of primitive objects is valid and useful. While other theories place different emphases on the relationship between complex and primitive objects, their focus clearly increases during the examination of complex objects as the expositions of the theories progress. However, the division of digital artifacts into only two classes is an oversimplification of the digital realm. The role of layers of metadata in, for example, databases [15] better reflect the nature of this realm in general. We suggest that an ideal theory would provide a natural layer of relevance for the forensic examiner and that the examiner should start the examination at this layer of abstraction; of course, the examiner should be able to delve deeper when necessary. As a simple example, a claim about a file would, in general, be independent of the filesystem (and hence, the sectors, clusters and other system structures on which the file is stored). One should be able to copy a signed file from a filesystem to another without affecting the properties of the signature. However, when an examination involves system attributes, such as the date of modification or the use of slack space, a lower level examination is clearly indicated.

4. **Science:** A distinction should be made between a science that may be trusted to produce scientifically-justifiable evidence and a science that may help expedite an investigation.

We further suggest that computations, rather than artifacts, should form the primary focus of a theory. A lack of space precludes a full exposition, so only a brief outline can be provided here. Computations usually manifest themselves by creating digital artifacts; these artifacts are the traditional objects of inquiry in digital forensics, but they often hint at the processes that created them. When computations are the units of an examination, the known postconditions of the computations indicate whether or not a given process could have been active. Moreover, it is possible to study combinations of computations by developing an algebra that determines the expected intermediate conditions and postconditions of the composite computation. Such a change in focus will facilitate the examination of real-world processes based on the algebra. Unfortunately, space does not permit the illustration of these claims. Note that a change to the examination of computations does not preclude the current focus on the study of artifacts. An artifact is typically the result of a computation; examining an artifact is, therefore, a special case of examining computations.

6.   Conclusions

The chapter has explored the forces that impact a foundational theory for digital forensic science. It has considered the scientific imperatives, the intended application and the needs of digital forensic science as embodied in current digital forensic science theories. Based on these requirements, the chapter has sketched the outlines of a possible new theory – one where scientifically-justifiable claims can be made about computations based on the discovered artifacts and the known or knowable postconditions of computations. The approach suggests that intermediate conditions and postconditions of computations can be used to compare hypothesized processes against the discovered artifacts. However, it remains to be shown that the process is indeed useful and practical. In particular, the expected simplicity with which compound computations can be characterized and examined has to be proven.

Acknowledgement

The author wishes to express his thanks to his colleague and friend, Professor Stefan Gruner, for many fruitful discussions about several issues raised in this chapter.

References

[1] M. Bunge, *Philosophy of Science: From Problem to Theory, Volume One*, Transaction Publishers, New Brunswick, New Jersey, 1998.

[2] D. Canter and D. Youngs, *Investigative Psychology: Offender Profiling and the Analysis of Criminal Action*, John Wiley and Sons, Chichester, United Kingdom, 2009.

[3] B. Carrier, A Hypothesis-Based Approach to Digital Forensic Investigations, CERIAS Technical Report 2006-06, Center for Education and Research in Information Assurance and Security, Purdue University, West Lafayette, Indiana, 2006.

[4] F. Cohen, *Digital Forensic Evidence Examination*, Fred Cohen and Associates, Livermore, California, 2013.

[5] M. Foucault, *Discipline and Punish – The Birth of the Prison*, Penguin, London, United Kingdom, 1991.

[6] S. French, *Science: Key Concepts in Philosophy*, Continuum, London, United Kingdom, 2007.

[7] GE Healthcare Life Science, DNAscan Rapid DNA Analysis System, Data File 29-0327-18 AB, Pittsburgh, Pennsylvania, 2014.

[8] P. Gladyshev, Formalizing Event Reconstruction in Digital Investigations, Doctoral Dissertation, Department of Computer Science, University College Dublin, Dublin, Ireland, 2004.

[9] W. Gratzer, *The Undergrowth of Science – Delusion, Self-Deception and Human Frailty*, Oxford University Press, Oxford, United Kingdom, 2000.

[10] S. Harding, *Whose Science? Whose Knowledge? Thinking from Women's Lives*, Cornell University Press, Ithaca, New York, 1991.

[11] K. Inman and N. Rudin, *Principles and Practice of Criminalistics: The Profession of Forensice Science*, CRC Press, Boca Raton, Florida, 2001.

[12] T. Kuhn, *The Structure of Scientific Revolutions*, University of Chicago Press, Chicago, Illinois, 1996.

[13] National Research Council, *Strengthening Forensic Science in the United States: A Path Forward*, National Academies Press, Washington, DC, 2009.

[14] T. Oberdan, Moritz Schlick, in *The Stanford Encyclopedia of Philosophy*, E. Zalta (Ed.), The Metaphysics Lab, Center for the Study of Language and Information, Stanford University, Stanford, California (`plato.stanford.edu/entries/schlick`), 2013.

[15] M. Olivier, On metadata context in database forensics, *Digital Investigation*, vol. 5(3-4), pp. 115–123, 2009.

[16] M. Olivier, On complex crimes and digital forensics, in *Information Security in Diverse Computing Environments*, A. Kayem and C. Meinel (Eds.), IGI Global, Hershey, Pennsylvania, pp. 230–244, 2014.

[17] M. Olivier, Towards a digital forensic science, in *Information Security for South Africa*, H. Venter, M. Loock, M. Coetzee, M. Eloff and S. Flowerday (Eds.), IEEE Press, Danvers, Massachusetts, 2015.

[18] O. Oyelami and M. Olivier, Using Yin's approach to case studies as a paradigm for conducting examinations, in *Advances in Digital Forensics XI*, G. Peterson and S. Shenoi (Eds.), Springer, Heidelberg, Germany, pp. 45–59, 2015.

[19] Scientific Working Group on Digital Evidence, Digital and Multimedia Evidence (Digital Forensics) as a Forensic Science Discipline, Version 2.0, 2014.

[20] E. Tal, Measurement in science, in *The Stanford Encyclopedia of Philosophy*, E. Zalta (Ed.), The Metaphysics Lab, Center for the Study of Language and Information, Stanford University, Stanford, California (`plato.stanford.edu/archives/sum2015/entries/measurement-science`), 2015.

[21] S. Tewelde, S. Gruner and M. Olivier, Notions of hypothesis in digital forensics, in *Advances in Digital Forensics XI*, G. Peterson and S. Shenoi (Eds.), Springer, Heidelberg, Germany, pp. 29–43, 2015.

[22] B. Turvey, *Forensic Fraud: Evaluating Law Enforcement and Forensic Science Cultures in the Context of Examiner Misconduct*, Academic Press, Waltham, Massachusetts, 2013.

[23] L. Wittgenstein, *Tractatus Logico-Philosophicus*, Routledge, Abingdon, United Kingdom, 2001.

Chapter 2

DATA PRIVACY PERCEPTIONS ABOUT DIGITAL FORENSIC INVESTIGATIONS IN INDIA

Robin Verma, Jayaprakash Govindaraj and Gaurav Gupta

Abstract   A digital forensic investigation requires an investigator to examine the forensic images of the seized storage media and devices. The investigator obtains full access to all the data contained in the forensic images, including private and sensitive data belonging to the individual being investigated that may be entirely unrelated to the case. Unrestricted access to forensic images poses a significant threat to data privacy. No legal or technical structures are in place to prevent abuse.

This chapter presents the results of three surveys, one for each stakeholder group in digital forensic investigations, namely investigators, lawyers and the general public, that sought to capture their data privacy perceptions regarding the investigative process. The survey responses show a lack of professional ethics among some of the investigators, lack of legal support for lawyers to protect data privacy and confusion among the general public regarding their data privacy rights. The results highlight a pressing need for a privacy-preserving digital forensic investigation framework. To this end, a simple, yet efficient, solution is proposed that protects data privacy without hindering forensic investigations.

Keywords: Data privacy, digital forensic investigations, stakeholders, survey

1.   Introduction

Privacy is a very complex term, primarily because there are different definitions of privacy in different contexts. An important aspect of privacy is the ability of an individual to control access to his/her personal space [11]. An individual's personal space in the digital world comprises data in the form of files. These personal files are stored on digital devices or on local or online storage.

© IFIP International Federation for Information Processing 2016
Published by Springer International Publishing AG 2016. All Rights Reserved
G. Peterson and S. Shenoi (Eds.): Advances in Digital Forensics XII, IFIP AICT 484, pp.25–45, 2016.
DOI: 10.1007/978-3-319-46279-0_2

A digital forensic investigation attempts to collect and analyze all the digital evidence related to the case at hand. A digital forensic investigator typically gains access to the entire contents of the seized storage media in order to collect and analyze all the evidence pertaining to the case. In addition to potential evidentiary files, the seized storage media also contain private data belonging to the owner, such as personal photographs, videos, business plans, email, medical documents, financial documents, music, movies, games and software. Unrestricted access to files that are unrelated to the case, including the owner's private files, poses a significant threat to data privacy. No well-defined standards or guidelines exist to assist an investigator in deciding when all the important evidence has been gathered. This lack of clarity motivates an investigator to search for more evidence, which tends to increase the possibility and scope of data privacy violations.

Legal assistance is necessary to safeguard the data privacy of suspects and victims during investigations and the subsequent court proceedings. Lawyers should be knowledgeable about all the legal provisions that protect data privacy. Suspects and victims should also be knowledgeable about their data privacy rights.

This research sought to collect the ground truth about the principal data privacy issues related to digital forensic investigations. Three surveys were conducted, one for each stakeholder group, namely investigators, lawyers and the general public. The survey instruments were designed to capture the data privacy perceptions of the three stakeholder groups regarding digital forensic investigations. Note that the general public group corresponded to the investigated entities (suspects and victims) whose storage media would be seized in investigations. The surveys focused on the Indian context and, hence, all the participants were from India. However, the results of the study, including the concerns raised, are relevant in countries around the world.

An analysis of the literature reveals that this is the first study of the perceptions of investigators, lawyers and members of the general public regarding data privacy during digital forensic investigations. The survey responses show a lack of professional ethics on the part of some investigators, a lack of legal support for lawyers to protect data privacy and confusion on the part of the general public regarding their data privacy rights. The results highlight a pressing need for a privacy-preserving digital forensic investigation framework. To this end, a simple, yet efficient, solution is proposed that protects privacy without hindering digital forensic investigations.

2.   Research Methodology

Surveys are a well-established research methodology. Researchers in digital forensics have used surveys to understand the opinions of target audiences on a variety of topics [12, 13]. The survey results have helped the researchers gain insights into particular problems and explore possible solutions.

The first step in the survey design involved personal interviews with one candidate each from the investigator and lawyer groups. Simultaneously, five potential candidates were interviewed from the general public group. The answers enabled the researchers to' identify closed sets of relevant questions for the surveys of the three groups of individuals.

The second step in the survey design involved the conversion of the subjective questions and responses to objective questions with comprehensive answer options. The initial questionnaires were shown to the interviewed candidates to collect their feedback on question formulation. The feedback enabled the researchers to improve the readability, relevance and comprehensiveness of the survey questionnaires. The three surveys were then posted on the Survey Monkey website (`surveymonkey.com`).

The questionnaire used in the investigator survey incorporated three subsections that focused on:

- Adherence to digital forensic procedures.

- Suitable time to stop gathering evidence in an investigation.

- Access to the private files of the investigated entities.

The questionnaire used in the lawyer survey incorporated four subsections that focused on:

- Minimum amount of evidence required in an investigation.

- Investigation of one case leading to the prosecution of another case.

- Concerns raised by the investigated entities about data privacy.

- Misuse of personal information collected during an investigation.

The questionnaire used in the general public survey comprised two subsections that focused on:

- Attitudes regarding the privacy of data and personally-identifiable information.

- Awareness of digital forensics and the investigative process.

Table 1. Digital forensic cases handled by investigators.

Cases Handled	Responses (Total: 15)	Response Rate
Less than 10	6	40.00%
10 to 29	2	13.33%
30 to 49	3	20.00%
50 to 69	2	13.33%
70 to 99	1	6.67%
100 or more	1	6.67%

The third and final step in the survey involved sending links to the surveys to the target audiences. The investigator and lawyer surveys were posted on Survey Monkey in August 2013. The last response in the investigator survey was received in January 2014 and the last response in the lawyer survey was received in February 2014. The public survey was posted on Survey Monkey in September 2013 and the last response was received in December 2014.

3.   Survey Participant Demographics

The investigator and the lawyer surveys included participants who were experts in their respective fields. All the participating investigators had undergone professional training and had received certifications in digital forensics. The participating lawyers were experts on Indian information technology law who had actively worked on cyber crime and computer fraud cases.

A total of fifteen digital forensic investigators responded to the survey. The investigators had experience working on criminal cases and corporate incidents. All the questions in the surveys were answered by the fifteen investigators. Eleven of the fifteen respondents were from private digital forensic laboratories or companies; the remaining four investigators worked at government forensic laboratories. Ten of the fifteen investigators had degrees in computer science; the remaining five investigators had various other academic backgrounds. Seven of the fifteen investigators had less than two years of work experience in digital forensics; four investigators had two to five years of experience; the remaining four investigators had five to ten years of experience. Table 1 shows the numbers of cases handled by the respondents during their investigative careers.

The lawyer survey respondents worked as cyber lawyers at reputed courts in India, including the Supreme Court of India. Five of the ten

Table 2. Experience levels of cyber lawyers.

Experience (Years)	Responses (Total: 10)	Responses Rate
0 to 2 years	4	40%
3 to 5 years	2	20%
6 to 8 years	2	20%
9 to 10 years	0	0%
More than 10 years	2	20%

respondents were with private firms (one of the five respondents owned a law firm); three respondents were independent legal consultants; the remaining two respondents worked at government agencies. All ten respondents answered all the questions in the survey. Table 2 presents the experience levels of the cyber lawyers who participated in the survey.

Table 3. Age distribution of general public respondents.

Age	Percentage
Up to 18	4.00%
19 to 24	61.10%
25 to 34	17.80%
35 to 44	6.80%
45 and above	10.30%

A total of 1,235 members of the general public completed the demographics section of the survey; 654 individuals quit before completing the demographics section. Male respondents constituted 66.6% of the participants and females constituted 33.4% of the participants. Table 3 shows the age distribution of the respondents.

Table 4 shows the educational qualifications of the survey participants from the general public. A total of 17.2% of the respondents had less than four years of experience using computing devices, 21.5% had four to six years of experience and 61.3% had more than six years of experience. The demographic data reveals that the survey participants were well educated and had adequate experience using computing devices.

A hypothesis was framed that the participants' levels of awareness about privacy issues related to digital documents were high. However, this hypothesis was rejected after a thorough analysis of the public survey results.

Table 4.   Educational qualifications of general public respondents.

Education	Percentage
High School Diploma	5.20%
Undergraduate Diploma	5.80%
Baccalaureate Degree	56.50%
Post-Graduate Degree	29.90%
Doctoral Degree	2.60%

4.   Investigator Perceptions of Privacy

The goal of the investigator survey was to assess how digital forensic investigators handled the personal data extracted from seized devices belonging to the subjects of investigations. Although the number of participants in the investigator survey was limited, the responses were valuable due to the expertise of the participants. The following subsections discuss the three components of the investigator questionnaire.

4.1   Following Forensic Procedures

The chain of custody is a legal document that tracks an exhibit (potential item of evidence) from the time of its seizure until it is presented in court or is returned to the owner after an investigation. The document contains information about the exhibit, along with the names of the individuals who had custody of the exhibit, their designations and periods of custody. The chain of custody is maintained to ensure accountability and fairness of the investigative process and judicial proceedings.

Two questions were framed on chain of custody procedures to assess if the investigators were well versed in the basics of their trade and took their jobs seriously. The first question asked the investigators if they filled out chain of custody forms – fourteen of the fifteen respondents responded in the affirmative; one respondent was unaware of chain of custody documentation.

The second question asked the investigators who filled out chain of custody forms about the frequency of filling out the forms – eleven of the fourteen did this every time; two did this most of the time, but not always; and one did this some of the time.

The next question asked the fourteen respondents who filled out chain of custody forms about when they filled out the forms. Two of the fourteen respondents said that they only filled out the forms for cases that were going to be tried in court. Three respondents did this only for important cases. The remaining nine respondents filled out the forms for all types of cases.

The responses to the last two questions are inconsistent. Eleven investigators said that they created chain of custody documentation every time, but only nine of them said that they created the documentation for all types of cases.

4.2   Completing the Evidence Gathering Phase

The first question on this topic asked investigators if they stopped gathering evidence after finding potentially relevant evidence or if they explored the forensic images further, increasing the probability of encountering personal files that were not relevant to the case. Eight of the fifteen investigators said that they stopped only after they had gathered all possible – pertinent and irrelevant – evidence. Six investigators stopped after they gathered all possible evidence related to a case. The remaining investigator stopped after collecting the minimum amount of evidence needed to prove or disprove a case.

The next question asked the investigators if they experienced situations where they collected evidence that was not related to the case at hand, but that could be used to make a separate case against the subject. Surprisingly, seven of the fifteen investigators said yes, most of the time; four responded yes, only sometimes; and four did not encounter situations where they collected such evidence.

The responses to the questions indicate that gathering excess evidence is a common practice among digital forensic investigators. The habit of searching for more evidence than required is due to an investigator's indecision about gathering adequate evidence to make a case or an attempt to enhance his/her professional reputation by discovering unrelated evidence that opens a new case against the subject. Both these situations increase the likelihood of data privacy breaches.

4.3   Accessing Private Files

The first question in this part of the survey asked investigators about their reactions after they encountered private files (e.g., personal photographs, videos, songs, business plans or intellectual property) during an investigation. Six of the fifteen investigators said that they viewed private files and copied the files related to the case being investigated as well as files that were not linked to the case, but appeared to be illegal or questionable. Four other investigators said that they viewed and copied private files because these files were more likely to contain evidence relevant to the case at hand as well as to other possible cases.

The remaining five investigators said that they viewed private files, but only copied the files that were relevant to the case at hand. The results reveal that all the surveyed investigators routinely accessed private files that may or may not be associated with the case at hand. Surprisingly, ten of the fifteen investigators would not hesitate to copy private files whether or not they found irregularities related to the case.

Another question asked the investigators if they had seen other investigators copy files such as wallpaper, songs, movies, games or commercial software from case images. Three of the fifteen respondents stated that they had seen their colleagues at their laboratories do such things. Four investigators said that they had seen investigators at other laboratories copy non-malicious personal files belonging to investigated entities. One investigator had not seen anyone copy such files, but she did not see any problem with such copying. The remaining investigators had not seen such copying and they felt that it was inappropriate.

Surprisingly, half the participants had seen investigators in their laboratories or elsewhere copy non-malicious content from forensic images. Such unprofessional behavior poses a serious threat to data privacy. If an investigator is willing to copy wallpaper, songs, movies, games and application software from media belonging to the subject of an investigation, then the security of the subject's private files, including personal photographs, audio and video files and countless other confidential documents, cannot be guaranteed.

The final question asked the investigators if they had heard of or been involved in a situation where a subject reported the misuse of information or evidentiary items being used to threaten him/her. Interestingly, only one of the fifteen investigators was aware of such a situation. Nine said that they had not heard of any misuse during their careers. The remaining five investigators doubted that such abuse could ever occur.

5.   Cyber Lawyer Perceptions of Privacy

The goal of the lawyer survey was to obtain insights into the legal aspects of privacy during digital forensic investigations and court proceedings. A pilot interview was conducted with a lawyer who had argued cases before the Supreme Court of India; the interview helped frame a comprehensive questionnaire for the survey. Although the number of participants in the lawyer survey were limited, the responses are valuable due to the expertise and prominence of the participants. The following subsections discuss the four components of the cyber lawyer questionnaire.

5.1   Completing a Case

The first question asked the respondents when a case of cyber crime or computer fraud was ready for trial. Seven of the ten respondents felt that a case was ready after all the possible evidence – relevant as well as irrelevant to the case – was collected and analyzed; some of this evidence could also be used in a fresh case. Two respondents felt they could stop after gathering all the evidence related to a case. The remaining respondent said that he would stop after collecting the minimum amount of potential evidence.

The next question asked about the minimum amount of evidence sufficient to prove or disprove a case. Four of the ten respondents said that one or two pieces of evidence would be sufficient. Three participants said three to five pieces of evidence would be enough while the remaining three respondents felt that six to ten pieces of evidence would be required.

The responses to this question are significant because they set an upper limit on the amount of evidence required in a typical case. It is interesting that digital devices containing hundreds or thousands of files are typically seized during an investigation; however, all the respondents felt that no more than ten pieces of evidence would be adequate. The remaining files on the seized digital devices would be irrelevant to the case and may well contain personal or private data belonging to the subject of the investigation.

5.2   Using Evidence in Other Cases

The first question in this subsection was designed to verify the results of the investigator survey, where the participants who collected evidence about activities not related to the case at hand used the evidence to open new cases. Asking the same question to cyber lawyers made sense because evidence collected by investigators is compiled and used by cyber lawyers in legal proceedings. One of the ten lawyer respondents always encountered situations where some of the evidence was used to start fresh cases. Five respondents experienced such situations most of the time while the remaining three respondents experienced these situations some of the time. One respondent had never encountered such a situation.

5.3   Protecting Data Privacy

The questions in this subsection focused on three privacy-related laws in the Constitution of India and the Information Technology Act of 2000 and its 2008 amendment [14]. The first question asked the lawyers about the numbers of cases they handled in which the investigated entity requested the right to privacy by referring to the freedom of speech and expression provided by Article 19(1)(a) or the right to life and personal liberty provided by Article 21 of the Constitution of India, or both. Five of the ten lawyers handled less than ten such cases and three encountered ten to 29 such cases. The remaining two respondents observed 30 to 49 and 50 or more such cases.

The second question asked about instances of investigated entities complaining about data privacy breaches under Section 72A of the (Indian) Information Technology Act of 2000. This section provides protection against the access and disclosure of private information belonging to an investigated entity that is irrelevant to the case at hand. An example is the access and/or disclosure of personal or family photographs and videos, when the owner of the material is being investigated for financial fraud. Six of the ten lawyers answered in the affirmative, with two to five instances of such cases. The remaining four lawyers answered in the negative.

The third question asked about instances of investigated entities complaining about data privacy breaches under Section 43A of the (Indian) Information Technology Act of 2000. This section provides protection against the improper or negligent handling of an individual's sensitive personal information during an investigation. Six of the ten lawyers answered in the affirmative, with one to five instances of such cases. The remaining four lawyers answered in the negative.

A subsequent question asked the lawyers about the numbers of cases they had worked on or had knowledge about, where an investigated entity requested the court to protect the private data or files residing on his/her seized digital devices. Three of the ten lawyers encountered up to ten such cases while two others encountered ten to 20 such cases. Interestingly, one respondent had knowledge of more than 90 cases. The remaining four respondents had never encountered such a case.

5.4   Misusing Personal Information

The last question asked the participants if they had heard of incidents where an investigated individual reported the misuse of personal information (especially, evidence being used after the completion of the investigation) as a threat or for purposes of intimidation. Two of the ten respondents knew about such cases; one respondent reported two cases of evidence mishandling while the other reported one case. Three of the ten respondents had never encountered such a case. Two respondents opted not to answer the question. The remaining three respondents were skeptical if such an abuse of evidence could ever occur.

6.   General Public Perceptions of Privacy

After acquiring images of the computing devices involved in a case, a digital forensic investigator has full access to the contents of the images. The owner of the devices has no way of ensuring that the investigator does not access private data unrelated to the case at hand. For example, if a person is suspected of financial fraud, then his family holiday photographs and videos – which are not related to the case – should not be accessed during the investigation.

Half of the investigators reported seeing fellow investigators copy private data belonging to investigated individuals that were completely unrelated to the cases at hand. Two respondents in the lawyer survey knew of instances where an investigator used the data gathered during a case to threaten the investigated individual. These reports raised serious privacy concerns and prompted the researchers to survey the general public to obtain insights into their sensitivity about data privacy. A hypothetical question was framed that asked the surveyed individuals if the seizure of their digital devices would affect their perceptions about data privacy. The following subsections discuss the two components of the general public questionnaire.

6.1   Attitudes Towards Privacy

The questions in this subsection focused on how people handled their private data. Specifically, the types of files that people considered to be private and where these files were stored. The protection of personally-identifiable information is another dimension of privacy in the digital world. Thus, the survey instrument created for the general public incorporated some questions related to personally-identifiable information.

Storage of Personal Information. The first question in this subsection asked the survey participants about the frequency with which they stored private data on digital devices. Table 5 summarizes the responses. Note that the percentage values in the table were obtained by summing the values corresponding to three responses: (i) sometimes; (ii) usually; and (iii) always.

Since considerable amounts of private data are stored on digital devices, the loss of a device could pose a serious privacy threat to its owner. Therefore, the next question asked the participants if they had lost any of their digital devices during the past five years. Table 6 summarizes

Table 5. Devices used to store private data.

Devices	Users
Mobile Phones	70.3%
Laptops	75.1%
Desktops	54.9%
Portable Hard Drives	45.4%
USB Drives	58.1%

Table 6. Devices lost during the past five years.

Devices	Users
Mobile Phones	33.0%
Tablets	0.7%
Laptops	3.1%
Portable Hard Drives	3.3%
USB Drives	39.9%
None	41.5%

the responses. The table shows that 59.5% of the respondents lost at least one digital device during the past five years. This high number implies that the device owners were not cautious about their devices or their devices were stolen at some point in time. Valuable items such as smartphones and laptops are attractive targets for thieves, but the loss of low-cost devices such as USB drives may be the result of careless behavior on the part of their owners. Indeed, 39.9% of the survey participants reported that they had lost at least one USB drive during the past five years.

Common Passwords for Different Accounts.   The survey revealed that 32.6% of the participants used common passwords for multiple accounts, whereas 45% of the participants used different passwords. The remaining 22.4% opted not to reveal any information about their passwords. The results show the casual behavior of people with regard to password security and data security as a whole.

Storage of Passwords on Devices.   The survey revealed that 24.6% of the participants stored their passwords on smartphones or tablets and 25.6% stored their passwords on laptops or desktops. Although the majority of the participants (63.9%) did not store passwords on their devices, one in three did, in fact, store their passwords on their devices. Thus, one can assume that one in three devices seized in investigations

Table 7. Personal files and documents stored on digital devices.

File/Document	Personal Computer	USB/Portable Hard Drive	Tablet	Smartphone
Photographs	81.50%	33.90%	6.70%	30.30%
Video Files	69.10%	23.10%	3.80%	20.50%
Audio Files	62.90%	20.70%	3.70%	22.00%
Bank Statements	43.60%	7.10%	1.50%	4.80%
Travel Bookings	50.40%	9.80%	3.10%	12.80%
Transcripts/Admit Card	67.30%	15.00%	3.10%	7.20%
Resume	71.90%	20.40%	4.10%	10.60%
Medical Reports	36.30%	6.30%	1.80%	3.10%
Job Offers	58.30%	10.80%	2.30%	5.90%
Passport	49.20%	10.70%	2.40%	5.00%
PAN Card	52.50%	10.20%	2.40%	4.90%
Aadhar Card	44.10%	8.60%	2.00%	4.40%
License	42.90%	8.10%	1.90%	4.80%
Voter ID	46.10%	8.40%	1.80%	4.40%
Birth Certificate	45.30%	8.20%	1.70%	3.10%
Credit/Debit Card Data	32.60%	5.20%	1.20%	3.70%

would contain stored passwords and that one in three investigated individuals would have common passwords for all their accounts.

Storage of Personal Files on Devices. This question was framed to make the survey participants aware of the private files stored on the digital devices they own or use. This would enable them to appreciate the risk they would incur if their devices were to be seized in digital investigations. The question asked the survey participants to specify the devices on which they stored certain types of private files. The participants were required to answer this question for all the listed private files. The responses provided a relative ranking of the devices on which individuals prefer to store various types of private files.

A total of 1,474 individuals answered this question. For reasons of space, only the notable findings are discussed. The survey revealed that 81.50% of the respondents stored their personal photographs on their laptops or desktops, and 30% to 35% stored personal photographs on USB drives, portable hard drives, online accounts and smartphones. Digital photographs were the most ubiquitous type of personal files stored across digital devices and online storage services.

Table 7 shows the percentages of survey participants who stored various personal files and documents on digital devices. Note that the PAN card is issued by the Income Tax Department of India, the Aadhar card

Table 8. Rankings of personal files/documents and PII stored on digital devices.

File/Document	Percentage	PII	Percentage
Credit/Debit Card Data	76.90%	Phone Number	74.60%
PAN Card	73.10%	PAN Card Data	72.30%
Transcripts/Admit Card	72.00%	Email Address	72.20%
Voter ID	71.40%	Full Name	70.39%
Passport	68.60%	Bank Data	69.90%
License	68.30%	Biometrics	69.10%
Aadhar Card	65.60%	Date of Birth	68.60%
Photographs	63.00%	Home Address	68.50%
Job Offers	62.80%	Passwords	68.30%
Birth Certificate	62.70%	Father's Name	67.66%
Resume	61.90%	Passport Data	65.60%
Bank Statements	61.20%	Aadhar Card Data	64.00%
		License Details	63.60%
		ATM PIN	62.20%
		Mother's Maiden Name	61.53%

is a biometric identity card issued by the Government of India and the Voter ID is issued by the Election Commission of India. For every type of private file or document specified in the question, the largest percentage of survey participants stored the file or document on their laptops or desktops. This finding supports the hypothesis that an individual's laptop and desktop tend to contain large amounts of personal data and that the individual's privacy is at risk when these devices are seized in digital forensic investigations.

Ranking Personal Files/Documents and PII. Two questions were framed to obtain the relative rankings of personal files/documents and personally-identifiable information (PII). The participants were asked to rank the entries on a scale of 1 to 5, where 1 corresponded to least important and 5 corresponded to most important. The motive was to have each participant assign relative priorities to personal files/documents and personally-identifiable information before the participant was introduced to the processes involved in evidence seizure and digital investigations. After obtaining the preliminary rankings for the first question, the second question asked the participants if they would change their rankings if their devices were seized for investigative purposes.

A total of 1,474 individuals responded to the first question. Upon counting only rating values of 4 and 5, a total of 63% of the respondents rated personal photographs as being important. Table 8 provides the corresponding percentages for other types of files/documents.

Table 9. Ratings after digital devices were hypothetically seized.

Private Data	No Effect	Increase	Decrease
Personal Files/Documents (1,304 responses)	47.3%	43.8%	8.8%
Personally-Identifiable Information (1,304 responses)	46.7%	46.6%	6.8%

A total of 1,287 individuals rated various personally-identifiable information on a scale of 1 to 5, where 1 corresponded to least important and 5 corresponded to most important. The results reveal that 70.39% of the survey participants felt that their full names were important, and 67.66% rated their father's name and 61.53% rated their mother's maiden name as important personally-identifiable information. Table 8 provides the corresponding percentages for other important types of personally-identifiable information.

6.2   Awareness of Investigations

The questions in this subsection were designed to understand how an individual's ratings of personal information would change if his/her digital devices were to be seized for investigative purposes. A drastic shift was anticipated in the privacy ratings in such a situation and the shift was expected to be inversely proportional to the trust that an individual had in investigative agencies. The change in attitude was also expected to depend on the individual's awareness of the digital forensic investigation process and the fact that most digital forensic tools can locate and extract hidden and deleted data.

Trust in Investigative Agencies. The survey participants tended to believe that law enforcement and other investigative entities would not misuse their personal data if their devices were to be seized for investigative purposes. Table 9 shows that 56.1% (= 47.3% + 8.8%) and 53.5% (= 46.7% + 6.8%) of the participants said that there would either be no effect on their previous privacy ratings for personal files/documents and personally-identifiable information, respectively, or their privacy ratings would decrease. It is especially interesting that the participants, who said that their privacy ratings would decrease, were actually less concerned about the privacy of their data after a hypothetical device seizure.

Awareness of Digital Forensics. Another question asked the survey participants if investigative agencies had tools to recover hidden or deleted data. The survey results indicate that 32.21% of the participants were not sure if this was possible and 20.25% believed that such data could not be recovered. Only 47.4% of the participants were aware that hidden or deleted data could be recovered. Despite the fact that nearly half of the survey participants knew that hidden or deleted data was recoverable, when answering the next question, 40.95% of the participants said that they temporarily stored their personal information on their office devices.

7.   Proposed Data Privacy Solution

The survey results indicate that the privacy of an investigated individual is at risk during a digital forensic investigation and that there is an urgent need to incorporate data privacy measures into the investigative process. A data privacy solution should protect the investigated individual while ensuring that neither the completeness of the investigation nor the integrity of the digital evidence are compromised. It is also highly desirable that the solution enhance investigator efficiency and save time and effort. Dehghantanha and Franke [4] have highlighted the importance of privacy-respecting digital investigations. The next section briefly discusses the research literature that addresses privacy in the context of digital forensic investigations. Following this discussion, the proposed data privacy solution is presented.

7.1   Privacy and Investigations

Aminnezhad et al. [1] have noted that digital forensic investigators find it difficult to strike the right balance between protecting the privacy of investigated individuals and performing complete investigations. They also observe that the general lack of awareness about data privacy on the part of digital forensic investigators could result in unintentional abuses.

Several researchers have attempted to use cryptographic mechanisms to protect data privacy during digital forensic investigations. Law et al. [10] have proposed a technique that encrypts data in an email server and simultaneously indexes case-related keywords. The investigator provides keywords to the server owner who has the encryption keys and uses them to decrypt emails containing the keywords, following which the emails are sent to the investigator.

Hou et al. [6, 9] have proposed mechanisms for protecting data residing at service provider storage centers using homomorphic, commutative encryption. The mechanisms also ensure that the service provider does not have any knowledge of the queries issued by an investigator. Hou et al. [7, 8] also present a similar solution for a remote server.

Shebaro and Crandall [15] have used identity-based encryption to conduct a network traffic data investigation in a privacy-preserving setting. Gou et al. [5] have specified generic privacy policies for network forensic investigations. Croft and Olivier [3] have proposed a technique that compartmentalizes data into layers of sensitivity, where less private data is in the lower layers and more private data is in the higher layers. Investigator access to private information is controlled by initially restricting access only to the lower layers. The investigator is required to demonstrate his knowledge and behavior in the lower layers to obtain access to information in the higher layers.

Van Staden [16] has proposed a privacy-enhancing technology framework for protecting the privacy of third parties during digital forensic investigations. The framework requires an investigator to write focused queries when searching for potential evidence. The framework evaluates whether or not the query results cause a privacy breach. If a breach is deemed to occur, then the investigator is asked to submit a more focused query. If an investigator overrides the query results and attempts to access private data, the framework logs the investigator's actions in a secure location.

7.2   Privacy Solution

The proposed data privacy solution does not interfere with the outcomes of a digital forensic investigation. The solution, which is presented in Figure 1, brings more transparency to the investigative process and increases investigator accountability.

The solution focuses on the analysis phase of a digital forensic investigation, during which an investigator analyzes images of the storage media in the seized digital devices. In addition to the images, the solution methodology takes two additional inputs, namely the learned knowledge of similar cases from a case profile database and the details of the case at hand. The case profile database is a collection of case-specific features that may be used to predict potential pieces of evidence for a particular case. The database contains a feature list based on the contents and metadata of evidence files and investigator reviews obtained from historical cases studies. The feature list selection for the database also requires taxonomic information about private data and files that exist on computer systems.

All the inputs are processed by a privacy-preserving forensic tool that identifies the pieces of evidence relevant to the case at hand. The forensic

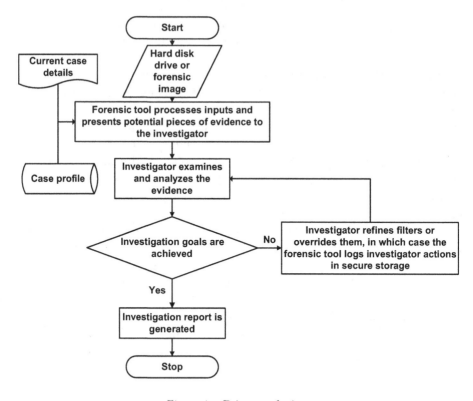

Figure 1.   Privacy solution.

tool needs to ensure the completeness of an investigation. The tool may generate false positives, but it should never report a false negative. The system proposed by van Staden [16] requires an investigator to submit focused queries to obtain potential evidence from an image. If the tool determines that the investigator's query results violate privacy, then the investigator has two options. The first option is to submit a fresh query that does not violate privacy. The second option is to override the privacy-filtering functionality and conduct the investigation in a conventional manner; in this case, the tool logs all the investigator's actions in secure storage to prevent tampering. As such, the tool adds an extra layer of search without any gain in knowledge or efficiency.

   The proposed privacy-preserving forensic tool simplifies the investigator's task by providing advice regarding potential evidence for the case at hand. If the investigator finds the results to be insufficient, then the investigator could mark the existing evidence and fine-tune the tool predictions by adding more information. Or, the investigator could override the prediction results and continue the investigation in a conventional manner; all the investigator's actions and their timestamps would then be logged in a secure manner. The authenticity of the logged actions are strengthened by obtaining the modification access change date and time-stamps corresponding to the actions directly from the operating system kernel [2, 17]. The logs are vital to resolving complaints about potential privacy breaches. After the investigator collects sufficient evidence from the output list, the investigative process is complete and the case report is generated.

The proposed privacy-preserving solution would not infringe on the powers of the investigator; it simply brings more accountability and transparency to the investigative process. The investigator would have a clear idea about the responsibilities with regard to data privacy and the performance of the investigator would not be compromised.

8. Conclusions

The surveys of investigators, lawyers and the general public provide valuable insights into their data privacy perceptions with regard to digital forensic investigations. The survey results reveal a lack of professional ethics on the part of some investigators, a lack of legal support for lawyers with regard to data privacy protection and confusion among the general public regarding their data privacy rights. While the numbers of participants in the investigator and lawyer surveys were limited, the survey responses were valuable due to the levels of expertise and experience of the participants. A total of 654 out of 1,889 (34.6%) participants in the general public survey did not complete the survey; their principal complaint was that the survey was very comprehensive and time-consuming. Nevertheless, the results and the concerns raised are relevant in India as well as in countries around the world.

The survey results demonstrate that there is an urgent need for a privacy-preserving digital forensic investigation framework that protects data privacy without compromising digital forensic investigations. The simple, yet efficient, privacy-protecting solution proposed in this work ensures the privacy of the subjects of investigations without compromising the completeness and efficiency of investigations. The solution also does not infringe on the powers of investigators; it simply brings more accountability and transparency to the investigative process.

Future research will focus on implementing the privacy-preserving digital forensic tool and evaluating its performance in real-world investigations. A key issue when using the tool is to choose the correct filters and parameters so that the probability of finding all possible evidence (before the filters are overridden) is maximized. Future research will also focus on methods for selecting appropriate filters and parameters.

References

[1] A. Aminnezhad, A. Dehghantanha and M. Abdullah, A survey of privacy issues in digital forensics, *International Journal of Cyber-Security and Digital Forensics*, vol. 1(4), pp. 311–323, 2012.

[2] M. Barik, G. Gupta, S. Sinha, A. Mishra and C. Mazumdar, An efficient technique for enhancing forensic capabilities of the Ext2 filesystem, *Digital Investigation*, vol. 4(S), pp. S55–S61, 2007.

[3] N. Croft and M. Olivier, Sequenced release of privacy-accurate information in a forensic investigation, *Digital Investigation*, vol. 7(1-2), pp. 95–101, 2010.

[4] A. Dehghantanha and K. Franke, Privacy-respecting digital investigation, *Proceedings of the Twelfth Annual International Conference on Privacy, Security and Trust*, pp. 129–138, 2014.

[5] H. Guo, B. Jin and D. Huang, Research and review in computer forensics, in *Forensics in Telecommunications, Information and Multimedia*, X. Lai, D. Gu, B. Jin, Y. Wang and H. Li (Eds.), Springer, Berlin Heidelberg, Germany, pp. 224–233, 2011.

[6] S. Hou, R. Sasaki, T. Uehara and S. Yiu, Verifying data authenticity and integrity in server-aided confidential forensic investigations, *Proceedings of the International Conference on Information and Communication Technology*, pp. 312–317, 2013.

[7] S. Hou, T. Uehara, S. Yiu, L. Hui and K. Chow, Privacy preserving confidential forensic investigation for shared or remote servers, *Proceedings of the Seventh International Conference on Intelligent Information Hiding and Multimedia Signal Processing*, pp. 378–383, 2011.

[8] S. Hou, T. Uehara, S. Yiu, L. Hui and K. Chow, Privacy preserving multiple keyword search for confidential investigations of remote forensics, *Proceedings of the Third International Conference on Multimedia Information Networking and Security*, pp. 595–599, 2011.

[9] S. Hou, S. Yiu, T. Uehara and R. Sasaki, Application of secret sharing techniques in confidential forensic investigations, *Proceedings of the Second International Conference on Cyber Security, Cyber Peacefare and Digital Forensics*, pp. 69–76, 2013.

[10] F. Law, P. Chan, S. Yiu, K. Chow, M. Kwan, H. Tse and P. Lai, Protecting digital data privacy in computer forensic examinations, *Proceedings of the Sixth International Workshop on Systematic Approaches to Digital Forensic Engineering*, 2011.

[11] A. Moore, Defining privacy, *Journal of Social Philosophy*, vol. 39(3), pp. 411–428, 2008.

[12] K. Ruan, J. Carthy and T. Kechadi, Survey of cloud forensics and critical criteria for cloud forensic capability: A preliminary analysis, *Proceedings of the Sixth Annual Conference on Digital Forensics, Security and Law*, pp. 55–69, 2011.

[13] K. Ruan, J. Carthy, T. Kechadi and I. Baggili, Cloud forensics definitions and critical criteria for cloud forensic capability: An overview of survey results, *Digital Investigation*, vol. 10(1), pp. 34–43, 2013.

[14] K. Seth, IT Act 2000 vs. 2008 – Implementation, challenges and the role of adjudicating officers, *Proceedings of the National Seminar on Enforcement of Cyberlaw*, 2010.

[15] B. Shebaro and J. Crandall, Privacy-preserving network flow recording, *Digital Investigation*, vol. 8(S), pp. S90–S100, 2011.

[16] W. van Staden, Protecting third party privacy in digital forensic investigations, in *Advances in Digital Forensics IX*, G. Peterson and S. Shenoi (Eds.), Springer, Berlin Heidelberg, Germany, pp. 19–31, 2013.

[17] R. Verma, J. Govindaraj and G. Gupta, Preserving dates and time-stamps for incident handling in Android smartphones, in *Advances in Digital Forensics X*, G. Peterson and S. Shenoi (Eds.), Springer, Berlin Heidelberg, Germany, pp. 209–225, 2014.

Chapter 3

A FRAMEWORK FOR ASSESSING THE CORE CAPABILITIES OF A DIGITAL FORENSIC ORGANIZATION

Ahmed Almarzooqi and Andrew Jones

Abstract   This chapter describes a framework for building and managing the capabilities of digital forensic organizations. The framework employs equations that express the relationships between core capabilities, enabling the definition of digital forensic capabilities. Straussian grounded theory is used to create the theoretical framework that is grounded in the data. The framework is also grounded in the literature on digital forensic capabilities, specifically research related to digital forensic readiness, capability maturity models, digital forensic management frameworks and best practices for building and managing digital forensic laboratories. Thus, the framework is readily integrated with other theories; indeed, it can identify gaps existing in the theories and provides opportunities to extend the theories.

Keywords: Digital forensic readiness, grounded theory, capability maturity model

1.   Introduction

Research in digital forensics primarily focuses on the quality of evidence, enhancing the investigation process and developing tools [3, 14]. However, limited research has focused on the decisions made when building and managing the capabilities of a digital forensic organization. To begin with, digital forensics lacks a definition of what constitutes the "capabilities" of a digital forensic organization.

This research surveyed more than thirty digital forensic experts from the United Kingdom and United Arab Emirates on building and managing the capabilities of a digital forensic organization. The participants discussed two types of capabilities. One type of capability covers the ability of an organization to perform digital forensic investigations. An-

G. Peterson and S. Shenoi (Eds.): Advances in Digital Forensics XII, IFIP AICT 484, pp. 47–65, 2016.
DOI: 10.1007/978-3-319-46279-0_3

other is an organization's capabilities as a whole, where digital forensic investigations are only part of the capabilities. For both types of capabilities, the survey participants were almost unanimous in stating the lack of, and the need for, guidance on specifying capabilities and standards for building and managing the capabilities of digital forensic organizations. While there have been numerous proposals on creating standards, models and frameworks for the digital investigation process [19], no unified standard or framework exists for developing, managing and implementing digital forensic capabilities in organizations, whether in the public (law enforcement) or private (corporate) domains.

This chapter proposes the Digital Forensic Organization Core Capability (DFOCC) Framework as a tool for understanding, improving and standardizing the creation and management of the capabilities of digital forensic organizations. The framework provides a roadmap for developing the capabilities of digital forensic organizations, identifying success factors and creating an attainable universal benchmark that could be used in place of timely and costly accreditation processes.

2.   Research Methodology

The proposed framework employs grounded theory [8], a method for discovering theories based on an analysis of the data and explaining participant behavior. Grounded theory focuses on actions and interactions. Since the research attempted to identify patterns in the actions and interactions involved in the development and management of the capabilities of a digital forensic organization, the questions of how and why digital forensic organizations and individual stakeholders understand and develop digital forensic capabilities are best suited to the application of grounded theory.

Martin and Turner [13] define a grounded theory methodology as "an inductive theory discovery methodology that allows the researcher to develop a theoretical account of the general features of a topic while simultaneously grounding the account in empirical observations or data." In short, the goal of grounded theory is to propose a theory. This research attempts to use the proposed DFOCC framework, which was discovered from the data and systematically obtained from social science research, to explore the integral social relationships and the behavior of groups in a digital forensic organization. The primary goal is to understand and explain the development and management of the capabilities of digital forensic organizations.

The core categories of the proposed framework emerged from the data through the three stages of coding processes in Straussian grounded theory, namely, open, axial and selective coding [4, 15]. After a review of the data using the grounded theory coding processes and after examining the relationships between the core categories at the dimensional level, four core categories emerged from the categories and subcategories: (i) policy; (ii) people; (iii) infrastructure; and (iv) investigation. By applying grounded theory, it was possible to understand the relationships between abstract concepts in digital forensic organizations that were derived from categories and grouped as core categories at abstract levels. Although a theory is automatically grounded when using a grounded theory method, it was possible to demonstrate specific instances where the theory connects to concepts and phenomena in the data and to validate the data during the axial and selective coding phases as required by grounded theory. Validation was performed through subsequent interviews and by examining the fit, relevance, workability and modifiability of the theory.

3. Related Work

A review of the literature was performed before conducting the participant interviews. This review also served as a form of validation in grounded theory. Straussian grounded theory allows researchers to consult the literature before starting data collection and data analysis [4]. Four areas of digital forensics research validated the focus on and the need to create a framework for building and managing the capabilities of digital forensic organizations: (i) digital forensic readiness [16]; (ii) capability maturity models [1, 12]; (iii) digital forensic management frameworks [9]; and (iv) best practices for building and managing digital forensic laboratories [11].

3.1 Digital Forensic Readiness

The research of Grobler [9] validates the need for creating a framework for building and managing the capabilities of digital forensic organizations. In particular, Grobler discusses the implementation of digital forensic capabilities in the context of digital forensic readiness, one of the principal challenges in digital forensics. According to Rowlingson [16], digital forensic readiness is "the ability of an organization to maximize its potential to use digital evidence when required." Digital forensic readiness, therefore, does not address the capabilities of a digital forensic organization that conducts investigations, but rather a non-digital-forensic organization that receives the services and/or products of a digital forensic organization. In this regard, digital forensic readiness is not only insufficient, but also not relevant to the capabilities of a digital forensic organization. Digital forensic readiness prepares the clients of digital forensic organizations whereas the proposed DFOCC framework prepares the digital forensic organizations themselves.

Regardless, digital forensic readiness is a key component of the digital forensic investigation process because its implementation assists digital forensic investigators even before incidents or crimes have occurred. Therefore, digital forensic readiness is proactive rather than reactive in nature. Von Solms et al. [20] have proposed a digital control framework that takes into account digital forensic readiness to provide governance for the digital forensic investigation process. However, this digital forensic control framework does not address the development and management of the capabilities of digital forensic organizations.

3.2   Capability Maturity Model

The literature survey also reviewed efforts focused on applying the capability maturity model to building and managing the capabilities of a digital forensic organization [1, 9, 12]. The capability maturity model has been applied in two contexts: (i) digital forensic investigation context; and (ii) digital forensic capability context. Before explaining the limits of the capability maturity model with regard to explaining digital forensic organization capabilities, it is important to first explain the capability maturity model and its origins. Next, the application of the capability maturity model in digital forensic investigations is discussed. This is followed by the application of the capability maturity model to digital forensic capabilities. Finally, it is shown that the capability maturity model can complement a digital forensic capability framework, but it does not, by itself, achieve a comprehensive view of digital forensic capabilities.

The capability maturity model is used to "describe the degree to which an organization applies formali[z]ed processes to the management of its various business functions" [12]. The model usually applies five levels of maturity in determining the capability levels of an organization's processes. The model was first used in software engineering as an objective assessment tool to measure the abilities of government contractor processes to perform software projects. The capability maturity model was later applied to other disciplines and process areas as a framework for process improvement.

Kerrigan [12] applied the capability maturity model to digital forensic investigations after reviewing several digital forensic investigation frameworks and models. Kerrigan specifically noted that the capability maturity model had to be applied keeping in mind three important and interrelated concepts: (i) people; (ii) process; and (iii) technology. Kerrigan identified five levels of maturity: (i) ad hoc; (ii) performed; (iii) defined; (iv) managed; and (v) optimized. The five levels were applied to the three key factors (people, process and technology) of organizational capabilities to conduct digital forensic investigations. Of the three key factors, only process was broken down to lower types of actions and interactions.

While Kerrigan [12] extended the capability maturity model to digital forensic investigations, the model was not applied to building and managing digital forensic organization capabilities. In other words, Kerrigan's focus was on the investigative process. An advantage of Kerrigan's approach is that it recognizes the role of people and technology in the digital forensic investigation process. However, the approach fails to express specific actions/interactions in the people and technology categories that would clarify the relationships between the categories.

Al-Hanaei and Rashid [1] have applied the capability maturity model to the capabilities of a digital forensic organization. Their model has six levels of maturity that are largely similar to Kerrigan's five levels. Additionally, like Kerrigan's model, the model considers improvements to the process, tools (technology) and skills (people). Unfortunately, like Kerrigan's model, the model of Al-Hanaei and Rashid does not address the development and management of the capabilities of digital forensic organizations. Also, it fails to clarify how the tools and technology are to be improved.

One reason for the silence of capability maturity models on the detailed relationships and requirements of people and technology is their inherent limitation in explaining the capabilities of a digital forensic organization. A capability maturity model focuses mainly on the process because, by definition, the model is a tool for improving or enhancing existing business processes. Furthermore, unlike the proposed DFOCC framework, a capability maturity model fails to take policy into full consideration as a core capability. Finally, because a capability maturity model is concerned more with improving existing processes within an organization, it is not helpful with regard to building or developing the capabilities of an organization or determining standard minimum requirements for the capabilities.

Nevertheless, the capability maturity model could enhance the proposed DFOCC framework, where DFOCC serves as the roadmap for a digital forensic organization to create a benchmark. While the capability maturity model literature suggests that the model can be used to set benchmarks, its application to a digital forensic organization is difficult because the model does not consider the detailed actions and

Table 1. Comparison of DFMF dimensions and DFOCC categories.

DFMF	DFOCC
Legal and Judicial	N/A
Governance	N/A
Policy	Policy
Process	Investigation
People	People
Technology	Infrastructure

interactions and the relationships between the capabilities. A capability maturity model, for example, would not suggest that there must be at least two types of tools and two investigators as a benchmark. This is because the model determines a benchmark based on the clients' existing capabilities, whether or not the perceived capabilities meet the definition of capabilities under the proposed DFOCC framework.

3.3   Digital Forensics Management Framework

The Digital Forensic Management Framework (DFMF) of Grobler [9] is most relevant to building and managing digital forensic organization capabilities. Grobler categorized individual actions in a comprehensive investigation model to identify the dimensions of digital forensics. He then constructed the framework based on these dimensions, which, interestingly, match the core categories of the DFOCC framework that is based on grounded theory.

Table 1 compares the DFMF dimensions with the DFOCC categories. The table clearly reveals the similarities and differences between DFMF and DFOCC. The basic similarities are the four common core capabilities of a digital forensic organization: (i) policy; (ii) process/investigation; (iii) people; and (iv) technology/infrastructure. DFMF adds legal and judicial and governance as additional dimensions whereas DFOCC identifies these two concepts using a conditional matrix as affecting capabilities, albeit not as core capabilities. It appears that the only differences are the wording – DFMF uses process and technology while DFOCC uses investigation and infrastructure, respectively.

A closer look at the DFMF requirements and deliverables levels reveals many similarities and concerns when compared with the categories and subcategories identified by DFOCC using grounded theory.

Tables 2 and 3 compare the DFMF requirements and deliverables against the DFOCC categories and subcategories. The similarities show that DFOCC, which is based on grounded theory, is consistent with

Table 2. Comparison of DFMF requirements and deliverables and DFOCC categories and subcategories.

DFMF Deliverable	DFMF Requirement	Core Category	DFOCC Category	DFOCC Subcategory
	Evidence handling and management policies	Policy	Facility building and management standards	Standards
				Best practices
				Guidelines
				Lab accreditation
	Incident management policies		Organizational policies	Information security policy
	Education, training and awareness policies			Physical security policy
	Management policies			Technology use policy
	Infrastructure policies			Confidentiality and NDA
				Standards/accreditation
Evidence management	Evidence handling procedures	Process	Investigation process	Scope of investigation
Digital evidence				Identification
Incident handling	Incident management procedures			Preservation
Investigation procedures				Analysis
				Reporting
				ACPO principles
BIA	Risk mgmt/contingency procedures		Evidence admissibility	Data verif/validation
IRP				Chain of custody
DRP				Investigator qualifications
BCP				Expert testimony
New technologies				Authentication
General management	Management procedures		Investigation procedures	Documentation Standard (ASCLD)
Use of forensics for non-forensics purposes				Pre-investigation
				Case management
Operational infrastructure	Infrastructure procedures			Post-investigation

Table 3. Comparison of DFMF requirements and deliverables and DFOCC categories and subcategories (continued).

DFMF Deliverable	DFMF Requirement	Core Category	DFOCC Category	DFOCC Subcategory
	Code of conduct	People	Knowledge/background	Information technology
				Law
Technical education and training	Awareness programs		Education	Discipline
				Degree
	Education and training programs		Experience	Industry experience
				Length of experience
First responder			Training and development	Types of training
Investigator				Training as qualifications
				Development
			Organizational hierarchy	Organization size
				Organization type
Expert witness			Investigator traits	Investigative
				Communicative
				Technical
				Analytical
Intrusion detection	Operational infrastructure	Technology	Tools	Tool selection
Systematic gathering				Forensic software
Monitoring				Standard tools
Networks				Hardware
Time synchronization				Software/hardware
				Peripherals
				Small-scale devices
Hardware	Investigation infrastructure		Building a facility	Process
Software				Facility requirements
Miscellaneous				Financial
			Virtual environment	Functionality/purpose
				Cloud

some initial findings in the literature. This is especially true with regard to the multi-dimensional approach used to develop DFMF. The multi-dimensional approach was drawn from the information security domain, which von Solms called a multi-dimensional discipline [10]. Specifically, von Solms identified various dimensions for information security, including people, policy, risk management, legal, ethical, insurance, technology, strategic governance and operational governance. The dimensions were also used to develop an assessment model for information security using the corporate governance, people, policy, legal, compliance and technology dimensions. These dimensions create the similarities between DFMF and DFOCC.

Most significantly, the DFOCC core categories and the DFMF dimensions were created using different methods. DFOCC is based on grounded theory, which means that its core categories were derived by grounding the data throughout data analysis. DFMF, on the other hand, does not rely on such a systematic method; instead, it is derived from the literature in the multi-dimensional discipline of information security. In other words, the DFOCC is grounded in data, while the DFMF is not. In such a case, according to Jones and Valli [11], grounded theory "can furnish additional value when literature fails to support the theoretical evolution of phenomena." This makes the use of grounded theory in this research even more appropriate.

Although the goals, application and methodology of DFMF differ from those of DFOCC, DFMF actually validates DFOCC. This is because the DFMF dimensions and the DFOCC core capabilities focus on the same four areas: policy, process/investigation, people and technology/infrastructure. The strong correlations between the two frameworks, coupled with the multidimensional nature of the information security domain, demonstrate that DFOCC and DFMF lead to the same end point despite using different paths to get there. Indeed, DFMF and DFOCC both establish that digital forensic organizations must consider the four core capabilities when making decisions about digital forensics regardless of whether they are viewed from a management, development or investigation perspective.

3.4 Digital Forensic Laboratory Development

DFOCC provides a framework for sorting through a complete list of needs when developing a digital forensic organization. The financial constraints and scope of a digital forensic organization impact the extent to which the organization will adopt the set of capabilities in the books. As stated by Jones and Valli [11], the minimum requirements of a digital forensic organization depends on factors such as the budget and scope of the organization's products and services. Jones and Valli also provide a "shopping list" of what an organization may or may not need according to its requirements. What is missing in the literature, therefore, is a guide on how to pick and choose the appropriate capabilities for a digital forensic organization to meet some minimum requirements. The difficulty, of course, is that the minimum requirements are subjective and highly dependent on the needs of an organization.

4. DFOCC Framework

DFOCC is a tool for building and managing the capabilities of digital forensic organizations. Note that DFOCC does not provide all the answers to developing and managing capabilities; such a task is beyond the scope of this research. Instead, the main goal of DFOCC is to make sense of the patterns identified in the data.

4.1 Equation Representation

DFOCC is based on an equation that concisely expresses the relationships in the data analyzed using grounded theory. The relationships between the four core categories are expressed using the equation:

$$C = P_1 \cdot (P_2 + I_1 + I_2) \tag{1}$$

where C denotes the capabilities of a digital forensic organization, $P1$ denotes policy, $P2$ denotes people, $I1$ denotes infrastructure and $I2$ denotes investigation. The equation was obtained using grounded theory, which involved the use of theoretical sensitivity and a conditional matrix, and grounding the theory in the data.

According to Equation (1), the capabilities of a digital forensic organization are obtained by multiplying policy (P_1) with the sum of people (P_2), infrastructure (I_1) and investigation (I_2). Thus, the capabilities cannot be achieved without policy. Policy is an overarching multiplier because each of the other three categories cannot exist without policies in place. Another consequence of using policy as a multiplier is that the equation can be expressed in partial terms as:

$$C = P_1 \cdot P_2 + P_1 \cdot I_1 + P_1 \cdot I_2 \tag{2}$$

This means that the core capabilities of people, infrastructure and investigation can be viewed separately, but each must be viewed with the policy multiplier. For example, it is not possible to have an infrastructure capability without policies in place that govern the use of software, the maintenance of software, access control, etc. The same is true for the relationship of policy with the capabilities of people and investigation.

The DFOCC equations express several observations and statements about digital forensics and the development and management of the capabilities of digital forensic organizations. One of them is the definition of the capabilities of a digital forensic organization as the sum of the core capabilities of people, infrastructure and investigation governed by a comprehensive set of policies as a unique capability.

This definition of capabilities does not set a comprehensive minimum standard of capabilities for all digital forensic organizations. Instead, it requires all digital forensic organizations to consider the four core capabilities. For example, a digital forensic organization that does not have any policy governing people should not be considered capable regardless of the quality of the people and technology in the organization.

The following sub-equation expresses the comparative weight of the capabilities:

$$P_1 \cdot I_2 = P_1 \cdot P_2 + P_1 \cdot I_1 \tag{3}$$

where the addition of the capabilities of people and infrastructure equals the capabilities of investigation. In other words, investigation is the sum of people and infrastructure because people (digital forensic investigators and managers) use the infrastructure (hardware, software and laboratory) to conduct successful investigations. It is important to note that policy remains an important multiplier. A statement that can be derived from this sub-equation relates to investigation capabilities as follows: the capabilities of a digital forensic organization with regard to conducting digital forensic investigations are determined by the organization's capabilities with regard to people and infrastructure, each of which is governed by a set of policies.

The above statement is a subset of the previous statement regarding organizational capabilities. However, it is important to clearly delineate the difference between organizational capabilities and investigation capabilities. A digital forensic organization may be able to conduct digital forensic investigations, but it may not necessarily be a capable digital forensic organization. In other words, investigation capabilities can exist absent policies because the investigation process has frameworks in place that can account for the lack of a comprehensive set of policies. The organization's capabilities, on the other hand, cannot exist without comprehensive policies.

4.2   Role of Policy

The DFOCC framework suggests that policy must be present in all aspects of capabilities within a digital forensic organization. In particular, a digital forensic organization must have a set of policies in place that govern people, infrastructure and investigations in order to be considered digital forensics capable.

The role of policy at the organizational level has already been identified in the digital forensic readiness literature [17, 18]. Organizational policy, therefore, has played a significant role in the digital forensic readiness literature. Policy is also prominent in digital forensic standards, accreditation and best practices – International Standards Organization (ISO) standards, Association of Chief Police Officers (ACPO) guidelines in the United Kingdom and American Society of Crime Lab Directors (ASCLD) accreditation standards in the United States all incorporate policies in their processes. DFOCC states in clear terms that policy is a requirement for all the core capabilities; thus, organization capabilities cannot be achieved without policies. A set of policies must exist for people, infrastructure and investigations, regardless of how extensive the policy set may be. At the minimum, a digital forensic organization should consider adopting policies across the core capabilities that enhance the admissibility of evidence. An example of such a policy is access control, which bolsters the credibility and reliability of the entire organization as well as the resulting evidence. A starting point for such an inquiry is the essential requirements imposed by the American Society of Crime Lab Directors [2]. These essential requirements are standards that directly affect and have a fundamental impact on the work product of a laboratory and/or the integrity of the evidence [7]. The DFOCC framework and its equations lend themselves to further observations and statements about what it means to be a digital forensics capable organization in the context of development and management.

5.   DFOCC Application

An important question is why DFOCC is important or even worth researching. Also, how exactly does DFOCC help digital forensic organizations? This section attempts to answer these questions and explain the applicability of the DFOCC framework to digital forensics. The DFOCC equations presented in the previous section can be applied to digital forensics in order to develop and manage digital forensic organizations. First, DFOCC can be used as a development tool to create a roadmap for building a digital forensic organization. Second, DFOCC can enhance evidence admissibility. Third, DFOCC can help improve the efficiency and effectiveness of a digital forensic organization by improving management and going after areas of success. Finally, DFOCC creates a universal benchmark for organization capabilities that also takes into account small and consultancy-level digital forensic organizations.

5.1 Roadmap for Organization Development

No standard framework is currently available for building a digital forensic organization. This observation was corroborated in the survey data when the participants were asked: "Do you know any guideline for developing digital forensic [capabilities], a standard guideline?" The majority of the survey participants indicated that no industry standard exists for developing or managing digital forensic capabilities. Some participants did mention the Association of Chief Police Officers guide and the International Standards Organization and American Society of Crime Lab Directors standards and best practices. However, most participants noted that these are not directly related to developing and managing digital forensic capabilities.

DFOCC surpasses the work of Jones and Valli [11] in that it provides a framework for sorting through a complete list of the needs for developing a digital forensic organization. This is the same position taken by Jones and Valli as well as the International Standards Organization and American Society of Crime Lab Directors publications. In fact, according to the FBI [7], "the fact that a laboratory chooses not to apply for [ASCLD] accreditation does not imply that a laboratory is inadequate or that its results cannot be trusted." Jones and Valli provide a comprehensive "shopping list" of what a digital forensic organization may or may not need according to its requirements.

At this time, a guide is needed to help select the appropriate capabilities of a digital forensic organization that meet some sort of minimum requirements. The difficulty is that the minimum requirements are highly dependent on the needs of an organization [11]. The DFOCC framework provides a potential roadmap that can guide a digital forensic organization in its decision making process. The framework states that, in order to be able to conduct digital forensic investigations, there must be people, infrastructure and a set of policies for people, infrastructure and investigations. DFOCC does not say what the policies are because they still have to be determined by factors such as the organization's budget, size and scope. DFOCC, however, gives a digital forensic organization a good starting point in the decision making process and a way to express a benchmark for the capabilities using the equation:

$$C = P_1 \cdot (P_2 + I_1 + I_2) \tag{4}$$

5.2   Evidence Admissibility

The DFOCC policy multiplier likely encourages digital forensic organizations to be more aware of the pitfalls of evidence admissibility. The survey participants stated that some reasons for the inadmissibility of digital forensic evidence were: (i) qualifications of digital forensic experts; (ii) authenticity of evidence via an unbroken chain of custody; and (iii) preservation of digital forensic evidence during investigations. Evidence likely becomes inadmissible because a digital forensic organization lacks the policies needed to ensure that the process it used satisfied the minimum threshold for admissibility.

The reasons for evidence becoming inadmissible can be connected to the DFOCC framework. For example, the qualifications of a digital forensic expert fall under the $P_1 \cdot P_2$ category, where digital forensic organizations ought to set a standard for educating and qualifying individuals as digital forensic experts, an issue that surprisingly is constantly debated in the discipline. Under the $P_1 \cdot P_2$ category, DFOCC would require a digital forensic organization to identify the qualifications of all its personnel. The digital forensic organization would have to create policies that cover the education and qualifications of its people. The lack of these policies and stated minimum requirements for qualifications would mean that a digital forensic organization does not have the requisite capabilities under DFOCC.

The chain of custody issue falls under the $P_1 \cdot I_2$ category of DFOCC, which requires organizations to create a documented policy for establishing chain of custody, a practice that is fortunately common in the discipline, but has not become a minimum standard for all digital forensic organizations to follow and for which all digital forensic organizations do not implement policies, as evidenced by the survey data. The lack of documented processes would mean that a digital forensic organization would not be deemed capable under DFOCC.

With regard to the preservation of the evidence during an investigation, the DFOCC framework would require the examination of an organization's evidence preservation practices, including the tools used and the processes followed to preserve the evidence. The tools should be accepted by the discipline as standard practice for preservation and digital forensic organizations should have policies in place that require the use of the tools to meet DFOCC capability requirements. The absence of tools for preserving evidence would mean that the digital forensic organization would not be deemed capable under the DFOCC framework. In other words, following the DFOCC framework would mean that a digital forensic organization has the minimum capabilities. Thus, the

Table 4. Sample application of the formula: $C = P_1 \cdot P_2 + P_1 \cdot I_1 + P_1 \cdot I_2$.

Policy and People $(\mathbf{P_1 \cdot P_2})$	Policy and Infrastructure $(\mathbf{P_1 \cdot I_1})$	Policy and Investigation $(\mathbf{P_1 \cdot I_2})$
People capabilities (more detailed than $P_1 \cdot I_1$ and $P_1 \cdot I_2$)	Infrastructure capabilities (less detailed than $P_1 \cdot P_2$)	Investigation capabilities (less detailed than $P_1 \cdot P_2$)
People policies (more detailed than $P_1 \cdot I_1$ and $P_1 \cdot I_2$)	Infrastructure policies (less detailed than $P_1 \cdot P_2$)	Investigation policies (less detailed than $P_1 \cdot P_2$)

digital evidence offered in court by a DFOCC-compliant organization would likely have a higher rate of admissibility.

5.3 Areas of Success

Another potential application of the DFOCC framework is to help identify areas of success in a digital forensic organization. Specifically, a digital forensic organization can use DFOCC to test whether perceived key factors of success match the organization's digital forensic capabilities. This can be done by first identifying a key success factor (e.g., quality of its people).

Next, the digital forensic organization must list all its digital forensic capabilities according to the DFOCC equation and examine if its capabilities match its key success factor. Table 4 shows how this works. The organization categorizes its capabilities according to the DFOCC equation by listing its people capabilities and people policy under the $P_1 \cdot P_2$ category, then its infrastructure capabilities and infrastructure polices under the $P_1 \cdot I_1$ category, and then its investigation capabilities and investigation polices under the $P_1 \cdot I_2$ category.

If the key success factor is really the quality of its people, then the list of people capabilities and people policies under the $P_1 \cdot P_2$ category would be comparatively more comprehensive and detailed than the $P_1 \cdot I_1$ and $P_1 \cdot I_2$ categories. The DFOCC framework potentially gives digital forensic organizations a systematic and simplified methodology for analyzing their capabilities and policies, and how the capabilities and policies relate to each other. Additionally, a digital forensic organization could perform comparisons across policies and, thus, create higher-level policies that cut across and unify the organization, possibly enhancing cohesion in the organization's processes.

5.4   Attainable Universal Benchmark

An important application of DFOCC is providing smaller organizations, even individual digital forensic consultants, with a means to create organizational benchmarks without undergoing a more expensive accreditation process. As one survey participant explained: "I don't believe you need to be accredited to [ISO] 27001 or 17025. I think those are good, but they're optional. They're a big burden. They are both ... big financial burdens."

Although additional data and research are needed to realize this potential, the DFOCC framework could serve a basis for identifying common benchmarks in digital forensic organizations that can be implemented without the burden of accreditation. For example, the survey reveals that the majority of participants use FTK from Access Data and/or EnCase from Guidance Software as their forensic analysis software. In other words, these two tools have become standard in the discipline. One survey participant stated the choice to use FTK and Encase as follows: "They are the industry standards. Everyone uses them, so we have to be able to read and write in their formats." Such observations could be established using quantitative research into digital forensic capabilities that leverages the DFOCC framework.

5.5   DFOCC Advantages

The DFOCC framework offers advantages in comparison with existing best practices and guidelines. First, the framework is simple and comprehensive. The framework narrows everything down to four variables: (i) policy; (ii) people; (iii) infrastructure; and (iv) investigation. Also, it can be expressed in equation form, which simplifies the expression of the relationships between the core capabilities as discussed above.

Another key advantage of DFOCC is that it is interconnected. The DFOCC equations recognize the interconnectedness of the core capabilities and policy acts as an adhesive for all the capabilities. Further, the survey data reveals that the interconnectedness also emerges in the category, subcategory and phenomenon levels. An example is the number of investigators (this corresponds to a dimension) that are needed in a laboratory. This issue initially affects the core people category by playing a key role in determining the scope and size of an organization. The same dimension, however, also appears in the investigation process with regard to the number of investigators needed to create a peer review system in a digital forensic investigation. The number of investigators also affects decisions regarding the infrastructure because the number of people in an organization is a factor in budgeting and creating software, hardware and facility requirements. Finally, the number of investigators affects policy because policies have to be specified for hiring and retaining people, performing validation and verification, and ensuring infrastructure efficiency.

Another advantage of the DFOCC framework is that it acts in a multilevel manner by considering the different types, sizes and scopes of digital forensic organizations. The framework could be applied to an individual as long as the individual has identified minimum benchmarks for each of the core categories using DFOCC. Finally, the formulation of the DFOCC framework using grounded theory is important; this ensures that the core categories and core capabilities are firmly grounded in data and that the data leads the application of the framework.

6. Conclusions

The DFOCC framework is designed specifically for building and managing the capabilities of digital forensic organizations. The framework employs equations that express the relationships between core capabilities, enabling the definition of digital forensic capabilities. The reliance of DFOCC on grounded theory means that the abstract notions of its core categories are themselves grounded in the data. Most importantly, the framework is also grounded in the literature on digital forensic capabilities, specifically research on digital forensic readiness, capability maturity models, digital forensic management frameworks and best practices for building and managing digital forensic laboratories. Therefore, the DFOCC framework is readily integrated with other theories; indeed, it identifies gaps existing in the theories and also provides opportunities to extend the theories.

References

[1] E. Al-Hanaei and A. Rashid, DF-C2M2: A capability maturity model for digital forensic organizations, *Proceedings of the IEEE Security and Privacy Workshops*, pp. 57–60, 2014.

[2] American Society of Crime Lab Directors/Laboratory Accreditation Board, Accreditation Programs, Garner, North Carolina, 2016.

[3] E. Casey, *Digital Evidence and Computer Crime: Forensic Science, Computers and the Internet*, Academic Press, Waltham, Massachusetts, 2011.

[4] J. Corbin and A. Strauss, *Basics of Qualitative Research: Techniques and Procedures for Developing Grounded Theory*, Sage Publications, Thousand Oaks, California, 2008.

[5] J. Creswell, *Research Design: Qualitative, Quantitative and Mixed Methods Approaches*, Sage Publications, Thousand Oaks, California, 2014.

[6] T. Ellis and Y. Levy, Towards a guide for novice researchers on research methodology: Review and proposed methods, *Issues in Informing Science and Information Technology*, vol. 6, pp. 323–337, 2009.

[7] Federal Bureau of Investigation, The accreditation decision, *Forensic Science Communications*, vol. 1(1), 1999.

[8] B. Glaser and A. Strauss, *The Discovery of Grounded Theory: Strategies for Qualitative Research*, Aldine Transaction, New Brunswick, New Jersey, 2009.

[9] C. Grobler, A Digital Forensic Management Framework, Ph.D. Thesis, Department of Informatics, Faculty of Science, University of Johannesburg, Auckland Park, South Africa, 2011.

[10] C. Grobler and B. Louwrens, Digital forensics: A multi-dimensional discipline, *Proceedings of the Information Security South Africa from Insight to Foresight Conference*, 2006.

[11] A. Jones and C. Valli, *Building a Digital Forensic Laboratory: Establishing and Managing a Successful Facility*, Butterworth-Heinemann and Syngress Publishing, Burlington, Massachusetts, 2009.

[12] M. Kerrigan, A capability maturity model for digital investigations, *Digital Investigation*, vol. 10(1), pp. 19–33, 2013.

[13] P. Martin and B. Turner, Grounded theory and organizational research, *Journal of Applied Behavioral Science*, vol. 22(2), pp. 141–157, 1986.

[14] M. Pollitt, An ad hoc review of digital forensic models, *Proceedings of the Second International Workshop on Systematic Approaches to Digital Forensic Engineering*, pp. 43–54, 2007.

[15] C. Robson, *Real World Research*, Blackwell Publishers, Malden, Massachusetts, 2002.

[16] R. Rowlingson, A ten-step process for forensic readiness, *International Journal of Digital Evidence*, vol. 2(3), 2004.

[17] R. Rowlingson, An Introduction to Forensic Readiness Planning, Technical Note 01/2005, National Infrastructure Security Coordination Centre, London, United Kingdom, 2005.

[18] C. Taylor, B. Endicott-Popovsky and D. Frincke, Specifying digital forensics: A forensics policy approach, *Digital Investigation*, vol. 4(S), pp. S101–S104, 2007.

[19] A. Valjarevic and H. Venter, A comprehensive and harmonized digital forensic investigation process model, *Journal of Forensic Sciences*, vol. 60(6), pp. 1467–1483, 2015.

[20] S. von Solms, C. Louwrens, C. Reekie and T. Grobler, A control framework for digital forensics, in *Advances in Digital Forensics II*, M. Olivier and S. Shenoi (Eds.), Springer, Boston, Massachusetts, pp. 343–355, 2006.

II

MOBILE DEVICE FORENSICS

Chapter 4

OPTIMIZING SHORT MESSAGE TEXT SENTIMENT ANALYSIS FOR MOBILE DEVICE FORENSICS

Oluwapelumi Aboluwarin, Panagiotis Andriotis, Atsuhiro Takasu and Theo Tryfonas

Abstract   Mobile devices are now the dominant medium for communications. Humans express various emotions when communicating with others and these communications can be analyzed to deduce their emotional inclinations. Natural language processing techniques have been used to analyze sentiment in text. However, most research involving sentiment analysis in the short message domain (SMS and Twitter) do not account for the presence of non-dictionary words. This chapter investigates the problem of sentiment analysis in short messages and the analysis of emotional swings of an individual over time. This provides an additional layer of information for forensic analysts when investigating suspects. The maximum entropy algorithm is used to classify short messages as positive, negative or neutral. Non-dictionary words are normalized and the impact of normalization and other features on classification is evaluated; in fact, this approach enhances the classification F-score compared with previous work. A forensic tool with an intuitive user interface has been developed to support the extraction and visualization of sentiment information pertaining to persons of interest. In particular, the tool presents an improved approach for identifying mood swings based on short messages sent by subjects. The timeline view provided by the tool helps pinpoint periods of emotional instability that may require further investigation. Additionally, the Apache Solr system used for indexing ensures that a forensic analyst can retrieve the desired information rapidly and efficiently using faceted search queries.

Keywords: Sentiment analysis, text mining, SMS, Twitter, normalization

© IFIP International Federation for Information Processing 2016
Published by Springer International Publishing AG 2016. All Rights Reserved
G. Peterson and S. Shenoi (Eds.): Advances in Digital Forensics XII, IFIP AICT 484, pp. 69–87, 2016.
DOI: 10.1007/978-3-319-46279-0_4

1.   Introduction

The ubiquity of mobile devices has redefined the communications landscape around the world. This has led to the creation of valuable individual data through conversational services such as SMS and micro blogging platforms such as Twitter. Mining the content of these interactions can provide valuable insights into the communicating entities. Information such as the time that an interaction occurred and the content of the communication can be useful to forensic analysts because it can reveal patterns that are hidden in the text.

Additional information about the disposition of conversations can be extracted using machine learning techniques. Sentiment analysis is the discipline concerned with retrieving opinion or emotion expressed in text. In the research literature, applications of sentiment analysis have been proposed in a variety of fields, especially related to social media and micro blogging services. As discussed in [1, 3], sentiment information can also be useful in forensic investigations of smartphones.

This chapter investigates the use of sentiment analysis to model the emotional swings of an individual as opposed to the emotional swings of a group of people towards a brand, which is more common in the research literature. Machine learning algorithms are employed for sentiment polarity classification. Normalization is used to account for lexically-incorrect terms that are prevalent in conversational texts; these invalid terms are known to negatively impact the efficiency of natural language processing [21]. A forensic tool with an intuitive user interface has been developed to support the extraction of sentiment information. The emotional timeline generated by the tool provides an additional layer of information about a person under investigation because it helps a forensic analyst identify periods of time during which the individual exhibited a volatile emotional state.

This research has several key contributions. First, the normalization of non-dictionary words alongside other sentence-level features is shown to improve sentiment polarity classification. Furthermore, the incorporation of a part-of-speech tagger (POS-Tagger) that is aware of the peculiarities of short messages enhances classifier performance. Another contribution is the analysis of how individual features affect the performance of the most efficient classifier of emotions in short text messages (SMS). Finally, the implemented forensic tool provides details about sentiment polarity expressed in an individual's SMS messages in a concise and intuitive manner to facilitate the rapid extraction of information by forensic analysts (see `github.com/Pelumi/ShortMsgAnalysis`).

2.   Related Work

The need to know the opinions of others on subjects of interest is valuable when attempting to make decisions in an unfamiliar terrain [6, 19, 22, 27]. The ubiquity of online reviews and recommendations makes the web a go-to place for individuals who seek such information. People rely on opinions posted on the web to guide decisions about products, movies, employers, schools, etc. Increased interest in this sort of information has been the major driver of research in sentiment analysis. Sentiment analysis started receiving increased attention in the research landscape in 2002 (see, e.g., [23, 27]) and has since been studied extensively, leading to its use in applications such as content advertising [15], election monitoring [29] and customer feedback data classification [11].

Sentiment analysis problems often take the form: given an instance of text, determine its polarity as either positive or negative, or identify its position within the extremes of both polarities [22]. Since some text instances are neither positive nor negative, sentiment analysis also involves identifying texts that do not convey any form of emotion (these are referred to as "neutral"). Hence, sentiment analysis problems are handled as classification or regression tasks. Deducing if a movie review is positive or negative is a binary classification task, while deducing how positive the review is on a scale of 1-10 is a regression task. In addition, sentiment analysis problems can be treated as multi-class classification tasks when the instances to be classified fall under categories such as positive, negative and neutral.

Sentiment analysis techniques include: (i) lexicon-based methods [3]; (ii) machine learning methods [1]; and (iii) hybrid approaches that combine lexicon-based and machine learning methods [1, 10]. When treating sentiment analysis as a classification task, machine learning algorithms that are known to perform well in text classification are often used. Some of the supervised learning algorithms commonly used in the literature are support vector machines (SVMs), multinomial naive Bayes (MNB) and maximum entropy (logistic regression) [12, 23, 26].

In digital forensics, text mining methods have been used for tasks such as authorship attribution in email [16] and text string search [4]. Support vector machine algorithms have also been used for email authorship attribution [9] and to identify the genders of the authors of SMS texts [8]. Authorship attribution experiments have also been conducted using machine learning techniques [14, 25]. The work of Mohammad et al. [20] is closely related to this research because it focuses on extracting sentiment polarity information from Twitter feeds (tweets). The work details the techniques used by the research team that obtained the highest accuracy (F-score) at the SemEval-2013 Task 2: Sentiment Analysis in Twitter Competition for Sentiment Polarity Classification.

Andriotis et al. [3] have applied sentiment analysis to augment digital forensic investigations by retrieving opinion information from SMS texts found in mobile devices. A lexicon-based technique was used for sentiment polarity classification and a proof-of-concept system was developed to visualize mood patterns extracted from SMS message databases. The maximum classification accuracy achieved was 68.8% (for positive SMS messages). The classification F-scores were improved in [1] and an F-score of 74.4% was obtained for binary classification (SMS: positive superclass and negative class). However, this work included neutral and positive messages in a superclass, which resulted in large false-positive rates. These error rates were decreased dramatically with a hybrid classifier [1], but the total estimated F-score also decreased (62%) when a three-class categorization (positive, neutral, negative) was performed. The best sentiment classification performance for SMS so far was achieved in SemEval-2014 Task 9: Sentiment Analysis in Twitter Contest. The winning team obtained an F-score of 70.28% for classifying SMS texts in three classes, but no published information is available about the false-positive rate.

Since machine learning techniques are known to outperform lexicon-based methods [12], this research focused on the use of machine learning methods for sentiment classification in an attempt to enhance the accuracy of the forensic tool. The research also has drawn cues from sentence-level features presented in [20]. However, the classification results have been improved by integrating the normalization of non-dictionary words. The work of Venkata Subramaniam et al. [28], which analyzes commonly-used techniques for handling noisy text, was also leveraged in this research. Finally, the statistical machine translation (SMT) technique for normalization presented in [13] served as the basis of the normalization task.

3.   Datasets and Classification

The classifier was trained using the multinomial logistic regression algorithm, also known as the maximum entropy (ME) algorithm. The maximum entropy algorithm makes it possible to apply logistic regression to multi-class classification problems like the three-class short message classification task considered in this work. Maximum entropy is usually preferred over the multinomial naive Bayes (MNB) algorithm because it does not assume the statistical independence of features. Therefore, it implicitly takes natural language processing properties like negation into consideration when creating models. While the training time for the maximum entropy algorithm is somewhat higher than that for the multinomial naive Bayes algorithm, the training time is much lower than those for other algorithms such as support vector machines [20]. The maximum entropy algorithm used in this work was implemented in Python using the `scikit-learn` library [24]. Parameter tuning was carried out by a `scikit-learn` process called Grid Search, which involves the specification of a range of parameters and allowing the system to run through the permutations to identify the optimal combination.

3.1   Datasets

The dataset used during the SemEval-2013 competition was utilized for training the models (`www.cs.york.ac.uk/semeval-2013/task2`). The training dataset contained 8,120 tweets (positive: 37.2%, negative: 14.7% and neutral: 48.1%). The testing dataset from [3] was also employed, making it possible to compare the results directly.

3.2   Pre-Processing

Pre-processing involves the cleaning of a raw dataset before applying a machine learning algorithm. It is a standard procedure in most machine learning tasks and the techniques used vary across domains. Pre-processing ensures that noisy data is in a proper shape for the application of machine learning algorithms. In text mining, pre-processing often involves normalization, spelling correction, managing text encoding, etc. Some of the techniques used in this research are described below.

- **Normalization:** In this context, normalization involves resolving lexically-incorrect monosyllabic terms to their correct form. The terms may be in the form of spelling mistakes or *ad hoc* social media short forms as defined in [18]. Normalization is known to improve the quality of some natural language processing tasks such as language translation [17, 18]. The normalization used in this research involved statistical machine translation; some of the techniques used are described in [18]. The outcome of the normalization task is a dictionary mapping of lexically-incorrect terms to their lexically-correct variants. An example is the mapping of each word in "raw text" to the corresponding word in "normalized text" in the following representation:

  - **Raw Text:** Hi ranger hw r u
  - **Normalized Text:** Hi ranger how are you

Statistical machine translation requires a parallel corpus – a list of messages containing lexically-incorrect terms mapped to their lexically-correct forms. In the dataset used in this research, the total number of "incorrect terms" mapped to "corrected terms" using statistical machine translation was 156. Thus, the generated normalization dictionary was quite small due to the limited size of the corpus. To address this disadvantage, the normalization dictionary in [13] containing more than 41,181 normalization candidates in the short message domain was also employed.

To apply the normalization dictionary to the corpus, each tweet was tokenized and lexically-correct tokens were filtered, leaving only lexically-invalid tokens. The lexically-correct terms were then identified based on their presence in an English dictionary using the Python Enchant spell-checking library; Enchant helps identify words that are not in the dictionary of a defined language (interested readers are referred to `bit.ly/pyench` for additional details). The remaining lexically-correct terms were identified by checking for their presence in online slang dictionaries (e.g., Urban Dictionary). The normalization of data instances before sentiment polarity classification is one of the main contributions of this work.

- **Data Cleaning:** Some terms specific to Twitter and SMS were cleaned to reduce the noise in the data. All occurrences of a user mention (e.g., @jack) and all web addresses in tweets were replaced with empty strings. In addition, occurrences of the term "RT," which means retweet on Twitter, were removed. These terms were removed to prevent the over-fitting of the model on the Twitter dataset (mentions, retweets and URLs are not as common in SMS texts as they are in tweets). Positive emoticons were replaced with words known to have positive connotations while negative emoticons were replaced with negative polarity words. This ensured that the information added by emoticons to the model was not lost during the tokenization process, since emoticons are prone to ambiguous tokenization.

  Data cleaning also involved the unification of elongated expressions. In this research, elongated expressions are terms with a sequence of three or more characters (e.g., "whyyyy"). These expressions are commonly used to convey emphasis in social media and the number of elongated characters varies across users. All elongated characters were trimmed to a maximum of two characters (e.g., "killll" was trimmed to "'kill"). This makes it easier to identify words that convey the same emotion.

- **Stemming:** This process reduces a word to its root form. For example, the words "simpler" and "simplest" are reduced to "simple" when stemmed. The goal of stemming is to ensure that words that carry the same meaning (but written in different forms) are transformed to the same format in order to unify their frequency counts. The Snowball Stemmer was used in this research because it exhibits better performance than the Porter Stemmer.

- **Stop Word Removal:** Stop words are words that are known to occur more frequently in a language than other words. In many natural language processing tasks, stop words are usually filtered because their presence biases the model. In this work, corpus-specific stop words were deduced based on the frequencies of the words in the dataset. Thus, frequently-occurring words in the corpus were filtered to make the model more robust in handling datasets from different sources.

  Corpus-specific keywords are the terms with the highest frequencies in a dataset. For example, terms that occurred in more than 20% of the dataset were considered stop words because they do not add much information to the classifier. Some of them were common stop words (e.g., "the" and "a") and others were just common expressions in the dataset (e.g., "RT" corresponding to retweet in the Twitter corpus). The percentage used (20%) was deduced experimentally by testing different ranges and sticking with the value that performed best. This also helped reduce the feature space.

3.3   Classifier Features

Various feature extraction techniques were used to generate the feature vectors. The features were determined from emoticons, lexicons, tweet content, part-of-speech tags present, etc. Details of the features are provided below. Note that unigram features correspond to single tokens while bigrams are two tokens that appear together in a data instance. For example, unigrams of the sentence "I am happy" are ["I," "am," "happy"] while the bigrams are ["I am," "am happy"].

- **Lexicon-Based Features:** Five distinct opinion lexicons were used as in [20]. Two of them were manually generated while the remaining three were created using the distant supervision learning scheme. The features extracted from each lexicon for the tweets were: number of positive tokens, score of the maximum scoring token, score of the last token and net score of a tweet using the sum of the scores of its tokens. The lexicons used were:

- **Bing Liu's Opinion Lexicon:** This is a manually-created lexicon with 2,006 positive words and 4,783 negative words. It includes common incorrectly-spelled terms, slang and social media lingo, making it more valuable than a pure English lexicon. The lexicon was compiled from 2004 to 2012 [10].

- **Multi-Perspective Question Answering Lexicon:** This lexicon contains 8,221 manually-labeled unigrams (available at mpqa.cs.pitt.edu/lexicons/subj_lexicon). It indicates the prior polarity of a word alongside its part-of-speech information.

- **NRC Word-Emotion Association Lexicon:** This unigram lexicon has 14,200 unique words manually-labeled as positive or negative.

- **Sentiment140 Lexicon:** This lexicon was automatically generated from Twitter data (1.6 million tweets) using distant supervision. The lexicon contains 62,468 unigrams and 677,698 bigrams.

- **NRC Hashtag Sentiment Lexicon:** This lexicon was generated using a similar technique to that used for the Sentiment140 lexicon. It contains 54,129 unigrams and 316,531 bigrams.

- **Emoticon Features:** Three features were generated based on emoticons. Two were binary features that indicate the presence or absence of positive or negative emoticons in tweets. The presence of the desired property sets the feature to one, while the absence sets it to zero. The third emoticon-based feature sets a binary feature to one or zero, if the tweet ends with a positive or negative emoticon, respectively. The last token of a tweet is significant because it provides valuable insights into the concluding message of the tweet.

- **Part-of-Speech Tagging:** This involves the assignment of part-of-speech information to a word in text. In natural language processing circles, it is well known that part-of-speech information provides important insights into sentiment information in text. However, part-of-speech tagging of tweets using traditional taggers tends to yield unusual results due to noise and the abundance of out-of-vocabulary (OOV) terms present in tweets. The NLTK Tagger [5] was augmented with a part-of-speech tagger that was aware of the nature of Twitter lingo. Owoputi et al. [21] have implemented a Twitter-aware part-of-speech tagger trained with manually-labeled part-of-speech-tagged tweets. After successfully retrieving the part-of-speech tags for each tweet, for each tag name in the tag set, the number of times each tag occurs was identified and accounted for by an integer value.

- **Sentence-Level Features:** The sentence-level features considered in this research were the upper case word count, elongated word count and presence of punctuation.

    - In each tweet, the number of words that appeared in upper-case was counted.
    - The number of words containing a character sequence greater than two (i.e., elongated words) was counted.
    - A binary feature was used to denote if the last token in a tweet was an exclamation point or question mark.
    - The number of continuous sequences of exclamation points or question marks was counted. Negation was handled using the method described in [23]; this is defined as the region of a tweet that starts with a negation term and ends with any of the punctuation marks: period, comma, question mark, colon, semi colon or exclamation point.

4.   Evaluation and Discussion

The raw maximum entropy classifier with default classifier parameters yielded an F-score of 64.62%, which served as the baseline for the experiments. The experiments were performed using the pre-processing techniques and feature extraction methods discussed above. The classifier parameters were also tuned and the optimal combination of features resulting in the best performance were identified via experimentation. Optimal performance was achieved with the parameters: C = 1.47; penalty = L1 (norm used in penalization) and tolerance = 0.6E-3 (tolerance for termination).

Table 1 shows the impact on the classifier F-score when one of the features is removed while retaining the others. The results indicate that Twitter-aware part-of-speech tagging [21] has the highest positive impact on the F-score followed by stemming, both of them increasing the F-score by a cumulative 3.46%. Experiments were also conducted using a traditional part-of-speech tagger, but it skewed the results by reducing the F-score. This further reinforces the need to use tools that are well suited to the short message domain. The use of normalization and the removal of stop words during the pre-processing phase boosted the F-score by a total of 1.62%. The introduction of some of these features

Table 1.   Effect of individual features on the F-score.

Experiments	F-Score % (Difference)
Optimal Features Combination	73.59 (—)
Part-of-Speech Tagging	71.59 (2.00)
Stemming	72.13 (1.46)
Stop Word Removal	72.27 (1.32)
Negation Handling	72.52 (1.07)
All Lexicons	72.82 (0.77)
Sentence-Level Features	73.18 (0.41)
(Capitalization, Term Elongation, Punctuation, Emoticons)	
Bigrams	73.27 (0.32)
Normalization	73.28 (0.31)

resulted in better classifier performance compared with related work [20], which did not use the features. Stop word removal involved identifying the domain-specific stop words based on word frequencies in the dataset.

Although the lexicon-based features improved the F-score by a total of 0.77%, they were not as effective as in [20], where they increased the F-score by approximately 8%. This can be explained by the use of a different machine learning algorithm in this research and the introduction of novel pre-processing techniques. The test set used in this research was the same as that used in [3], where an F-score of 68.8% was obtained. Based on the F-score of 73.59% obtained in this work, it can be deduced that the current classifier achieved a percentage increase of 6.96%.

The current work is similar to that of Mohammad et al. [20] due to an intersection in the feature extraction techniques used. In particular, the lexicons came from the same source, identical datasets were used and some similar sentence-level features (e.g., number of capitalized words and presence of emoticons) were employed. However, the primary difference between the two works is that Mohammad et al. [20] focused on sentiment polarity classification while the goal of this research was to make the output of a sentiment analysis system useful to forensic investigators by making it easy to extract insights from the results obtained using the forensic tool. Additionally, the machine learning algorithms used for classification differed. Mohammad et al. [20] used a support vector machine whereas the present work employed a logistic regression based classifier.

It is important to note that the test dataset did not contain neutral instances. This is because the focus was on enabling forensic analysts to identify fluctuations in emotions, the most important being positive

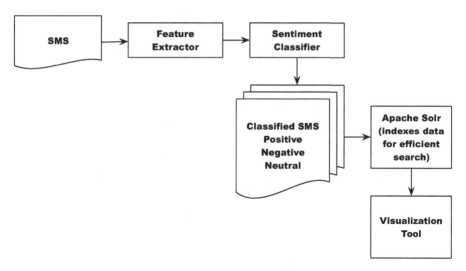

Figure 1.   Sentiment visualization tool.

to negative sentiments or vice versa. However, when experiments were conducted with neutral SMS instances, the resulting F-score dropped by 3.6%, but this score is still higher than the score reported in [3]. This result is also better that that obtained in previous work featuring a hybrid classifier [1], which yielded an F-score of 62% for three-class classification. Moreover, the F-score (73.59% – 3.6% = 69.99%) obtained in this work approximates the current best score (70.28%) achieved with a support vector machine classifier in the SemEval-2014 Task 9: Sentiment Analysis in Twitter Contest. However, maximum entropy models are known to be faster than support vector machine models. Thus, the classifier presented in this work is competitive compared with existing systems.

5.   Sentiment Visualization Tool

A web visualization tool was implemented with an easy-to-use interface for extracting relevant sentiment information from SMS texts (Figure 1). The implementation leveraged the Python Flask library and the Bootstrap framework for the front-end. The classifier, which was trained using the feature set that yielded the best F-score, was used to predict the sentiments of SMS texts created by unknown individuals. Note that, although the classifier was trained with tweets, not SMS messages, the visualization tool used SMS messages as a test case. This is because tweets and SMS messages are strikingly similar in terms of structure. Both formats set restrictions on length using character limits and they also include words and symbols with common characteristics (e.g., emoticons) – interested readers are referred to [3] for details about the similarities between tweets and SMS messages. Furthermore, the test results obtained for the unseen SMS dataset presented in Table 1 demonstrate that the classifier performs well on SMS datasets.

The messages used to showcase the forensic tool were extracted from the NUS SMS dataset [7]. The version used contained 45,062 messages sent by more than 100 people from 2010 to 2014. The messages were in the XML format and each message tag contained metadata about the SMS messages (the new version of the dataset contains anonymous information). Each message tag contained: (i) sender phone number; (ii) recipient phone number; (iii) time message was sent; (iv) sender age; and (v) city and country where the message was sent.

After parsing the XML message data, the sender, recipient and time fields were retrieved for each SMS message. The sender age, city and country fields were not used in this research. Each SMS message was then pre-processed by applying the same techniques that were used when training the classifier. Features were extracted and fed to the classifier as test input data for sentiment polarity classification.

The classifier outputted the polarity of each SMS message and the classified messages were moved to the Apache Solr system for storage and indexing. Apache Solr is a fast, open-source, enterprise search system built on the Apache Lucene system used in previous research [3]. Solr allows faceted search, which involves dynamic clustering of search results to enable users to drill down to the answers they desire. An example of a faceted search in the context of this research is to find messages that have negative polarity and are sent by a particular user S after a given time T. The ability to have such a strong grip on the data retrieval process was the rationale for pushing data into Solr. Additional functionality can be built into the forensic tool in the future because of the features provided by Solr.

After the visualization software interface is launched, it accesses the relevant Solr core and provides information about the individuals who communicated with the person under investigation. The names of these individuals are pre-loaded into a dropdown list. An individual of interest can then be selected and information about the polarity of messages sent by the selected individual can be visualized. The pre-loaded data creates an avenue for showcasing the features of the forensic tool.

In a real-world use case, the following steps would be performed during a forensic investigation: (i) obtain a physical image from a mobile device; (ii) fetch the SMS messages from the SQLite database (`mmssms.db` for an Android device); (iii) classify the messages with the trained classifier;

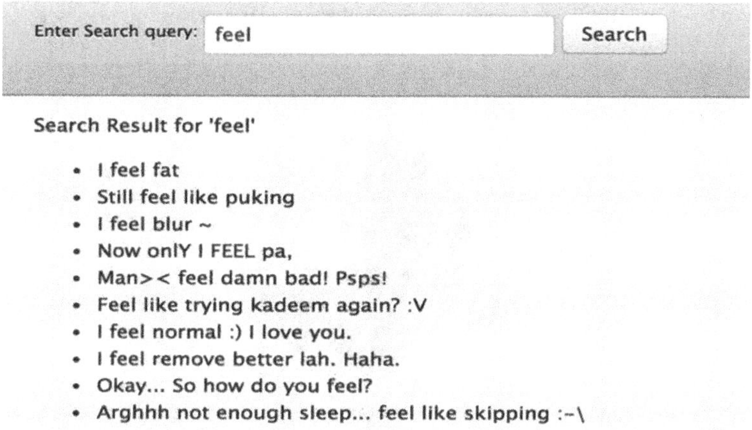

Enter Search query: feel   Search

Search Result for 'feel'

- I feel fat
- Still feel like puking
- I feel blur ~
- Now onlY I FEEL pa,
- Man>< feel damn bad! Psps!
- Feel like trying kadeem again? :V
- I feel normal :) I love you.
- I feel remove better lah. Haha.
- Okay... So how do you feel?
- Arghhh not enough sleep... feel like skipping :-\

Figure 2. Screenshot of the search component.

and (iv) push the results into Solr to enable access by the visualization tool. Note that the techniques for extracting messages from a mobile device are outside the scope of this research. However, interested readers are referred to [2, 3] for details about extracting physical images and SMS messages from Android devices.

The visualization tool provides the following features:

- **Search Interface:** A search tool was implemented to enable users to search for occurrences of any desired term in SMS messages. For example, an analyst may be interested in identifying all the messages that mention the word "feel." The search box shown in Figure 2 can be used to enter a search query; the figure also shows the output with the relevant results. While the search tool is useful when an analyst knows what to look for, it is not very helpful in situations where there is no prior knowledge about the keywords that reveal interesting patterns. To address this problem, a sentiment timeline view (discussed below) was developed to help an analyst discover patterns. Additionally, a tag cloud view was implemented to provide information about the most common keywords in SMS messages.

- **Polarity Distribution View:** This view provides a pie chart that presents the percentage polarity distributions of sent and received messages. Figure 3 displays the polarity distribution of sent messages for a person of interest as seen in the dashboard of the sentiment visualization system.

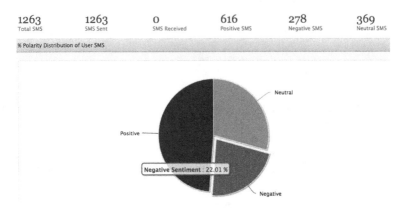

Figure 3.   Screenshot of the polarity distribution of an individual's SMS messages.

Figure 4.   Screenshot of the tag cloud of an individual's SMS messages.

- **Tag Cloud View:** A tag cloud is used to render the most common words in messages with negative or positive polarities. This gives an analyst a feel for the terms that are often associated with a specific emotion of an individual. The tag cloud implementation is interactive in that it responds to mouse clicks. When a word in the tag cloud is clicked, SMS messages containing the word are returned. Figure 4 shows a screenshot of the tag cloud generated for a sample individual.

- **Sentiment Timeline View:** A sentiment timeline view (first presented in [3]) was implemented to help analyze the mood swings of an individual over time. Figure 5 shows a screenshot of the timeline view – the horizontal axis represents time and the vertical axis represents the number of messages sent. The sentiment timeline view is at the core of the visualization tool because it provides insights into the emotional swings of an individual in an automated manner.

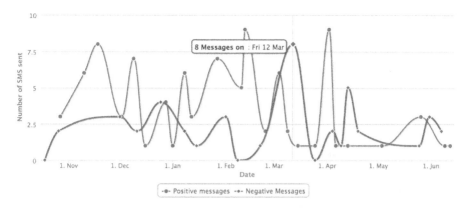

Figure 5. Screenshot of the sentiment timeline component.

When the mouse cursor hovers over a node, a tooltip is used to display the number of SMS messages that the node represents. The node may then be clicked to view the contents of the sent messages. As seen in the screenshot, the user experienced a sudden emotional spike on Friday, March 12. This is because the user sent eight negative messages on that day, but did not send any negative messages the previous day. The forensic tool extracts patterns of this nature and reveals emotional fingerprints that would otherwise have been hidden. This feature is more important than a search feature because it reveals insights that a forensic analyst could not acquire via keyword searches. Indeed, sentiment timeline analysis provides very valuable information about the emotionally-volatile periods of a person under investigation.

6.   Conclusions

This research has attempted to address some of key problems plaguing sentiment analysis in the short message domain. The proposed solution incorporates a sentiment-aware tokenizer, a part-of-speech tagger created for the short message domain, and implementations of normalization and negation. Among all the features considered, part-of-speech tagging proved to be the most effective, followed by stemming. The use of normalization, domain-specific stop words (based on term frequencies) and bigram features absent in previous work further improved the results. Experiments demonstrate that the resulting classifier performs well on an SMS message dataset, validating the similarities existing between SMS messages and tweets, and affirming that the model does not over-fit the data. Additional experimentation with several sentence-level features demonstrates the utility of normalization in sentiment polarity classification.

A forensic tool was developed to extract sentiment information from short messages sent by persons of interest. The tool also helps visualize the mood swings of subjects over time, assisting forensic analysts in pinpointing periods of emotional instability that may require further investigation.

Future research will focus on the topics discussed in messages. A keyword-based preliminary version of this feature is already provided by the tool in a tag cloud view. Attempts will be made to display topical summaries of a group of messages and correlate these topics with the emotional states of the message sender. To further improve the F-score and classification efficiency, established techniques such as principal component analysis will be used to reduce the feature space. Additionally, receiver operating characteristic analysis will be employed to identify the optimal thresholds for improving classifier accuracy.

References

[1] P. Andriotis and G. Oikonomou, Messaging activity reconstruction with sentiment polarity identification, in *Human Aspects of Information Security, Privacy and Trust*, T. Tryfonas and I. Askoxylakis (Eds.), Springer International Publishing, Cham, Switzerland, pp. 475–486, 2015.

[2] P. Andriotis, G. Oikonomou and T. Tryfonas, Forensic analysis of wireless networking evidence of Android smartphones, *Proceedings of the IEEE International Workshop on Information Forensics and Security*, pp. 109–114, 2012.

[3] P. Andriotis, A. Takasu and T. Tryfonas, Smartphone message sentiment analysis, in *Advances in Digital Forensics X*, G. Peterson and S. Shenoi (Eds.), Springer, Heidelberg, Germany, pp. 253–265, 2014.

[4] N. Beebe and J. Clark, Digital forensic text string searching: Improving information retrieval effectiveness by thematically clustering search results, *Digital Investigation*, vol. 4(S), pp. 49–54, 2007.

[5] S. Bird, NLTK: The Natural Language Toolkit, *Proceedings of the Association for Computational Linguistics Workshop on Effective Tools and Methodologies for Teaching Natural Language Processing and Computational Linguistics*, vol. 1, pp. 63–70, 2002.

[6] E. Cambria, B. Schuller, Y. Xia and C. Havasi, New avenues in opinion mining and sentiment analysis, *IEEE Intelligent Systems*, vol. 28(2), pp. 15–21, 2013.

[7] T. Chen and M. Kan, Creating a live, public short message service corpus: The NUS SMS corpus, *Language Resources and Evaluation*, vol. 47(2), pp. 299–335, 2013.

[8] N. Cheng, R. Chandramouli and K. Subbalakshmi, Author gender identification from text, *Digital Investigation*, vol. 8(1), pp. 78–88, 2011.

[9] O. de Vel, A. Anderson, M. Corney and G. Mohay, Mining e-mail content for author identification forensics, *ACM Sigmod Record*, vol. 30(4), pp. 55–64, 2001.

[10] X. Ding, B. Liu and P. Yu, A holistic lexicon-based approach to opinion mining, *Proceedings of the International Conference on Web Search and Web Data Mining*, pp. 231–240, 2008.

[11] M. Gamon, Sentiment classification on customer feedback data: Noisy data, large feature vectors and the role of linguistic analysis, *Proceedings of the Twentieth International Conference on Computational Linguistics*, pp. 841–847, 2004.

[12] A. Go, R. Bhayani and L. Huang, Twitter Sentiment Classification using Distant Supervision, CS224N Final Project Report, Department of Computer Science, Stanford University, Stanford, California, 2009.

[13] B. Han, P. Cook and T. Baldwin, Lexical normalization for social media text, *ACM Transactions on Intelligent Systems and Technology*, vol. 4(1), article no. 5, 2013.

[14] F. Iqbal, H. Binsalleeh, B. Fung and M. Debbabi, Mining writeprints from anonymous e-mails for forensic investigation, *Digital Investigation*, vol. 7(1-2), pp. 56–64, 2010.

[15] X. Jin, Y. Li, T. Mah and J. Tong, Sensitive webpage classification for content advertising, *Proceedings of the First International Workshop on Data Mining and Audience Intelligence for Advertising*, pp. 28–33, 2007.

[16] P. Juola, Authorship attribution, *Foundations and Trends in Information Retrieval*, vol. 1(3), pp. 233–334, 2006.

[17] C. Kobus, F. Yvon and G. Damnati, Normalizing SMS: Are two metaphors better than one? *Proceedings of the Twenty-Second International Conference on Computational Linguistics*, vol. 1, pp. 441–448, 2008.

[18] W. Ling, C. Dyer, A. Black and I. Trancoso, Paraphrasing 4 microblog normalization, *Proceedings of the Conference on Empirical Methods in Natural Language Processing*, pp. 73–84, 2013.

[19] E. Martinez-Camara, M. Martin-Valdivia, L. Urena Lopez and A. Montejo-Raez, Sentiment analysis in Twitter, *Natural Language Engineering*, pp. 1–28, 2012.

[20] S. Mohammad, S. Kiritchenko and X. Zhu, NRC-Canada: Building the state-of-the-art in sentiment analysis of tweets, *Proceedings of the Seventh International Workshop on Semantic Evaluation Exercises*, 2013.

[21] O. Owoputi, B. O'Connor, C. Dyer, K. Gimpel, N. Schneider and N. Smith, Improved part-of-speech tagging for online conversational text with word clusters, *Proceedings of the Conference of the North American Chapter of the Association of Computational Linguistics*, pp. 380–390, 2013.

[22] B. Pang and L. Lee, Opinion mining and sentiment analysis, *Foundations and Trends in Information Retrieval*, vol. 2(1-2), pp. 1–135, 2008.

[23] B. Pang, L. Lee and S. Vaithyanathan, Thumbs up? Sentiment classification using machine learning techniques, *Proceedings of the Association for Computational Linguistics Conference on Empirical Methods in Natural Language Processing*, vol. 10, pp. 79–86, 2002.

[24] F. Pedregosa, G. Varoquaux, A. Gramfort, V. Michel, B. Thirion, O. Grisel, M. Blondel, P. Prettenhofer, R. Weiss, V. Dubourg, J. Vanderplas, A. Passos, D. Cournapeau, M. Brucher, M. Perrot and E. Duchesnay, `scikit-learn`: Machine learning in Python, *Journal of Machine Learning Research*, vol. 12, pp. 2825–2830, 2011.

[25] A. Stolerman, R. Overdorf, S. Afroz and R. Greenstadt, Breaking the closed-world assumption in stylometric authorship attribution, in *Advances in Digital Forensics X*, G. Peterson and S. Shenoi (Eds.), Springer, Heidelberg, Germany, pp. 185–205, 2014.

[26] J. Suttles and N. Ide, Distant supervision for emotion classification with discrete binary values, *Proceedings of the Fourteenth International Conference on Computational Linguistics and Intelligent Text Processing*, vol. 2, pp. 121–136, 2013.

[27] P. Turney, Thumbs up or thumbs down? Semantic orientation applied to unsupervised classification of reviews, *Proceedings of the Fortieth Annual Meeting of the Association for Computational Linguistics*, pp. 417–424, 2002.

[28] L. Venkata Subramaniam, S. Roy, T. Faruquie and S. Negi, A survey of types of text noise and techniques to handle noisy text, *Proceedings of the Third Workshop on Analytics for Noisy Unstructured Text Data*, pp. 115–122, 2009.

[29] H. Wang, D. Can, A. Kazemzadeh, F. Bar and S. Narayanan, A system for real-time Twitter sentiment analysis of the 2012 U.S. presidential election cycle, *Proceedings of the Association for Computational Linguistics 2012 System Demonstrations*, pp. 115–120, 2012.

Chapter 5

IMPACT OF USER DATA PRIVACY MANAGEMENT CONTROLS ON MOBILE DEVICE INVESTIGATIONS

Panagiotis Andriotis and Theo Tryfonas

Abstract   There are many different types of mobile device users, but most of them do not seek to expand the functionality of their smartphones and prefer to interact with them using predefined user profiles and settings. However, "power users" are always seeking opportunities to gain absolute control of their devices and expand their capabilities. For this reason, power users attempt to obtain "super user" privileges (root) or jailbreak their devices. Meanwhile, the "bring your own device" (BYOD) trend in the workplace and increased numbers of high profile users who demand enhanced data privacy and protection are changing the mobile device landscape. This chapter discusses variations of the Android operating system that attempt to bypass the limitations imposed by the previous Android permission model (up to version 5.1) and highlights the fact that forensic analysts will encounter devices with altered characteristics. Also, the chapter discusses the Android permission model introduced in the latest operating system (version M or 6.0) that will likely change the way users interact with apps.

Keywords: Android devices, privacy, trust, power users, anti-forensics

1.   Introduction

Android is an open source project that enables developers to alter operating system characteristics according to their preferences. Data privacy and the lack of user controls on installed apps have always been major concerns for security-aware developers and users. The previous – but still dominant – permission model of Android operating systems (up to version 5.1) has been criticized for limiting the ability of users to control the private data that apps may access.

© IFIP International Federation for Information Processing 2016
Published by Springer International Publishing AG 2016. All Rights Reserved
G. Peterson and S. Shenoi (Eds.): Advances in Digital Forensics XII, IFIP AICT 484, pp. 89–105, 2016.
DOI: 10.1007/978-3-319-46279-0_5

This chapter focuses on mobile devices that run variations of the Android Open Source Project (AOSP). It highlights the various approaches that deal with the fact that the previous – but still dominant – permission model of Android operating systems (up to version 5.1) is not flexible and does not allow users to restrict access to specific resources. Furthermore, it demonstrates that evidence derived from devices may contain falsified data due to app utilization that employs obfuscation measures to protect user data and privacy. This fact raises the specter that the probative value of "evidence" extracted from such devices can be put into question.

2.   Data Privacy Concerns

Contemporary mobile devices are equipped with many sensors. The Android documentation lists at least twenty variables (e.g., TYPE_AC-CELEROMETER) that can be used by developers to access various sensors and enrich the functionality of their apps. The sensors are essentially divided into hardware- and software-based sensors. Apps normally use sensors to measure orientation, motion and other environmental conditions and provide the expected functionality to users. A portion of the data produced by the apps contains information derived from sensors. This information is stored internally on the device or in the cloud. Some of the information may be encrypted (e.g., locations from Google Maps).

For example, a call to the camera or microphone of an Android device requires the inclusion of the appropriate permissions in the manifest xml file from the developer so that a user can be informed about the resources required by the specific app. Next, the user has to decide if he/she will accept the stated policy and download the app from the Play Store. The previous Android permission model has a binary accept-reject character. Therefore, if an app needs access to a user's contact list, it has to ask the user for permission to access it; then, the user is informed that his/her contact list will be shared via content providers to other ecosystems. Figure 1 presents screenshots of Android's privacy management control variations (left to right: permissions, incognito mode and Privacy Guard).

In theory, the Android permission model assures that data privacy is not violated without the knowledge of the user. But this is not always the case. In fact, privacy in the smartphone ecosystem is not only related to the stored data accessible by third-party applications via the aforementioned route, but privacy is also associated with the sensors themselves. For example, an Android device does not require permissions to be declared by an app for access to a number of device sensors

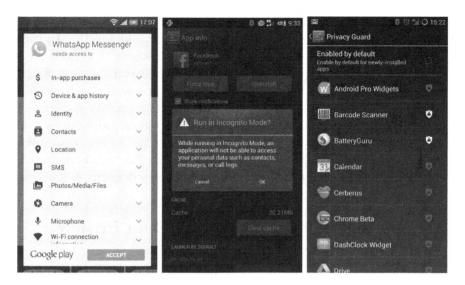

Figure 1. Android's privacy management control variations.

(e.g., light sensor) [16]. This potentially violates user privacy because an adversary could utilize the sensors to intercept information about users' private lives. For example, the information provided by an accelerometer in a mobile device could be used to determine if its user is moving, sitting at a table, or even sleeping.

Data sharing in ecosystems that run the Android operating system provides flexibility and limitless functionality. The sharing enables developers to implement apps that can communicate with data containers (e.g., contact lists) and obtain information from sensors (e.g., location services). Recent research has shown that forensic analyses can benefit from such capabilities because data availability becomes easier via applications that merge similar functionalities. An example is the Google Hangouts app, primarily a chatting app, which now serves as a text messaging app (SMS) [2] because it makes it much easier for users to send SMS messages with embedded information. As a consequence, valuable data is stored in databases (e.g., `babel1.db`) internal to mobile devices that are potentially the targets of forensic analyses. However, users are the vulnerable entities in this model because they install applications that request access to most of the available resources.

Mobile device users must be aware of the resources (data containers, software and hardware sensors) used by apps. Hence, according to their preferences, the operating system should provide solutions that satisfy their privacy concerns. This can be achieved by restricting access to categories of data (e.g., contact lists) if users so desire, as well as by informing them about the specific portions of their devices that will be utilized by apps. The previous data management model of the Android operating system covers the latter situation. However, the need for a model that creates unique trust relationships between developers and users has been apparent for some time, and it is now available in version 6.0 of the Android operating system. The revised security model may well force consumers to understand the risks of downloading apps that require multiple resources from their devices. In the future, consumers could be even more cautious by consciously controlling the actions that the apps are allowed to perform in the ecosystems defined by their devices [3].

3.   Mechanisms for Enhancing Data Privacy

In recent years, several data privacy preservation models have been implemented in Android devices. The approaches for handling the problems of data leakage and permission handling in Android environments fall into three categories: (i) app-based models; (ii) Android Open Source Project variations; and (iii) secure container models, which are essentially used in enterprise environments. Each of the three categories of approaches handles the weaknesses of Android's binary accept-reject model in a distinct manner.

3.1   App-Based Model

The first approach includes applications targeted for rooted devices. These applications mimic the privacy framework introduced in Android version 4.3 (Apps Ops), which is shown in Figure 2 [13]. In this environment, users can restrict access to data sources and sensors. For example, if a GPS navigation application requires access to the GPS sensor and contact list of a phone, the user could allow access to the GPS and restrict access to the contact list. Unfortunately, this feature was removed in version 4.4 – Android developers declared that the Apps Ops framework was created only for internal use and testing purposes.

However, the control privacy feature was well received by XDA Developers as well as by power users. Apps Ops allowed users to have absolute control of the services that apps could access. As a result, developers brought back the Apps Ops functionality. For example, one XDA forum member created the Xposed framework that provided the services that were removed in the official release. However, the disadvantage of this method is that an Android device must be rooted (super-user privileges) to allow the installation of the Xposed application package file (apk).

Figure 2. Apps Ops privacy management control [13].

App Ops variants created by several developers are available at the Google Play Store. However, numerous users have expressed their concerns about the effectiveness of these apps and whether or not they protect privacy. Reviews indicate the need for a universal approach that is safe to use and that restores the privacy controls that were removed after Android operating system version 4.3. The new runtime permission model seems to fill this gap.

The AppsOpsExposed framework is an open source project that is downloadable from Github (`repo.xposed.info/module/at.jclehner.appopsxposed`). AppsOpsExposed is essential and should be installed on a device so that other applications can restore the Apps Ops functionality. One example is XPrivacy, an award-winning application that uses the framework and utilizes obfuscation techniques to prevent sensitive data leakage. XPrivacy restricts the categories of data that an application can access by feeding the application with fake data or no data. It is also an open source project, but an Android device has to be rooted to provide its functionality.

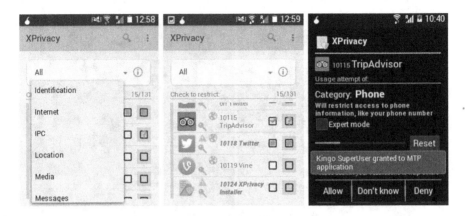

Figure 3. XPrivacy setup.

Experiments were conducted with XPrivacy (version 3.6.19) installed on a Samsung Galaxy Pocket 2 (SM-G110H) running Android operating system version 4.4.2. First, the device had to be rooted using Kingoroot, a popular exploit. Note that this rooting exploit was selected purely for experimental reasons. Such exploits could introduce additional security vulnerabilities and most vendors discourage their installation. The XPrivacy installer from the Google Play Store is useful for installing the Xposed framework and the XPrivacy app. After the installation, the user can choose the functions that should be restricted for specific apps (Figure 3).

Experiments were conducted with the location services and phone contact list. The primary testing location (PTL) was (51.4558270, −2.6034071) (Figure 4). The phone was used for a period of time before XPrivacy was installed. Thus, the SIM contact list, SMS messages and other information were already registered in the internal storage of the device. After XPrivacy was installed, direct access to the location services, contact list and other accounts was restricted. As a consequence, some apps did not work as expected. For example, Twitter required a new log in every time the app was invoked, Facebook Friend Finder was unable to find any new friends by reaching the contact list and Yelp could not function properly (Figure 4).

Further research demonstrated that, when location services were used for Twitter posts, accurate locations were not included in the tweets (Figure 5). Also, other apps such as Facebook and Swarm were fed with false data provided by XPrivacy according to the relevant settings (Figure 5). Thus, a cautious − or malicious − user could benefit from similar apps and utilize them to hinder forensic investigations. Forensic

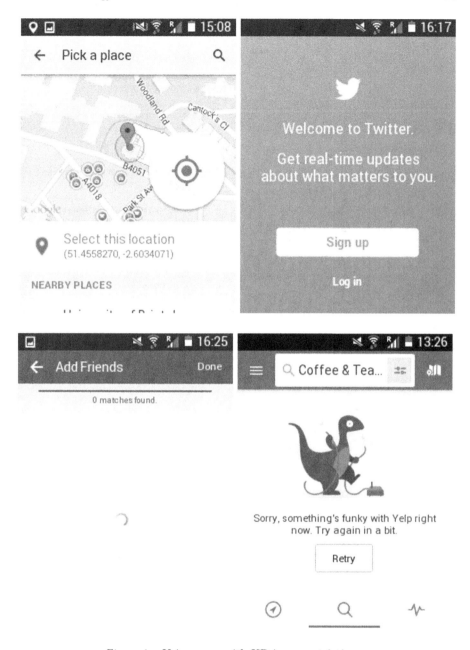

Figure 4. Using apps with XPrivacy restrictions.

analysts should be aware of these practices and should be very careful when presenting evidence from rooted devices in court because such applications could have been installed and used on the devices. These

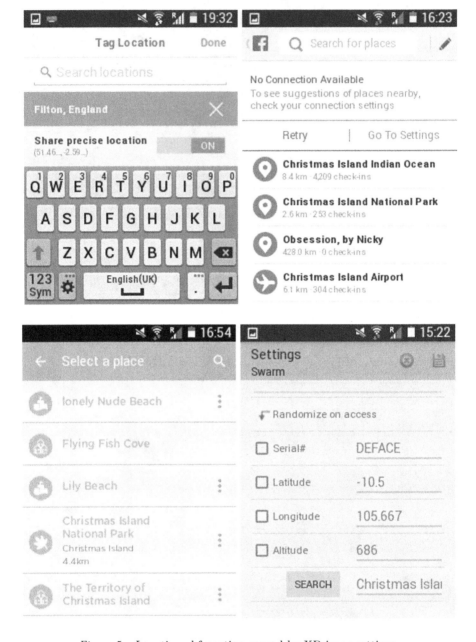

Figure 5.   Location obfuscation caused by XPrivacy settings.

applications increase the likelihood that evidence has been manipulated or falsified.

Forensic analysis was also performed on the experimental smartphone using the data acquisition and analysis strategy described in [1]. Interestingly, the app databases that locally store various app related data did not contain any information that pointed to the original primary testing location. For example, the `fsq.db` database in the "venues" table contained the location (105.667, –10.5) corresponding to the longitude and latitude of Christmas Island National Park provided by XPrivacy (Figure 5). Despite the fact that apps such as XPrivacy can mislead forensic analysts, other apps (e.g., Google Maps and the Location Tagger on the Camera app) worked flawlessly. If a forensic analyst is able to extract data from these apps, there is a possibility that portions of the retrieved data might have been manipulated. Thus, the trustworthiness of the extracted evidence can be put into question.

3.2   Android Open Source Project Variations

The second category of proposals for data privacy management for the Android operating system includes a few key (firmware) variations of the Android Open Source Project. The Android Open Source Project offers a common platform that enables developers to modify the orientation of the operating system in various directions. CyanogenMod is among the most popular variations of the Android Open Source Project and it implements a different approach to Android's data privacy management. For example, the CM11 version based on Android KitKat (version 4.4) features the Privacy Guard permission manager app. Privacy Guard (Figure 1) provides the same functionality with the XPrivacy app (i.e., it uses obfuscation, a technique proposed in several technical papers [6]) and is essentially an evolution of the incognito mode (Figure 1). Specifically, CyanogenMod offers the incognito mode privacy management feature for older versions (starting from CM7). Another popular example of a modified Android operating system version is OxygenOS, which runs on OnePlus 2 phones.

The CyanogenMod installer web page suggests that it is not necessary for a phone to be rooted to install and run the latest version. However, users who are not familiar with technology might find the installation process obscure. Privacy Guard enables users to turn on or off any feature that they feel is not necessary for an app to function. For example, a user may decide that a social media app such as Twitter should not have access to location data on the phone. Privacy Guard either restricts access to the information or it supplies the app with limited resources. The main limitations of Privacy Guard are that it does not anonymize users and prevent apps from tracking their sessions. Another problem is that some apps might throw exceptions during runtime that cause them to crash.

Android Open Source Project variations like CyanogenMod demonstrate that rooted phones are not the only devices that may potentially have anti-forensic capabilities. Indeed, apps such as those discussed above could create similar anti-forensic environments. Therefore, smartphone ecosystems defined by such devices may also contain modified or falsified data. Forensic analysts should be cautious and take strong steps to validate data originating from the devices.

3.3   Secure Container (BYOD) Model

Blackphone (and Blackphone 2) implement a different approach to the problem of data privacy preservation. Their SilentOS operating system (previously known as PrivatOS) is also based on the Android platform. The concept behind this Android Open Source Project variation is that data privacy and security should be the most powerful features of an operating system. This is why the Blackphone has built-in apps such as the Blackphone Security Center. It also features third-party services that enable Blackphone users to remotely wipe and gain control of their data from anywhere in the world. Users can also use encryption for secure search and browsing, data transfer and storage, and voice calls and chats.

These devices offer an adequate solution in corporate environments that have a bring your own device policy. However, most of the provided security services come with some cost – they may be free of charge for a period of time, but users may eventually have to pay subscription fees to maintain high levels of security. Obviously, standard forensic analysis tools and practices cannot be applied to such devices. Forensic analysts should expect to use sophisticated hardware and software to extract useful information from these devices.

Finally, the rapid proliferation of mobile devices across society, the alarming increase and sophistication of malware and grave concerns about data privacy have led companies such as Samsung to offer security frameworks targeted for corporate environments. An example is the Samsung KNOX framework, which enhances trust by implementing robust, multi-layered mobile security. In fact, this framework has created a separate data privacy management category for itself. KNOX offers its own workspace above the Android stack where distinct applications can work safely. It also features hardware components and advanced cryptographic services.

The enhancements presented by KNOX have made it a pioneer in the Android enterprise mobility space. Users can customize their personal space to share data with their (corporate) secure containers. The data could be contacts, calendars, browser bookmarks, etc. The new generations of the Android operating system are empowered by such enterprise capabilities. They add value to data privacy by separating personal and corporate data by essentially creating different user accounts on the same device. In the case of forensic analysis, these systems will likely require special techniques to uncover evidence because they engage proprietary cryptographic protocols.

The Android for Work framework is another emerging technology that uses containerization. The framework separates business apps and personal apps, enabling Android smartphone and tablet users to use the same devices for their professional and personal lives. This is accomplished by setting up dedicated work profiles for business content that do not interfere with their personal profiles. Corporate IT management services cannot reach or manipulate personal data belonging to users. Users enjoy familiar experiences when using their devices in the workplace and gain control over the data to be shared. Security is enhanced via sandboxing, security policies, app verification and encryption. Furthermore, an enterprise mobility management (EMM) system can be used to manage all the engaged mobile devices, (enterprise) apps and business data from a single console. Clearly, forensic analysts will face considerable obstacles when they attempt to obtain data related to enterprise environment activities without the assistance of the enterprise mobility management system vendor.

3.4 Towards a New Era of Mobile Computing

A new trend in the smartphone market is the merging of the enterprise mobility and bring your own device concepts in a single environment. Enterprise mobility management applications enable IT administrators to enforce a wide range of policies by possibly following the KNOX paradigm. However, these advancements may well be overwhelming for the average user. Usability, flexibility and simplicity should be the most critical concepts underlying data protection schemes. The sixth version of the Android operating system (version M) has brought a radical change to the operating system security model (Figure 6) – it allows users to control the data they share using runtime permissions. This means that future forensic analysts will encounter cases where smartphone users have restricted data sharing between apps, significantly complicating forensic investigations of the mobile devices. Also, apps

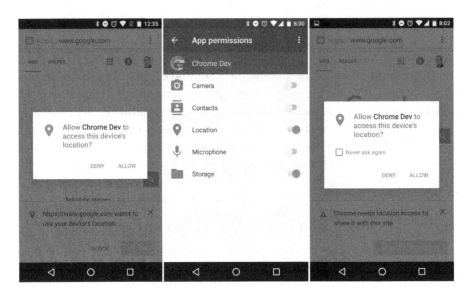

Figure 6. New runtime permissions model.

in the near future will be more personalized due to advancements and restrictions. Thus, generic (traditional) digital forensic models will likely be inadequate in the new era that embraces the permission paradigm.

4.   Other Open Source Operating Systems

Other open source platforms, such as the Mozilla Firefox operating system and Tizen, follow different security and privacy models. As in the case of Android, they rely on Linux kernels, but they are also equipped with web runtime layers on top of the kernels. This improvement enables developers to create apps (webapps) using only web technologies (e.g., HTML5, CSS and Javascript).

Mozilla has developed proprietary APIs for the Firefox operating system in which the handling of app permissions is different for hosted apps and packaged apps. Hosted apps are downloaded from websites while packaged apps are already installed on devices. Packaged apps are divided into three categories: (i) web apps, which do not use privileged or certified APIs; (ii) privileged apps, which use privileged APIs (distributed through the Firefox Marketplace); and (iii) certified apps (preinstalled), which can access privileged and certified APIs. Privileged and certified apps have content security policies, but each app is required to invoke an installation method. This procedure validates the app and asks the user to approve its installation. In other words, depending on the app type (e.g., if it is certified or privileged), the Firefox operating system implicitly grants some of the permissions and then asks the user to approve other permissions (using prompts during runtime as in the case of the upcoming Android version). However, this model does not give the user the power to invoke or deny permissions for certified apps.

Tizen, on the other hand, has a predefined set of APIs that are divided into specific categories. The communications API, for example, provides functionality for Bluetooth control and messaging; also, it provides email services, access to near field communication devices and push notifications. Web apps require authorization to access restricted APIs via a manifest file, which lists the required features from the apps following a (subject, object, permission)-based access control model. Tizen is still in its early days and its developers intend to create a multi-purpose operating system that will serve mobile devices, wearables, vehicle infotainment systems and smart TVs. The proliferation of Android devices makes it unlikely that a forensic analyst would encounter a smartphone that runs a Tizen (or similar) operating system. However, forensic analysts should be aware that these new technologies may well enter the market; because they are open source, there is an increased likelihood that they could be incorporated in smartphones targeted for underdeveloped or developing countries. Thus, digital forensic research should focus on techniques and tools for handling cases where the evidence container is a device that runs one of the aforementioned operating systems or some other emerging operating system that could acquire a significant market share (e.g., Ubuntu Touch operating system).

5. Android Version 6

The advent of Android version M (version 6.0) will likely change the way users interact with their apps, given the runtime permissions model that was revealed at the M Developer Preview. The new permission model ensures that developers will build apps that request user permissions only for a limited number of resources. Other permissions will have to be requested and granted by users at runtime. This novel permission system will make smartphone ecosystems unique. The advancements in data sharing between apps will change the way forensic analysis is performed because the devices will restrict access to resources. Hence, an analyst may only be able to find limited data in a database on a device. On the other hand, users with limited privacy and security concerns or awareness may enjoy all the new functionalities provided by the installed apps while knowingly or unknowingly allowing access to all resources.

Version	Codename	API	Distribution
2.2	Froyo	8	0.2%
2.3.3 - 2.3.7	Gingerbread	10	3.0%
4.0.3 - 4.0.4	Ice Cream Sandwich	15	2.7%
4.1.x	Jelly Bean	16	9.0%
4.2.x		17	12.2%
4.3		18	3.5%
4.4	KitKat	19	36.1%
5.0	Lollipop	21	16.9%
5.1		22	15.7%
6.0	Marshmallow	23	0.7%

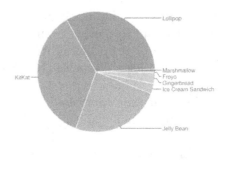

Figure 7. Developer Dashboard (January 2016).

User adoption of the new model and user reactions would be an interesting subject for future research. However, history has shown that all Android users do not immediately download and install the latest operating system versions on their devices; in fact, a large number of users prefer to use older operating systems. Figure 7 shows that four months after the release of the sixth version, only 0.7% of the devices that visited the Google Play Store were running the Marshmallow edition. Thus, earlier versions of the Android operating system will persist in the user community for several years.

6.   Related Work

Data privacy protection mechanisms will be vital in the new era of mobile computing where data sharing can create risks. Small- and medium-sized enterprises appear to be more vulnerable to data leakage because they often do not have advanced IT resources and capabilities [9]; thus, they may not implement strong bring your own device models.

Several approaches have been proposed to protect personal mobile computing from unlimited data sharing. The MyShield system [4] supplies anonymized data if requested by users and incorporates Secure Circles, a control mechanism that enables users to manage app access to sensitive data based on the level of trust.

Other approaches have focused on location services [5], providing an opportunity for mobile device users to protect their privacy by adjusting the accuracy of their locations in order to use location-based apps while simultaneously securing their private data using on-device or service-based obfuscation [11]. Bernheim Brush et al. [7] note that, when individuals agree to share their location data using existing obfuscation methods, their decisions are consistent with their personal privacy concerns. Also, Tang et al. [15] suggest that, when abstract location descriptions are included in privacy protection schemes, location sharing is more likely to occur.

Henne et al. [10] have proposed a crowd-based recommendation system for Android devices that allows users to configure the accuracy of location data provided to apps based on five precision levels; they also claim that unskilled users benefit from such an approach. Crowdsourcing for location-based privacy settings is discussed in [14]. Beresford et al. [6] have developed MockDroid, a modified version of the Android operating system, which works like XPrivacy; however, its principal difference is that it essentially feeds "empty" resources to apps that require access to potentially sensitive data. This reduces app functionality, but the vast majority of apps on the device work without any problems. AppFence is a data protection mechanism that uses shadowing and exfiltration blocking on apps while reducing adverse side effects [12]. According to its developers, the mechanism did not cause problems to 66% of the tested applications. Finally, Fisher et al. [8] have demonstrated that iOS users can be classified into three categories according to their location privacy settings: those who deny access to all apps, those who allow access to all apps and those who selectively permit access to the apps they trust.

7. Conclusions

This chapter has discussed a variety of mobile device ecosystems that emerge from the fact that advanced users tend to change – and sometimes dramatically change – the expected behavior of their smartphones. The chapter has also highlighted variations in the data privacy and security models developed by the Android Open Source Project. The implication for forensic analysts is that when smartphones are rooted and/or obfuscation apps are installed, forensic analyses will likely provide limited or false evidence. Security models used by other open source systems have also been discussed, along with the projected limitations of the current Android operating system version. This chapter has not considered Apple (iOS) devices because they use a different permission system that enables users to restrict data sharing and deny access to specific resources. Clearly, the trend is that future smartphones will provide ever-increasing privacy and security functionality to users. Forensic researchers and analysts should be aware of this trend and attempt to develop sophisticated techniques and tools that maximize evidence recovery while ensuring the probative value of the recovered evidence.

References

[1] P. Andriotis, G. Oikonomou and T. Tryfonas, Forensic analysis of wireless networking evidence of Android smartphones, *Proceedings of the IEEE International Workshop on Information Forensics and Security*, pp. 109–114, 2012.

[2] P. Andriotis, G. Oikonomou, T. Tryfonas and S. Li, Highlighting relationships of a smartphone's social ecosystem in potentially large investigations, to appear in *IEEE Transactions on Cybernetics*, 2016.

[3] P. Andriotis, T. Tryfonas, G. Oikonomou and I. King, A framework for describing multimedia circulation in a smartphone ecosystem, in *Advances in Digital Forensics XI*, G. Peterson and S. Shenoi (Eds.), Springer, Heidelberg, Germany, pp. 251–267, 2015.

[4] R. Beede, D. Warbritton and R. Han, MyShield: Protecting Mobile Device Data via Security Circles, Technical Report CU-CS-1091-12, Department of Computer Science, University of Colorado Boulder, Boulder, Colorado, 2012.

[5] M. Benisch, P. Kelley, N. Sadeh and L. Cranor, Capturing location-privacy preferences: Quantifying accuracy and user-burden trade-offs, *Personal and Ubiquitous Computing*, vol. 15(7), pp. 679–694, 2011.

[6] A. Beresford, A. Rice, N. Skehin and R. Sohan, MockDroid: Trading privacy for application functionality on smartphones, *Proceedings of the Twelfth Workshop on Mobile Computing Systems and Applications*, pp. 49–54, 2011.

[7] A. Bernheim Brush, J. Krumm and J. Scott, Exploring end user preferences for location obfuscation, location-based services and the value of location, *Proceedings of the Twelfth ACM International Conference on Ubiquitous Computing*, pp. 95–104, 2010.

[8] D. Fisher, L. Dorner and D. Wagner, Location privacy: User behavior in the field, *Proceedings of the Second ACM Workshop on Security and Privacy in Smartphones and Mobile Devices*, pp. 51–56, 2012.

[9] M. Harris and K. Patten, Mobile device security considerations for small- and medium-sized enterprise business mobility, *Information Management and Computer Security*, vol. 22(1), pp. 97–114, 2014.

[10] B. Henne, C. Kater and M. Smith, Usable location privacy for Android with crowd recommendations, *Proceedings of the Seventh International Conference on Trust and Trustworthy Computing*, pp. 74–82, 2014.

[11] B. Henne, C. Kater, M. Smith and M. Brenner, Selective cloaking: Need-to-know for location-based apps, *Proceedings of the Eleventh International Conference on Privacy, Security and Trust*, pp. 19–26, 2013.

[12] P. Hornyack, S. Han, J. Jung, S. Schechter and D. Wetherall, These aren't the droids you're looking for: Retrofitting Android to protect data from imperious applications, *Proceedings of the Eighteenth ACM Conference on Computer and Communications Security*, pp. 639–652, 2011.

[13] T. Kaiser, Google removes "App Ops" privacy control feature from Android 4.4.2, *DailyTech*, December 16, 2013.

[14] J. Lin, S. Amini, J. Hong, N. Sadeh, J. Lindqvist and J. Zhang, Expectation and purpose: Understanding users' mental models of mobile app privacy through crowdsourcing, *Proceedings of the ACM International Conference on Ubiquitous Computing*, pp. 501–510, 2012.

[15] K. Tang, J. Hong and D. Siewiorek, The implications of offering more disclosure choices for social location sharing, *Proceedings of the SIGCHI Conference on Human Factors in Computing Systems*, pp. 391–394, 2012.

[16] T. Vidas and N. Christin, Evading Android runtime analysis via sandbox detection, *Proceedings of the Ninth ACM Symposium on Information, Computer and Communications Security*, pp. 447–458, 2014.

Chapter 6

ANALYZING MOBILE DEVICE ADS TO IDENTIFY USERS

Jayaprakash Govindaraj, Robin Verma and Gaurav Gupta

Abstract   User browsing behavior is tracked by search providers in order to construct activity profiles that are used to fine-tune searches and present user-specific advertisements. When a search input matches a commercial product or service offering, ads based on the previously-saved interests, likes and dislikes are displayed. The number of web searches from mobile devices has exceeded those conducted from desktops. Mobile devices are being used for critical business tasks such as e-commerce, banking transactions, video conferences, email communications and confidential data storage. Companies are moving towards mobile-app-only strategies and advertisers are displaying ads on mobile apps as well. Mobile device ads can often reveal information such as location, gender, age and other valuable data about users. This chapter describes a methodology for extracting and analyzing ads on mobile devices to retrieve user-specific information, reconstruct a user profile and predict user identity. The results show that the methodology can identify a user even if he or she uses the same device, multiple devices, different networks or follows different usage patterns. The methodology can be used to support a digital forensic readiness framework for mobile devices. Additionally, it has applications in context-based security and proactive and reactive digital forensic investigations.

Keywords: Smartphones, advertisements, user behavior, user identification

1.   Introduction

A 2014 mobile security survey by Checkpoint [5] reported that 64% of Android devices, 16% of Apple/iOS devices, about 16% of Windows phones and about 36% of BlackBerry devices are vulnerable to security threats. Insecure web browsing accounted for 61% of the total factors impacting the safety of mobile data. Meanwhile, 82% of security professionals expect mobile security incidents to increase, 98% have concerns

© IFIP International Federation for Information Processing 2016
Published by Springer International Publishing AG 2016. All Rights Reserved
G. Peterson and S. Shenoi (Eds.): Advances in Digital Forensics XII, IFIP AICT 484, pp. 107–126, 2016.
DOI: 10.1007/978-3-319-46279-0_6

about the impact of mobile security incidents and 95% face challenges with bring your own device (BYOD) policies.

Mobile devices can be taken anywhere, increasing the possibility of the devices getting stolen or tampered with. Smartphones enable users to access the Internet from anywhere. Mobile devices are vulnerable to remote attacks through SMS/MMS or via the exploitation of insecure connections. Unlike hard disk drives, it is challenging to forensically-image phones without changing the states of the devices. Since phones use flash memory, every time an extraction is made, a different hash value is obtained.

All forensic images of phones are not equal. Logical extraction only provides a dump of the existing files such as call history, SMS and text messages; it does not acquire a dump of the unused space on the phone. Physical extraction can obtain a complete memory dump, but the process is difficult to perform without invasive techniques that could damage the phone. Most commercial forensic tools cannot bypass passcodes of smartphones [1]. Smartphones have to be jailbroken or rooted to access evidence required in digital forensic investigations.

Most mobile forensic solutions and products are designed for use in post-incident scenarios. At this time, there is no well-defined digital forensic readiness framework for mobile devices. Data collection is a key requirement in readiness scenarios [6, 10]. However, it is not clear what evidence to collect, how to handle situations where the collected evidence has been tampered with [11] and how to monitor and target particular evidence. Without question, there is a great need for new ways to identify users before security incidents occur as well as after the incidents.

Tracking a user's search keywords is one way search providers are gathering user preferences and targeting the most appropriate ads to display to users [13]. It is often the case that potential criminals plan their crimes using Internet searches or make purchases of objects or services needed to perpetrate their crimes. Knowledge of an accused's ad preferences could be useful in attempting to establish the sequence of events involved in the planning and execution of the crime. If the suspect had used mobile devices, the kind of ads that he clicked/viewed could reveal information about himself, including his motives and behavior. Although browser history may reveal more information, the specific ads that the suspect clicked and the websites he visited can reveal valuable information about his interests and behavior [4]. This is the principal motivation for analyzing the ads clicked by a user to identify the user.

This chapter describes a system that can track clicked ads in real time, extract the ads, analyze them to retrieve personal information and use

Table 1. Types of mobile ads.

Ad Type	Description
Video Ads	These ads are displayed during a game; a user has the option to skip after certain amount of time or watch the ads
Interactive Ads	These ads are similar to video ads; however, the user also has the opportunity to interact with the ads
Banner Ads	These ads are displayed within an app or site; the ads can be displayed in any location within the display limit based on the developers' intentions
Native Ads	The contents of these ads are aligned with the content of the app; the user does not feel that he/she is viewing ads
Pop-Up and Takeover Ads	These ads are displayed as dedicated full screen pages, requiring users to click to get to the original pages
Lock-Screen Ads	These ads are displayed whenever a device is locked
Notification Ads	These ads are displayed as notifications by apps belonging to a brand or company; the ads notify users of events and sales, and strengthen customer relationships
Rich Media Mobile Ads	These interactive ads provide rich user experiences using the mobile device gyroscope, camera and/or accelerometer
Branded Mobile Ads	These ads are specifically developed by advertisers and uploaded to an app store

this information to construct a user profile. The utility of the system is demonstrated via experiments involving multiple users, multiple devices and the collection and analysis of more than 5,000 ads. It is shown that, if a user operates a mobile phone in an office environment with restricted network access and uses the same device in a home environment with unrestricted network access, the two different usage patterns can still be used to identify the user. The system can also be used as a digital forensic readiness framework for mobile devices. Additionally, it has applications in context-based security and proactive and reactive digital forensic investigations. Finally, the system can be used to identify ads that violate constraints imposed by enterprises or government.

2. Background

This section provides background information on the main aspects of this research, including mobile ads, mobile ad targeting and mobile ad architecture. Ads are displayed to mobile device users via SMS, MMS, phone calls, web browsers and mobile applications. Table 1 presents the

Table 2. Mobile ad targeting methods.

Ad Targeting	Description
Content Targeting	Based on the app or the site where ads are displayed
Behavioral Targeting	Based on user behavior, browsing, recent downloads and interests by analyzing recent device locations
Device- or Carrier-Based Targeting	Based on the type of device or carrier used; ads for iPhone cases would only be displayed on iPhone devices
Demographic Targeting	Based on information such as user age, gender, ethnicity and language preference
Geographic Targeting	Based on the user location obtained from the device GPS or nearest cell tower location
Re-Targeting	Based on users who viewed or clicked the ad in the past
Time-Based Targeting	Based on the particular time of day

various types of mobile ads [14]. Different types of mobile ad targeting [7] are used by advertisers to reach users. Table 2 describes the various mobile ad targeting methods.

2.1   Information Revealed by Ads

An ad may reveal private information about a user that the user would not otherwise disclose. This corresponds to an unintended data leakage vulnerability [2]. The following information about a user or device may be leaked:

- App name and version of the ad that was clicked.
- List of device capabilities.
- Name of network operator.
- User-provided age.
- User-provided gender.
- Ad publisher account ID.
- Type of network used (e.g., 3G, 4G or Wi-Fi).
- User-set system language.
- App-supplied keywords.

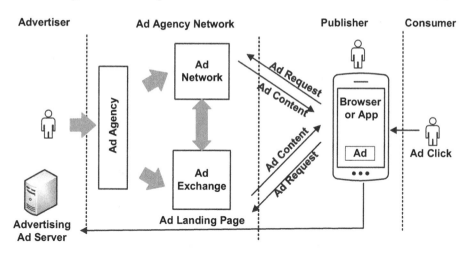

Figure 1. Mobile advertisement architecture.

- User location.

- Time zone.

- User demographic information.

- User emotional state (e.g., anger, fear, sadness, depression or hopelessness).

2.2 Mobile Advertisement Architecture

Figure 1 presents the mobile advertisement architecture. The workflow includes four participants: (i) advertisers; (ii) ad agency network; (iii) publishers; and (iv) consumers [8].

- Advertisers are commercial entities that wish to promote their products and services. An advertiser contracts an ad network for an ad campaign. The ad campaign typically specifies the advertising budget and the target numbers of clicks and impressions over a certain time period. An ad agency manages marketing, advertising and public relations services on behalf of the advertiser.

- An ad agency network consists of three components: (i) ad agency; (ii) ad network; and (iii) ad exchange:

  - An ad agency handles the marketing and branding strategies of advertisers.

- An ad network collects ad space from publishers and segments the space to offer specialized groups of ads that match advertiser needs. An ad network participates in the exchange of ads and places bids on behalf of advertisers. An ad network receives information such as user profiles, contexts and device types from an ad exchange server. An ad exchange server also collects and shares ad metrics such as the numbers of clicks and impressions.

- An ad exchange is a marketplace for publishers and advertisers to buy and sell ad space. It connects publishers with multiple ad networks. Buying and selling in an ad exchange occur via real-time auctions. An ad exchange is a neutral party that collects ads from different ad networks. An ad exchange server tracks down the list of displayed and clicked ads and determines the fees that an advertiser has to pay; some of the collected fees are passed to the publishers of the apps where the ads were displayed.

■ Publishers develop mobile applications for mobile device users (consumers). A mobile application includes an ad control module that notifies the associated ad exchange server that there is an available slot for an ad on a user's device. The app also sends user information such as the user profile, context and device type to an ad exchange. The ad exchange server decides how to monetize the particular ad slot.

■ Consumers are the end users of mobile apps who actually click on the ads.

3.   Related Work

Toubiana et al. [12] have demonstrated that Google web search session cookies can expose personal user data. They claim that the cookies capture as much as 80% of a user's search/click history. Castelluccia et al. [3] have also shown how private user information is leaked during the web searches.

Korolova [9] has shown how the micro-targeted ads on Facebook leak private information belonging to users. Castelluccia et al. [4] show that knowledge of only a small number of websites containing Google ads can reveal an individual's interests with an accuracy of 79%. In fact, up to 58% of an individual's Google ad profile can be reconstructed using this information. Castelluccia et al. reportedly accessed the ads (which are almost always served in the clear) by capturing data packets over a network.

Most recent research has focused on desktop web searches, browsing histories and ads displayed on desktop browsers, in the process demonstrating that private user information is leaked. In contrast, the system described in this chapter captures user URLs from mobile device cache files, cookies and the history database. The system retrieves ad-specific URLs and extracts private information that can be deduced from the ads. The system then reconstructs user behavior and sequences of events with the goal of establishing user identity. The system is capable of identifying users across multiple networks, even when they exhibit different usage patterns on a single device or on multiple devices.

4. Methodology

Ads are of various types, including location-based ads, content-based ads and targeted ads. Ads often reveal some private information about the user that the user would normally not disclose. An experimental setup was created to capture and analyze the ads. The targeted operating systems were iOS and Android. The targeted browsers were Safari and Chrome. Experiments were conducted with apps belonging to popular categories on four different devices and with four different users. More than 5,498 ads were captured.

The methodology involved four steps: (i) simulation of the mobile ad ecosystem; (ii) ad extraction; (iii) ad analysis; and (iv) inferences based on ad analysis (i.e., reconstructing a user identity).

5. Mobile Devices

Mobile devices display ads at two locations: (i) on the app itself; and (ii) on the search browser.

5.1 iOS Ad Architecture

As shown in Figure 2, whenever a user clicks on an ad on an iOS app, the ad information is stored in cookies (Figure 3(a)) and cache files (Figure 3(b)) in the corresponding app folder. Additionally, an entry is logged in the Safari history database.

Whenever a user clicks on an ad on the Safari browser or on an ad on an app itself, an entry is logged in the history database in the format shown in Table 3.

Figure 4 shows that the Safari history database is the common location for ad-related information.

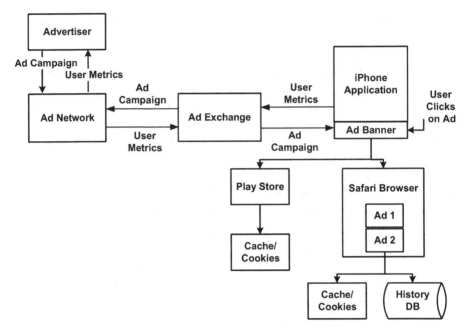

Figure 2.   iOS ad architecture.

Table 3.   Ad information format.

Timestamp	URL	Ad
10-Jun-2015 20:13:40	www.googleadservices.com/pagead/aclk?sa= L&aiCnX3vFT&adurl=http://99acres.com	99acres

iOS Ad Extraction.   The Safari history database was accessed after jailbreaking the iOS device. Ads in the history database were tagged with `googleads.g.doubleclick.net` or `adclick.g.doubleclick.net`. As shown in Table 3, the history database contains the ad timestamp and URL. The ad URLs were extracted from the history database by searches using the keywords "adurl," "googleads" and "doubleclick." The ads sent to the app store had intermediate links that opened in the browser and were then redirected to the app store. These intermediate ad URLs were also stored in the history database, but the actual ad URLs were not stored. The intermediate URLs were extracted from the history database. A custom app was then used to replay the intermediate URLs and capture the actual ad URLs and other ad information.

To capture the ads in real time, the iOS device had to be jailbroken and some browser and app store functions had to be hooked. Figure 5(a) presents the iOS ad extraction process.

(a) Cookies.   (b) Cache Files.

Figure 3. Cookies and cache information.

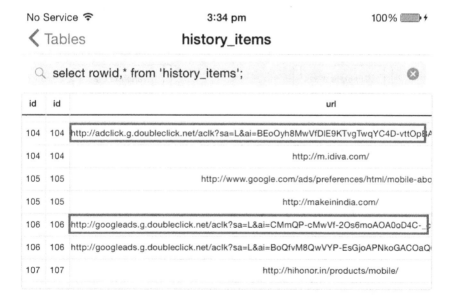

Figure 4. Safari history database information.

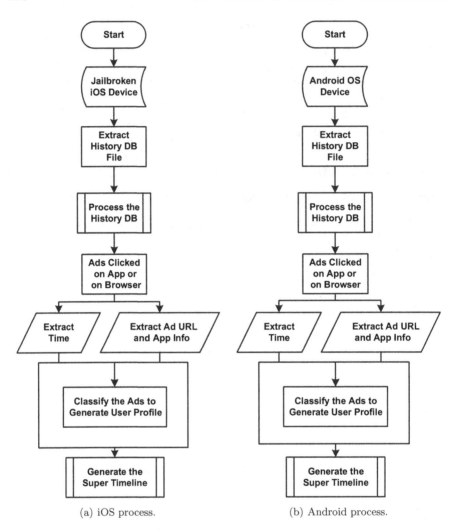

(a) iOS process.　　　　　　(b) Android process.

Figure 5. iOS and Android ad extraction processes.

5.2　Android Ad Architecture

As shown in Figure 6, when a user clicks on an ad on an Android app, the ad information is stored in a `logcat` file. Figure 7 presents the information stored in the `logcat` file.

On the other hand, when a user clicks on an ad in the Chrome browser, an entry is logged in the history database as shown in Figure 8. However, user clicks on some ads are redirected to the Google Play Store and the corresponding entries are logged in the `logcat` file.

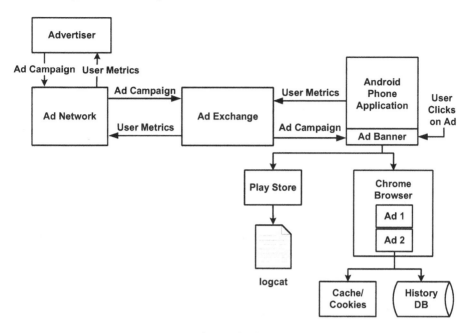

Figure 6. Android ad architecture.

```
Bangalore(UCA)&gclid=CM2IrcXX-sQCFRUVjgodaTQALQ

V/timeIds ( 8368): 16-4-2015 06:22:35

V/titleIds( 8368): Online Shopping India, Search and Buy Product Deals for Cheap

V/urlIds  ( 8368): http://www.askmebazaar.com/product.php?app_data=cHJvZHVjdF9pZ

V/timeIds ( 8368): 17-4-2015 02:08:58

V/titleIds( 8368): New Cars, Used Cars, Car Prices, Reviews & Photos in India -

V/urlIds  ( 8368): http://www.carwale.com/m/?ltsrc=l7831&gclid=COn-tJn4_MQCFYEoj

V/timeIds ( 8368): 17-4-2015 04:08:06

V/titleIds( 8368): Idea Cellular - Cell Phone Services | 3G, Prepaid, Postpaid &

V/urlIds  ( 8368): https://m.ideacellular.com/mobile/default/index.html?pn=insta

V/timeIds ( 8368): 17-4-2015 04:09:38

V/titleIds( 8368): Ford Figo Price in India, Photos & Review - CarWale

V/urlIds  ( 8368): http://www.carwale.com/m/ford-cars/figo/?ltsrc=21545&gclid=C:
```

Figure 7. Android `logcat`.

Android Ad Extraction. Android in-app ads and browser ads either open in the browser or in the Play Store. Information about in-app ads

```
http://www.zomato.com/bangalore/tamarind-banaswadi?adref=043000-0050957-0000006&gclid=CJKhkZf9ubsCFWlT4godVWs
https://www.tapjoy.com/?gclid=CMr8k9ac6cQCFRQqjgodWyoApQ
http://www.askme.com/bangalore/taxi-cab-services?gclid=cn3o3o-p68qcfrcmjgodpieapq&utm_source=google&utm_medium=s
http://www.askme.com/bangalore/taxi-cab-services?gclid=cmzr-9dd68qcfqesiqod23oalw&utm_source=google&utm_medium=s
http://lp.startapp.com/?mc=2&pid=3&cmpid=381&countid=WW&gclid=CMnr3sXe68QCFUQojgodKLwAWA
https://paytm.com/airtel-prepaid-mobile-online-recharge.htm?gclid=COCs2qT38sQCFQwnjgodgEwA3g
http://m.gaadi.com/used_car_result.php?campaign_type=search&make=Land+Rover&gclid=CJelv8qP88QCFRcMjgod-3AACg
http://www.carwale.com/m/landrover-cars/?ltsrc=1123&gclid=CIOu4tGP88QCFRcXjgod4hUAgg
http://www.webcrawler.com/info.wbcrwl.305.10/search/web?q=land+rovers+used+for+sale&cid=135636324&ad.network=g&a
```

Figure 8.   Android history database.

that open in the browser and information about browser ads are stored
in the browser history database. The challenge was to extract the history
database and separate the ad URLs from normal web browsing URLs
stored in the database. Typically, an Android device must be rooted to
access the browser history database. However, it was discovered that the
APIs provided by the Android SDK, corresponding to content providers
of Chrome and the Android default browser, enable the extraction of
history data without having to root an Android device.

After extracting the history database, it was necessary to separate
the ad URLs from the normal web browsing URLs. After analyzing
the ad URLs, it was discovered that they had some unique keywords
such as "googleadsservices," "adclick" and "adurl." These keywords
were employed as distinguishing features to separate ad URLs from web
browsing URLs. Figure 5(b) presents the Android ad extraction process.

Based on this research, an Ad Extractor Android app was implemented to save the date, time, title and URL of each ad in the browser
history database to the `logcat` file. As mentioned above, an algorithm
was implemented to separate ad URLs based on specific keywords. The
ad URLs were separated from the other URLs and copied to a file using ADB commands. Whenever the Ad Extractor app was launched, it
dumped all the ad data to a specified file. Thus, the ads on a browser
as well as ads from apps that go to a browser were captured.

The next task was to capture the ads that go to the Play Store from
the app or browser. The URLs of these ads are not recorded in the
browser history file. It was discovered that around 40% of the ads in
Android apps (in-app ads) go to the Play Store. These ad URLs are
also not stored in the browser history. However, because no Play Store
history database exists, it was not possible to capture the required ad
information.

To address this problem, a custom app that uses the Play Store URL
schema is required. The idea is to open an app using the URL schema
and enable the user to select whether to go to the Play Store or to use
the custom-created URL schema app. Two URL schema exist for the

Table 4. Genymotion emulators.

Devices	Description
Nexus (Device 1)	Google Nexus 4
Samsung (Device 1)	Galaxy S3
Nexus (Device 2)	Google Nexus 4
Nexus (Device 2)	Google Nexus 4

Play Store – `market` and `play.google.com`. Thus, a URL schema app was developed with the same URL schema as the Play Store. When this custom app is used, instead of an ad going directly to the Play Store upon being clicked by a user, two options are provided to the user:

- Google Play Store app (built-in app).

- URL schema app (custom-built app).

Upon selecting the URL schema app, an ad is opened in the app, enabling the capture of the ad URL. Two URL schema apps were developed, one for capturing ads with the URL scheme `market:` and the other for ads with the URL scheme `play.google.com`.

All the steps (browser ad extraction and Google Play Store ad extraction) and the individual app functionality were consolidated into a single app that was deployed in the experiments. When a user clicked on ads, the consolidated app captured all the ads, stored them in temporary locations and sent the collected information via email to the researchers based on a predefined schedule.

In order to simulate a mobile ad ecosystem, an experimental system was created using Genymotion emulators. This system automated the ad clicking process for in-app banner ads (i.e., ads that appear in apps). Five apps were selected for the experiments: (i) Cricbuzz; (ii) Reddit Sync; (iii) 4 Pics 1 Word; (iv) Times of India; and (v) Advanced Permission Manager. The five apps were selected based on their popularity and coverage of categories such as sports, news and games; a controller app was also included. All the apps had banner ads at fixed locations that made automated clicking more efficient.

The five apps mentioned above and the two URL schema apps were installed in Genymotion emulators (see Table 4). A shell script was created to launch each app in turn and click on the ad. This process was repeated 1,000 times. In the simulations, ads that go to the browser directly from the history database were captured; in the case of ads that go to the Google Play Store, the ad URLs were captured using the URL

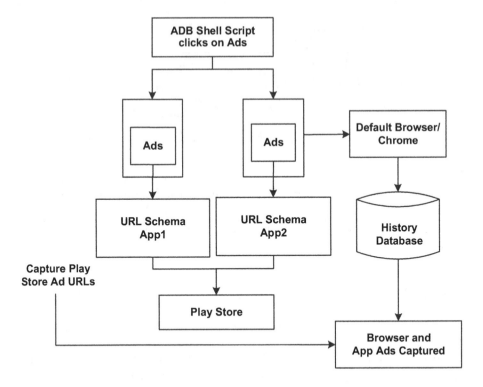

Figure 9.   Experimental setup for Android ad extraction.

schema apps that logged them to separate text files along with their timestamps.

The experiments with the five apps were conducted by two different users (running two emulators per user) over a period of eight weeks. The ad data was subsequently collected from the history database and analyzed to construct user behavior profiles. Figure 9 summarizes the ad extraction process.

Android Ad Analysis. The experiments captured more than 5,498 ads from the four emulators (see Table 4). The ads were mined to collect the following data:

- **Ad Category Information:** To understand the different categories of ads.

- **Ad Interest Information:** To understand the different types of user interests that ads reveal.

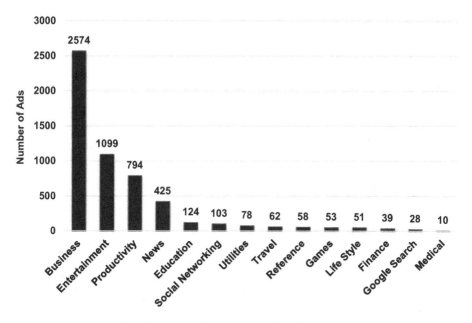

Figure 10. Ad category distribution.

- **User Information:** To obtain user-related information for constructing user profiles and generating user preferences based on the clicked ads.

Two Google accounts (User1 and User2) were set up and an automated program was created to read the URLs and browse the links. In the first experiment, User1 logged in and the automated program was executed to read the URLs and browse the links for one device in an office environment (restricted network). In the second experiment, User2 logged in and the automated program was executed to read the URLs and browse the links for one device in a home environment (unrestricted environment). Two user profiles were created and the results were compared. The next section presents the experimental results and inferences.

6. Results and Discussion

More than 5,499 ads were captured using the four emulators. This section discusses the statistics related to the captured results.

6.1 Ad Category

Figure 10 shows that 47% of the ads deal with business, 20% with entertainment, 14% with productivity and 8% with news.

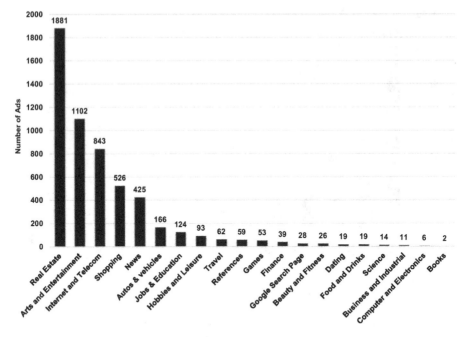

Figure 11. Ad interest distribution.

6.2   Ad Interest

Figure 11 shows that 34% of the ads deal with real estate, 20% with arts and entertainment, 15% with the Internet and telecommunications, and 10% with shopping.

6.3   User Information

Analysis indicated that 36% of the ads contained location information, 33% time information, 13% language information and 5% app information. If the ads are assumed to be clicked by the user more than 100 times, then 38% would contain location information, 34% time information and 14% language information (see Figure 12).

If the ads are assumed to be clicked by the user less than 100 times, then 22% would contain information about financial transactions, 21% about mobile phone account recharges, 10% about offers, 10% about cars and 7% about marital status (see Figure 13).

Figure 14 shows the preferences generated for a user who used two different environments. Based on this information, it was possible to link the user preferences to the same user.

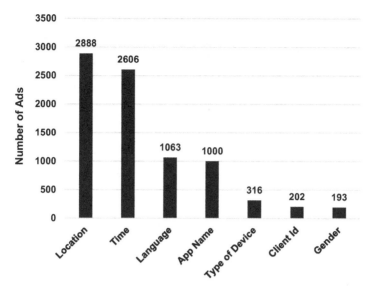

Figure 12. User information based on ads clicked more than 100 times.

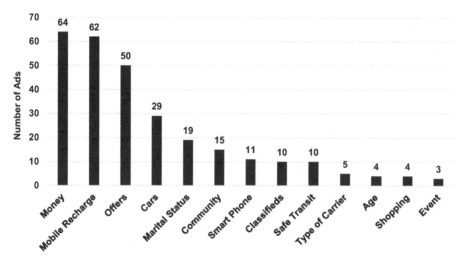

Figure 13. User information based on ads clicked less than 100 times.

6.4 Observations and Inferences

The following observations and inferences were made using the data collected from ads displayed in Android apps:

- Ads provided information relevant to events, offers and events. For example, a real estate offer lasted for five days and it was observed that the ads during the five days were related to the offer.

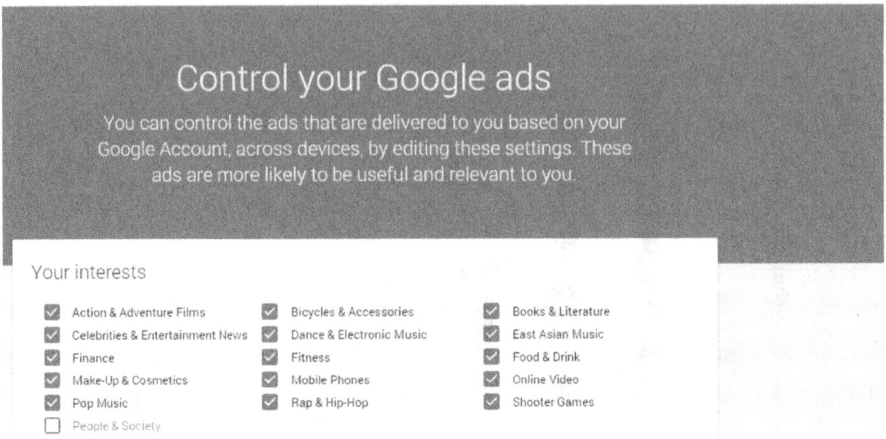

Figure 14. User preferences generated via Google.

- Ads provided information about user locations. For example, an ad for a jeweler showed the store locations and offers in the city of Bangalore; another ad was about a Kannada news app (Kannada is the regional language).

- No significant difference was observed in the displayed ads with respect to the user who was logged in.

The following observations and inferences were made using the data collected from ads displayed in Google search:

- Ads provided information about regional festivals, events and occasions (e.g., Diwali, Christmas and New Year festival offers, and sports events).

- Ads customized for geolocation provided information about user locations (e.g., `taxiwala.com`, a taxi service located in Delhi).

- The average database size of ads corresponding to a keyword was between five and ten; ads were almost always getting picked up from this database of ads.

- The percentage of ads displayed from the database ranged from 30% to 100%

- In the case of some search keywords, more ads seemed to appear late in the evening, thereby disclosing information about time of the day.

- No significant difference was observed in the displayed ads with respect to the user who was logged in.

From these results, it was possible to construct user profiles, predict user locations, days, dates and times, regional festivals and other events.

7. Conclusions

This research has demonstrated how information gleaned from ads on a mobile device can be used to identify users. The methodology can be used to identify a user even if he or she uses the same device, multiple devices, different networks or follows different usage patterns. Also, the methodology can support a digital forensic readiness framework for mobile devices. Additionally, it has applications in context-based security and proactive and reactive digital forensic investigations.

The current research has focused extensively on the Android environment. Future research will examine iOS devices as well as desktop systems, laptops and tablets. Furthermore, the methodology will be extended to link a user across multiple devices and systems. Finally, future research will attempt to track and capture live ads at the network and firewall levels, which could support proactive crime prevention efforts.

References

[1] D. Abalenkovs, P. Bondarenko, V. Pathapati, A. Nordbo, D. Piatkivskyi, J. Rekdal and P. Ruthven, Mobile Forensics: Comparison of Extraction and Analyzing Methods of iOS and Android, Gjovik University College, Gjovik, Norway, 2012.

[2] T. Book and D. Wallach, An Empirical Study of Mobile Ad Targeting, Department of Computer Science, Rice University, Houston, Texas, 2015.

[3] C. Castelluccia, E. De Cristofaro and D. Perito, Private information disclosure from web searches, in *Privacy Enhancing Technologies*, M. Atallah and N. Hopper (Eds.), Springer-Verlag, Berlin Heidelberg, Germany, pp. 38–55, 2010.

[4] C. Castelluccia, M. Kaafar and M. Tran, Betrayed by your ads! Reconstructing user profiles from targeted ads, in *Privacy Enhancing Technologies*, S. Fischer-Hubner and M. Wright (Eds.), Springer-Verlag, Berlin Heidelberg, Germany, pp. 1–17, 2012.

[5] Dimensional Research, The Impact of Mobile Devices on Information Security: A Survey of IT and IT Professionals, San Francisco, California, 2014.

[6] A. Guarino, Digital forensics as a big data challenge, in *ISSE 2013 Securing Electronic Business Processes*, H. Reimer, N. Pohlmann and W. Schneider (Eds.), Springer Fachmedien, Wiesbaden, Germany, pp. 197–203, 2013.

[7] O. Hamoui, Targeting an Ad to a Mobile Device, U.S. Patent Application US20080059300 A1, 2007.

[8] Interactive Advertising Bureau, IAB Platform Status Report: A Mobile Advertising Overview, New York, 2008.

[9] A. Korolova, Privacy violations using microtargeted ads: A case study, *Proceedings of the IEEE International Conference on Data Mining Workshops*, pp. 474–482, 2010.

[10] G. Mohay, Technical challenges and directions for digital forensics, *Proceedings of the First IEEE International Workshop on Systematic Approaches to Digital Forensic Engineering*, pp. 155–161, 2005.

[11] R. Rowlingson, A ten-step process for forensic readiness, *International Journal of Digital Evidence*, vol. 2(3), 2004.

[12] V. Toubiana, V. Verdot and B. Christophe, Cookie-based privacy issues on Google services, *Proceedings of the Second ACM Conference on Data and Application Security and Privacy*, pp. 141–148, 2012.

[13] J. Yan, N. Liu, G. Wang, W. Zhang, Y. Jiang and Z. Chen, How much can behavioral targeting help online advertising? *Proceedings of the Eighteenth International Conference on the World Wide Web*, pp. 261–270, 2009.

[14] J. Yu, You've got mobile ads! Young consumers' responses to mobile ads with different types, *International Journal of Mobile Marketing*, vol. 8(1), pp. 5–22, 2013.

Chapter 7

A FORENSIC METHODOLOGY FOR ANALYZING NINTENDO 3DS DEVICES

Huw Read, Elizabeth Thomas, Iain Sutherland, Konstantinos Xynos and Mikhaila Burgess

Abstract   Handheld video game consoles have evolved much like their desktop counterparts over the years. The most recent eighth generation of game consoles are now defined not by their ability to interact online using a web browser, but by the social media facilities they now provide. This chapter describes a forensic methodology for analyzing Nintendo 3DS handheld video game consoles, demonstrating their potential for misuse and highlighting areas where evidence may reside. Empirical research has led to the formulation of a detailed methodology that can assist forensic examiners in maximizing evidence extraction while minimizing, if not preventing, the destruction of information.

Keywords: Video game consoles, Nintendo 3DS, forensic analysis methodology

1.   Introduction

The 3DS, released in Japan in February 2011, is Nintendo's latest handheld platform. At the time of writing this chapter, more than 45 million units have been sold worldwide [17], making the 3DS one of the most popular eighth generation handheld video game consoles. Nintendo has upgraded the 3DS over its lifespan and has created several revisions with features such as larger screens (3DS XL), improved hardware ("new" Nintendo 3DS) and a "lite" version (2DS).

Like its predecessor, the Nintendo DS, the 3DS is Wi-Fi enabled and connects to the Internet. It has a built-in web browser, an email-like system and, as in the case of the DSi, a digital camera. The defining changes to the 3DS over its predecessors are enhanced social media, new sharing features and access to an app store from the device. Built-in functionality such as StreetPass enables the exchange of data with

© IFIP International Federation for Information Processing 2016
Published by Springer International Publishing AG 2016. All Rights Reserved
G. Peterson and S. Shenoi (Eds.): Advances in Digital Forensics XII, IFIP AICT 484, pp. 127–143, 2016.
DOI: 10.1007/978-3-319-46279-0_7

other 3DS consoles in close proximity even when the console is in the sleep mode [19]. The Nintendo eShop [20] supports the downloading of software directly to the device.

The Nintendo 3DS is primarily designed for playing games, but the features mentioned above enable it to be used in many other activities that may be of interest in forensic investigations. One way to determine the 3DS customer profiles (and the types of users) is to consider the Pan European Game Information (PEGI) classifications for video games [21]. The Nintendo 3DS has two games rated as 18-year-old and 397 games rated as three-year-old. In contrast, the Sony PlayStation Vita has eighteen 18-year-old rated games and 112 3-year-old rated games [21]. The figures are similarly skewed towards the 3DS in the 7-year-old rating category. Thus, it is reasonable to conclude that, if a 3DS is seized as part of an investigation, the case would likely involve a young child. This was demonstrated in a case where the previous generation DSi was used by a ten-year-old girl to take a picture of her attacker during an assault [10]. A more recent case involved a man who encouraged two 11-year old girls to send naked pictures via the email-like service provided by the 3DS [3].

2.   Related Work

The published literature suggests that the 3DS platform can be misused [3, 16]. However, there is no evidence to suggest that the Nintendo 3DS has been explored as a potential container of forensic artifacts, although it may provide information relating to misuse and user activities such as network communications. Research on other entertainment systems (described below) has shown that the forensic methods and the types of artifacts recovered depend largely on whether the system is unencrypted and whether the main storage is a hard drive. If the answer is no to either of these questions, then a forensic investigator could attempt to extract information via the native interface.

2.1   Devices with Hard Drives

Microsoft's Xbox 360 is not encrypted, but it has the non-standard XTAF filesystem. The approach proposed by Xynos et al. [28] is to carve files and perform string searches for dates and times. Filesystem drivers [26] and forensic tools [13] are also available that can simplify the analysis.

Conrad et al. [7] conducted a series of tests on a Sony PlayStation 3 to determine the optimum method for analyzing the console. Although encryption is used to protect data, the PlayStation 3 does have a standard 2.5" hard drive for storage. Conrad et al. recommend that an analyst extract a forensically-sound duplicate of the drive and use the duplicate to perform the investigation via the native PlayStation 3 interface.

Microsoft's Xbox One also contains encrypted files. An analysis of the hard drive [14] has shown that the files are contained in an NTFS filesystem, which opens the possibility of analyzing date and time entries in the MFT. However, the Sony PlayStation 4 does not have an immediately-recognizable filesystem. Forensic analysis recommendations are similar to those for the PlayStation 3: forensically image the hard drive and proceed to analyze the system via the native PlayStation 4 interface [9]. The PlayStation 4 analysis process described in [9] employed a special write blocker, VOOM Shadow 3, to write hard drive changes to an intermediate buffer that facilitated system navigation without any instabilities.

2.2   Devices without Hard Drives

The Nintendo Wii uses onboard storage that is soldered onto the motherboard. Similar to the PlayStation 4, a forensic analysis of the Wii [27] demonstrated that it is possible to recover data from the device via the user interface. However, this "live analysis" methodology has the potential to alter the data if performed incorrectly.

Desoldering the onboard memory is an option, but the high skill level needed and the potential for damage rule it out as a possible investigative method. Sutherland et al. [25] have described the analysis of an LG Smart TV entertainment system. Although a Smart TV is not a game console, the forensic analysis approach is relevant. In particular, an empirical analysis was performed via the user interface of the LG Smart TV, not unlike the methodologies used on the Wii and PlayStation 4 described above. However, as in the case of the Wii, it was difficult to extract a physical image of the onboard memory. Thus, the Smart TV analysis concentrated on what could be recovered via the user interface.

The device with the greatest similarity to the Nintendo 3DS that has been forensically analyzed and documented is the Sony PlayStation Portable (PSP) [8]. Although its updated sibling, the Sony PlayStation Vita, is technically a more direct rival to the Nintendo 3DS, at the time of this writing, no forensic research related to this device could be found. The Sony PlayStation Portable has Internet connectivity and a web browser. The browser stores artifacts on a removable, unencrypted FAT16-formatted memory stick. Conrad et al. [8] describe the process of forensically imaging the memory stick and analyzing files for web browsing artifacts, including deleted entries.

3.   Forensic Value

The Nintendo 3DS can hold two types of media simultaneously, a game cartridge and an SD card. 3DS game cartridges primarily store game data, but are also used by some games to record save game data. The SD card stores images and videos taken with the camera, and applications downloaded from the eShop. Additionally, there is internal storage capacity on a NAND flash memory chip soldered onto the motherboard [11].

The closed console has several LED indicators that provide information about the system state. A blue power LED on the front of the console indicates that the device is in the standby mode. A charging LED indicates the power status and if the battery is running low. Red indicates that the device has to be charged, orange indicates that it is currently charging, while yellow indicates that the device is fully charged. Note that, if the device loses power, running applications may not be written to the device; for example, web browser history may be lost if the browser is not closed properly.

An LED on the top right of the device indicates if notifications have been received. There are four possibilities for this LED: (i) blue – SpotPass data has been received; (ii) green – StreetPass data has been received; (iii) orange – a friend's device is online; and (iv) red – the device needs to be charged. A slider on the right-hand side of the device controls wireless connectivity; the LED alongside it turns yellow when wireless is on.

Upon powering a 3DS, the last application that ran on the device is selected and the corresponding game logo is displayed on the top screen. If the notification LED is lit, a glowing dot appears on the icon of the application that received the notification.

Several features are potentially of interest to a forensic investigator. The 3DS offers Wi-Fi connectivity. The WLAN subsystem is a single-chip 802.11b/g device [12]. Connection information is easily accessible via the settings menu; this includes information about the current connection used by the device along with the MAC address. Up to three access points can be stored.

The activity log keeps a record of the applications launched on the system, including the first and most recent date that each application was used. This information is updated during a live investigation if any applications are executed, so it is important that the information is collected early in the analysis.

The 3DS incorporates a Netfront browser based on the WebKit engine, which enables images to be downloaded to the SD card [18]. The built-in web browser has forensic significance because it provides a history of up to 32 web pages viewed by the user. However, neither date nor time information are available. It should be noted that, if a link is followed from an older web page, then a new history list is generated from that point onwards. Cached information includes the website favicon, title and URL. The web browser history can be viewed using the left and right arrows on the touch screen. A maximum of 64 bookmarks may be stored.

The camera serves as the access point for the image gallery. An investigator can use the camera to view images stored on the device, including images downloaded via the web browser. The date and time of a viewed image are displayed in the top screen. In addition, there is a note indicating where the image is stored, either on the SD card or in internal NAND memory.

The Nintendo eShop is used to purchase downloadable content. Information stored in the eShop could be of value because some credit card details may be saved, such as the last four digits of a credit card number and its expiration date.

The friends list contains friends who have connected locally or over the Internet using a "friend code." Users can see when their friends are online and can update their status, which is shared with others.

Until October 2013, the Swapnote message exchange service (Letter Box in some regions) could be used to exchange messages and photos with other users via the Internet using the SpotPass service. However, Nintendo terminated this service because some consumers, including minors, were posting their friend codes on Internet bulletin boards and then using Swapnote to exchange offensive material [16]. Although no new messages can be sent via SpotPass, historical data may be available on a device. Messages and pictures can still be exchanged using StreetPass (Figure 1), which requires the two devices to be in close proximity.

Unofficial cartridges (flashcarts) can offer additional functionality for the 3DS, with some cartridges providing data storage for user files. An example is Acekard 3 game cartridges that are often used for pirating software or running homebrew applications. However, the 3DS device itself supports miniSD cards, enabling users to store a range of files, including music, images and documents [22]. It is, therefore, vital to thoroughly examine game cartridges to confirm their functionality and ensure that no evidence is missed.

Several hacks have been developed that circumvent the security measures on the 3DS and allow third-party (homebrew) applications to be installed. As discussed in [23], these mechanisms could be used as new vectors to extract data from embedded systems. In the case of the

Figure 1. StreetPass service for exchanging pictures and messages.

3DS, a number of applications and game titles have been shown to be exploitable. A comprehensive list can be found in [24]. Several FTP homebrew applications have also been released [2], but at the time of this writing, they only allow access to the miniSD card, not the internal NAND flash memory.

Table 1 summarizes the 3DS device features that would be of interest in a forensic investigation. These features must be examined very carefully to ensure that the investigation is conducted in a forensically-sound manner and/or no evidence is missed.

Barriers to using standard imaging methods on a 3DS device include the lack of common interfaces (e.g., USB) and encryption of the internal NAND flash memory. Imaging a 3DS NAND chip is possible using JTAG or chip-off. JTAG guidance for forensically imaging NAND flash memory using a tool such as FTK Imager is presented in [5]; the image can be flashed back later to verify the results. Chip-off is more invasive and

Table 1. Features of interest.

Features	Reason
LEDs	Different color states indicate that data exchange has occurred
Wi-Fi	Associated access points reveal where the 3DS was used
Web Browser	Provides recent history (maximum 32 pages) and bookmarks (maximum 64 pages)
Camera	Provides access to image gallery, views of images created by the 3DS and images saved from webpages; indicates the locations of stored images (internal NAND memory and miniSD card)
eShop	Provides the last four digits of credit card numbers and their expiration dates
Friends List	Contains the list of friends (on the Internet and/or in close proximity); owners can share their status
Swapnote	Email-like service used to send text and images from the gallery; SpotPass and StreetPass services used to send text and images over the Internet and to users in close proximity, respectively
Unofficial Game Cards	May contain additional embedded media (e.g., microSD), homebrew software (potential for further communications options) and pirated software
Activity Log	Provides coarse indications of application usage patterns (e.g., pedometer indicates user perambulations)
Game Notes	Contains hand-written notes created by the user

requires the desoldering of the NAND chip. To avoid these challenges, a 3DS device can be investigated live, but this may have an impact on the state of the device (i.e., alter or even add data). The forensic analysis methodology described in the next section considers all these issues while adhering to the ACPO Good Practice Guide for Digital Evidence [4] to minimize alterations, tampering and modifications of the original evidence to the extent possible.

4. Forensic Analysis Methodology

As discussed in the previous section, the most appropriate approach for acquiring evidence from a 3DS device is via the user interface. This empirical approach ensures that investigators do not lose evidence due to unfamiliarity with the device.

The 3DS has two displays, but only the lower screen is touch-sensitive. Underneath the screen are three buttons, SELECT, HOME and START.

The most important is the HOME button, which allows a user to return to the main screen at any time. A stylus located next to the game card slot on the back of the 3DS makes it easier to interact with the device. Alternatively, a user can employ two navigational buttons: A to select an item from the menu and B to move back to the previous menu. The lower touch-sensitive screen contains applications with several built-in utilities along the top.

Figure 2 presents the forensic analysis methodology for Nintendo 3DS devices. The methodology has the following steps:

- **Step 1: Start the video camera to record all interactions:** The recommended ACPO best practice [4] when examining a live device is to record the process and capture all the actions involved in the examination for later scrutiny and to provide a strong record of the procedures used in the analysis. In addition, a written record should be kept of every action performed, including its time and duration.

- **Step 2: Check the device status:** Before the SD and application cards are removed, it is important to ensure that the 3DS is actually turned off (i.e., it is not in the suspend mode). If the cards are removed when the system is in the suspend mode, then running applications are forcibly closed and potential evidence held in memory may be lost.

  The power indicator light must be checked first. If the light is blue, then the system is on. Next, the Wi-Fi indicator light on the right-side of the 3DS must be checked. If the light is amber, then the slider must be depressed to disable Wi-Fi. Following this, the console is opened – this resumes the suspended applications. Observations of interest are then recorded, following which the power button is pressed and held down to close the software and expose the power off function. This updates the activity log, but it was discovered that the log is updated even if the application card is forcibly removed. Finally, the device should be powered off.

- **Step 3: Remove, write-protect and analyze the SD card separately; clone the image to a new SD card; insert the clone:** The SD card is not encrypted and can be imaged separately using a suitable forensic tool. The card is formatted as FAT16 (up to 2 GiB) or FAT32 (up to 32 GiB). Data can be extracted via carving, which also retrieves images (including their EXIF data) that can be important depending on the case. Specifically, the following information can be extracted:

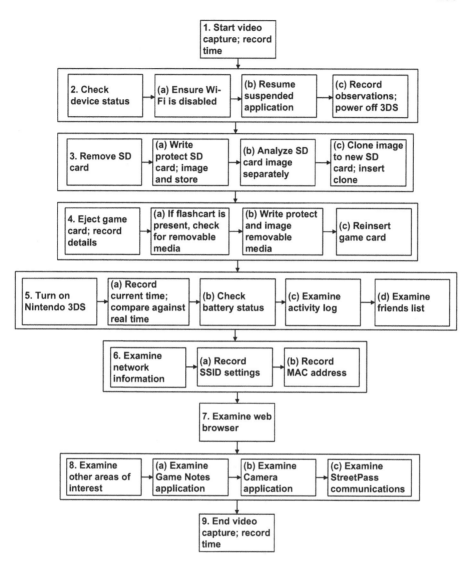

Figure 2. Forensic analysis process for Nintendo 3DS devices.

- Exif.Image.Make: Nintendo
- Exif.Image.Model: Nintendo 3DS
- Exif.Image.DateTime: 2012:01:27 13:37:00

Images downloaded via the web browser can be seen in the DCIM folder, but no information about the sources of the images is stored. Therefore, it is necessary to rely on the web browser history data.

Videos taken by a 3DS are stored in the AVI format, 3D images are stored in the MPO format and voice notes are stored in the M4A format.

Applications downloaded to the SD card from the eShop are encrypted; extensive information about the layout and file structure can be found in [1]. Experiments revealed that launching different applications known to exist on an SD card did not change the MAC (modification, access, creation) times of application files. The only times that are provided relate to the initial installations of applications on the SD card; therefore, an investigator should not rely on a timeline analysis of this nature. Furthermore, applications are stored in folders with names containing hexadecimal characters. To compile a list of applications on the SD card, an investigator would need to cross-reference the list as described in [15].

Applications that can store or process user data should be noted and appended to the end of Step 7 (described below). A clone of the SD card should be inserted into the 3DS device without write-protection. Later steps (e.g., Steps 8(a) and 8(b)) may require an investigator to export files to the SD card. Using a clone ensures that application data on the SD card can be analyzed via the console interface while maintaining the forensic integrity of the original SD card.

- **Step 4: Eject the game card; record the card details:** The game card should be formally recorded to confirm that it is a game or application. Recording and analyzing the title, type and code found on the card can confirm its functionality. If the game Cubic Ninja, in particular, is found, the presence of homebrew applications on the SD card is indicated. Investigators should cross-reference the homebrew application list available in [2] against the SD card from Step 3 to determine if other useful forensic artifacts can be found. At the time of writing this chapter, FTP servers (ftPONY and ftBRONY), a Facebook client (fb43ds) and a video player (vid3o) would be of interest to investigators. Furthermore, if an unofficial flashcart is found, there may be a removable microSD card, which should be write-protected, imaged and analyzed separately. The microSD should be cloned and the clone inserted without write-protection into the flashcart.

- **Steps 5(a), 5(b): Power on the Nintendo 3DS:** The Wi-Fi starts when the 3DS is powered up if the Wi-Fi was turned on previously. If the amber indicator light is lit on the right-side of the

3DS, then the Wi-Fi must be disabled by pushing the slider or the device must be in a Faraday cage. If the device detects that new firmware is available, then it prevents access to some areas until the update has been applied. At the top-right-hand corner is the battery icon, which indicates the battery power level using blue bars and if the device must be charged. Alongside this is the current date and time. The date and time are not updated automatically; this must be taken into account when examining timestamps retrieved from the device because they may have to be offset against the current time. The top-left-hand corner displays the connectivity status – a blue bar containing the word "Internet" indicates an active connection. The main menu displays the applications available in a grid format; these provide valuable information about the possible uses of the 3DS.

- **Step 5(c): Examine the activity log:** The activity log provides a record of recent activities on the device. Upon opening an application, a record is made in the activity log. Hence, the activity log should be one of the first items examined by an investigator.

  The activity log has two distinct views as part of the application. The first view enables a user to examine daily records of usage, which can be adjusted for daily, weekly, monthly or yearly totals. Figure 3 shows the daily view of an activity log; the analyst can scroll through and select the date on the bottom screen while the top screen defaults to a graph representation of the usage. A list view provides a different representation of the data. This view may be used, for example, to examine the results of a pedometer that indicates the numbers of steps taken by a user and the corresponding times.

  The second view in the activity log is of the software library. An analyst can navigate the application icons on the bottom screen while the top screen displays the corresponding usage. The dates of the first use and most recent use are presented, but timestamps are not provided.

- **Step 5(d): Examine the friends list:** The friends list contains friends' names, friend codes, whether friends are online or not, and a user-editable message of up to 16 characters that can be broadcast to everyone in the friends list.

- **Step 6: Examine network information:** Networking information can be found under the Settings menu. Upon selecting

Figure 3. Daily view of activity log events.

Internet Settings, the new menu contains the items: Connection Settings, SpotPass, Nintendo DS Connections, Other Information.

Upon selecting Connection Settings, a list of three possible connections are displayed. If the Connection has "None" written alongside it, no connection is established. However, if it has an entry such as "Connection 1: mySSID," then a connection is established. A lock symbol indicates the security status of the connection.

To obtain the MAC address of the device, it is necessary to access Internet Settings and select Other Information. The MAC address may be needed during an investigation to confirm or eliminate that the device was used to perform certain actions.

- **Step 7: Examine the web browser:** The 3DS web browser appears in the top-right-hand corner of the touch screen. When the browser is opened, the last page viewed is the first to open. From this point on, the left arrow at the bottom of the screen can be used to navigate through previously-viewed pages. Clicking on the Menu button provides access to the bookmarks list and an "i" icon provides page information, including the address (i.e., URL).

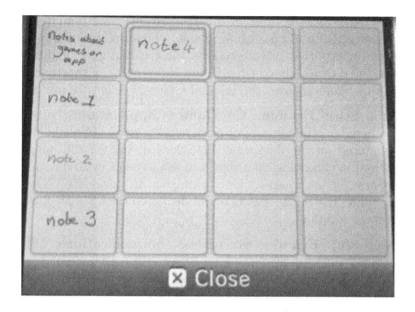

Figure 4.   Game Notes application with handwritten messages.

The Bookmarks item contains a maximum of 64 entries. A bookmark can be opened for editing, which displays the complete website URL. The web browser design poses a challenge to forensic investigators because no permanent record of the browser history is recorded; only the most recent 32 pages can be viewed. Other information can be confirmed via the web browser, such as the current network connection and proxy settings. The menu contains a setting tab, which displays information as follows:

– Connection Type: Wireless LAN (Connection 1)

– Connection (SSID): mySSID

– Security: WPA2-PSK (AES)

In addition, the user can use the menu to delete the history, cookies and save data.

- **Step 8(a): Examine the Game Notes application:** As shown in Figure 4, Game Notes supports handwritten notes made by users. Date/time information is not stored by a 3DS device, but a user may write the time on the note itself. The application stores the handwritten messages in onboard memory. However, export functions are provided that enable an investigator to save notes of interest such as pictures on the SD card by default and in internal memory if the SD card unavailable. Timestamp data associated with an exported picture reflects the creation date of the image, not the creation date of the Game Notes entry. Exporting images in this manner leaves the original Game Note entries intact.

- **Step 8(b): Examine the Camera application:** The camera icon enables the viewing of photos and videos. These images can be stored on the device or the SD card, but all the images are viewed in chronological order from left to right, with date markers separating the images. By clicking on an image, the date/time at which the image was taken is displayed, along with the image storage location.

- **Step 8(c): Examine StreetPass communications:** Mii characters (Nintendo avatars) from other 3DS consoles can be transferred when the consoles are in close proximity to each other. The number of times the Miis have met is displayed alongside an indicator of the software used (e.g., "met via StreetPass"). A Mii creator can register information to be transferred with the Mii, including the nickname, Mii's birthday, creator, StreetPass hits and plaza population. A coarse timestamp indicates when the Mii was linked to the 3DS device (e.g., "3 hours ago" or "4 days ago").

5.   Conclusions

The phrase "End of the Age of Nintendo Forensics" was coined by Carvey [6] to emphasize that forensic investigators must have detailed knowledge about the systems and files they analyze and that they should not merely rely on digital forensic tools. We are currently in the "New Age of Nintendo Forensics," where game consoles – both desktop and handheld – can contain significant amounts of digital evidence about user actions and possible criminal activity. This is especially true of the eighth generation of game consoles that provide advanced Internet functionality and applications, including web browsers, email and social media.

This chapter has highlighted cases in which Nintendo handheld consoles have provided evidence of illegal activity and has identified areas on the devices where data relevant to forensic investigations may be stored. The forensic analysis methodology for Nintendo 3DS devices was developed using empirical research. The methodology maximizes data retrieval and minimizes evidence loss or corruption; this is important because certain sequences of events can trigger the modification of forensically-relevant data.

Unfortunately, retrieving a dump of the internal device memory is difficult without hardware modifications and analyzing the dump is extremely difficult due to encryption. Future research should focus on these problems. For example, if an FTP server could run with root privileges, it may be possible to obtain and analyze a logical image of the files stored in the internal NAND memory. Analyzing and understanding the raw files that store data could reveal valuable artifacts pertaining to user communications. If Linux tools (e.g., dd) compiled for use on a 3DS are available, it may be possible to obtain unencrypted images of internal NAND memory. Existing forensic techniques such as file carving could then be used to identify and recover deleted data and temporary files.

References

[1] 3DBrew, Title Data Structure (3dbrew.org/wiki/Title_Data_Structure), 2014.

[2] 3DBrew, Homebrew Applications (www.3dbrew.org/wiki/Homebrew_Applications), 2016.

[3] B. Ashcroft, Accused child predator allegedly used Nintendo's Swapnote service, *Kotaku* (kotaku.com/child-predators-were-using-nintendos-swapnote-service-1459304126), November 6, 2013.

[4] Association of Chief Police Officers, Good Practice Guide for Digital Evidence, London, United Kingdom, 2012.

[5] Ate0Eight, DIY 3DS XL NAND Dumping-R/W pt. 1 (www.youtube.com/watch?v=n5Aa88HCK6g), 2013.

[6] H. Carvey, The age of "Nintendo forensics" ..., Windows Incident Response (windowsir.blogspot.no/2005/12/age-of-nintendo-forensics.html), December 22, 2005.

[7] S. Conrad, G. Dorn and P. Craiger, Forensic analysis of a PlayStation 3 console, in *Advanced in Digital Forensics VI*, K. Chow and S. Shenoi (Eds.), Springer, Heidelberg, Germany, pp. 65–76, 2010.

[8] S. Conrad, C. Rodriguez, C. Marberry and P. Craiger, Forensic analysis of the Sony PlayStation Portable, in *Advances in Digital Forensics V*, G. Peterson and S. Shenoi (Eds.), Springer, Heidelberg, Germany, pp. 119–129, 2009.

[9] M. Davies, H. Read, K. Xynos and I. Sutherland, Forensic analysis of a Sony PlayStation 4: A first look, *Digital Investigation*, vol. 12(S1), pp. S81–S89, 2015.

[10] C. Hanlon, Quick-thinking girl, 10, traps paedophile by using her games console to take picture of him molesting her, *Daily Mail*, March 28, 2012.

[11] iFixit, Nintendo 3DS Teardown, San Luis Obispo, California (www.ifixit.com/Teardown/Nintendo+3DS+Teardown/5029), 2016.

[12] IHS Technology, Nintendo 3DS Carries $100.71 Bill of Materials, IHS iSuppli Physical Teardown Reveals, Press Release, Engelwood, Colorado, March 28, 2011.

[13] Magnet Forensics, Magnet Forensics releases Internet Evidence Finder v6.3, Waterloo, Canada (www.magnetforensics.com/magnet-forensics-releases-internet-evidence-finder-v6-3), February 5, 2014.

[14] J. Moore, I. Baggili, A. Marrington and A. Rodrigues, Preliminary forensic analysis of the Xbox One, *Digital Investigation*, vol. 11(S2), pp. S57–S65, 2014.

[15] Mtheall, List of Application Identifiers (mtheall.com/~mtheall/tmdlist.php), 2014.

[16] Nintendo, Notice about Service for Nintendo 3DS Software Swapnote, Redmond, Washington (www.nintendo.com/whatsnew/detail/UHQZFP2Jxcll_Vm-PsZpxNIK5920bRRK), October 31, 2013.

[17] Nintendo, Hardware and Software Sales Units, Kyoto, Japan (www.nintendo.co.jp/ir/en/sales/hard_soft/index.html), 2016.

[18] Nintendo, Internet Browser Specifications for Nintendo 3DS, Redmond, Washington (www.nintendo.com/3ds/internetbrowser/specs), 2016.

[19] Nintendo, Welcome to StreetPass: What is StreetPass? Frankfurt, Germany (www.nintendo.co.uk/Nintendo-3DS/StreetPass/What-is-StreetPass-/What-is-StreetPass--827701.html), 2016.

[20] Nintendo, What is Nintendo eShop? Redmond, Washington (www.nintendo.com/eshop/what-is-eshop), 2016.

[21] Pan European Game Information, Search a Game, Brussels, Belgium (www.pegi.info/en/index/id/509), 2016.

[22] R4town.com, Acekard 3 Card for Nintendo 3DS and DSi (r4town.com/products/Acekard-3-card-for-Nintendo-3DS-and-DSi.html), 2016.

[23] H. Read, I. Sutherland, K. Xynos and F. Roarson, Locking out the investigator: The need to circumvent security in embedded systems, *Information Security Journal: A Global Perspective*, vol. 24(1-3), pp. 39–47, 2015.

[24] smea, The Homebrew Launcher (`smealum.github.io/3ds`), 2016.

[25] I. Sutherland, K. Xynos, H. Read, A. Jones and T. Drange, A forensic overview of the LG Smart TV, *Proceedings of the Twelfth Australian Digital Forensics Conference*, pp. 102–108, 2014.

[26] I. Tepper, A set of tools for working with the Xbox 360 (`code.google.com/p/x360`), 2016.

[27] B. Turnbull, Forensic investigation of the Nintendo Wii: A first glance, *Small Scale Digital Device Forensics Journal*, vol. 2(1), pp. 1–7, 2008.

[28] K. Xynos, S. Harries, I. Sutherland, G. Davies and A. Blyth, Xbox 360: A digital forensic investigation of the hard disk drive, *Digital Investigation*, vol. 6(3-4), pp. 104–111, 2010.

III

NETWORK FORENSICS

Chapter 8

RECONSTRUCTING INTERACTIONS WITH RICH INTERNET APPLICATIONS FROM HTTP TRACES

Sara Baghbanzadeh, Salman Hooshmand, Gregor Bochmann, Guy-Vincent Jourdan, Seyed Mirtaheri, Muhammad Faheem and Iosif Viorel Onut

Abstract   This chapter describes the design and implementation of ForenRIA, a forensic tool for performing automated and complete reconstructions of user sessions with rich Internet applications using only the HTTP logs. ForenRIA recovers all the application states rendered by the browser, reconstructs screenshots of the states and lists every action taken by the user, including recovering user inputs. Rich Internet applications are deployed widely, including on mobile systems. Recovering information from logs for these applications is significantly more challenging compared with classical web applications. This is because HTTP traffic predominantly contains application data with no obvious clues about what the user did to trigger the traffic. ForenRIA is the first forensic tool that specifically targets rich Internet applications. Experiments demonstrate that the tool can successfully handle relatively complex rich Internet applications.

Keywords: Rich Internet applications, user session reconstruction, HTTP logs

1.   Introduction

Over the past few years, an increasing number of application developers have opted for web-based solutions. This shift has been possible due to the enhanced support of client-side technologies, mainly scripting languages such as JavaScript [11], asynchronous JavaScript and XML (Ajax [13]).

JavaScript enables application developers to modify the document object model (DOM) [23] via client-side scripting while Ajax provides asyn-

G. Peterson and S. Shenoi (Eds.): Advances in Digital Forensics XII, IFIP AICT 484, pp. 147–164, 2016.
DOI: 10.1007/978-3-319-46279-0_8

chronous communications between scripts executing on a client browser and web server. The combination of these technologies has created rich Internet applications (RIAs) [12]. These web-based applications are highly dynamic, complex and provide users with an experience similar to "native" (i.e., non-web) applications.

Typically, in a web application, the client (i.e., user web browser) exchanges messages with the server using HTTP [10] over TCP/IP. This traffic is partially or entirely logged by the web server that hosts the application. The traffic is easily captured as it traverses a network (e.g., using a proxy). The captured traffic generated by a user during a session with a web application is called a user session log.

A user session log can be used to reconstruct user browser interactions for forensic analysis after a incident has been detected. For example, suppose the owner of a web application discovers that a hacker had exploited a vulnerability a few months earlier. The system administrator is tasked to find out what happened and how it happened using the only available resource – the server-generated logs of previous user sessions. This task would not be too challenging for a classical web application because tools have been developed for this purpose (e.g., [18]). However, if the web application is a modern rich Internet application, then manual reconstruction would be extremely difficult and time consuming, and no tools are available that could help with the task.

This chapter describes the design and implementation of ForenRIA, a tool intended to help recover information about an intrusion using the available logs. ForenRIA reconstructs screenshots of user sessions, recovers user inputs and all the actions taken by a user during a session. The tool satisfies two important design goals with regard to digital forensics [5]. First, as a result of security concerns, the forensic analysis should be sandboxed; in other words, connections to the Internet are minimized. Second, the reconstructed pages are rendered as closely as possible to the pages viewed at the time of the incident. The first goal is achieved by the offline replay of traffic in a browser. The second goal is met by preserving the correct state of the document object model.

This research was conducted in collaboration with the IBM QRadar Incident Forensic Team. When it comes to recovering user interactions from HTTP logs of rich Internet applications, QRadar forensics relies on a mix of tools and expert knowledge. Thus, the research goal was to develop a general and fully-automated method for inferring user interactions with complex rich Internet applications.

The ForenRIA tool described in this chapter automatically reconstructs user interactions with rich Internet applications using only previously-recorded user session logs as input. Efficient methods are proposed to find user actions; these are based on the notions of "early-action" and "non-existent" clicks that prioritize candidate clicks based on the event history. New techniques are described for inferring user inputs from HTTP traces. Also, a method is presented for handling random parameters in requests during offline traffic replay.

2. Session Reconstruction Methodology

This section describes the user session reconstruction methodology and its implementation in the ForenRIA tool.

2.1 Inputs, Outputs and Assumptions

The goal of this research was to automatically reconstruct entire sessions involving user interactions with rich Internet applications using only HTTP logs as input. During an interaction with a rich Internet application, a user is presented with the rendering of the current document object model by the browser. Some of the user actions (e.g., mouse moves and clicks) trigger the execution of client-side code. In this work, the execution of this code is referred to as an "event."

Events are usually triggered by user actions on HTML elements or automatically by scripts, for example, after a delay or timeout. Some of these event executions trigger requests back to the server. Some of these requests are synchronous while others are asynchronous (i.e., a response might arrive later, and several other requests/responses might occur in the meantime). It is also common for a user to provide inputs via menu selections or as text. These inputs are typically sent along with some requests and the responses that are returned usually depend on the user inputs. Thus, reconstructing user interactions involves the recovery of the series of document object models rendered by the browser as well as all the events executed during the session. Typically, for each event, it is necessary to know the type of event (click, mouse hover, etc.) as well as the XPath of the HTML element on which the event occurred. It is also necessary to recover all user inputs, including the values that were provided and where the values were provided.

It is relatively straightforward to reconstruct user interactions from the log in a "traditional" web application because the data sent by the server is more or less what was displayed by the browser. The situation is very different for rich Internet applications where many requests are generated by script code running on the browser and the responses typically contain only a small amount of data used by the receiving scripts to partially update the document object models (Figure 1 shows an example). Thus, many of the request-response pairs are part of a series

```
{"soapenv:Body":{"response":{"returnValue":{"value":{"ImplClassName":
"com.ibm.team.service.jts.internal.mailer.MailerService","properties":[{
"defValue":"false",...,"eQClassName":"http:\/\/schemas.xmlsoap.org"}}}}}}
```

Figure 1. Body of a typical HTTP response.

of interactions and cannot be analyzed in isolation. Consequently, it is difficult to infer all the steps taken by the user, the inputs provided and the elements that were clicked when the only information provided is in the recorded user session log. The ForenRIA tool described in this chapter addresses these challenges and obtains the details of a security incident by automatically recovering every user interaction.

The input to the tool is a sequence of previously-captured HTTP traffic $\{t_1, t_2, ..., t_n\}$ where t_i is the ith request-response pair. It is necessary to identify the set of actions $\{a_1, a_2, ..., a_m\}$ performed by the user. If the execution of a_i generates a set of requests T_i, then the requests in T_i should directly follow T_{i-1} in the input log.

The following information is of interest with regard to the outputs:

- **User Actions:** The precise sequence of actions performed by a user during a session (clicks, selections, etc.) and the exact elements of the document object models on which the actions were performed.

- **User Inputs:** The exact inputs provided by a user during a session and the fields in which the inputs were provided.

- **Document Object Models:** The series of document object models that appeared in a user's browser during a session, including information such as the values and parameters of cookies.

- **Screenshots:** The series of screens that were displayed to a user.

It is assumed that the input is the log corresponding to a single user. Extracting the trace for an individual user from server logs is a well-studied problem (see e.g., [21]) that is outside the scope of this research. In the context of this research, the traffic has already been recorded and no additional instrumentation of the user's browser is possible. In addition, the reconstruction is performed offline with no access to the original rich Internet application.

2.2   Architecture and Approach

Figure 2 presents the architecture of the ForenRIA tool. The input is a previously-recorded user session access log with two instances of

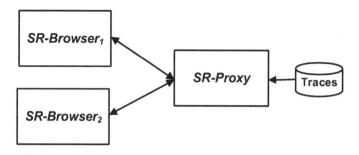

Figure 2. ForenRIA tool architecture.

a programmable browser (SR-Browser$_1$ and SR-Browser$_2$) and a proxy (SR-Proxy) that reconstructs user interactions.

The two browsers re-enact the user actions and the proxy plays the role of the original web server. When the browsers generate the correct actions, the proxy receives a set of requests that match the pre-recorded requests and sends the corresponding responses. Otherwise, an error is returned and another action is selected by the browsers. Note that the two browsers implement the same deterministic algorithm and, thus, always select the same actions.

Algorithm 1. : SR-Browser algorithm.

1: **while** not finished **do**
2:      LoadAndInstrumentLastKnownGoodDOM(*ReconstructedActionsList*);
3:      *ActionCandidate* = ChooseAndExecuteNextAction();
4:      WaitForStableCondition();
5:      **if** SequenceCheck() **then**
6:          *ReconstructedActionsList*.push(*ActionCandidate*);
7:      **end if**
8: **end while**
9: **return** *ReconstructedActionsList*;

Algorithm 1 specifies the steps executed by SR-Browser$_1$ and SR-Browser$_2$. At each step, a browser reloads the last known-correct state (or the initial URL) if necessary, and instruments the document object model by overwriting JavaScript functions such as **addEventListener** and **setTimeout** to control the subsequent execution of JavaScript code (Line 2). Next, it is necessary to find the next user interaction candidate. To decide efficiently, SR-Browser and SR-Proxy collaborate on the selection. After the next user interaction candidate (and possibly the corresponding user inputs) is chosen, the corresponding event is triggered by the browser (Line 3). SR-Browser then waits until a stable state is reached (Line 4) and verifies the correctness of the selected action by

Algorithm 2. : SR-Proxy algorithm.

1: **while** not finished **do**
2:      *req* := GetCommonRequestsFromBrowsers();
3:      **if** *req is an "HTTP" request* **then**
4:          **if** matchFound(req) **then**
5:              ReturnMassagedResponse*req*;
6:          **else**
7:              Return404NotFound();
8:          **end if**
9:      **else**
10:          respondToCtrlMessage(*req*);
11:      **end if**
12: **end while**

asking SR-Proxy about the previously-generated sequence of requests (Line 5). If the selected action is correct, then the action is added to the output (i.e., actual user interaction along with the XPath of the element on which it was exercised, possible user input, copy of the current document object model, reconstructed screenshot of the state of the browser, etc.).

Algorithm 2 specifies the steps executed by SR-Proxy. SR-Proxy waits for requests sent by the browser. If the request received is a normal HTTP request (Line 3), then it attempts to find the request in the user logs. If the request is found (Line 4), then the corresponding response is sent to the browser with some modifications (Line 5); otherwise, an error message is returned to the browser (Line 7). If the request is not a normal HTTP request, then it is a control message (e.g., a collaboration message to find the next user interaction candidate or a sequence check) that must be answered (Line 10).

Loading the Last Known-Good State. Frequently, during the reconstruction process, SR-Browser is not in the correct client state. This could be because the reconstruction has not yet started or because SR-Proxy has signaled that a generated request does not match the recorded request. When SR-Browser is not in the correct client state, then it needs to restore the previous state and try another user action. In traditional web applications, it is sufficient to reload the previous URL. However, the situation is more complex with rich Internet applications because the previous state is usually the result of the execution of a series of scripts and interactions with the browser. The proposed approach is to clear the browser cache, reload the initial URL and re-execute all the previously-detected interactions to bring SR-Browser back to the previous state. A

```
XMLHttpRequest.prototype.sendOriginal = XMLHttpRequest.prototype.send;
XMLHttpRequest.prototype.send = function (x){
        var onreadyStateChangeOriginal = this.onreadystatechange;
        this.onreadystatechange = function(){
                onreadystatechangeOriginal(this);
                parent.ajaxFinishNotification();
        }
        parent.ajaxStartNotification();
        this.sendOriginal(x);
}
```

Figure 3. Hijacking Ajax calls to detect when a callback function completes.

more efficient alternative is to implement the technique described in [19] and directly reload the previous document object model.

Thus, the state that is reached needs to be instrumented by overwriting a range of base JavaScript calls in order to fully control what happens next. The basic idea is to overwrite methods such as addEventListener, setTimeout and XMLHttpRequest.prototype.send so that SR-Browser code is executed when these calls are triggered. Figure 3 shows an example involving the function XMLHttpRequest.prototype.send. The other methods are overwritten in a similar manner.

Finding the Next User Interaction Candidate. At each step, the browser has to find the correct user action and, possibly, the correct user inputs. There are typically hundreds, if not thousands, of possible events for each document object model, so a blind search is not practical. Thus, SR-Browser and SR-Proxy collaborate to create a list of possible choices in decreasing likelihood as follows:

- **Actionable Elements:** Priority is given to document object model elements that are actionable – these are visible elements with some JavaScript attached. Sometimes, this code is assigned explicitly to an attribute of an element (e.g., the onclick attribute of a div tag), but in other cases the listener is added dynamically to the element using methods like addEventListener. Having overwritten these methods as explained previously, ForenRIA can keep track of these elements as well. The algorithm then prioritizes actionable elements by increasing the distances to leaves in the document object model tree.

- **Explicit Clues:** In some cases, it is easy to guess the next action taken by the user simply by examining the next requests in the log. For example, the user may have clicked on a simple hyperlink and SR-Browser can find an anchor element (i.e., <a href=...>) in the current document object model with the corresponding URL

```
window.onload = function(){
    var all_tds = document.getElementsByTagName("td");
    for (var e = 0; e < all_tds.length; e++){
        all_tds[e].onClick = function(){
            id = this.getElementsByTagName('strong')[0].firstChild.nodeValue;
            getAjax("GET", "content/content" + id + ".html", true);
            }
        }
}
```

Figure 4. Example of an onclick handler created dynamically.

in its **href** tag; or, when an obvious clue is found, such as the parameters of the next URL in the **href** or the **onclick** handler of an element in the document object model. These cases, which were the norm in older web sites, are rarely encountered in rich Internet applications.

- **Implicit Clues:** In a rich Internet application, there are usually no obvious clues about the element that triggered an HTTP request. Figure 4 presents an example involving PeriodicTable, a simple rich Internet application. In this case, a single event handler **onclick** is attached to the common parent of several elements in a document object model. Its execution triggers an Ajax call that dynamically detects the element that was originally clicked. The following steps are taken to tackle such situations:

  - *Known JavaScript Libraries:* Many rich Internet applications are built using popular JavaScript libraries such as JQuery, Dojo and Angular. It is often relatively easy to detect the fingerprints of these libraries. Each library has a standard way of generating requests when a user interacts with an element. By implementing code specific to each library, elements can be mapped to clues in the requests dynamically, essentially turning implicit clues into explicit clues.

  - *Early Action:* An incorrect action may be selected during the course of a reconstruction. In some cases, the action on an element *e* generates a series of unexpected requests (i.e., they are not the next ones in the traces), but these requests still appear as a block later in the trace. This can mean that algorithm has taken the action on *e* too early. This situation is remembered and the same action on *e* is taken when the corresponding block is next in the queue.

    Figure 5 demonstrates the situation. In Figure 5(a), the tool has selected an element early and the requests are found in

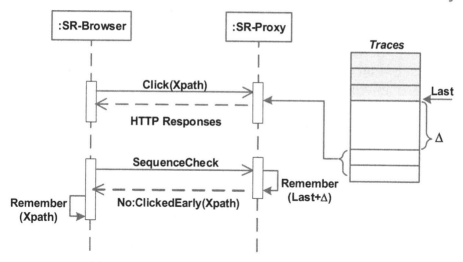

(a) Requests found in the log further down the queue.

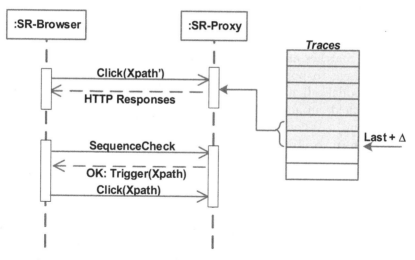

(b) Requests become the next unconsumed requests in the queue.

Figure 5. Early action handling.

the recorded log, but further down the queue. As shown in Figure 5(b), the requests subsequently become the next unconsumed requests in the queue. SR-Proxy then instructs SR-Browser to select the same element. Note that "Last" refers to the last consumed resource in the trace.

– *Non-Existent Action:* The dual notion of early action is a non-existent action. This is triggered when a request generated by selecting an element e does not exist in the trace. This is an indication that e was not used in the session and the priority of e can be reduced.

■ **Finding User Inputs:** User input is an integral part of a web application and recovering the input is necessary for a forensic analysis as well as to perform a successful reconstruction. In web applications, user inputs are usually captured in fields that can be grouped into a form. However, in a rich Internet application, interacting with a single field may trigger network traffic; for example, typing in a search box can load partial results. This is a common behavior that does not follow the HTTP standard for form submission, which involves several input fields being submitted at one time to the server. The standard specifies that the user input values should be encoded as <name, value> pairs. To address this situation, SR-Proxy scans the log for occurrences of <name, value> pairs (encoded in one of the standard formats). When matches are found, the pairs are sent to SR-Browser, which uses them to populate input fields in the current document object model. If a single value is sent, corresponding to a single input field, an action is attempted on the field (e.g., onchange or onkeyup). When a set of values is sent back, SR-Browser looks for a form containing input fields with all the given names and attempts to submit the form.

Client-Side Randomness. One difficulty to overcome is randomness. Server-side randomness is not an issue because the same traffic is replayed. However, if the client includes some randomly-generated values in its requests (e.g., random selection of a news feed), then the requests do not match those saved in the log file.

To address this problem, two concurrent instances of SR-Browser, both running the same deterministic algorithm, are used. The two browsers select the same action and the same user input in the same sequence, and send the same requests to SR-Proxy. SR-Proxy compares the requests received from the two browsers. Usually, the requests are identical. However, when client-side randomness is involved, some requests do not match. The parts that do not match are deemed to be randomly generated by the client and are not expected to match the recorded traffic. In such cases, the proxy looks for partial matches in the log file.

Temporal Headers in Responses. HTTP responses have temporal headers such as `date`, `expires` and `last-modified` that may impact replay; this is because the time of replay does not correspond to the time of capture. For example, if a resource has an `expires` header set to time t_1 and it is replayed at time $t_2 > t_1$, then SR-Browser automatically requests the resource again, impacting the replay. Therefore, SR-Proxy updates all the headers using the current time and the relative time offset at the time of recording.

Browser Stable Condition. After executing an event, SR-Browser waits until it reaches a stable condition, a state in which no further changes occur unless a new event is executed. SR-Browser decides if the state is stable or not by overwriting JavaScript functions. In particular, it keeps track of pending requests by overwriting the methods used to send and receive requests (e.g., `send` and `onreadystateschange` methods of the *XMLHttpRequest* object; Figure 3 shows an example). Additionally, some scripts can be executed after a given delay via a JavaScript timeout. In order to keep track of these events, SR-Browser also redefines the built-in `settimeout` method.

Sequence Check. After an element is clicked, if no error is returned by SR-Proxy, then SR-Browser interacts with SR-Proxy to confirm that the clicked element was chosen correctly. One difficulty with this approach is that a single click can generate multiple calls to the server, so several requests and responses can occur after a single click. Another difficulty is that the asynchronous nature of server calls (i.e., Ajax) means that requests may be received in different orders in different runs. Thus, it is not simply a matter of going down a list in the correct order on the SR-Proxy side. Instead, the entire set of requests and responses should eventually form a gapless block in the recorded trace after SR-Browser reaches the stable condition, and this gapless block should be right after the previous block. SR-Proxy checks for this situation upon receiving the sequence check message from SR-Browser after it reaches a stable condition.

Basic Solution. Any system that attempts to reconstruct user interactions with rich Internet applications must be able to handle user input recovery, client-side randomness, sequence checks and previous state restoration; otherwise, reconstruction may not be possible. A basic solution is to perform an exhaustive search on the elements of a document object model to find the next action; this solution does not use the techniques proposed in ForenRIA. A search of the literature reveals that no other published solution has the characteristics of the basic solution. Thus, no other solution can help reconstruct rich Internet application sessions, even in an inefficient manner.

3.   Experimental Results

This section presents the experimental results obtained using the ForenRIA tool. The SR-Browser implementation uses the PhantomJS headless programmable browser. PhantomJS supports the recreation of the document object models, the creation of screenshots and the retrieval of the XPaths of elements on which inputs and actions are performed. SR-Proxy is implemented as a PHP application.

The experimental evaluation limited the test cases to rich Internet applications because other tools already perform user interaction reconstruction on non-Ajax web applications (e.g. [18]). The test applications included: OpenCart, an open-source e-commerce solution; OSCommerce, an e-commerce platform; IBM's Rational Team Concert (RTC), an agile application lifecycle management rich Internet application based on DOJO; El-Finder, an open-source file manager for the web; (v) Engage, a web-based goal setting and performance management application built using the Google web toolkit; Test RIA, Altoro Mutual and PeriodicTable, three simple rich Internet applications built for testing purposes; and a Joomla test site, a popular content management system that uses jQuery. The complete HTTP traffic corresponding to user interactions was captured for each test application using `fiddler` and `mitmproxy` (for sites using SSL/TLS).

The experiments measured the effectiveness of reconstructing user interactions. Two factors were considered: (i) time taken; and (ii) cost (i.e., number of actions required by SR-Browser to reconstruct all the user interactions). The experiments were run on Linux computers with an Intel Core i7 2.7 GHz CPU and 4 GB RAM. The ForenRIA results were compared with those obtained using the basic solution.

Table 1 compares the reconstruction times and costs for ForenRIA and the basic method. Note that Actions is the number of user actions and Requests is the number of HTTP requests in a recorded session. ForenRIA successfully reconstructed the interactions in all the test cases, including recovering all the document object models, the XPaths of the elements on which actions were taken, the user inputs, and the details of all the cookies and screen captures of the rich Internet applications as originally presented to the user. The lengths of the captured sessions ranged from 25 to 150 user actions, with many forms being filled in several complex scenarios. For example, the OpenCart session required 150

Table 1. Reconstruction times and costs for ForenRIA and the basic method.

RIA	Actions	Requests	Time (hh:mm:ss)		Cost	
			ForenRIA	Basic	ForenRIA	Basic
OpenCart	150	325	0:10:26	76:10:45	3,221	1,808,250
OSCommerce	150	532	0:02:44	21:23:15	150	501,806
RTC	30	218	0:46:54	50:53:44	1,423	94,242
El-Finder	150	175	0:14:55	07:24:40	12,533	376,820
Engage	25	164	0:31:13	01:47:02	7,834	17,052
Test Ria	31	74	0:00:37	00:22:51	302	15,812
PeriodicTable	89	94	0:07:38	36:20:45	4,453	1,559,796
AltoroMutual	150	204	0:01:41	25:24:30	358	815,302
Joomla	150	253	0:48:20	N/A	344	N/A

actions, including 101 user inputs to register a user, add products to the shopping cart and check out. On average, ForenRIA required 59 events and 23 seconds to find the next action. In contrast, the basic method required on average 5,034 events and 1,503 seconds to find the next action. The basic method on Joomla was stopped after reconstructing only 22 actions because it was too slow. The time required for these 22 actions was 15:24:30 with a cost of 2,274; however, since the basic method was terminated, the corresponding entries in Table 1 are marked as N/A.

In addition, El-Finder and Engage had random parameters in their requests. Without detecting these parameters, it was not possible to even load the first pages of these sites. However, ForenRIA correctly found all the random parameters for these websites, enabling the complete reconstruction of the sessions.

The experimental results demonstrate the effectiveness of the proposed approach for reconstructing user interactions with rich Internet applications. No current tool can reconstruct user interactions only using HTTP traces.

To demonstrate the capabilities of ForenRIA, an attack scenario involving a vulnerable banking application was created by IBM for test purposes. In the scenario, an attacker visits the vulnerable web site and uses an SQL injection attack to gain access to private information and then transfers a considerable amount of money to another account. The attacker also discovers a cross-site scripting vulnerability that could be exploited later against other users.

Given the full HTTP traces, ForenRIA was able to fully reconstruct the attack in just six seconds. The output included screenshots of all the pages seen by the hacker, document object models of all the pages and the steps and inputs used for the unauthorized login, SQL injection attack and cross-site scripting vulnerability. A forensic analysis of the attack would have been quite straightforward using ForenRIA, including the discovery of the cross-site scripting vulnerability. In contrast, the same analysis without ForenRIA would have taken much longer and the cross-site scripting vulnerability would probably have been missed. A demonstration of this case study as well as sample inputs/outputs of the ForenRIA tool are available at `ssrg.site.uottawa.ca/sr/demo.html`.

4.   Related Work

A survey paper by Cornelis et al. [6] reveals that deterministic replay has been investigated for many years in a variety of contexts. Some of the systems were designed to debug operating systems or analyze cache coherence in distributed shared memory systems [17, 25]. However, these systems do not handle client-side non-determinism in the parameters sent to the server, which is critical to dealing with rich Internet applications.

The Selenium IDE (implemented as a Firefox plugin) [20] records user actions and replays traffic. Recording can only be done using Firefox, but replays can be performed across browsers using synthetic JavaScript events. A number of methods have been proposed to capture and replay user actions in JavaScript applications (e.g., Mugshot [16] and WaRR [1]). The client-side of Mugshot records events in in-memory logs; Mugshot also creates a log entry containing the sequence number and clock time for each recorded event. The WaRR [1] recorder is also embedded in a web browser and captures a complete interaction trace; it logs a sequence of commands, where each command is a user action. Atterer et al. [3] have used a proxy to inject a script that hijacks all JavaScript events triggered by a user. However, all these approaches require an alteration of the live rich Internet application to record all the user action information needed to recreate the events at replay time. As mentioned above, the goal of the research discussed in this chapter was to reconstruct a user session from raw traces without instrumenting the client or the modifying rich Internet application. Thus, none of the above solutions satisfy the required goal.

Some traffic replay systems [2, 14] have focused on replaying traffic at the IP or TCP/UDP levels. Hong and Wu [14] have implemented a system that interactively replays traffic by emulating a TCP protocol stack. However, these levels are too low for efficient reconstructions of user interactions with rich Internet applications.

WebPatrol [4] has introduced the concept of automated collection and replay of web-based malware scenarios. The prototype has two components, a scenario collection component and a scenario replay component. The scenario collection component automatically gathers malware infection trails using its own "honey clients" and builds a web-based malware scenario repository. The scenario replay component reconstructs the original infection trail at any time from the stored data. WebPatrol is not designed to reconstruct generic rich Internet application interactions from traces; therefore, it cannot be used for this purpose.

Historically, session reconstruction has meant finding the pages visited by users and distinguishing between different users in server logs, often as a pre-processing step for web usage mining (see e.g., [7, 8, 22]). However, the proposed work assumes that individual user sessions have already been extracted from logs, perhaps using one of these techniques.

ReSurf [24] is a referrer-based click inference tool; however, it is of limited use for rich Internet applications. Spiliopoulou et al. [21] have discussed the importance of noisy and incomplete server logs and have evaluated several heuristics for reconstructing user sessions. Their experiments demonstrate that there is no single best heuristic and that heuristic selection depends on the application at hand. Such a method, which is based on server logs, is termed as "reactive" by Dohare et al. [9].

The tool that is most closely related to ForenRIA is ClickMiner [18]. ClickMiner also reconstructs user sessions from traces recorded by a passive proxy. Although ClickMiner has some level of JavaScript support, it is unable to handle rich Internet applications.

5. Conclusions

The ForenRIA tool described in this chapter can automatically reconstruct user interactions with rich Internet applications solely from HTTP traces. In particular, ForenRIA recovers all the application states rendered by the browser, reconstructs screenshots of the states and lists every action taken by the user, including recovering user inputs. ForenRIA is the first forensic tool that specifically targets rich Internet applications. Experiments demonstrate that the tool can successfully handle relatively complex rich Internet applications.

From a digital forensic point of view, ForenRIA has several advantages. The reconstruction process is performed offline to minimize security concerns, it is fully automated and it is even able to render the pages seen by users. ForenRIA also saves precious time during an investigation. Nevertheless, it is intended to complement – not replace – other tools: ForenRIA focuses on the application user interface and works at the HTTP level whereas other tools operate at the lower network level. ForenRIA is, thus, unsuitable when an attack bypasses the user interface; however, in such a case, it is quite straightforward to understand the attack directly from the log, without having to use an advanced tool. It is important to note that ForenRIA is not limited to forensic analyses. It can be used in other situations, such as to automatically retrace the steps that led to any (non-necessarily security-related) incident and to automatically reproduce the steps involved in a bug report.

Future research will test ForenRIA on a larger set of rich Internet applications. Also, it will attempt to enhance the algorithm to discover implicit clues. Additionally, a more efficient technique will be developed to restore the previous state when the selected element is not the right one; this technique will leverage the approach described in [15].

The effective handling of browser caching is an open problem. In particular, SR-Browser has to automatically adapt to the caching strategies adopted by user browsers. The behavioral differences between browsers is a problem that requires more research. Finally, some user actions may not generate any traffic, but the actions are, nevertheless, necessary to continue the session. Dealing with this issue when reconstructing user sessions is also an open question.

Acknowledgement

This research was supported by the IBM Center for Advanced Studies, the IBM Ottawa Software Lab and the Natural Sciences and Engineering Research Council of Canada (NSERC).

References

[1] S. Andrica and G. Candea, WaRR: A tool for high-fidelity web application record and replay, *Proceedings of the Forty-First IEEE/IFIP International Conference on Dependable Systems and Networks*, pp. 403–410, 2011.

[2] AppNeta, Tcpreplay, Boston, Massachusetts (`tcpreplay.appneta.com`), 2016

[3] R. Atterer and A. Schmidt, Tracking the interaction of users with AJAX applications for usability testing, *Proceedings of the SIGCHI Conference on Human Factors in Computing Systems*, pp. 1347–1350, 2007.

[4] K. Chen, G. Gu, J. Zhuge, J. Nazario and X. Han, WebPatrol: Automated collection and replay of web-based malware scenarios, *Proceedings of the Sixth ACM Symposium on Information, Computer and Communications Security*, pp. 186–195, 2011.

[5] M. Cohen, PyFlag – An advanced network forensic framework, *Digital Investigation*, vol. 5(S), pp. S112–S120, 2008.

[6] F. Cornelis, A. Georges, M. Christiaens, M. Ronsse, T. Ghesquiere and K. Bosschere, A taxonomy of execution replay systems, *Proceedings of the International Conference on Advances in Infrastructure for Electronic Business, Education, Science, Medicine and Mobile Technologies on the Internet*, 2003.

[7] R. Dell, P. Roman and J. Velasquez, Web user session reconstruction using integer programming, *Proceedings of the IEEE/WIC/ACM International Conference on Web Intelligence and Intelligent Agent Technology*, pp. 385–388, 2008.

[8] R. Dell, P. Roman and J. Velasquez, Web user session reconstruction with back button browsing, in *Knowledge-Based and Intelligent Information and Engineering Systems*, J. Velasquez, S. Rios, R. Howlett and L. Jain (Eds.), Springer, Berlin Heidelberg, Germany, pp. 326–332, 2009.

[9] M. Dohare, P. Arya and A. Bajpai, Novel web usage mining for web mining techniques, *International Journal of Emerging Technology and Advanced Engineering*, vol. 2(1), pp. 253–262, 2012.

[10] R. Fielding, J. Gettys, J. Mogul, H. Frystyk, L. Masinter, P. Leach and T. Berners-Lee, Hypertext Transfer Protocol – HTTP/1.1, RFC 2616, 1999.

[11] D. Flanagan, *JavaScript: The Definitive Guide*, O'Reilly Media, Sebastopol, California, 2011.

[12] P. Fraternali, G. Rossi and F. Sanchez-Figueroa, Rich Internet applications, *IEEE Internet Computing*, vol. 14(3), pp. 9–12, 2010.

[13] J. Garrett, Ajax: A new approach to web applications, Adaptive Path, San Francisco, California (www.adaptivepath.com/ideas/ajax-new-approach-web-applications), February 18, 2005.

[14] S. Hong and S. Wu, On interactive Internet traffic replay, *Proceedings of the Eighth International Conference on Recent Advances in Intrusion Detection*, pp. 247–264, 2006.

[15] J. Lo, E. Wohlstadter and A. Mesbah, Imagen: Runtime migration of browser sessions for JavaScript web applications, *Proceedings of the Twenty-Second International Conference on World Wide Web*, pp. 815–826, 2013.

[16] J. Mickens, J. Elson and J. Howell, Mugshot: Deterministic capture and replay for JavaScript applications, *Proceedings of the USENIX Conference on Networked Systems Design and Implementation*, 2010.

[17] S. Narayanasamy, G. Pokam and B. Calder, BugNet: Recording application-level execution for deterministic replay debugging, *IEEE Micro*, vol. 26(1), pp. 100–109, 2006.

[18] C. Neasbitt, R. Perdisci, K. Li and T. Nelms, ClickMiner: Towards forensic reconstruction of user-browser interactions from network traces, *Proceedings of the ACM SIGSAC Conference on Computer and Communications Security*, pp. 1244–1255, 2014.

[19] J. Oh, J. Kwon, H. Park, and S. Moon, Migration of web applications with seamless execution, *Proceedings of the Eleventh ACM SIGPLAN/SIGOPS International Conference on Virtual Execution Environments*, pp. 173–185, 2015.

[20] Selenium, Selenium Web Application Testing System (`seleniumhq. org`), 2015.

[21] M. Spiliopoulou, B. Mobasher, B. Berendt and M. Nakagawa, A framework for the evaluation of session reconstruction heuristics in web-usage analysis, *INFORMS Journal on Computing*, vol. 15(2), pp. 171–190, 2003.

[22] J. Srivastava, R. Cooley, M. Deshpande and P. Tan, Web usage mining: Discovery and applications of usage patterns from web data, *ACM SIGKDD Explorations Newsletter*, vol. 1(2), pp. 12–23, 2000.

[23] World Wide Web Consortium, Document Object Model (DOM) Level 3 Core Specification, Version 1.0, W3C Recommendation, Cambridge, Massachusetts (`www.w3.org/TR/DOM-Level-3-Core`), 2004.

[24] G. Xie, M. Iliofotou, T. Karagiannis, M. Faloutsos, and Y. Jin, ReSurf: Reconstructing web-surfing activity from network traffic, *Proceedings of the IFIP Networking Conference*, 2013.

[25] M. Xu, R. Bodik and M. Hill, A "flight data recorder" for enabling full-system multiprocessor deterministic replay, *Proceedings of the Thirtieth Annual International Symposium on Computer Architecture*, pp. 122–135, 2003.

Chapter 9

RECONSTRUCTING TABBED BROWSER SESSIONS USING METADATA ASSOCIATIONS

Sriram Raghavan and S.V. Raghavan

Abstract   Internet browsers support multiple browser tabs, each browser tab capable of initiating and maintaining a separate web session, accessing multiple uniform resource identifiers (URIs) simultaneously. As a consequence, network traffic generated as part of a web request becomes indistinguishable across tabbed sessions. However, it is possible to find the specificity of attribution in the session-related context information recorded as metadata in log files (in servers and clients) and as network traffic related logs in routers and firewalls, along with their metadata. The forensic questions of "who," "what" and "how" are easily answered using the metadata-based approach presented in this chapter. The same questions can help systems administrators decide on monitoring and prevention strategies. Metadata, by definition, records context information related to a session; such metadata recordings transcend sources.

This chapter presents an algorithm for reconstructing multiple simultaneous browser sessions on browser applications with multi-threaded implementations. Two relationships, coherency and concurrency, are identified based on metadata associations across artifacts from browser history logs and network packets recorded during active browser sessions. These relationships are used to develop the algorithm that identifies the number of simultaneous browser sessions that are deployed and then reconstructs the sessions. Specially-designed experiments that leverage timing information alongside the browser and session contexts are used to demonstrate the processes for eliciting intelligence and separating and reconstructing tabbed browser sessions.

Keywords: Tabbed browser sessions, metadata association, session reconstruction

© IFIP International Federation for Information Processing 2016
Published by Springer International Publishing AG 2016. All Rights Reserved
G. Peterson and S. Shenoi (Eds.): Advances in Digital Forensics XII, IFIP AICT 484, pp. 165–188, 2016.
DOI: 10.1007/978-3-319-46279-0_9

1.   Introduction

The main function of a browser application is to present a web service by requesting it of a server and displaying it in a browser window. In practice, whenever a browser engages in a web session, it records information in its log files, usually meant for troubleshooting purposes. The browser and the associated logs work as follows: when a browser application is deployed, a process is created that interacts with the network socket (through one or more open ports) to access services from the network. The browser application logs the server responses and caches one or more of the resources received. In a generic browser, a parent browser process controls the overall operation and launches one or more rendering engines and loads plug-in modules as required [5]. The parent process is responsible for disk interactions, the user interface and the network. Every time a new browser window or tab is spawned, a new browser process is initiated to monitor the modules executing within its framework. Over a period of time, browser applications have evolved to create and maintain multiple simultaneous sessions [1, 6].

A single browser session may be defined as a sequence of browser requests and corresponding server responses that are received by the browser application; to start with, these are pivoted on a single browser tab. As the interactions progress, a user may optionally open more tabs and possibly more windows, but the manner of recording session information remains the same. However, the volume of information recorded to answer the forensic questions "who," "what" and "how" can grow significantly over time. The proposed approach for reconstructing browser sessions by associating session log information with a network trace converts the problem to a progressive and incremental one, thereby enabling the forensic or security context usage to be natural, easy and real time.

There are several important aspects related to reconstructing browser sessions and the relative browser tab sessions. Specifically, browser sessions are reconstructed to understand the number of simultaneous sessions operated by the browser. Additionally, when a user selects a new tab or clicks on a link from an existing tab to open a new browser session on another tab, the browser application has a unique way of opening the session. This relative positioning of browsers can help identify if a causal relationship existed; however, this task requires further analysis of the individual sessions and parsing the HTML pages to identify the hyperlinks involved in creating the session. It is possible to establish if two or more browser tabs placed close together connect to the same domain server and then, if necessary, identify the sequence in which the web pages were opened by studying the hyperlinks in each of the pages.

Such an investigation involves significant parsing effort and can become challenging when obfuscated code or malware is involved. However, this is outside the scope of this work; in fact, Neasbitt et al. [7] study the problem of differentiating user-clicked pages from auto-load components that are parts of an active browser rendering.

This research establishes the feasibility of isolating multiple simultaneous browser sessions on multi-threaded browser applications based on browser application logs and network traffic logs at the host end. In order to do so, a metadata-based approach is used to determine the contextual relationships between artifacts within and across the browser logs and network packets. The proposed algorithm based on the identified metadata relationships is applied to specially-designed experiments for a usage scenario involving a Firefox application with five tabbed sessions across two browser windows.

2. Related Work

Xie et al. [11] and Neasbitt et al. [7] have recognized the importance of recovering browser activities to aid forensic analyses of web traffic traces in investigations of user-browser interactions involved in security incidents, albeit from a purely user standpoint. In doing so, it is recognized that most browser applications implement a recovery feature that enables the browser to restore a session when an application crashes or does not undergo a proper termination procedure [6]. The recovery features ensure continuity when the context breaks down or drastically changes for operational reasons. While these appear to be similar, they vary in their details; both have a definite need, but different goals. The purpose of this research is not to reconstruct sessions when browser session crashes are involved; rather, the intention is to reconstruct browser sessions regardless of the nature in which the browser applications were terminated. This is particularly necessary when the actions of a suspected perpetrator must be tracked sequentially to determine the why more than the how during an investigation. The ability to reconstruct user sessions independent of the underlying browser process and application execution contexts is emerging as a requirement when applications are subject to compromise. Such as approach is discussed in this chapter.

In order to reconstruct a communications session from network traffic, network packets can be analyzed to determine the parties engaged in the communications, time of communications and type of information exchanged; such analysis enables the recorded information to be organized sequentially into logical sessions. However, when browsers use multiple tabbed sessions, building such logical sequences for each session, that too individually, is non-trivial [2]. In fact, browser logs do not contain sufficient information to identify the number of parallel sessions deployed [8]. It is, therefore, necessary to associate artifacts recorded across all independent sources and correlate the events to reconstruct the browser sessions.

The goal of this research is multi-fold and there are several important contributions. First, when reconstructing browser sessions, each request is mapped to its corresponding response. Further, when a web page has animations or active content, it often tends to initiate separate requests that are not part of the original page; these requests are initiated when the page is being rendered in the browser window. Such requests are identified and their responses, where applicable, are mapped. Second, not all responses are initiated based on their corresponding requests. In such cases, requests that are likely to initiate multiple responses are mapped and the responses are suitably chained to their corresponding origins to determine the communications streams to which they belong. Third, the procedure is automated as an algorithm designed to operate in high-bandwidth environments while enabling analyses of the computations and memory use during browser session reconstruction.

3.   Multi-Threaded Browser Application Design

A browser subsystem [4] consists of several components, including a parent browser process, logging agent, one or more network sockets to maintain the browser sessions, plug-ins to decode interactive content and maintain encrypted sessions, and one or more rendering engines associated with the user interface. Popular browser applications include Internet Explorer (Microsoft), Chrome (Google), Safari (Apple), Firefox (Mozilla) and Opera (Opera). This research focuses on browser applications that have multi-threaded implementations.

In multi-threaded browser applications, there is exactly one parent browser process that manages the individual sessions using threads, regardless of whether they were initiated using browser (application) windows or browser tabs. Therefore, when tracing the path of these browser sessions to the respective browser windows or tabs, it is sufficient to establish a one-to-one relationship between the window or tab and the session that was supported. This is possible because there is exactly one process through which information passes from the network to the application.

The Mozilla Firefox browser, a multi-threaded browser application, contains a single parent process and spawns a thread for each sub-operation. The Firefox browser launches a new process for the first instance of a browser window and maintains individual web sessions as threads. Since browser windows and browser tabs are interchangeable, creating a second browser window (either independently or by separating a tabbed browser session) does not give rise to a new process, but it continues as a thread executing off the original parent process. In other words, regardless of the number of Firefox browser windows or tabs, there exists only one process with one or more threads maintaining the different web sessions. Since a single process manages multiple browser sessions, an active Firefox browser process consumes much more memory than other browsers that do not adopt this approach. Furthermore, from an implementation standpoint, the Firefox browser parent process executes purely as a 32-bit process regardless of the underlying hardware platform; and consequently, the addressable space for the entire browser application is limited to 4 GB, which is must be managed across multiple sessions.

Despite the existence of multiple browser threads that process simultaneous sessions, web requests and responses are interleaved when they are logged by the application; the logged events appear as a single session because the application does not log information related to the number of simultaneously active sessions. However, a systematic analysis based on the proposed methodology can break down this apparent singular session into the respective tabbed sessions as described below.

4. Mapping Browser Actions

A browser process localizes itself with respect to its network when it is activated (i.e., an active session is initiated by a user). This activity requires a series of message exchanges between the local host and the network. Typically, this involves a link-local host localization that is achieved at layer-2 of the network stack. Following the localization, the host engages in name resolution with one or more DNS servers listed in its network registry. This action is followed by a TCP engagement with the server itself.

The browser application can engage with one or more TCP sessions with the server. When a new server needs to be identified, it is preceded with the name resolution phase. The sessions can be TCP or secure TCP (i.e., HTTPS on server port 443). The number of sessions is dependent on the original server response and can vary depending on the context. When multiple TCP sessions are in play, a browser can maintain multiple sessions using multiple network ports on the browser host machine; each session is maintained until the browser host sends a FIN request to terminate the session. During a browser session, a user may make additional web requests until the user terminates the browser window or tab.

4.1 Browser Sessions and Logging

At any time, an active browser session requires the browser host machine to identify its position in the network (using ARP request-responses) before requesting information about the server from where a service is to be requested (using DNS request-responses). The network packets transmitted and received during this period (ARP-DNS-TCP/UDP-HTTP) can be sensed and their network packet attributes can be used as parameters associated with the corresponding browser session.

Consider the sequence of network transactions that occur when a user attempts to download a resource from the Internet. Initially, the user makes a web request through a web browser, which initiates an ARP request to identify itself within its local network (or subnet), following which it makes a DNS request to the local web proxy to identify the IP address of the server where the resource resides. After the DNS response is received, the browser host machine initiates a TCP connection with the particular server and makes a request for the resource. This request may or may not include an HTTP session, where the web server responds to the browser host machine with one or more web pages through which the resource request can be made. After the request is made, the resource is transmitted from the server to the browser host machine as a file transfer action, which is, in essence, a sequence of TCP packets.

This behavior of the browser session along with network address resolutions and network-based communications leave adequate information about all the activities and the associated events. This information can be analyzed as required during reconstruction. The most significant aspect of browser session reconstruction is that neither the browser log file nor the network packets captured have any information about the specific browser window or browser tab responsible for generating a web session. For each browser event that is a web response from some server, the browser logs the URL corresponding to the request, the title of the page as defined on the server, the domain in which the server resides (e.g., google.com), the timestamp corresponding to the response in the UNIX time format and structure information specifying how the response is to be rendered by the browser. As a result, a complete and rich web session in a browser window is represented in the form of a textual log entry. Normally, logs do not record the numbers of active browser windows or tabs and, therefore, reverse tracking remains a challenge.

Xie et al. [11] have proposed a method for reconstructing web browser activity by pruning a referrer-based graph; specifically, the method reconstructs web surfing activities from traffic traces by analyzing the referrer headers. Neasbitt et al. [7] have implemented the ClickMiner system for reconstructing user-browser interactions from network traces. ClickMiner uses referrer-click inference to prune a user browser activity graph based on referrer re-redirections to ascertain the points where a user actively participated in generating new web requests. Through a user study, Neasbitt et al. demonstrated that ClickMiner can correctly reconstruct up to ninety percent of user-browser interactions.

Raghavan and Raghavan [10] have presented an approach for identifying the source of a downloaded resource based on relationships established using browser logs, network packets and file metadata. They demonstrated the use of metadata-based associations to determine relationships between different sources of digital evidence (e.g., user filesystem, browser logs and temporary Internet files) to determine the origins of digital image files downloaded from the Internet. The metadata in a file is used to track alternate copies of the file and log events that created or affected the file during a user session. Using metadata associations, they determined file-to-file, file-to-log-event and log-event-to-log-event relationships, which were then traced to the source URL of the downloaded file. This research extends the work presented in [10] to identify the causal relationships between event sources. In particular, network parameters and browser history logs are used to distinguish as well as identify concurrent events across sessions and coherent events belonging to a single session while handling multiple simultaneous browser sessions of a browser application.

4.2   Tracking a Browser Session

When a browser interprets a web response and displays the corresponding HTML page, many aspects of the response can be logged by the browser. Normally, some of the entries that can be recorded in the browser history log are the page rendered (i.e., URL), domain corresponding to the URL, date and time when the web response was received, name of the referral server, number of visits in a given duration and the user under whose account the access was logged. Browser windows and tabs are interchangeable in most browser applications and the window or tab that generates a specific web response is not recorded or logged. As a consequence, the entries in the browser history log file appear in a sequential manner. Moreover, the web request responsible for the response is transparent to the utility that logs browser history in-

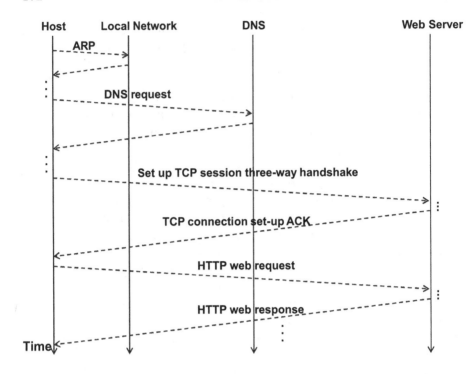

Figure 1.   Space-time diagram corresponding to a web request.

formation. The missing relationship information must be obtained from the network packet log.

When a packet capture utility captures network packets entering and leaving a host machine, it uses filters to recognize and log network packets according to the protocol used in the communications. A simple web request leaving a host machine requires the machine to send ARP packets to identify the gateway in a given network and then request address resolution of the server with which the browser is attempting to communicate. After the address resolution yields an IP address, the browser attempts to set up a TCP channel with the server, following which the request is sent. Figure 1 displays this sequence as a space-time (S-T) diagram.

Note that a large number of packets enter and leave the host machine, but only the browser process makes the web request while the network stack on the host handles the rest internally. As a result, the HTTP request contains insufficient information to enable a trace back to a specific browser window or browser tab. Therefore, it is essential that any proposed method relies on a sequence of transactions that exhibit the characteristics shown in Figure 1 instead of a single HTTP request.

Each browser response in the browser history log is associated with a sequence of network packet transactions that correspond to the web request made by the browser on the host.

While the browser application tracks web responses that are recorded sequentially, network packets are needed to decipher web requests. Additionally, the packet capture must be timed so that it coincides with the browser sessions in question. This requires the capture utility to be positioned to have complete visibility of the sequence of network packets exchanged in the same sequence as shown in the space-time diagram in Figure 1. Such a task can be achieved in any organizational LAN by triggering a packet dump for the machine host where a browser application is launched and filtering for network packets initiated by the host in question.

5.   Eliciting Session-Based Relationships

The browsing application history is stored on the host machine when browsing the web. It includes information entered into forms, passwords and sites that were visited. The browser history log records the requests sequentially; in the presence of multiple tabs, subsequent requests across tabs are interleaved as the browser continues to generate additional web requests. In such a scenario, network packets are collocated in time, but belong to different browser sessions. It is interesting to note that the browser tabs (browser session) may generate web traffic and network packets to different servers, thereby establishing distinct streams of web responses and network packet flows. Associating a browser log event with its corresponding sequence of network packets requires the careful identification of the relevant characteristics of the browser log entry that can aid this activity. Figure 2 shows the generic layout of a browser history log entry [8] along with the metadata of interest.

Network packets have many useful attributes (or metadata) that may be used to associate the packets with a particular network session. The information includes the source and destination IP addresses, protocol, timestamp corresponding to when a packet was seen leaving or entering the browser host machine, host browser (TCP) process port and server port numbers, and session sequence number. Figure 3 shows the generic layout of a network packet [3] with the relevant metadata highlighted.

The proposed approach identifies specific network packet sessions in accordance with the space-time sequence shown in Figure 1 and constructs a high-level transaction that results from the web request generated by the browser process. As discussed in the previous section, these have one-to-one correspondence with the browser history log entries.

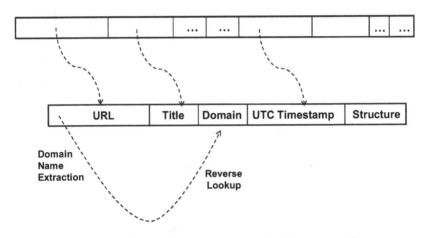

Figure 2. Browser history log entry with relevant metadata.

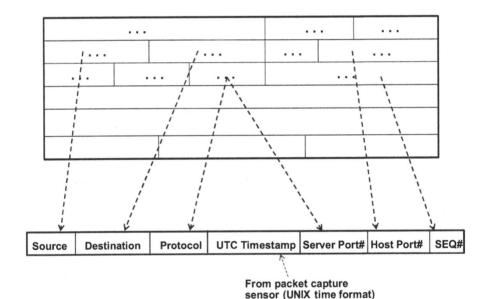

Figure 3. Generic layout of a network packet with relevant metadata.

The distinction across simultaneous browser sessions (using multiple windows or tabbed sessions) is not apparent when a browser log or network packet trace are seen in isolation. In contrast, the browser logs and network packets together provide a session context that the proposed approach leverages to elicit the relationship between the two information sources. This relationship is extracted using knowledge of the sequence of actions that govern a browser-based interaction (space-time diagram) and the timing information associated with the network packets exchanged between the host and the respective web servers with which the browser application on the host interacts. This is discussed further in the following subsections.

5.1 Modeling Browser Sessions

A browser session is modeled by selecting a browser that satisfies the specifications of this research (e.g., Mozilla Firefox browser) and a basic static homepage (e.g., `google.com`). This ensures that the homepage consumes minimum additional memory and time as it loads and also allows a focus on the dynamics of the browser rather than on the web page. A list of web pages is prepared that contain a mixture of static pages as well as dynamic pages with animations and plug-ins. In sequence, additional tabs are created in an open browser window with each of these pages opened one at a time; each time, the increase in memory consumption, network ports used, number of additional network connections established and the memory locations used by the multi-threaded browser process are noted. This provides an estimate of how much additional memory is consumed when a page is opened as a second tab, where the first tab is always set to the homepage. This exercise is then repeated on a browser window for each of the web sites. In each case, the additional tab or window opened that directs to the homepage is used as a control.

In the next step, keeping two fixed tabs, the exercise outlined above is repeated for each of the websites in the list and records are made of the memory consumed, network ports used, number of additional network connections established and memory locations used by the browser process. This is repeated for the browser windows in the same manner. Iterations are performed from two tabs to eight tabs and observations are made about how the browser behaves along with the parameters listed above. The case is also repeated for browser windows starting with two and increasing the number of windows in steps to eight and noting the parameters for each case. This process provides a representation of a browser session.

In the case of a single browser session, network packets are causally related with the respective browser events that, in turn, are structurally tied to the session – this can include the use of a specific process $\mathbf{p}$ and network ports n_1, n_2, n_3 to send and receive the network packets corresponding to the browser web request and its corresponding server response. Naturally, all the communications sent and received during the session are maintained through the network ports that bind them structurally to the browser session tab.

5.2   Developing a Browser Session State Space

An active browser session is characterized by a web request q, a browser host forward network session np_{fwd}^{host}, server response r and a browser host return network session np_{ret}^{host}. The network sessions np_{fwd}^{host} and np_{ret}^{host} are maintained by a browser process $\mathbf{p}$ on network port n. Thus, a simple browser session s with a single web request followed by a single server response is represented as:

$$s = (q, np_{fwd}^{host}, r, np_{ret}^{host}, \mathbf{p}, n) \tag{1}$$

When the browser maintains the session over a period of time T, it can make multiple web requests q_1, q_2, q_3 and receive an equal number of responses r_1, r_2, r_3 for a specific browser process $\mathbf{p}$ on network port n. The web requests q_1, q_2, q_3 are grouped into a request set Q and the server responses r_1, r_2, r_3 into a response set R. As shown in Equation (1), each web request from the host machine is associated with a unique network port number and timestamp. When a server response is observed for the host on the same network port, the association is established on a first-in-first-out basis. Server responses observed on other ports meant for the same destination are identified as referred responses launched by the browser during page rendering. In this manner, user requests are separated from referred requests and a one-to-one correspondence is established between the elements in set Q and the elements in set R.

The sequence of network packets transmitted from the browser host machine is grouped in set NP_{fwd}^{host} while the sequence of network packets received at the browser host machine from the server is grouped in set NP_{ret}^{host}. Timing information associated with session information is quite critical in the reconstruction. This requires the association of time with the progress of a session that can be utilized during the reconstruction. The proposed approach does not represent time explicitly; however, readers should note that every request and response observed in the network is implicitly associated with a timestamp. As a consequence, both NP_{fwd}^{host} and NP_{ret}^{host} have elements (individual requests and responses seen in the network) that are mapped one-to-one on the timeline. Therefore the browser session S maintained by browser process $\mathbf{p}$ on network port n over a time period T is given by:

$$S = (Q, NP_{fwd}^{host}, R, NP_{ret}^{host}, \mathbf{p}, n) \tag{2}$$

Using this representation of the state space of a single browser session, two relationships are elicited to define a coherent session and distinguish it from a concurrent session. A coherent session is one where the tagged activities correspond to a single browser session. A concurrent session is one where the tagged activities co-occur in time and belong to distinct browser sessions without any further relationships. These relationships are defined by matching metadata values. A metadata value match is an exact match or a threshold-based match using a predetermined threshold δ to accommodate network delays. The two relationships are used to group related artifacts from the recorded evidence and reconstruct parallel browser sessions across multiple browser tabs.

5.3   Coherent Event Relationship

When a metadata match occurs across two artifacts a_1 and a_2 in a browser session S, where a_1 and a_2 belong to the events from the browser log or from observed network traffic originating from the same server (domain), a coherent event relationship exists when the two artifacts a_1 and a_2 belong to a single browser session. The coherent event relationship is expressed as $a_1 R_{coh} a_2$. By definition, the relationship R_{coh} is reflexive and associative:

- $a_1 R_{coh} a_2 \Leftrightarrow a_2 R_{coh} a_1$

- $(a_1 R_{coh} a_2) \cap (a_2 R_{coh} a_3) \Rightarrow (a_1 R_{coh} a_3)$

When all the artifacts $a_1, a_2, a_3, \ldots, a_m$ exhibit identical associations with each other, the relationship is expressed as $R_{coh}(a_1, a_2, a_3, \ldots, a_m)$.

5.4   Concurrent Event Relationship

When a metadata match occurs across two artifacts a_1 and a_2 in a subset of the state space $(R, \ NP_{ret}^{host})$ in a given time interval T, where a_1 and a_2 belong to the events from a browser log or from the observed network traffic packets, a concurrent event relationship exists when the two artifacts a_1 and a_2 share concurrency in time but belong to different browser sessions. The concurrent event relationship is expressed as $a_1 R_{ccn} a_2$. By definition, the relationship R_{ccn} is reflexive but not associative:

- $a_1 R_{ccn} a_2 \Leftrightarrow a_2 R_{ccn} a_1$

- $(a_1 R_{ccn} a_2) \cap (a_2 R_{ccn} a_3) \not\Rightarrow (a_1 R_{ccn} a_3)$

When all the artifacts $a_1, a_2, a_3, \ldots, a_n$ exhibit identical associations with each other, the relationship is expressed as $R_{ccn}(a_1, a_2, a_3, \ldots, a_m)$.

Algorithm 1. : Rachna – Browser session reconstruction algorithm.

Input: Browser request list $Q = \{q_1, q_2, q_3, ...\}$, server responses $R = \{r_1, r_2, r_3, ...\}$, observed network traffic at the browser host NP_{fwd}^{host} and NP_{ret}^{host}, browser process **p** and network ports $\{n_1, n_2, n_3, ...\}$

Output: Simultaneous browser sessions for each corresponding (Q, R)

  1: num-sessions ← 0

  2: **for all** num-sessions = $\|$largest set $R_{ccn}(...)\|$ **do**

  3:     **if** server response $R \neq \emptyset$ **then**

  4:         num-sessions ← num-sessions + 1

  5:     **end if**

  6:     **for all** server responses $r \in R$ **do**

  7:         l ← list of referenced resources found in the response

  8:         **for all** resource items $\in l$ **do**

  9:            Map the resource in l to TCP sessions from $NP_{fwd}^{host}, NP_{ret}^{host}$

10:         **end for**

11:         Create the state $(q, np_{fwd}^{host}, r, np_{ret}^{host}, \mathbf{p}, n)$ for server response $r \in R$ for each unique network port n

12:     **end for**

13:     num-sessions ← num-sessions + 1

14:     Group all requests Q corresponding to responses in l for a single session to derive the session state $(Q, NP_{fwd}^{host}, R, NP_{ret}^{host}, (p), n)$ for browser process **p** for each unique network port n

15:     Stagger the session states so formed and order them chronologically with respect to the web requests in Q for each session state

16: **end for**

17: Display num-sessions as the number of simultaneous browser sessions

18: **for all** distinct sessions **do**

19:     Display $(Q, NP_{fwd}^{host}, R, NP_{ret}^{host}, \mathbf{p}, n)$

20: **end for**

When this condition holds, it can be interpreted as evidence of at least m distinct browser sessions because any two artifacts, taken two at a time, exhibit the concurrence relationship. With regard to ordering and prioritizing relationships, a coherency relationship supersedes a concurrency relationship where applicable. Consequently, if two artifacts a_1 and a_2 exhibit a concurrency relationship as well as a coherency relationship, then coherency is given priority and concurrency is dropped. This condition accounts for artifacts that belong to the same session, but may be recorded in parallel TCP sessions of a browser.

Algorithm 1 formalizes the process of reconstructing browser sessions. The algorithm is named Rachna, which means "to form" or "to construct" in Sanskrit.

Figure 4 shows the reconstruction of multiple browser sessions using network packets and the corresponding browser history log entries. The browser history log events show the web responses as presented by a

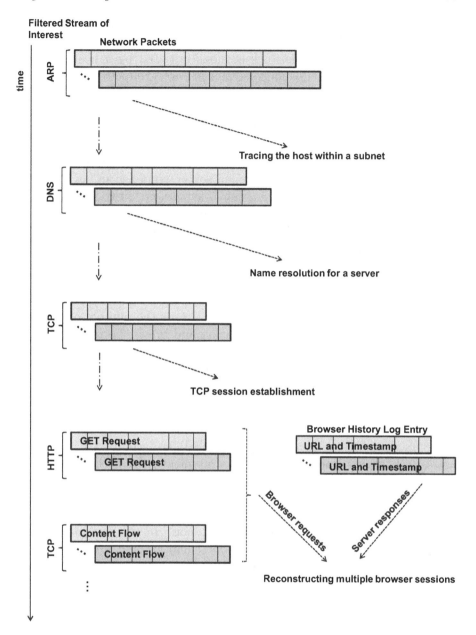

Figure 4. Reconstruction of multiple browser sessions.

browser window or tab. However, the request that led to a response being generated is implicit. Naturally, during the reconstruction it becomes necessary to trace its origin. Such a request is derived by parsing the server response to determine the list of resources, which are referenced to identify their respective sources.

For each resource, the network sessions initiated by a host are correlated and the request-response sequences are grouped to create the tuple $(q, np_{fwd}^{host}, r, np_{ret}^{host}, \mathbf{p}, n)$ for the browser process $\mathbf{p}$. Having identified such sequences, the number of simultaneous sessions deployed is updated.

The network packets in Figure 4 that are colored differently have a concurrency relationship. When network packets demonstrate a coherency relationship with a particular server response in set R, they are grouped together to indicate a coherent session. Such groupings are performed to reconstruct each coherent session.

Artifacts that do not exhibit coherency relationships have concurrency relationships because they do not share a session context beyond the obvious. Such artifacts are represented by $R_{ccn}()$. By definition, each pair of artifacts is concurrent and not coherent – thus, for each pair, there must exist two sessions that do not share a context. Hence, the cardinality of the largest set defined by $R_{ccn}()$ is the number of distinct browser sessions for a browser application and browser process $\mathbf{p}$.

6.   Identifying Browser Artifact Relationships

An experiment was performed to identify the relationships between browser artifacts using metadata associations.

A user was asked to launch a Mozilla Firefox browser (with developer mode and network request tracker enabled) and conduct a browsing session. The user opened the browser application with three tabs on the first browser window and then opened a separate window with two additional tabs. The default homepage was set to google.com.

In the first window, the user connected to securecyberspace.org and the online TV news guide sidereel.com. In the second window, the user logged into his personal Yahoo! email account and the second tab was connected to youtube.com. Next, the user modified the browser tab connected to Yahoo! email to become a separate window. In each of the two browser tabs connected to sidereel.com and youtube.com, the user executed a search and selected an item from the search list to be played. The entire session was captured using Wireshark over a ten-minute period. The relevant browser history sessions were also recorded. The network packets and browser logs were then analyzed. Table 1 summarizes the dataset collected in the experiment. Since the entire session was closely monitored and tracked, Wireshark was used to

Table 1. Experimental dataset.

Evidence	Number
Browser history	32
GET resource requests	1,489
Network packets	52,692

extract the SSL session keys and decipher the encrypted sessions after obtaining permission from the user.

The AssocGEN analysis engine [9] was adapted to identify the coherency and concurrency relationships based on the metadata determined from the browser log entries and network packets captured during the active network sessions. The browser history log entries and the individual network packets associated via their respective parameters identified in Figures 2 and 3, respectively, were grouped together depending on the relationships exhibited. Specifically, the simultaneous tabbed browser sessions that exhibited coherent event relationships on artifacts belonging to a single tabbed session exhibited both causality and session dependence (browser process to port binding) across browser log entries and network packets. This was used to separate the different simultaneous sessions.

The number of sessions was initially set to zero and, because the server response was non-null, the number of sessions was incremented to one. The original HTML responses for each session were parsed to obtain a total of 1,489 resource requests spread across five browser sessions and more than 52,692 network packets captured over the entire browsing duration. To eliminate requests generated from the browser during the rendering process, metrics provided by the developer mode of the Firefox browser were used to isolate HTML content from the remaining elements such as JavaScript, JPG, CSS and XML.

The origin server was identified for every reference resource that was downloaded. Each time a response from a new server was identified, the number of sessions was incremented. After the origin server for each resource was identified, coherency relationships between the corresponding server responses and network packets were discovered. The coherent artifacts (server response r, resource list l, network traffic np_{fwd}^{host}, network traffic np_{ret}^{host}) were grouped under a single browser session. As described in the algorithm, each referrer connection initiated by the browser during rendering was conducted on a network port other than the one where the main HTML page was being rendered. This enabled the main elements of the page and the add-on elements to be distinguished. The distinction enabled the linking and chaining of server responses from the streaming server (`youtube.com`), where a single request can contain a response that initiates a new request.

While establishing the coherency between the artifacts from a single browser session, resource lists across sessions were compared with the aggregated network traffic at the browser host machine. This revealed concurrency relationships between the resources and network packets. Next, the largest set of artifacts for which concurrency relationships could be established was determined ($\|R_{ccn}\|$). The number of sessions was updated for each new element discovered in this set; in the experiment, the number of sessions was five.

7.   Results and Discussion

After the artifacts were grouped according to the R_{coh} and R_{ccn} relationships, the network traffic that serviced each web request sent by the browser was aggregated. Thirteen distinct web requests were generated by user browser actions during the period of observation. The host was isolated using the network traffic; this revealed that the browser had a total of five tabbed browser sessions.

Two static page connections from the first browser window were identified (`google.com` and `securecyberspace.org`). These connections did not generate repeated reconnections and it was determined that the sessions were associated with a single browser window. This was determined based on the memory locations allocated to the browser window (first window), which contained the session context in memory for browser process **p**. However, the user subsequently requested a page named "Practicing Security" on the page connected to `securecyberspace.org`. No further activity was observed on the pages.

The tabbed sessions connected to the two online media servers generated the most rendered requests: 189 resource requests for `sidereel.com` and 158 resource requests for `youtube.com`. The pop-up and dynamic prompts were not included in the count. During the analysis, these request elements did not provide a precise source of origin; this contributed to the ambiguity. The connection with the email server also had a large number of requests, although they were restricted to the server homepage. After the user requests progressed to the mail login pages, the number of requests were reduced drastically. It should be noted that this was primarily due to the advertisements provided on the website that contained referred elements from the parent server (i.e., `au.yahoo.com`), which generated new connections on behalf of the server. Further analysis of the browser cache and stored information on

Table 2. Reconstructed browser sessions.

Tabbed Session ID	Timestamp	URL
1	13-08-2015 PM 02:52:15	`www.google.com`
2	13-08-2015 PM 02:52:37	`www.securecyberspace.org`
3	13-08-2015 PM 02:53:12	`www.sidereel.com`
2	13-08-2015 PM 02:53:28	`http://www.securecyberspace.org/` `practicing_security`
4	13-08-2015 PM 02:55:32	`https://www.youtube.com`
5	13-08-2015 PM 02:55:57	`https://au.yahoo.com/?p=us`
3	13-08-2015 PM 02:56:46	`www.sidereel.com/_television/` `search?utf8=%E2%9C%93&amp;q=` `thewestwing`
4	13-08-2015 PM 02:57:21	`https://www.youtube.com/results?` `search_query=arrow+season+2`
3	13-08-2015 PM 02:57:58	`http://www.sidereel.com/The_West_` `Wing`
5	13-08-2015 PM 02:59:35	`https://login.yahoo.com/config/` `mail?&.src=ym&.intl=au`
5	13-08-2015 PM 02:59:46	`https://edit.yahoo.com/config/` `change_pw?.done=https%3A%2F%` `2Fmail.yahoo.com&.src=ym&.intl=` `au&.spreg=4&.scrumb=z9e3gjYzlQb&.` `lang=en-AU&.asdk_embedded=&.` `appsrc=&.appsrcv=&.srcv=&.smc=` `&sts=1441272728&sig=2c1bb1d2`
4	13-08-2015 PM 02:58:36	`https://www.youtube.com/watch?v=` `wYnOI9gtoKw`
5	13-08-2015 PM 03:00:17	`https://edit.yahoo.com/config/` `change_pw?.scrumb=z9e3gjYzlQb&.` `done=https%3A%2F%2Fmail.yahoo.` `com&.src=ym&.st=4`
5	13-08-2015 PM 03:01:42	`https://au-mg5.mail.yahoo.com/` `neo/launch?.rand=4vfcsaqi45krv`

the host machine helped identify the user's stored email login credentials (recovering user details and identifying the account accessed by the user are added benefits of brower sesssion reconstruction). The email server and `youtube.com` repeatedly refreshed their page contents identified in page elements such as JavaScript, JPG and XML, and some ActiveX content generated new host-server connections on new network ports.

7.1   Results

Table 2 presents the reconstructed browser sessions (server responses R). The results were validated by repeating the activity on the same browser providing the URL as identified by the browser history log for each tabbed session and comparing the generated records. The analysis engine was used to first process the browser history logs and load the log records and their parsed metadata into the engine repository. After the browser logs were traversed completely, the network packets obtained during the capture were traversed. Following this, a procedure call was used to generate all object relationships based on associations identified in their metadata across the browser history log entries, TCP connections, browser process information and network port information from memory, and network packets in the packet capture.

After the associations were generated and stored in the repository, the syntactic relationships between artifacts of the same type (i.e., among network packets and browser history logs) and the semantic relationships across types were elicited to discover the origins of the web sessions. Artifacts that belonged to the same application were determined to have coherent event relationships R_{coh}. This is typically true for all records from a browser history log or between network packets.

The concurrent event relationships R_{ccn} were determined to exist between artifacts that occurred at the same time but contained different session contexts, and belonged to distinct browser sessions. This is true of browser history records captured across tabs running simultaneous sessions or between network packets that service parallel sessions across different browser tabs. Based on the reconstruction, the sessions were replayed on a Firefox browser to corroborate the evidence. Figure 5 shows a snapshot of the replayed Firefox browser sessions consisting of three browser windows and five tabbed browser sessions. Note that, while the algorithm could distinguish the sessions carried out across two browser windows and over five tabbed sessions, the algorithm did not discern the change when the two browser windows were expanded to three windows during the session. It is believed that the browser process **p** maintains the same memory locations and session ID to service this session, but the special identifiers that separate a tabbed session as a new browser window remain to be identified. Current research is exploring this aspect of browser behavior.

7.2   Discussion

The proposed method for distinguishing multiple simultaneous sessions leverages artifact relationships derived from metadata-based associations. Coherency relationships are employed to establish connectedness between artifacts belonging to a single session and concurrency relationships are used to distinguish between artifacts that share the

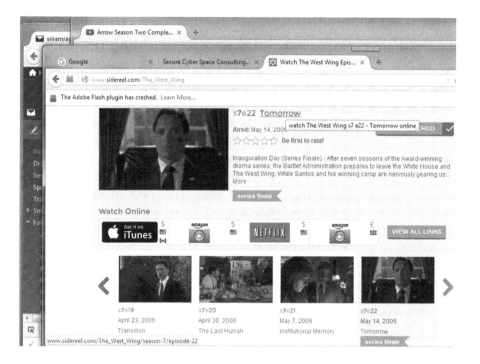

Figure 5. Reconstructed Firefox browser sessions.

time of occurrence, but not the session context. However, some special cases must be considered due to the assumption that multiple browser sessions may exist at the point of initiation.

It is also necessary to consider cases where new tabs are created along the way and to detect them effectively using the Rachna algorithm, especially when the new session communicates with the same server as the immediately-previous tab. In this case, while the resources from the server can be mapped after parsing the original server response as described in the algorithm, the newly-deployed tab may share resources with the original session and this may not warrant a new network session – this could create a miss when the resources list is mapped against the network traffic. This can be identified by tracking the network ports on the host to determine when a new connection is requested from a server that has an existing connection with browser process **p**. There is some scope for refining the detection method in such an approach.

A browser application can host one or more browser sessions, which are hosted on one or more browser windows. The transactions conducted across such sessions are recorded in the browser logs. The information processed by the browser application is volatile. Between the parent process and the threads maintaining multiple browser sessions, there are two-way communications that ensure that each thread receives its unique commands.

When the parent process needs to create and maintain a network session, it makes a request to the network stack and this communication is unidirectional – in the sense that the network stack does not track the origin of the request. All the completed network services are generically returned through the network stack to host memory (shared memory implementation), from where the process responsible for making the call reads the information for further processing. It was also observed that the Rachna algorithm could not deal with pop-up windows and dynamic prompts with page timeouts. This is because the algorithm cannot associate the precise origin of a pop-up on a page with a request originating from the host machine.

While the approach may appear to be efficient in terms of operating the application and not losing information when sessions may need to be sandboxed, the lack of explicit two-way attribution remains a challenge with regard to efficient and timely reconstructions performed when investigating security incidents. Providing attribution by ensuring two-way information recording can go a long way in developing attack-resilient browsers in the future.

8.   Conclusions

This research has demonstrated the feasibility of isolating multiple simultaneous browser sessions on multi-threaded browser applications based on browser application logs and network traffic logs on a browser host machine. Metadata-based associations were leveraged to identify and reconstruct all tabbed sessions that are part of a typical browser interaction. Coherency and concurrency relationships between artifacts derived from browser history logs and network traffic were used to identify the number of simultaneous sessions. The Rachna algorithm was developed to identify these relationships, discover the number of simultaneous browser sessions deployed and reconstruct the sessions. The effectiveness of the approach was demonstrated by conducting an analysis of a five-tabbed Mozilla Firefox browser session reconstructed using browser history logs and network packets. Finally, it was shown that the cardinality of the largest set of concurrent artifacts from a collection can be used to identify the number of simultaneous sessions by tracking the main page elements and distinguishing them from the rendered elements and the active elements that request reconnections from the same server.

Many current browsers provide an "incognito" or "silent" option to prevent browser activities from being recorded in browser application logs. This can have a significant impact on the reconstruction method presented in this chapter and may impede the identification of coherency and concurrency relationships. However, the incognito mode simply cuts off the logging module while the actual information continues to reside with the application and is usually held by the parent process. Future research will extend the approach to deal with such scenarios. Also, research will explore the minimum information needed to reconstruct browser sessions with acceptable accuracy. Many active pages, especially those associated with online media, contain pop-ups and dynamic prompts; current research is attempting to identify the distinguishing features of a pop-up on a web response and to incorporate these features in the Rachna algorithm. The knowledge gained from these efforts may lead to fundamental changes in the specification of future Internet-related active devices and applications.

References

[1] Chromium Projects, Multi-Process Architecture (`www.chromium.org/developers/design-documents/multi-process-architecture`), 2016.

[2] M. Cohen, PyFlag – An advanced network forensic framework, *Digital Investigation*, vol. 5(S), pp. S112–S120, 2008.

[3] G. Combs, Wireshark (`www.wireshark.org/about.html`), 2016.

[4] A. Grosskurth and M. Godfrey, A reference architecture for web browsers, *Proceedings of the Twenty-First IEEE International Conference on Software Maintenance*, pp. 661–664, 2005.

[5] N. Lwin, Agent based web browser, *Proceedings of the Fifth International Conference on Autonomic and Autonomous Systems*, pp. 106–110, 2009.

[6] Mozilla, Mozilla Browser Architecture, Mountain, View, California, 2014.

[7] C. Neasbitt, R. Perdisci and K. Li, ClickMiner: Towards forensic reconstruction of user-browser interactions from network traces, *Proceedings of the ACM Conference on Computer and Communications Security*, pp. 1244–1255, 2014.

[8] J. Oh, S. Lee and S. Lee, Advanced evidence collection and analysis of web browser activity, *Digital Investigation*, vol. 8(S), pp. S62–S70, 2011.

[9] S. Raghavan and S. Raghavan, AssocGEN: Engine for analyzing metadata-based associations in digital evidence, *Proceedings of the Eighth International Workshop on Systematic Approaches to Digital Forensic Engineering*, 2013.

[10] S. Raghavan and S. Raghavan, Determining the origin of down-loaded files using metadata associations, *Journal of Communications*, vol. 8(12), pp. 902–910, 2013.

[11] G. Xie, M. Iliofotou, T. Karagiannis, M. Faloutsos and Y. Jin, ReSurf: Reconstructing web-surfing activity from network traffic, *Proceedings of the IFIP Networking Conference*, 2013.

Chapter 10

A PROBABILISTIC NETWORK FORENSIC MODEL FOR EVIDENCE ANALYSIS

Changwei Liu, Anoop Singhal and Duminda Wijesekera

Abstract   Modern-day attackers use sophisticated multi-stage and/or multi-host attack techniques and anti-forensic tools to cover their attack traces. Due to the limitations of current intrusion detection systems and forensic analysis tools, evidence often has false positive errors or is incomplete. Additionally, because of the large number of security events, discovering an attack pattern is much like finding a needle in a haystack. Consequently, reconstructing attack scenarios and holding attackers accountable for their activities are major challenges.

    This chapter describes a probabilistic model that applies Bayesian networks to construct evidence graphs. The model helps address the problems posed by false positive errors, analyze the reasons for missing evidence and compute the posterior probabilities and false positive rates of attack scenarios constructed using the available evidence. A companion software tool for network forensic analysis was used in conjunction with the probabilistic model. The tool, which is written in Prolog, leverages vulnerability databases and an anti-forensic database similar to the NIST National Vulnerability Database (NVD). The experimental results demonstrate that the model is useful for constructing the most-likely attack scenarios and for managing errors encountered in network forensic analysis.

Keywords: Network forensics, logical evidence graphs, Bayesian networks

1.   Introduction

Digital forensic investigators use evidence and contextual facts to formulate attack hypotheses and assess the probability that the facts support or refute the hypotheses [5]. However, due to the limitations of forensic tools and expert knowledge, formulating a hypothesis about

G. Peterson and S. Shenoi (Eds.): Advances in Digital Forensics XII, IFIP AICT 484, pp. 189–210, 2016.
DOI: 10.1007/978-3-319-46279-0_10

a multi-step, multi-host attack launched on an enterprise network and using quantitative measures to support the hypothesis are major challenges. This chapter describes a model that helps automate the process of constructing and analyzing quantitatively-supportable attack scenarios based on the available evidence. The applicability and utility of the model are demonstrated using a network attack case study.

The proposed method uses a Bayesian network to estimate the likelihood and false positive rates of potential attack scenarios that fit the discovered evidence. Although several researchers have used Bayesian networks for digital evidence modeling [3, 5, 12, 13], their approaches construct Bayesian networks in an *ad hoc* manner. This chapter shows how the proposed method can help automate the process of organizing evidence in a graphical structure (called a logical evidence graph) and apply Bayesian analysis to the entire graph. The method provides attack scenarios with acceptable false positive error rates and dynamically updates the joint posterior probabilities and false positive error rates of attack paths when new items of evidence for the attack paths are presented.

2. Background and Related Work

Bayesian networks have been used to express the credibility and relative weights of digital and non-digital evidence [2, 3, 5, 12, 13]. Several researchers have used Bayesian networks to model dependencies between hypotheses and crime scene evidence, and have employed these models to update the belief probabilities of newly-discovered evidence given the previous evidence [2–4, 12–14].

Digital forensic researchers have used Bayesian networks to reason about evidence and quantify the reliability and traceability of the corresponding hypotheses [5]. However, these Bayesian networks were custom-built without using a uniform model. In contrast, the proposed model is generic and helps address the problems posed by false positive errors, analyze the reasons for missing evidence and compute the posterior probabilities and false positive rates of attack scenarios constructed using the available evidence.

Meanwhile, few, if any, tools directly support the automated construction of Bayesian networks based on the available evidence and estimate belief probabilities and potential error rates. A software tool for network forensic analysis was developed for use with the proposed probabilistic model. The tool, which is written in Prolog, leverages the MulVAL reasoning system [1, 10] and employs system vulnerability databases and an anti-forensic database similar to the NIST National Vulnerability

Database (NVD). The experimental results demonstrate that the tool facilitates the construction of most-likely attack scenarios and the management of errors encountered in network forensic analysis.

3.   Logical Evidence Graphs

This section defines logical evidence graphs and shows how rules are designed to correlate attack scenarios with the available evidence. Because logical reasoning is used to link observed attack events and the collected evidence, the evidence graphs are referred to as logical evidence graphs.

Definition 1 (Logical Evidence Graph (LEG)):   A logical evidence graph $LEG = (N_f, N_r, N_c, E, L, G)$ is a six-tuple where N_f, N_r and N_c are three disjoint sets of nodes in the graph (called fact, rule and consequence fact nodes, respectively), $E \subseteq ((N_f \cup N_c) \times N_r) \cup (N_r \times N_c)$ is the evidence, L is a mapping from nodes to labels and $G \subseteq N_c$ is a set of observed attack events.

Every rule node has one or more fact nodes or consequence fact nodes from prior attack steps as its parents and a consequence fact node as its only child. Node labels consist of instantiations of rules or sets of predicates specified as follows:

1. A node in N_f is an instantiation of predicates that codify system states, including access privileges, network topology and known vulnerabilities associated with host computers. The following predicates are used:

   - hasAccount(_principal, _host, _account), canAccessFile(_host, _user, _access, _path) and other predicates model access privileges.

   - attackerLocated(_host) and hacl(_src, _dst, _prot, _port) model network topology, including the attacker's location and network reachability information.

   - vulExists(_host, _vulID, _program) and vulProperty(_vulID, _range, _consequence) model node vulnerabilities.

2. A node in N_r describes a single rule of the form $p \leftarrow p_1 \wedge p_2 \cdots \wedge p_n$. The rule head p is an instantiation of a predicate from N_c, which is the child node of N_r in the logical evidence graph. The rule body comprises p_i ($i = 1..n$), which are predicate instantiations of N_f from the current attack step and N_c from one or more prior attack steps that comprise the parent nodes of N_r.

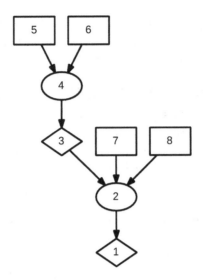

Figure 1.   Example logical evidence graph.

3. A node in N_c represents the predicate that codifies the post-attack
state as the consequence of an attack step. The two predicates
execCode(_host, _user) and netAccess(_machine, _protocol, _port)
are used to model the attacker's capability after an attack step.
Valid instantiations of these predicates after an attack update valid
instantiations of the predicates listed in (1).

Figure 1 shows an example logical evidence graph; Table 1 describes
the nodes in Figure 1. In Figure 1, fact, rule and consequence fact nodes
are represented as boxes, ellipses and diamonds, respectively. Facts
(Nodes 5, 6, 7 and 8) include network topology (Nodes 5 and 6), computer configuration (Node 7) and software vulnerabilities obtained by
analyzing evidence captured by forensic tools (Node 8). Rule nodes
(Nodes 2 and 4) represent rules that change the attack status using attack steps. These rules, which are based on expert knowledge, are used
to link chains of evidence as consequences of attack steps. Linking a
chain of evidence using a rule creates an investigator's hypothesis of an
attack step given the evidence. Consequence fact nodes (Nodes 1 and
3) codify the attack status obtained from event logs and other forensic
tools that record the postconditions of attack steps.

Lines 9 through 17 in Figure 2 describe Rules 1 and 2 in Table 1. The
rules use the Prolog notation ":-" to separate the head (consequence
fact) and the body (facts). Lines 1 through 8 in Figure 2 list the fact
and consequence fact predicates of the two rules.

Table 1. Descriptions of the nodes in Figure 1.

Node	Notation	Resource
1	execCode(workStation1, user)	Evidence obtained from event log
2	THROUGH 3 (remote exploit of a server program)	Rule 1 (Hypothesis 1)
3	netAccess(workStation1, tcp, 4040)	Evidence obtained from event log
4	THROUGH 8 (direct network access)	Rule 2 (Hypothesis 2)
5	hacl(internet, workStation1, tcp, 4040)	Network setup
6	attackerLocated(internet)	Evidence obtained from log
7	networkServiceInfo(workStation1, httpd, tcp, 4040, user)	Computer setup
8	vulExists(workStation1, 'CVE-2009-1918', httpd, remoteExploit, privEscalation)	Exploited vulnerability alert from intrusion detection system

Rule 1 in Lines 9 through 12 represents an attack step that states: if (i) the attacker is located in a "Zone" such as the "internet" (Line 10: attackerLocated(Zone)); and (ii) a host computer "H" can be accessed from the "Zone" using "Protocol" at "Port" (Line 11: hacl(Zone, H, Protocol, Port)); then (iii) host "H" can be accessed from the "Zone" using "Protocol" at "Port" (Line 9: netAccess(H, Protocol, Port)) via (iv) "direct network access" (Line 12: rule description).

Rule 2 in Lines 13 through 17 states: if (i) a host has a software vulnerability that can be remotely exploited (Line 14: vulExists(H, _, Software, remoteExploit, privEscalation)); and (ii) the host can be reached using "Protocol" at "Port" with privilege "Perm" (Line 15: networkServiceInfo(H, Software, Protocol, Port, Perm)); and (iii) the attacker can access host using "Protocol" at "Port" (Line 16: netAccess(H, Protocol, Port)); then (iv) the attacker can remotely exploit host "H" and obtain privilege "Perm" (Line 13: execCode(H, Perm)) via (v) "remote exploit of a server program" (Line 17: rule description).

4. Computing Probabilities

Bayesian networks can be represented as directed acyclic graphs whose nodes represent random variables (events or evidence in this work) and arcs model direct dependencies between random variables [11]. Every

Rule Head – Post-attack status as derived fact obtained via evidence analysis
1. Consequence: execCode(_host, _user).
2. Consequence: netAccess(_machine, _protocol, _port).
Rule Body – Access privilege
3. Fact: hacl(_src, _dst, _prot, _port).
Rule Body – Software vulnerability obtained from a forensic tool
4. Fact: vulExists(_host, _vulID, _program).
5. Fact: vulProperty(_vulID, _range, _consequence).
Rule Body – Network topology
6. Fact: hacl(_src, _dst, _prot, _port).
7. Fact: attackerLocated(_host).
Rule Body – Computer configuration
8. Fact: hasAccount(_principal, _host, _account).

Rule 1:
9. (netAccess(H, Protocol, Port) :-
10. attackerLocated(Zone),
11. hacl(Zone, H, Protocol, Port)),
12. rule_desc('direct network access', 1.0).

Rule 2:
13. (execCode(H, Perm) :-
14. vulExists(H, _, Software, remoteExploit, privEscalation),
15. networkServiceInfo(H, Software, Protocol, Port, Perm),
16. netAccess(H, Protocol, Port)),
17. rule_desc('remote exploit of a server program', 1.0).

Figure 2.   Example rules expressing attack techniques.

node has a table that provides the conditional probability of the node's variable given the combination of the states of its parent variables.

Definition 2 (Bayesian Network (BN)): Let X_1, X_2, $\cdots$, X_n be n random variables connected in a directed acyclic graph. Then, the joint probability distribution of $X_1, X_2, ..., X_n$ can be computed using the Bayesian formula:

$$P(X_1, X_2, \ldots, X_n) = \prod_{i=1}^{n} [P(X_i)|parent(P(X_i))] \tag{1}$$

A Bayesian network helps model and visualize dependencies between a hypothesis and evidence, and calculate the revised probability when new evidence is presented [9]. Figure 3 presents a causal view of hypothesis H and evidence E. Bayes' theorem can be used to update an investigator's belief about hypothesis H when evidence E is observed:

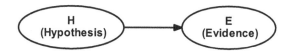

Figure 3. Causal view of evidence.

$$P(H|E) = \frac{P(H) \cdot P(E|H)}{P(E)}$$

$$= \frac{P(H) \cdot P(E|H)}{P(E|H) \cdot P(H) + P(E|\neg H) \cdot P(\neg H)} \quad (2)$$

where $P(H|E)$ is the posterior probability of an investigator's belief in hypothesis H given evidence E. $P(E|H)$, which is based on expert knowledge, is a likelihood function that assesses the probability of evidence assuming the truth of H. $P(H)$ is the prior probability of H when the evidence has not been discovered and $P(E) = P(E|H) \cdot P(H) + P(E|\neg H) \cdot P(\neg H)$ is the probability of the evidence regardless of expert knowledge about H and is referred to as a normalizing constant [5, 9].

4.1 Computing $P(H|E)$

A logical evidence graph involves the serial application of attack steps that are mapped to a Bayesian network as follows:

- N_c as the child of the corresponding N_r shows that an attack step has occurred.

- N_r is the hypothesis of the attack step and is denoted by H.

- N_f from the current attack step and $N_{c'}$ from the previous attack step as the parents of N_r correspond to the attack evidence, showing the exploited vulnerability and the privilege the attacker used to launch the attack step.

- N_c propagates the dependency between the current attack step and the next attack step. N_c is also the precondition of the next attack step.

Computing $P(H|E)$ for a Consequence Fact Node. Equation (2) can be used to compute $P(H|E)$ for a consequence fact node of a single attack step when the previous attack step has not been considered. Because the rule node N_r provides the hypothesis H and both the fact node N_f and the consequence fact node from a previous attack step $N_{c'}$ provide evidence E, the application of Bayes' theorem yields:

$$P(H|E) = P(N_r|E) = \frac{P(N_r) \cdot P(E|N_r)}{P(E)} \qquad (3)$$

The fact nodes from the current attack step and the consequence fact node from a previous attack step are independent of each other. They constitute the body of a rule, deriving the consequence fact node for the current attack step as the head of the rule. Consequently, their logical conjunction provides the conditions that are used to arrive at the rule conclusion. Accordingly, if a rule node has k parents $N_{p1}, N_{p2}, \ldots, N_{pk}$ that are independent, then $P(E) = P(N_{p1}, N_{p2}, \ldots, N_{pk}) = P(N_{p1} \cap N_{p2} \cap \cdots \cap N_{pk}) = P(N_{p1}) \cdot P(N_{p2}) \cdots P(N_{pk})$ (note that $\cap$ denotes the AND operator). Due to the independence, given rule N_r, $P(E|N_r) = P(N_{p1}, N_{p2}, \ldots, N_{pk}|N_r) = P(N_{p1}|N_r) \cdot P(N_{p2}|N_r) \cdots P(N_{pk}|N_r)$. Hence, by applying Equation (3), where H is N_r and E is $N_{p1} \cap N_{p2} \cap \cdots \cap N_{pk}$, $P(H|E)$ for a consequence fact node is computed as:

$$\begin{aligned} P(H|E) &= P(N_r|N_{p1}, N_{p2}, \cdots, N_{pk}) \\ &= \frac{P(N_r) \cdot P(N_{p1}|N_r) \cdot P(N_{p2}|N_r) \cdots P(N_{pk}|N_r)}{P(N_{p1}) \cdot P(N_{p2}) \cdots P(N_{pk})} \qquad (4) \end{aligned}$$

However, because $P(E|N_r)$ represents the subjective judgment of a forensic investigator, it would be difficult for human experts to assign $P(N_{p1}|N_r)$, $P(N_{p2}|N_r)$, $\cdots$, $P(N_{pk}|N_r)$ separately. Therefore, the forensic investigator has the discretion to use Equation (3) to compute $P(E|N_r)$ directly.

Computing $P(H|E)$ for the Entire Graph. Next, it is necessary to compute $P(H|E)$ for the entire logical evidence graph comprising the attack paths. Any chosen attack path in a logical evidence graph is a serial application of attack steps. An attack step only depends on its direct parent attack steps and is independent of all the ancestor attack steps in the attack path. Upon applying Definition 2, the following equation is obtained:

$$\begin{aligned} P(H|E) &= P(H_1, H_2 \cdots H_n | E_1, E_2, E_3 \cdots E_n) \\ &= P(S_1)P(S_2|S_1) \cdots P(S_n|S_{n-1}) \end{aligned} \qquad (5)$$

where S_i ($i = 1..n$) denotes the ith attack step in an attack path.

Let $N_{i,f}, N_{i,r}$ and $N_{i,c}$ be the fact, rule and consequence fact nodes, respectively, at the ith attack step. Then, Equation (5) may be written as:

$$P(H|E) = P(S_1) \cdots P(S_i|S_{i-1}) \cdots P(S_n|S_{n-1})$$
$$= P(N_{1,r}|N_{1,f}) \cdots P(N_{i,r}|N_{i-1,c}, N_{i,p}) \cdots P(N_{n,r}|N_{n-1,c}, N_{n,p})$$
$$= \frac{P(N_{1,r})P(N_{1,f}|N_{1,r})}{P(N_{1,f})} \cdots \frac{P(N_{n,r})P(N_{n-1,c}, N_{n,f}|N_{n,r})}{P(N_{n-1,c}, N_{n,f})}$$
$$\tag{6}$$

where $P(S_1)P(S_2|S_1) \cdots P(S_i|S_{i-1})$ is the joint posterior probability of the previous i attack steps (i.e., $1..i$) given all the evidence from the attack steps (e.g., evidence for attack step 1 is $N_{1,f}$; the evidence for attack step i includes $N_{i-1,c}$ and $N_{i,f}$ where $i = 2..n$.

$P(S_1)P(S_2|S_1) \cdots P(S_i|S_{i-1})$ is propagated to the $i + 1^{th}$ attack step by the consequence fact node $N_{i,c}$, which is also the precondition of the $i + 1^{th}$ attack step. Algorithm 1 formalizes the computation of $P(H|E)$ for the entire logical evidence graph.

Because a logical evidence graph may have several attack paths, to compute the posterior probability of each attack path, all the nodes are marked as WHITE (Lines 2 through 4 in Algorithm 1) and all the fact nodes are pushed from the first attack step of all attack paths to an empty queue (Lines 1 and 5). If the queue is not empty (Line 7), a fact node is taken out of the queue (Line 8) and a check is made to see if its child that is a rule node is WHITE (Lines 9 and 10). If the rule node is WHITE, a new attack path is created (Line 11), upon which Equation (6) is used recursively to compute the joint posterior probability of the entire attack path (Lines 16 through 30) and the node is marked as BLACK (Line 13) after the computation of the function PATH($N_{1,r}$) in Line 12 is complete. The above process is repeated until the queue holding the fact nodes from the first attack steps of all the attack paths is empty.

4.2 Computing the False Positive Rate

False positive and false negative errors exist in logical evidence graphs. A false negative arises when the investigator believes that the event was not caused by an attack, but was the result of an attack. A false positive arises when the investigator believes that an event was caused by an attack, but was not. Clearly, it is necessary to estimate both types of errors.

Because a logical evidence graph is constructed using attack evidence chosen by the forensic investigator, there is always the possibility of false positive errors. Therefore, the cumulative false positive rate of the constructed attack paths must be computed. False negative errors are not computed in this work.

Algorithm 1. : Computing $P(H|E)$ for the entire graph.

Input: A LEG $= (N_r, N_f, N_c, E, L, G)$ with multiple attack paths and $P(N_{i,r})$ $(i = 1..n)$, $P(N_{1,f}|N_{1,r})$, $P(N_{1,f})$, $P(N_{i-1,c}, N_{i,f}|N_{i,r})$, $P(N_{i-1,c}, N_i, f)$ $(i = 2..n)$ obtained from expert knowledge about each attack path. $N_{1,f}$, $N_{i-1,c}$ and $N_{i,f}$ $(i \geq 2)$ correspond to evidence E. $N_{i,r}$ $(i \geq 1)$ corresponds to H.

Output: The joint posterior probability of the hypothesis of every attack path $P(H|E)=P(H_1, H_2 \cdots H_n|E_1, E_2, E_3 \cdots E_n)$ given all the evidence represented by fact nodes $N_{i,f}$ and $N_{i,c}$ $(i = 1..n)$. ($P(H|E)$ is written as P in the algorithm.

1: $Q_g \leftarrow \emptyset$　　　　　　　　　　　　　　　　　　　　　　▷ set Q_g to empty
2: **for** each node n $\in$ LEG **do**
3: 　　color[n] $\leftarrow$ WHITE　　　　　　　▷ mark every node in the graph as white
4: **end for**
5: ENQUEUE($Q_g, N_{1,f}$)　　▷ push all fact nodes from the first attack step to queue Q_g
6: j $\leftarrow$ 0　　　　　　　　　▷ use j to identify the attack path being computed
7: **while** $Q_g \neq \emptyset$ **do**　　　　　　　　　　▷ when queue Q_g is not empty
8: 　　n $\leftarrow$ DEQUEUE(Q_g)　　　　　　　　　　　▷ remove fact node n
9: 　　$N_{1,r} \leftarrow$ child[n]　　　　　　▷ find a rule node as the child node of n
10: 　　**if** $(color[N_{1,r}] \equiv$ WHITE) **then** ▷ if the rule node is not traversed (white)
11: 　　　　j $\leftarrow$ j+1　　　　　　　　　　　　▷ must be a new attack path
12: 　　　　P[j] $\leftarrow$ PATH($N_{1,r}$)　　▷ compute joint posterior probability of the path
13: 　　　　color[$N_{1,r}$] $\leftarrow$ BLACK　　　　　　▷ mark the rule node as black
14: 　　**end if**
15: **end while**

16: **PATH($N_{1,r}$)** {　　　　　▷ compute the posterior probability of an attack path
17: $N_{1,c} \leftarrow$ child[$N_{1,r}$]　　　　▷ consequence fact node of the first attack step
18: E $\leftarrow$ parents[$N_{1,r}$]　　　　　　　▷ E is the evidence for the first attack step
19: $P[N_{1,c}] \leftarrow \frac{P(N_{1,r})P(E|N_{1,r})}{P(E)}$　　　　　　▷ probability of the first attack step
20: color[E] $\leftarrow$ BLACK　　　　　　　▷ mark all traversed evidence as black
21: P $\leftarrow$ $P[N_{1,c}]$　　　　　　　　　▷ use P to do the recursive computation
22: **for** $i \leftarrow$ 2 to n **do**　　　　▷ from the second attack step to the last attack step
23: 　　$N_{i,r} \leftarrow$ child[$N_{i-1,c}$]　　　　　　▷ rule node as H of the ith attack step
24: 　　E $\leftarrow$ parents[$N_{i,r}$]　　　　　　　▷ evidence for the ith attack step
25: 　　$N_{i,c} \leftarrow$ child[$N_{i,r}$]　　　▷ consequence fact node of the ith attack step
26: 　　$P[N_{i,c}] \leftarrow P(N_{i,r}|E) \leftarrow \frac{P(N_{i,r})P(E|N_{i,r})}{P(E)}$
　　　　　　　　　　　　　　　　▷ posterior probability of the ith attack step
27: 　　color[E] $\leftarrow$ BLACK　　　　　　　▷ mark all traversed evidence as black
28: 　　P $\leftarrow$ P $\times P(N_{i,c})$　　　▷ joint posterior possibility of attack steps (1..i)
29: **end for**
30: **Return** P　　　　▷ return the posterior attack possibility of the attack path

The individual false positive estimate for an attack step is expressed as $P(E|\neg H)$, where $\neg H$ is the alternative hypothesis, usually written as "not H," and the value of $P(E|\neg H)$ can be obtained from expert knowledge. To demonstrate the computation of the cumulative false positive rate of an entire attack path, let $N_{i,f}$, $N_{i,r}$ and $N_{i,c}$ correspond to the fact, rule and consequence fact nodes, respectively, of the ith attack step. Then, the cumulative false positive rate of the entire attack path is computed as follows:

$$
\begin{aligned}
P(E|\neg H) &= P(E_1, E_2, \cdots, E_n | \neg(H_1, H_2, \cdots, H_n)) \\
&= \bigcup_{i=1}^{n} P(E_i | \neg N_{i,r}) \\
&= 1 - (\cdots(1 - (1 - P(E_2|\neg N_{2,r}) \cdot (1 - P(E_1|\neg N_{1,r})))))) \\
&\quad \cdot (1 - P(E_n|\neg N_{n,r}))
\end{aligned}
\tag{7}
$$

Note that all the evidence supporting an attack step is independent of the evidence supporting the other attack steps.

As mentioned above, E_1 in Equation (7) is $N_{1,f}$ and E_i includes $N_{i-1,c}$ and $N_{i,f}$ ($i = 2..n$). The symbol $\cup$ denotes the noisy-OR operator [7]. For a serial connection, if any of the attack steps is a false positive, then the entire attack path is considered to be a false positive. Algorithm 2 formalizes the computation of $P(E|\neg H)$ for the entire evidence graph.

Lines 1 through 15 in Algorithm 2 are the same as in Algorithm 1 (i.e., they find a new attack path). Lines 16 through 29 use Equation (7) to recursively compute the cumulative false positive rate of an entire attack path.

5.   Case Study

This case study demonstrates how probabilistic attack scenarios can be reconstructed using Bayesian analysis [13].

5.1   Experimental Network

Figure 4 shows the experimental network [6] used to generate a logical evidence graph from post-attack evidence. In the network, the external Firewall 1 controls Internet access to a network containing a Portal Web Server and Product Web Server. The internal Firewall 2 controls access to a SQL Database Server that can be accessed from the web servers and workstations. The Administrator Workstation has administrative privileges to the Portal Web Server that supports a forum for users to chat with the administrator. In the experiment, the Portal and Product Web Servers and the Database Server were configured to log all accesses and queries as events and Snort was used as the intrusion detection

Algorithm 2. : Computing $P(E|\neg H)$ for the entire graph.

Input: A LEG $=$ (N_r, N_f, N_c, E, L, G) and $P(N_{1,f}|N_{1,r})$ as $P(E_1|H_1)$,
$P(N_{i-1,c}, N_{i,f}|N_{i,r})$ as $P(E_i|H_i)$ $(i = 2..n)$ for every attack path.

Output: The cumulative false positive rate of each attack path $P(E|\neg H) =$
$P(E_1, E_2, \cdots, E_n|\neg(H_1, H_2 \cdots H_n)$. $P(E|\neg H)$ is written as P_f in the algorithm.

```
 1: Q_g ← ∅                                    ▷ set Q_g to empty
 2: for each node n ∈ LEG do
 3:     color[n] ← WHITE              ▷ mark every node in the graph as white
 4: end for
 5: ENQUEUE(Q_g, N_{1,f})   ▷ push all fact nodes from the first attack step to queue
    Q_g
 6: j ← 0                      ▷ use j to identify the attack path being computed
 7: while Q_g ≠ ∅ do                       ▷ when queue Q_g is not empty
 8:     n ← DEQUEUE(Q_g )                         ▷ remove fact node n
 9:     N_{1,r} ← child[n]              ▷ find a rule node as the child node of n
10:     if (color[N_{1,r}] ≡ WHITE) then  ▷ if the rule node is not traversed (white)
11:         j ← j+1                            ▷ must be a new attack path
12:         P_r[j] ← PATH(N_{1,r})  ▷ compute the cumulative false positive rate of the
        path
13:         color[N_{1,r}] ← BLACK                ▷ mark the rule node as black
14:     end if
15: end while

16: PATH(N_{1,r}) {                ▷ compute the false positive rate of an attack path
17:     N_{1,c} ← child[N_{1,r}]        ▷ consequence fact node of the first attack step
18:     E ← parents[N_{1,r}]             ▷ E is the evidence for the first attack step
19:     P[N_{1,c}] ← P(E|¬N_{1,r})        ▷ false positive rate of the first attack step
20:     color[E] ← BLACK                  ▷ mark all traversed evidence as black
21:     P_f ← P[N_{1,c}]                  ▷ use P_f to do the recursive computation
22:     for i ← 2 to n do           ▷ from the second attack step to the last attack step
23:         N_{i,r} ← child[N_{i-1,c}]           ▷ rule node as H of the i^{th} attack step
24:         N_{i,c} ← child[N_{i,r}]     ▷ consequence fact node of the i^{th} attack step
25:         E ← parents[N_{i,r}]               ▷ evidence for the i^{th} attack step
26:         P_f ← 1 − (1 − P_f) × (1 − P(E|¬N_{i,r}))        ▷ cumulative false positive rate
27:         color[E] ← BLACK                 ▷ mark all traversed evidence as black
28: end for
29: Return P_f       ▷ return the cumulative false positive rate of the attack path
```

system. The evidence in the case study constituted the logged events
and intrusion alerts.

By exploiting vulnerabilities in a Windows workstation and a web
server with access to the Database Server, the attacker was able to successfully launch two attacks on the Database Server and a cross-site
scripting (XSS) attack on the Administrator Workstation. The attacks
involve: (i) using a compromised workstation to access the Database

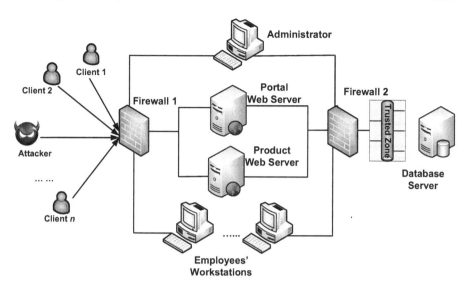

Figure 4. Experimental network.

Table 2. Evidence comprising logged events and alerts.

Timestamp	Source IP	Destination IP	Content	Vulnerability
08\13-12:26:10	129.174.124.122 Attacker	129.174.124.184 Workstation1	SHELLCODE x86 inc ebx NOOP	CVE-2009-1918
08\13-12:27:37	129.174.124.122 Attacker	129.174.124.185 Workstation2	SHELLCODE x86 inc ebx NOOP	CVE-2009-1918
08\13-14:37:27	129.174.124.122 Attacker	129.174.124.53 Product Web Server	SQL Injection Attempt	CWE89
08\13-16:19:56	129.174.124.122 Attacker	129.174.124.137 Administrator	Cross Site Scripting	XSS
08\13-14:37:29	129.174.124.53 Product Web Server	129.174.124.35 Database Server	name='Alice' AND password="alice' OR '1'='1'	CWE89
...	...	...	...	...

Server (CVE-2009-1918); (ii) exploiting a vulnerability in the web application (CWE89) in the Product Web Server to attack the Database Server; and (iii) exploiting the XSS vulnerability in the chat forum hosted by the Portal Web Server to steal the Administrator's session ID, enabling the attacker to send phishing emails to the clients and trick them to update their confidential information.

Table 3.   Post-attack evidence.

Timestamp	Attacked Computer	Attack Event	Post Attack Status
08\-14:37:29	129.174.124.35 Database Server	Information Retrieved Maliciously	Malicious Access
...	...	...	...

Observed Attack Events
1. attackGoal(execCode(workStation1, _)).
2. attackGoal(execCode(dbServer, user)).
3. attackGoal(execCode(clients, user)).

Network Topology
4. attackerLocated(internet).
5. hacl(internet, webServer, tcp, 80).
6. hacl(internet, workStation1, tcp, _).
7. hacl(webServer, dbServer, tcp, 3660).
8. hacl(internet, admin, _, _).
9. hacl(admin, clients, _, _).
10. hacl(workStation1, dbServer, _, _).

Computer Configuration
11. hasAccount(employee, workStation1, user).
12. networkServiceInfo(webServer, httpd, tcp, 80, user).
13. networkServiceInfo(dbServer, httpd, tcp, 3660, user).
14. networkServiceInfo(workStation1, httpd, tcp, 4040, user).

Information from Table 2 (Software Vulnerability)
15. vulExists(webServer, 'CWE89', httpd).
16. vulProperty('CWE89', remoteExploit, privEscalation).
17. vulExists(dbServer, 'CWE89', httpd).
18. vulProperty('CWE89', remoteExploit, privEscalation).
19. vulExists(workStation1, 'CVE-2009-1918', httpd).
20. vulProperty('CVE-2009-1918', remoteExploit, privEscalation).
21. timeOrder(webServer, dbServer, 14.3727, 14.3729).

Figure 5.   Input file for generating the logical evidence graph.

The logging system and intrusion detection system captured evidence of network attack activities. Table 2 presents the processed data. Table 3 presents the post-attack evidence obtained using forensic tools.

5.2   Constructing the Graph

To employ the Prolog-based rules for evidence graph construction, the evidence and system state were codified as instantiations of the rule predicates as shown in Figure 5. In Figure 5, Lines 1 through 3 model evidence related to the post-attack status (Table 3), Lines 4 through 10 model the network topology (system setup), Lines 11 through 14 model system configurations and Lines 15 through 21 model vulnerabilities obtained from the captured evidence (Table 2).

The input file with rules representing generic attack techniques was submitted to the reasoning system along with two databases, including an anti-forensic database [6] and MITRE's CVE [8], to remove irrelevant evidence and obtain explanations for any missing evidence.

The results are: (i) according to the CVE database, Workstation 2, which is a Linux machine using Firefox as the web browser, rendered an attack using CVE-2009-1918 unsuccessful because the exploit only succeeds on Windows Internet Explorer; (ii) a new attack path expressing that the attacker launched phishing attacks at the clients using the Administrator's stolen session ID was found; and (iii) an attack path between the compromised Workstation 1 and the Database Server was found.

The network forensic analysis tool created the logical evidence graph shown in Figure 6. The nodes in Figure 6 are described in Tables 4 and 5. The third column of each table lists the logical operators used to distinguish fact nodes, rule nodes and consequence fact nodes. A fact node is marked as LEAF, a rule node is marked as OR and a consequence fact node is marked as AND.

Figure 6 has three attack paths:

- The attacker used an XSS attack to steal the Administrator's session ID and obtain administrator privileges to send phishing emails to clients (Nodes: $11 \to 9 \to 8 \to 7 \to 6 \to 4 \to 3 \to 2 \to 1$) (Left).

- The attacker used a buffer overflow vulnerability (CVE-2009-1918) to compromise a workstation and then obtain access to the Database Server (Nodes: $34 \to 33 \to 32 \to 31 \to 30 \to 28 \to 18 \to 17 \to 16$) (Middle).

- The attacker used a web application that does not sanitize user input (CWE89) to launch a SQL injection attack at the Database Server (Nodes: $11 \to 24 \to 23 \to 22 \to 21 \to 19 \to 18 \to 17 \to 16$) (Right).

5.3 Computations

This section uses Algorithms 1 and 2 to compute $P(H|E_1, E_2, \cdots, E_n)$ and $P(E_1, E_2, \cdots, E_n|\neg H)$ for the attack paths in Figure 6 (H corresponds to $H_1 \cap H_2 \cdots \cap H_n$).

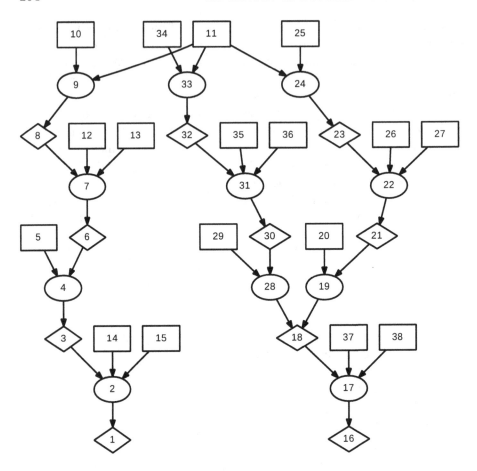

Figure 6. Constructed logical evidence graph.

Using Algorithm 1 to Compute $P(H|E1, E2..En)$. Algorithm 1 requires $P(N_{1,r})$, $P(N_{1,f})$, $P(N_{1,f}|N_{1,r})$, $P(N_{i,r})$, $P(N_{i-1,c}, N_{i,f}|N_{i,r})$, $P(N_{i-1,c}, N_{i,f})$ $(i = 2..n)$. All these probabilities are derived from expert knowledge. To minimize subjectivity, the average value of the probability based on the judgments of multiple experts should be computed [5]. Because the case study is intended to demonstrate the computations, for simplicity, all $P(H_i) = P(\neg H_i) = 50\%$, $P(E_i) = k \in [0,1]$ (k obviously would differ for different evidence in a real scenario). Also, the $P(E_i|H_i)$ values were assigned based on the judgment of the authors of this chapter; the probability values of $P(E_i|H_i)$ are listed in Table 6.

Table 4. Descriptions of the nodes in Figure 6.

Node	Notation	Relation
1	execCode(clients, user)	OR
2	THROUGH 3 (remote exploit of a server program)	AND
3	netAccess(clients, tcp, _)	OR
4	THROUGH 7 (multi-hop access)	AND
5	hacl(admin,clients, tcp, _)	LEAF
6	execCode(admin, apache)	OR
7	THROUGH 3 (remote exploit of a server program)	AND
8	netAccess(admin, tcp, 80)	OR
9	THROUGH 8 (direct network access)	AND
10	hacl(internet, admin, tcp, 80)	LEAF
11	attackerLocated(internet)	LEAF
12	networkServiceInfo(admin, httpd, tcp, 80, apache)	LEAF
13	vulExists(admin,'XSS', httpd, remoteExploit, privEscalation)	LEAF
14	networkServiceInfo(clients, httpd, tcp, _, user)	LEAF
15	vulExists(clients, 'Phishing', httpd, remoteExploit, privEscalation)	LEAF
16	execCode(dbServer, user)	OR
17	THROUGH 3 (remote exploit of a server program)	AND
18	netAccess(dbServer, tcp, 3660)	OR
19	THROUGH 7 (multi-hop access)	AND
20	hacl(webServer, dbServer, tcp, 3660)	LEAF
21	execCode(webServer, user)	OR
22	THROUGH 3 (remote exploit of a server program)	AND
23	netAccess(webServer, tcp, 80)	OR

Thus, $P(H_i|E_i)$ for each attack step without considering the other attack steps is given by:

$$\frac{P(H_i)P(E_i|H_i)}{P(E_i)} = \frac{0.5 \cdot P(E_i|H_i)}{k}$$

$$= \frac{P(E_i|H_i)}{2k} \qquad (8)$$

$$= c \cdot P(E_i|H_i)$$

Table 5. Descriptions of the nodes in Figure 6 (continued).

Node	Notation	Relation
24	THROUGH 8 (direct network access)	AND
25	hacl(internet, webServer, tcp, 80)	LEAF
26	networkServiceInfo(webServer, httpd, tcp, 80, user)	LEAF
27	vulExists(webServer, 'CWE89', httpd, remoteExploit, privEscalation)	LEAF
28	THROUGH 7 (multi-hop access)	AND
29	hacl(workStation1, dbServer, tcp, 3660)	LEAF
30	execCode(workStation1, user)	OR
31	THROUGH 3 (remote exploit of a server program)	AND
32	netAccess(workStation1, tcp, 4040)	OR
33	THROUGH 8 (direct network access)	AND
34	hacl(internet, workStation1, tcp, 4040)	LEAF
35	networkServiceInfo(workStation1, httpd, tcp, 4040, user)	LEAF
36	vulExists(workStation1, 'CVE-2009-1918', httpd, remoteExploit, privEscalation)	LEAF

where $c = \frac{1}{2k}$. Algorithm 1 is used to compute $P(H|E_1, E_2, \cdots E_n)$ as shown in the last column of Table 6.

Note that Node 17 has two joint posterior probabilities, which are from the middle path and right path, respectively. Note also that the middle attack path has a lower probability than the right attack path. This is because the attacker destroyed the evidence obtained from the middle path that involved using a compromised workstation to gain access to the database. Additionally, the $P(E|H)$ value is lower. Therefore, the corresponding hypothesized attack path has a much lower probability $P(H|E_1, E_2, \cdots, E_n)$. In reality, it is unlikely that the same attacker would attempt a different attack path to attack the same target if the previous attack had already succeeded. A possible scenario is that the first attack path was not anticipated, so the attacker attempted to launch the attack via the second attack path. The joint posterior probability $P(H|E_1, E_2, \cdots, E_n)$ could help an investigator select the most pertinent attack path.

Table 6. Computation of $P(H|E_1, \cdots, E_n)$ for the attack paths.

Attack Step	H1	Attack Step 1			H$_2$	Attack Step 2		
		$P(E_1|H_1)$	$P(H_1|E_1)$	$P(H|E_1)$		$P(E_2|H_2)$	$P(H_2|E_2)$	$P(H|E_1, E_2)$
Left	Node 9	0.90	0.90c	0.90c	Node 7	0.80	0.80c	$0.720c^2$
Middle	Node 33	0.99	0.99c	0.99c	Node 31	0.87	0.87c	$0.861c^2$
Right	Node 24	0.99	0.99c	0.99c	Node 22	0.85	0.85c	$0.842c^2$

Attack Step	H$_3$	Attack Step 3			H$_4$	Attack Step 4		
		$P(E_3|H_3)$	$P(H_3|E_3)$	$P(H|E_1, E_2, E_3)$		$P(E_4|H_4)$	$P(H_4|E_4)$	$P(H|E_1, E_2, E_3, E_4)$
Left	Node 4	0.90	0.90c	$0.648c^3$	Node 2	0.75	0.75c	$0.486c^4$
Middle	Node 28	0.87	0.87c	$0.750c^3$	Node 17	0.75	0.75c	$0.563c^4$
Right	Node 19	0.97	0.97c	$0.817c^3$	Node 17	0.95	0.95c	$0.776c^4$

Using Algorithm 2 to Compute $P(E_1, E_2, \cdots, E_n | \neg H)$. Algorithm 2 requires $P(N_{1,f} | N_{1,r})$ corresponding to $P(E_1 | \neg H_1)$ and $P(N_{i-1,c}, N_{i,f} | N_{i,r})$ corresponding to $P(E_i | \neg H_i)$ ($i = 2..n$) to recursively compute $P(E_1, E_2, \cdots, E_n | \neg H)$. As an example, $P(E_i | \neg H_i)$ was assigned to each attack step in the three attack paths and $P(E_1, E_2, \cdots, E_n | \neg H)$ was computed (Table 7). The results show that the right attack path has the smallest cumulative false positive estimate.

Values computed for $P(H | E_1, E_2, \cdots, E_n)$ and $P(E_1, E_2, \cdots, E_n | \neg H)$ show the beliefs in the three constructed attack paths given the collected evidence. The right attack path (Nodes: $11 \rightarrow 24 \rightarrow 23 \rightarrow 22 \rightarrow 21 \rightarrow 19 \rightarrow 18 \rightarrow 17 \rightarrow 16$) is the most convincing attack path because it has the largest $P(H | E)$ value and smallest $P(E | \neg H)$ value. The left attack path is not convincing because its joint posterior probability is less than $0.5c^4$. The middle path is not so convincing because it has a higher cumulative false positive rate, suggesting that the attack path should be re-evaluated to determine if it corresponds to a real attack scenario.

6. Conclusions

The principal contribution of this research is a method that automates the construction of a logical evidence graph using rules and mapping the graph to a Bayesian network so that the joint posterior probabilities and false positive rates corresponding to the constructed attack paths can be computed automatically. The case study demonstrates how the method can guide forensic investigators to identify the most likely attack scenarios that fit the available evidence. Also, the case study shows that the method and the companion tool can reduce the time and effort involved in network forensic investigations. However, the method cannot deal with zero-day attacks; future research will attempt to extend the underlying model to address this deficiency.

This paper is not subject to copyright in the United States. Commercial products are identified in order to adequately specify certain procedures. In no case does such an identification imply a recommendation or endorsement by the National Institute of Standards and Technology, nor does it imply that the identified products are necessarily the best available for the purpose.

References

[1] Argus Cyber Security Lab, MulVAL: A Logic-Based Enterprise Network Security Analyzer, Department of Computer Science and Engineering, University of South Florida, Tampa, Florida (www.arguslab.org/mulval.html), 2016.

Table 7. Computation of $P(E_1, E_2, \cdots, E_n | \neg H)$ for the attack paths.

Attack Step	H_1	Attack Step 1		H_2	Attack Step 2	
		$P(E_1|\neg H_1)$	$P(E_1|\neg H_1)$		$P(E_2|\neg H_2)$	$P(E_1, E_2|\neg H)$
Left	Node 9	0.002	0.002	Node 7	0.001	0.0030
Middle	Node 33	0.002	0.002	Node 31	0.003	0.0050
Right	Node 24	0.002	0.002	Node 22	0.001	0.0030

Attack Step	H_3	Attack Step 3		H	Attack Step 4	
		$P(E_3|\neg H_3)$	$P(E_1, E_2, E_3|\neg H)$		$P(E_4|\neg H_4)$	$P(E_1, E_2, E_3, E_4|\neg H)$
Left	Node 4	0.004	0.007	Node 2	0.030	0.0368
Middle	Node 28	0.003	0.008	Node 17	0.040	0.0477
Right	Node 19	0.002	0.005	Node 17	0.007	0.0120

[2] B. Carrier, A Hypothesis-Based Approach to Digital Forensic Investigations, Ph.D. Thesis, Department of Computer Science, CERIAS Tech Report 2006-06, Center for Education and Research in Information Assurance and Security, Purdue University, West Lafayette, Indiana, 2006.

[3] A. Darwiche, *Modeling and Reasoning with Bayesian Networks*, Cambridge University Press, Cambridge, United Kingdom, 2009.

[4] N. Fenton, M. Neil and D. Lagnado, A general structure for legal arguments about evidence using Bayesian networks, *Cognitive Science*, vol. 37(1), pp. 61–102, 2013.

[5] M. Kwan, K. Chow, F. Law and P. Lai, Reasoning about evidence using Bayesian networks, in *Advances in Digital Forensics IV*, I. Ray and S. Shenoi (Eds.), Springer, Boston, Massachusetts, pp. 275–289, 2008.

[6] C. Liu, A. Singhal and D. Wijesekara, A logic-based network forensic model for evidence analysis, in *Advances in Digital Forensics XI*, G. Peterson and S. Shenoi (Eds.), Springer, Heidelberg, Germany, pp. 129–145, 2015.

[7] Y. Liu and H. Man, Network vulnerability assessment using Bayesian networks, *Proceedings of SPIE*, vol. 5812, pp. 61–71, 2005.

[8] MITRE, Common Vulnerabilities and Exposures, Bedford, Massachusetts (`cve.mitre.org`), 2016.

[9] B. Olshausen, Bayesian Probability Theory, Redwood Center for Theoretical Neuroscience, Helen Wills Neuroscience Institute, University of California at Berkeley, Berkeley, California, 2004.

[10] X. Ou, W. Boyer and M. McQueen, A scalable approach to attack graph generation, *Proceedings of the Thirteenth ACM Conference on Computer and Communications Security*, pp. 336–345, 2006.

[11] J. Pearl, Fusion, propagation and structuring in belief networks, *Artificial Intelligence*, vol. 29(3), pp. 241–288, 1986.

[12] F. Taroni, A. Biedermann, P. Garbolino and C. Aitken, A general approach to Bayesian networks for the interpretation of evidence, *Forensic Science International*, vol. 139(1), pp. 5–16, 2004.

[13] F. Taroni, S. Bozza, A. Biedermann, G. Garbolino and C. Aitken, *Data Analysis in Forensic Science: A Bayesian Decision Perspective*, John Wiley and Sons, Chichester, United Kingdom, 2010.

[14] C. Vlek, H. Prakken, S. Renooij and B. Verheij, Modeling crime scenarios in a Bayesian network, *Proceedings of the Fourteenth International Conference on Artificial Intelligence and Law*, pp. 150–159, 2013.

IV

CLOUD FORENSICS

Chapter 11

API-BASED FORENSIC ACQUISITION OF CLOUD DRIVES

Vassil Roussev, Andres Barreto and Irfan Ahmed

Abstract   Cloud computing and cloud storage services, in particular, pose new challenges to digital forensic investigations. Currently, evidence acquisition for these services follows the traditional method of collecting artifacts residing on client devices. This approach requires labor-intensive reverse engineering effort and ultimately results in an acquisition that is inherently incomplete. Specifically, it makes the incorrect assumption that all the storage content associated with an account is fully replicated on the client. Additionally, there is no current method for acquiring historical data in the form of document revisions, nor is there a way to acquire cloud-native artifacts from targets such as Google Docs.

This chapter introduces the concept of API-based evidence acquisition for cloud services, which addresses the limitations of traditional acquisition techniques by utilizing the officially-supported APIs of the services. To demonstrate the utility of this approach, a proof-of-concept acquisition tool, kumodd, is presented. The kumodd tool can acquire evidence from four major cloud drive providers: Google Drive, Microsoft OneDrive, Dropbox and Box. The implementation provides command-line and web user interfaces, and can be readily incorporated in established forensic processes.

Keywords: Cloud forensics, cloud drives, API-based acquisition

1.   Introduction

Cloud computing is emerging as the primary model for delivering information technology services to Internet-connected devices. It abstracts away the physical computing and communications infrastructure, and enables customers to effectively rent (instead of own and maintain) as much infrastructure as needed. According to NIST [14], cloud computing has five essential characteristics that distinguish it from previous

© IFIP International Federation for Information Processing 2016
Published by Springer International Publishing AG 2016. All Rights Reserved
G. Peterson and S. Shenoi (Eds.): Advances in Digital Forensics XII, IFIP AICT 484, pp. 213–235, 2016.
DOI: 10.1007/978-3-319-46279-0_11

service models: (i) on-demand self service; (ii) broad network access; (iii) resource pooling; (iv) rapid elasticity; and (v) measured service.

The underpinning technological development that has made the cloud possible is the massive adoption of virtualization on commodity hardware systems. Ultimately, this allows for a large pool of resources, such as a data center, to be provisioned and load-balanced at a fine granularity, and for the computations of different users (and uses) to be strongly isolated.

The first public cloud services – Amazon Web Services (AWS) – were introduced by Amazon in 2006. According to a 2015 report by RightScale [18], cloud adoption has become ubiquitous: 93% of businesses are experimenting with cloud deployments, with 82% adopting a hybrid strategy that combines the use of multiple providers (usually in a public-private configuration). Nonetheless, much of the technology transition is still ahead, as 68% of enterprises have less than 20% of their application portfolios running in cloud environments. Gartner [8] predicts that another two to five years will be needed before cloud computing reaches the "plateau of productivity" [9], heralding a period of mainstream adoption and widespread productivity gains.

Meanwhile, cloud forensics is in its infancy. Few practical solutions exist for the acquisition and analysis of cloud evidence, and most of them are minor adaptations of traditional methods and tools. Indeed, NIST, the principal standardization body in the United States, is still attempting to build consensus on the challenges involved in performing forensics of cloud data. A recent NIST report [14] identifies 65 separate challenges involved in cloud forensics.

This research focuses on a specific problem – the acquisition of data from cloud storage services. Cloud storage services are extremely popular, with providers such as Google Drive, Microsoft OneDrive, Dropbox and Box offering consumers between 2 GB and 15 GB of free cloud storage. Cloud storage is also widely used by mobile devices to share data across applications that are otherwise isolated from each other. Therefore, a robust evidence acquisition method is a necessity. Additionally, due to the wide variety of cloud storage services and the rapid introduction of new services, evidence acquisition methods and tools should be adaptable and extensible.

In traditional forensic models, an investigator works with physical evidence containers such as storage media or integrated embedded devices such as smartphones. In these scenarios, it is easy to identify the processor that performs the computations as well as the media that store traces of the computations, and to physically collect, preserve and analyze the relevant information content. As a result, research has focused on discovering and acquiring every little piece of log and timestamp information, and extracting every last bit of discarded data that applications and the operating system leave behind.

Conceptually, cloud computing breaks this model in two major ways. First, resources such as CPU cycles, RAM and secondary storage are pooled (e.g., RAID storage) and then allocated at a fine granularity. This results in physical media that usually contain data owned by many users. Additionally, data relevant to a single case can be spread across numerous storage media and (potentially) among different providers responsible for different layers in the cloud stack. Applying the conventional model introduces several procedural, legal and technical problems that are unlikely to have an efficient solution in the general case. Second, computations and storage records are ephemeral because virtual machine (VM) instances are continually created and destroyed and working storage is routinely sanitized.

As discussed in the next section, cloud storage forensics treats the problem as just another instance of application forensics. It applies basic differential analysis techniques [7] to gain an understanding of the artifacts present on client devices by taking before and after snapshots and deducing the relevant cause and effect relationships. During an actual investigation, an analyst would be interpreting the state of the system based on these known relationships.

Unfortunately, there are several problems with the application of existing client-side methods:

- **Completeness:** The reliance on client-side data can exclude critical case data. An example is the selective replication of cloud drive data, which means that a client device may not have a local copy of all the stored data. As usage grows – Google Drive already offers up to 30 TB of storage – this will increasingly be the typical situation.

- **Correctness and Reproducibility:** It is infeasible to reverse engineer all the aspects of an application's functionality without its source code; this immediately calls into question the correctness of the analysis. Furthermore, cloud storage applications on a client are updated frequently with new features introduced on a regular basis. This places a burden on cloud forensics to keep up the reverse engineering efforts, making it harder to maintain the reproducibility of analyses.

- **Cost and Scalability:** Manual client-side analysis is burdensome and does not scale with the rapid growth and the variety of services (and service versions).

This chapter presents an alternative approach for acquiring evidence from cloud storage services by leveraging the official APIs provided by the services. This approach, which eliminates the need for reverse engineering, has the following conceptual advantages:

- APIs are well-documented, official interfaces through which cloud applications on a client communicate with services. They tend to change slowly and any changes are clearly marked; new features may be incorporated incrementally in an acquisition tool.

- It is easy to demonstrate completeness and reproducibility using an API specification.

- Web APIs tend to follow patterns, which makes it possible to adapt existing code to a new (similar) service with modest effort. It is often practical to write an acquisition tool for a completely new service from scratch in a few hours.

To demonstrate the feasibility of the approach and to gain firsthand experience with the acquisition process, a proof-of-concept tool named `kumodd` has been developed. The tool can perform complete (or partial) acquisition of cloud storage account data. It works with four popular services, Google Drive, Microsoft OneDrive, Dropbox and Box, and supports the acquisition of revisions and cloud-only documents. The prototype is written in Python and offers command line and web-based user interfaces.

2.   Related Work

This section summarizes essential cloud terminology and discusses related work.

2.1   Cloud Computing

The National Institute of Standards and Technology (NIST) [14] defines cloud computing as "a model for enabling ubiquitous, convenient, on-demand network access to a shared pool of configurable computing resources (e.g., networks, servers, storage, applications and services) that can be rapidly provisioned and released with minimal management effort or service provider interaction." With respect to public cloud services – the most common case – this means that the physical hardware on which computations take place is owned and maintained by the provider, and is, thus, part of the deployed software stack. Generally, customers have the option to pay per unit of CPU, storage and network use, although other business arrangements are also possible.

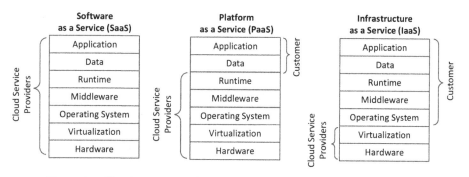

Figure 1. Cloud service models and ownership of layers (public cloud).

Cloud computing services are commonly classified into three canonical models: (i) software as a service (SaaS); (ii) platform as a service (PaaS); and infrastructure as a service (IaaS). In practice, the distinctions are often not clear cut and practical information technology cloud solutions – and potential investigative targets – may incorporate elements of all three canonical models. As illustrated in Figure 1, it is useful to decompose a cloud computing environment into a stack of layers (from low to high): (i) hardware; (ii) virtualization (consisting of a hypervisor that enables the installation of virtual machines); (iii) operating system (installed on each virtual machine); (iv) middleware; (v) runtime environment; (vi) data; and (vii) application.

Depending on the deployment scenario, different layers may be managed by different parties. In a private deployment, the entire stack is hosted by the owner and the overall forensic picture is very similar to that of a non-cloud information technology target. Data ownership is clear, as are the legal and procedural paths to obtain the data; indeed, the very use of the term "cloud" is mostly immaterial to forensics.

In a public deployment, the SaaS/PaaS/IaaS classification becomes important because it defines the ownership and management responsibilities over data and services (Figure 1). In hybrid deployments, layer ownership can be split between the customer and the provider and/or across multiple providers. Furthermore, this relationship may change over time; for example, a customer may handle the base load on an owned infrastructure, but burst to the public cloud to handle peak demand or system failures.

Due to the wide variety of deployment scenarios, the potential targets of cloud forensics can vary widely. Thus, the most productive approach for developing practical solutions is to start with specific (but common) cases and, over time, attempt to incorporate an expanding range. The focus of this discussion is the forensics of cloud drive services, starting with the acquisition process.

2.2 Cloud Drive Forensics

The concept of a "cloud drive" is closely related to network filesystem shares and is almost indistinguishable from versions of the i-drive (Internet drive) that were popular the late 1990s. The main difference is that of scale – today, wide-area network (WAN) infrastructures have much higher bandwidth, which makes real-time file synchronization much more practical. Also, there are many more providers, most of which build their services in top of third-party IaaS offerings such as AWS.

Over the last few years, a number of forensic researchers have worked on cloud drives. Chung et al. [1] analyzed four cloud storage services (Amazon S3, Google Docs, Dropbox and Evernote) in search of traces left on client systems that could be used in criminal cases. They reported that the analyzed services may create different artifacts depending on specific features of the services and proposed a forensic investigative process for cloud storage services based on the collection and analysis of artifacts of cloud storage services recovered from client systems. The process involves gathering volatile data from a Mac or Windows system (if available) and then retrieving data from the Internet history, log files and directories. In the case of mobile devices, Android phones are rooted to collect data and iTunes is used to obtain information for iPhones (e.g., backup iTunes files). The objective was to check for traces of a cloud storage service in the collected data.

Hale [11] analyzed the Amazon Cloud Drive and discusses the digital artifacts left behind after an Amazon Cloud Drive account has been accessed or manipulated from a computer. Two methods may be used to manipulate an Amazon Cloud Drive Account: one is via the web application accessible using a web browser and the other is via a client application from Amazon that can be installed on the system. After analyzing the two methods, Hale found artifacts of the interface in the web browser history and cache files. Hale also found application artifacts in the Windows registry, application installation files in default locations and a SQLite database for tracking pending upload/download tasks.

Quick and Choo [16] discuss the artifacts left behind after a Dropbox account has been accessed or manipulated. Using hash analysis and keyword searches, they attempted to determine whether the client software provided by Dropbox had been used. This involved extracting the account username from browser history (Mozilla Firefox, Google Chrome and Microsoft Internet Explorer) and pursuing avenues such as directory listings, prefetch files, link files, thumbnails, registry, browser history and memory captures. In a follow-up work, Quick and Choo [17] used a similar conceptual approach to analyze the client-side operation and artifacts of Google Drive and provide a useful starting point for investigators.

Martini and Choo [13] have researched the operation of ownCloud, a self-hosted file synchronization and sharing solution. As such, it occupies a slightly different niche because it is much more likely for the client and server sides to be under the control of the same person or organization. Martini and Choo were able to recover several artifacts, including sync and file management metadata (logging, database and configuration data), cached files describing the files the user stored on the client device and uploaded to the cloud environment or vice versa, and browser artifacts.

Outside of forensics, there has been some interest in analyzing the implementation of cloud drive services. An example is the work by Drago et al. [3, 4]. However, its focus was on performance and networking issues, and, although the results are interesting, their application to forensic practice is very limited.

2.3   Forensic Uses of Cloud Service APIs

Huber et al. [12] were among the first to utilize cloud service APIs as part of the forensic process. However, their main goal was to provide a context for an investigation by acquiring a snapshot of the social network of the investigative target via the Facebook Graph API.

With regard to commercial tools, Cloud Data eXplorer from ElcomSoft [6] offers the ability to acquire (via a service API) user artifacts from Google accounts, including profile information, messages, contacts and search history. However, no facilities are available to acquire cloud drive data, nor is there any support for services other than Google.

2.4   Summary

Previous work on cloud storage forensics has primarily focused on adapting the traditional application forensics approach to finding client-side artifacts. This involves blackbox differential analysis, where before and after images are created and compared to deduce the essential functions of the application. Clearly, the effectiveness of this approach depends on the comprehensiveness of the tests performed on a target system; ultimately, it is nearly impossible to enumerate all the eventualities that may have affected the state of an application. The process involves a labor-intensive reverse engineering effort, which requires sub-

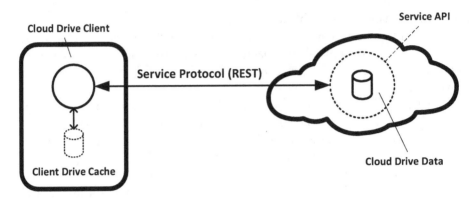

Figure 2. Cloud drive service architecture.

stantial human resources. Nevertheless, as discussed in the next section, the biggest limitation of client-side forensics is that it cannot guarantee the complete acquisition of cloud drive data.

3. Rationale for API-Based Acquisition

This section discusses the limitations of client-side acquisition and the benefits of API-based acquisition.

3.1 Limitations of Client-Side Acquisition

The fundamental limitation of client-side acquisition of cloud data is that it is an acquisition-by-proxy process. In other words, although it resembles traditional acquisition from physical media, the method does not target the authoritative source of the data, namely the cloud service. As illustrated in Figure 2, client content is properly viewed as a cached copy of cloud-hosted data. This simple fact has crucial implications for forensic acquisition.

Partial Replication. The most obvious problem is that there is no guarantee that any of the clients attached to an account have a complete copy of the cloud drive content. As a point of reference, Google Drive currently offers up to 30 TB of online storage (at a monthly cost of $10/TB) whereas Amazon offers unlimited storage at $60/year. As data accumulates, it will become impractical to maintain complete replicas of all devices. Indeed, based on current trends, it is likely that most users will not have a single device containing a complete copy of the data. From the forensic perspective, direct access is needed to cloud drive metadata to ascertain its contents. The alternative, blindly relying on client cache, would result in an inherently incomplete acquisition with unknown gaps.

Revisions. Most drive services provide some form of revision history; the lookback period varies from 30 days to unlimited revision history depending on the service and subscription terms. This new source of valuable forensic information has few analogs in traditional forensic targets (e.g., Volume Shadow Copy service on Windows), but forensic investigators are not yet familiar with this evidentiary source. Revisions reside in the cloud and clients rarely have anything but the most recent versions in their caches. Thus, a client-side acquisition will miss prior revisions and will not even know that they are missing.

Cloud-Native Artifacts. Due to the wholesale movement to web-based applications, the digital forensics community must learn to handle a new problem – digital artifacts that do not have serialized representations in local filesystems. For example, Google Docs documents are stored locally as links to the documents that can only be edited via a web application. Acquiring an opaque link, by itself, is borderline useless – it is the content of the document that is of primary interest. It is often possible to obtain a usable snapshot of the web application artifact (e.g., in PDF), but this can only be accomplished by requesting it from the service directly; again, this cannot be accomplished by an acquisition-by-proxy process.

To summarize, the brief examination in this section reveals that the client-side approach to drive acquisition has major conceptual flaws that are beyond remediation. Clearly, what is needed is a different method that can obtain data directly from the cloud service.

3.2 Benefits of API-Based Acquisition

Fortunately, cloud services provide a front door – an API – to directly acquire cloud drive content. In broad terms, a cloud drive provides a storage service similar to that of a local filesystem; specifically, it enables the creation and organization of user files. Therefore, its API loosely resembles that of the filesystem API provided by the local operating system. Before the technical details of the proof-of-concept tool are described, it is necessary to make the case that the use of the API is forensically sound.

The main issue to address is that an API-based approach results in a logical – not physical– evidence acquisition. Traditionally, it has been an article of faith that obtaining data at the lowest possible level of abstraction results in the most reliable evidence. The main rationale is that the logical view of the data may not be forensically complete because data marked as deleted is not shown. Also, a technically-sophisticated adversary may be able to hide data from the logical view. Until a few years ago, this view would have been reasonably justified.

However, it is important to periodically examine the accepted wisdom in order to account for new technological developments. It is outside the scope of this chapter to make a more general argument, but it should be noted that solid-state drives (SSDs) and even newer generations of high-capacity hard drives resemble autonomous storage computers rather than the limited peripherals of ten or more years ago. Some of them contain ARM processors and execute complex load-balancing and wear-leveling algorithms, which include background data relocation. Although they support, for example, block-level access, the results do not directly map to physical data layouts; this makes the acquired images logical, rather than physical. To obtain (and make sense of) a truly low-level representation of the data would increasingly require hardware blackbox reverse engineering. More than likely, this would lead to the wider acceptance of *de facto* logical acquisition as forensically sound.

In the case of cloud forensics, the case for adopting API-mediated acquisition is simple and unambiguous. According to Figure 2, the client component of the cloud drive (that manages the local cache) utilizes the exact same interface to perform its operations. Thus, the service API is the lowest available level of abstraction and is, therefore, appropriate for forensic processing. Furthermore, the metadata of individual files often include cryptographic hashes of their contents, which provide strong integrity guarantees during acquisition.

The service APIs (and the corresponding client software development kits for different languages) are officially supported by providers and have well-defined semantics and detailed documentation; this allows for a formal and precise approach to forensic tool development and testing. In contrast, blackbox reverse engineering can never achieve provable perfection. Similarly, acquisition completeness guarantees can only be achieved via an API – the client cache contains an unknown fraction of the content.

Finally, software development is almost always easier and cheaper than reverse engineering followed by software development. The core of the prototype tool described in this chapter is less than 1,600 lines of Python code (excluding the web-based GUI) for four services. An experienced developer could easily add a good-quality driver for a new (similar) service in a day or two, including test code. The code needs to be updated infrequently as providers strive to provide continuity and

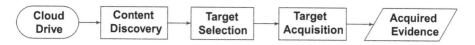

Figure 3. Acquisition phases.

backward compatibility; any relevant additions to the API can easily be identified and adopted incrementally.

4. Tool Design and Implementation

Conceptually, acquisition involves three core phases: (i) content discovery; (ii) target selection; (iii) and target acquisition (Figure 3). During content discovery, the acquisition tool queries the target and obtains a list of artifacts (files) along with their metadata. In a baseline implementation, this can be reduced to enumerating all the available files; in an advanced implementation, the tool may leverage the search functionality provided by the API (e.g., Google Drive). During the selection process, the list of targeted artifacts can be filtered by automated means or by soliciting user input. The result is a (potentially prioritized) list of targets that is passed to the tool for acquisition.

Traditional approaches largely short-circuit this process by attempting to blindly acquire all the available data. However, this "acquire first, filter later" approach is not sustainable for cloud targets – the amount of data could be enormous and the available bandwidth could be up to two orders of magnitude less than the local storage.

The kumodd prototype described in this chapter is designed to be a minimalistic tool for research and experimentation that can also provide a basic practical solution for real cases. In fact, kumodd has been made as simple as possible to facilitate its integration with the existing toolset. Its basic function is to acquire a subset of the content of a cloud drive and place it in an appropriately-structured local filesystem tree.

4.1 Architecture

The kumodd tool is split into several modules and three logical layers: (i) dispatcher; (ii) drivers; and (iii) user interface (Figure 4). The dispatcher is the central component, which receives parsed user requests, relays them to the appropriate driver and returns the results. The drivers (one for each service) implement the provider-specific protocols via the respective web APIs. The tool provides two interfaces, a command-line interface (CLI) and a web-based GUI.

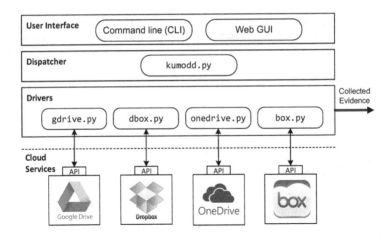

Figure 4. kumodd architecture.

4.2   Command-Line Interface

The general format of kumodd commands is:

python kumodd.py -s [service] [action] [filter]

The [service] parameter specifies the target service. Currently, the supported options are gdrive, dropbox, onedrive and box corresponding to Google Drive, Dropbox, Microsoft OneDrive and Box, respectively.

The [action] argument instructs kumodd on the action to be performed on the target drive:

- -l lists stored files as a plaintext table.

- -d downloads files subject to the [filter] specification.

- -csv <file> downloads the files specified by <file> in CSV format.

The -p <path> option is used to specify the path to which the files should be downloaded (and override the default, which is relative to the current working directory).

The [filter] parameter specifies the subset of files to be listed or downloaded based on file type: all (all files present); doc (Microsoft Office/Open Office document files: .doc/.docx/.odf), xls (spreadsheet files), ppt (PowerPoint presentation files); text files (text/source code); and pdf files.

In addition, some general groups of files can be specified: `officedocs` (all document, spreadsheet and PowerPoint presentation files); `image` (all image files); `audio` (all audio files); and `video` (all video files). Some example commands are:

- List all the files stored in a Dropbox account:

  - `python kumodd.py -s dbox -l all`

- List the images stored in a Box account:

  - `python kumodd.py -s box -l image`

- Download the PDF files stored in a Microsoft OneDrive account to the Desktop folder:

  - `python kumodd.py -s onedrive -d all -l -p /home/ user/Desktop/`

- Download the files listed in `gdrive_list.csv` from Google Drive:

  - `python kumodd.py -s gdrive -csv /home/user/Desktop/ gdrive_list.csv`

User Authentication. All four services use the OAuth2 (`oauth.net/ 2`) protocol to authenticate a user and to authorize access to an account. When `kumodd` is used for the first time to connect to a cloud service, the respective driver initiates the authorization process, which requires the user to authenticate with the appropriate credentials (username/password). The tool provides the user with a URL that must be opened in a web browser, where the standard authentication interface for the service requests the relevant username and password.

The process for using Google Drive is as follows:

```
[title=Authentication Step 1: connect to \emph{Google Drive}]
kumo@ubuntu:~/kumodd$ python kumodd.py -s gdrive -d all
Your browser has been opened to visit:
https://accounts.Google.com/o/oauth2/auth?scope=
https%3A%2F%2Fwww.www.Googleapis.com...
    ...
```

Figure 5 shows the authentication steps: provide account credentials (left) and authorize application (right). After supplying the correct credentials and authorizing the application, the service returns an access code that the user must input in the command line to complete the authentication and authorization processes for the account. If the authentication is successful, the provided access token is cached persistently in

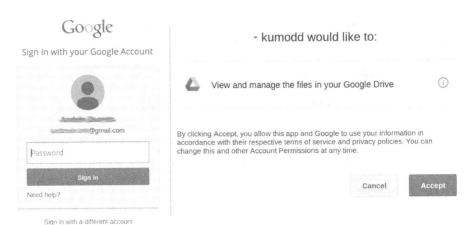

Figure 5.   Authentication steps.

```
[caption=Sample processing output (with cached authorization token),
   label=lst:auth4]
kumo@ubuntu:~/kumodd$ python kumodd.py -s gdrive -d all
Working...
TIME(UTC) APPLICATION  USER FILE-ID REMOTE PATH REVISION LOCAL PATH
   HASH(MD5)
2015-06-25 03:48:43.600028 kumodd-1.0 example.dev@gmail.com
   1L-7o0rgPT2f6oX600PtF4ZUFOmOJW1Crktr3DPril8o My Drive/ppt test
   v.2 downloaded/example.dev@gmail.com/My Drive/ppt test -
2015-06-25 03:48:44.951131 kumodd-1.0 example.dev@gmail.com
   1huaRTOudVnLe4SPMXhMRnNQ9Y_DUr69m4TEeD5dIWuA My Drive/revision doc
   test v.3 downloaded/example.dev@gmail.com/My Drive/revision doc
   test -
...
2015-06-25 03:48:54.254104 kumodd-1.0 example.dev@gmail.com
   OB4wSliHoVUbhUHdhZlF4NlR5c3M My Drive/test folder/stuff/more stuff/
   tree.py v.1 downloaded/example.dev@gmail.com/My Drive/test folder/
   stuff/more stuff/tree.py 61366435095ca0ca55e7192df66a0fe8
9 files downloaded and 0 updated from example.dev@gmail.com drive
Duration: 0:00:13.671442
```

Figure 6.   Sample processing output (with cached authorization token).

a `.dat` file saved in the `/config` folder with the name of the service. Future requests will find the token and will not prompt the user for credentials (Figure 6).

Content Discovery. In the current implementation, content discovery is implemented by the `list` (`-l`) command, which acquires the file

```
[caption=List of all files in a \emph{Google Drive} account
   (trimmed),label={lst:gdrive-ls}]
andres@ubuntu:~/kumodd$ python kumodd.py -s gdrive -l all
Working...
FILE-ID REMOTE PATH REVISION HASH(MD5)
...1qCepBpY6Nchklplqqqc My Drive/test 1 -
...oVUbhaG5veSO3UkJiU1U My Drive/version_test 3 ...bcdee370e5
...
...oVUbhUHdhZ1F4N1R5c3M My Drive/test folder/stuff/more stuff/
   tree.py ...2df66a0fe8
```

Figure 7. List of all files in a Google Drive account (trimmed).

metadata from the drive. As with most web services, the response is in the JSON format; the amount of attribute information varies based on the provider and can be quite substantial (e.g., Google Drive). Since it is impractical to show all the output, the kumodd list command provides an abbreviated version with the most essential information formatted as a plaintext table (Figure 7). The rest is logged as a CSV file in the /localdata folder with the name of the account and service.

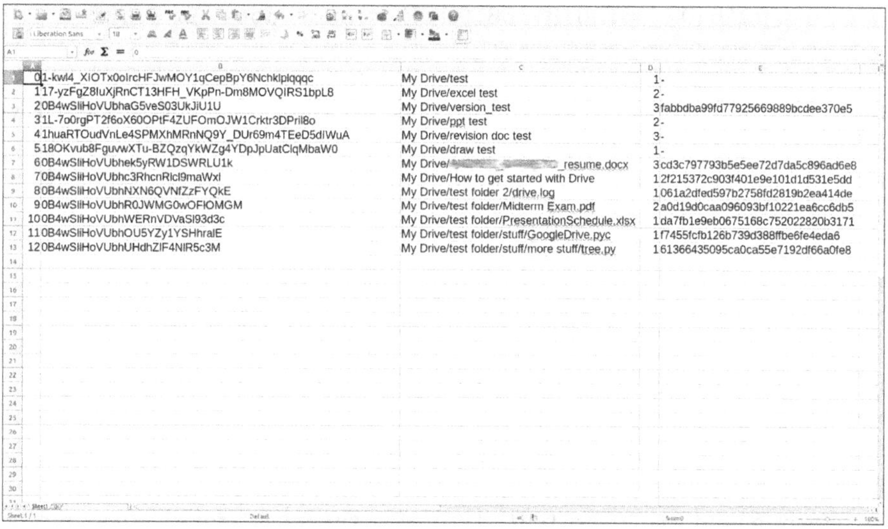

Figure 8. Contents of the generated CSV file.

The stored output can be processed interactively using a spreadsheet program (Figure 8) or using Unix-style command line tools, thereby enabling a subsequent selective and/or prioritized acquisition.

Acquisition. As discussed above, the acquisition is performed by the download command (-d) and can be performed as a single discovery-and-acquisition step or it can be targeted by providing a list of files using the -csv option.

A list of downloaded files is displayed with information such as download date, application version, username, file ID, remote path, download path, revisions and cryptographic hashes. This information is also logged in the file /downloaded/<username>/<service-name>.log. Downloaded files are located in the /downloaded/<username>/ directory. The complete original metadata files with detailed information about the downloaded files is stored in /downloaded/<username>/meta data/ in the JSON format.

Revisions: The tool automatically enumerates and downloads all the revisions of the files selected for acquisition. The number of available revisions can be previewed as part of the file listing (Figure 8). During the download, the filenames of the individual revisions are generated by prepending the revision timestamp to the base filename. The filenames can be viewed using the regular file browser:

```
(2015-02-05T08:28:26.032Z) resume.docx    8.4kB
(2015-02-08T06:31:58.971Z) resume.docx    8.8kB
```

Arguably, other naming conventions are also possible, but the ultimate solution likely requires a user interface similar to the familiar file browser, but which also understands the concept of versioning and allows an analyst to trace the history of individual documents and obtain snapshots of a drive at particular points in time.

Cloud-Native Artifacts (Google Docs): A new challenge presented by the cloud is the emergence of cloud-native artifacts – data objects that have no serialized representation on local storage and, by extension, cannot be acquired by a proxy. Google Docs is the primary service considered in this work; however, the problem readily generalizes to many SaaS/web applications. A critical difference between native applications and web applications is that the code for the latter is dynamically downloaded at runtime and the persistent state of artifacts is stored back in the cloud. Thus, the serialized form of the data (usually in JSON) is an internal application protocol that is not readily rendered by a standalone application.

In the case of Google Docs, the local Google Drive cache contains only a link to the online location, which creates a problem for forensics. Fortunately, the API offers the option to produce a snapshot of the

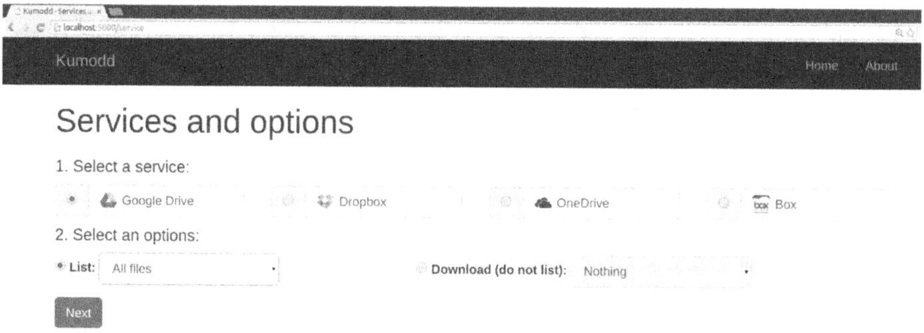

Figure 9. Web-based GUI: Service selection.

document/spreadsheet/presentation in several standard formats [10], including text, PDF and MS Office. At present, `kumodd` automatically downloads PDF snapshots of all Google Docs encountered during acquisition. Although this is a better solution than merely cloning the link from the cache, forensically-important information is lost because the internal artifact representation contains the complete editing history of the document. This problem is discussed later in the chapter.

4.3   Web-Based GUI

The `kumodd` tool provides an interactive web-based GUI that is designed to be served by a lightweight local web server. The GUI is started using the `kumodd-gui.py` module:

```
[title=Starting the web GUI]
python kumodd-gui.py
kumo@ubuntu:~/kumodd$ python kumodd-gui.py
* Running on http://127.0.0.1:5000/ (Press CTRL+C to quit)
* Restarting with stat
```

After starting the server, the `kumodd` web-based GUI becomes available at `localhost:5000` and is accessible via a web browser. Note that, at this stage, the server should only be run locally; however, with some standard security measures, it could be made available remotely.

The web module employs the same drivers used with the command line application for authentication, discovery and acquisition. Its purpose is to simplify user interactions. For the simple case of wholesale data acquisition, the process can be accomplished in three button clicks.

After pressing the Get Started! button, the user is presented with the choice of the target service and the action to perform (Figure 9). After this step, a detail window presents a list of files and the option of choosing the files to be downloaded (Figure 10). After the files are

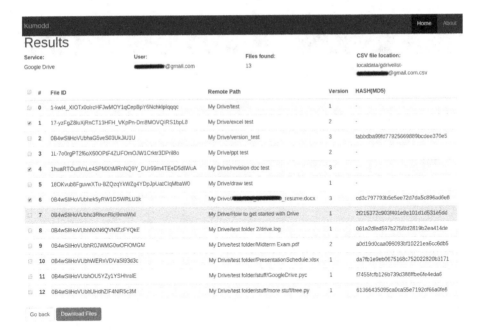

Figure 10.   Web-based GUI: Target selection.

Figure 11.   Web-based GUI: Acquisition results.

selected, a results screen presents the paths to the files and other relevant information (Figure 11). Note that every step of the process is also shown on the terminal.

4.4   Validation

To validate the tool, accounts were created with all the services and known seed files. Using the normal web interface for the respective

Table 1. **kumodd** download times and throughput.

Service	Average time (mm:ss)	Throughput (MB/s)
Google Drive	17:22	1.01
OneDrive	18:21	0.95
Dropbox	17:00	1.03
Box	18:22	0.95
Average	17:46	0.98

service, revisions were created and several Google Docs artifacts were created for Google Drive. A complete acquisition was performed using **kumodd** and the cryptographic hashes of the targets were compared. In all cases, successful acquisitions of all revisions were completed and snapshots were obtained of the cloud-only artifacts.

To obtain a sense of the acquisition rates, 1 GiB of data was split and stored in 1,024 files of 1 MiB each. The data was sourced from the Linux pseudorandom number generator to eliminate the potential influence of behind-the-scenes compression or de-duplication. The preliminary tests, which used the campus network, measured the throughput at different times of the day over a period of one week. No consistent correlations were observed.

To eliminate potential constraints stemming from the local-area network and Internet service provider infrastructure, the experiments were moved to Amazon EC2 instances (US-West, Northern California). For each of the four supported services, complete acquisition jobs were executed for seven days at 10:00 AM (PDT) in order to approximate daytime acquisition. Table 1 shows the average download times and throughput.

The Amazon EC2 results were entirely consistent with the on-campus results, which also averaged around 1 MB/s. The most likely explanation is that the bottleneck was caused by bandwidth throttling on the part of the cloud drive provider. It would appear that, at the free level, 1 MB/s is the implied level of service (at least for third-party applications).

5. Discussion

Several issues arose during the research and experimentation.

Integrity Assurance. An issue of concern is that not all services provide cryptographic hashes of file content as part of the metadata. In the experiments, this includes Dropbox (one of the largest providers), which only provides a "rev" attribute that is guaranteed to be unique and is referred to as a "hash" in the API documentation [5]. However, the generating algorithm is unknown and the observed values are much too short (they fit in 64 bits) to be of cryptographic quality. However, it is known that, as of 2011, Dropbox was using SHA256 on 4 MiB blocks for backend de-duplication that, along with an incorrect implementation, led to the Dropship attack [2]. It is also known that the same provider uses cryptohashes to prevent the sharing of files for which it has received DMCA notices [15]. Therefore, providing a cryptohash for data object content would be a reasonable requirement for any cloud API used for forensic purposes.

Pre-Acquisition Content Filtering. One aspect not addressed in this work is the need to provide access to the search capability built into many of the more advanced services. This would allow triage and exploration with zero pre-processing overhead; some services also provide preview images that could be used for this purpose. Even with the current implementation, it is possible to filter data in/out by cryptohashes without the overhead of computing them.

Multi-Service Management and Forward Deployment. Cloud storage is a *de facto* commodity business with numerous providers vying for consumer attention. Thus, a number of cloud storage brokers have emerged to help users manage multiple accounts and optimize their services (often at the free level). For example, Otixo supports 35 different services and facilitates data movement among them. Forensic software needs similar capabilities to support cloud forensics.

In the near term, solutions that can be forward-deployed on a cloud provider infrastructure will be required. This will become necessary as cloud data grows much faster than the available bandwidth in a wide-area network, making full remote acquisitions impractical. The kumodd web interface is a sketch of such a solution; the forensic virtual machine instance could be co-located in the same data center as the target while the investigator controls it remotely. In this scenario, forensic analysis could begin immediately while the data acquisition could be performed in the background.

Long-Term Preservation of Cloud-Native Artifacts. It is mentioned above that Google Docs data objects are very different from most serialized artifacts that are familiar to analysts [19]. The most substantial difference is that the latter are snapshots of the states of artifacts whereas the former is literally a log of user edit actions since the creation of the document. This presents a dilemma for forensics. Should a snapshot be acquired in a standard format such as PDF (like `kumodd`) and, thereby, lose all historical information? Or should the `changelog` be acquired and, thus, be dependent on the service provider (Google) to render it at any point in the future? Since neither option on its own is satisfactory, future research will attempt to develop a third option that will maintain the log and replay it independently of the service provider.

6. Conclusions

This research has three principal contributions. The first is a new acquisition model. It is clear that cloud drive acquisition cannot be performed on a client in a forensically-sound manner. This is because the client is not guaranteed to mirror all the data and has no facilities to represent file revisions and the content of cloud-native artifacts. The proper approach is to go directly to the source – the master copy maintained by the cloud service – and acquire the data via the API. In addition to being the only means for guaranteeing a forensically-complete copy of the target data, the API approach supports the reproducibility of results, rigorous tool testing (based on well-defined API semantics) and triage of the data (via hashes and/or search APIs). The overall development effort is significantly lower because the entire blackbox reverse engineering component of client-centric approaches is eliminated. As a reference, each of the four drivers for the individual services contains between 232 and 620 lines of Python code.

The second contribution is a new acquisition tool. The `kumodd` tool can perform cloud drive acquisition from four major providers: Google Drive, Microsoft OneDrive, Dropbox and Box. Although its primary purpose is to serve as a research platform, the hope is that it will quickly evolve into a reliable, open-source tool that will cover an expanding range of cloud services.

The third contribution is the elicitation of new research questions. This research has identified certain problems that must be addressed by the digital forensics community. In particular, it is necessary to develop a means for extracting, storing and replaying the history of cloud-native artifacts such as Google Docs. Additionally, a mechanism is needed to ensure the integrity of the data acquired from all providers. Moreover, it is necessary to build tools that can handle multi-service cases and operate in forward deployment scenarios.

Finally, it is hoped that this research will stimulate a new approach to cloud forensics and that it will serve as a cautionary note that simply extending client-side forensics holds little promise. Over the short term, this will mean expending extra effort to develop a new toolset. Over the medium-to-long term, the emphasis on logical acquisition – which this work promotes – will help realize much greater levels of automation in the acquisition and processing of forensic targets.

References

[1] H. Chung, J. Park, S. Lee and C. Kang, Digital forensic investigation of cloud storage services, *Digital Investigation*, vol. 9(2), pp. 81–95, 2012.

[2] D. DeFelippi, Dropship (`github.com/driverdan/dropship`), 2016.

[3] I. Drago, E. Bocchi, M. Mellia, H. Slatman and A. Pras, Benchmarking personal cloud storage, *Proceedings of the ACM Internet Measurement Conference*, pp. 205–212, 2013.

[4] I. Drago, M. Mellia, M. Munafo, A. Sperotto, R. Sadre and A. Pras, Inside Dropbox: Understanding personal cloud storage services, *Proceedings of the ACM Internet Measurement Conference*, pp. 481–494, 2012.

[5] Dropbox, Core API Best Practices, San Francisco, California (`www.dropbox.com/developers/core/bestpractices`), 2016.

[6] ElcomSoft, ElcomSoft Cloud eXplorer, Moscow, Russia (`www.elcomsoft.com/ecx.html`), 2016.

[7] S. Garfinkel, A. Nelson and J. Young, A general strategy for differential forensic analysis, *Digital Investigation*, vol. 9(S), pp. S50–S59, 2012.

[8] Gartner, Gartner's 2014 hype cycle for emerging technologies maps the journey to digital business, Stamford, Connecticut (`www.gartner.com/newsroom/id/2819918`), August 11, 2014.

[9] Gartner, Gartner Hype Cycle, Stamford, Connecticut (`www.gartner.com/technology/research/methodologies/hype-cycle.jsp`), 2016.

[10] Google, Drive, Mountain View, California (`developers.google.com/drive`), 2016.

[11] J. Hale, Amazon Cloud Drive forensic analysis, *Digital Investigation*, vol. 10(3), pp. 295–265, 2013.

[12] M. Huber, M. Mulazzani, M. Leithner, S. Schrittwieser, G. Wondracek and E. Weippl, Social snapshots: Digital forensics for online social networks, *Proceedings of the Twenty-Seventh Annual Computer Security Applications Conference*, pp. 113–122, 2011.

[13] B. Martini and R. Choo, Cloud storage forensics: ownCloud as a case study, *Digital Investigation*, vol. 10(4), pp. 287–299, 2013.

[14] P. Mell and T. Grance, The NIST Definition of Cloud Computing, NIST Special Publication 800-145, National Institute of Standards and Technology, Gaithersburg, Maryland, 2011.

[15] K. Orland, Dropbox clarifies its policy on reviewing shared files for DMCA issues, *Ars Technica*, March 30, 2014.

[16] D. Quick and R. Choo, Dropbox analysis: Data remnants on user machines, *Digital Investigation*, vol. 10(1), pp. 3–18, 2013.

[17] D. Quick and R. Choo, Google Drive: Forensic analysis of data remnants, *Journal of Network and Computer Applications*, vol. 40, pp. 179–193, 2014.

[18] RightScale, RightScale 2015 State of the Cloud Report, Santa Barbara, California (`assets.rightscale.com/uploads/pdfs/Right Scale-2015-State-of-the-Cloud-Report.pdf`), 2015.

[19] V. Roussev and S. McCulley, Forensic analysis of cloud-native artifacts, *Digital Investigation*, vol. 16(S), pp. S104–S113, 2016.

Chapter 12

THE CLOUD STORAGE ECOSYSTEM – A NEW BUSINESS MODEL FOR INTERNET PIRACY?

Raymond Chan, Kam-Pui Chow, Vivien Chan and Michael Kwan

Abstract   Cloud storage, also known as "one-click file hosting," is the easiest method to share files. It enables users to upload any files without providing any information or installing any software. This chapter discusses the development of the cloud storage ecosystem before and after the Megaupload case of 2012. The roles and relationships of the key contributors in the cloud storage ecosystem are highlighted. Also, the manner in which the key contributors generate revenue is discussed and revenue estimates are provided based on Internet traffic data and domain information.

Keywords: Cloud storage ecosystem, file sharing, business model

1.   Introduction

Cloud storage is widely used to share files that infringe copyright laws. Downloading files from cloud storage sites does not expose IP address information to parties other than the cloud storage provider. Hence, some cloud storage sites encourage users to upload and share files by paying them rewards [7]. To receive these rewards, cloud storage users upload their files to various public forums and encourage other users to download them. The greater the number of downloads from the shared links, the greater the income earned by the file uploaders. P2P file sharing networks do not have a financial reward component, which is why increasing numbers of users are sharing files using cloud storage.

In January 2012, the Megaupload cloud storage site was shut down by the United States in collaboration with New Zealand and Hong Kong [5]. It was estimated that Megaupload was making millions dollars in profits

© IFIP International Federation for Information Processing 2016
Published by Springer International Publishing AG 2016. All Rights Reserved
G. Peterson and S. Shenoi (Eds.): Advances in Digital Forensics XII, IFIP AICT 484, pp. 237–255, 2016.
DOI: 10.1007/978-3-319-46279-0_12

at the time. The charges against Megaupload included money laundering, racketeering and copyright infringement [13].

The Megaupload shutdown does not appear to have had a major impact on the cloud storage business. A 2014 report, Good Money Gone Bad, commissioned by the Digital Citizen Alliance [3], details how huge amounts of advertising revenue are earned by cloud storage sites as well as by other service providers (including P2P sites) that facilitate file sharing that involves copyright infringement. Clearly, increasing numbers of businesses – legal, dodgy and illegal – are leveraging cloud storage for their operations. However, it appears that there have been some observable changes in the cloud storage ecosystem after the 2012 Megaupload case. This chapter discusses the cloud storage ecosystem and the recent changes in the ecosystem. It highlights the roles and relationships of the key contributors in the ecosystem. Also, it discusses the manner in which key contributors generate income in the ecosystem and estimates their revenue using Internet traffic data and domain information.

2.   Cloud Storage Ecosystem

Cloud storage or one-click file hosting provided by entities such as MEGA, Rapidshare and Mediafire offer rapid and convenient methods for uploading and sharing files. A user uploads a file to cloud storage and the cloud storage provider generates a uniform resource locator (URL) that contains meta-information about the shared file. The uploader then disseminates the URL to other users who are interested in downloading the file. Compared with earlier file sharing methods, such as FTP and P2P networks, cloud storage services provide tremendous availability, flexibility and anonymity to uploaders [1]. Moreover, file uploaders do not need to stay online in order to share files.

Uploading and Sharing Links.   To upload a file, the file owner selects a cloud storage website. The website displays a file upload button to upload files. The user then chooses the file to upload and presses the upload button, upon which the file is submitted to the cloud storage site. The website then generates a unique download URL on the screen for the user to copy and share with others. A user who receives the URL can download the file directly. Some cloud storage sites also provide a URL to the uploader for deleting the file. Depending on the popularity of the file, the download URL and file are deleted after a certain period of time.

Ecosystem Changes.   In 2011, Megaupload was ranked first in the top-ten list of file-sharing hosts, eight of them cloud storage sites [14].

This shows the popularity of cloud storage sites in 2011. According to Mahanti et al. [8], before the shutdown of Megaupload in 2012, the cloud storage ecosystem primarily comprised two major contributors: (i) file hosting cloud storage service providers; and (ii) linker sites providing search services to users. Mahanti et al. concluded that one of the drivers of file hosting service growth was the incentive schemes run by cloud storage providers such as Megaupload to attract uploaders to provide copyright-infringing content to increase traffic. This was also a key allegation against Megaupload in the 2012 U.S. Department of Justice indictment [5].

Following the indictment, Megaupload appears to have lost millions of users. One possibility is that the users moved to other file sharing technologies such as BitTorrent. Another is that they subscribed to other cloud storage sites. A piracy analysis study by Price [11] reports that the number of BitTorrent users increased 3.6% in 2013 compared with 2011. On the other hand, the number of cloud storage users decreased 7.7% in 2013 compared with 2011, which appears to be a direct result of the Megaupload case.

Despite the downward trend in the use of cloud storage sites for file sharing soon after the Megaupload shutdown in 2012, cloud storage has become a huge market on the Internet with increasing profits. According to a 2014 report commissioned by Digital Citizens Alliance [4], the most profitable cloud storage site had annual profits of $17.6 million. In order to increase cloud storage business, the cloud storage ecosystem reacted quickly to the law enforcement actions against Megaupload. The following trends have been observed:

- **Change in Operation Mode:** Ad-link shortening services now hide the original file download links. Also, social media platforms remove the ad-link shortening links that are shared by file uploaders on social media.

- **Uploading to Multiple Sites:** Since the file links at cloud storage sites expire after a period of time, it is now common practice for uploaders to upload files to multiple cloud storage sites so that, when a file link on one cloud storage system expires, a number of active links persist at other cloud storage sites. This resilience feature enables uploaders to continue to operate after cloud storage sites are shut down by law enforcement.

- **Premium Downloading Without Subscriptions:** According to a 2014 report by NetNames [4], a major portion of the income (70%) of cloud storage sites comes from premium accounts. Indeed, premium account subscriptions are a proven gold mine for

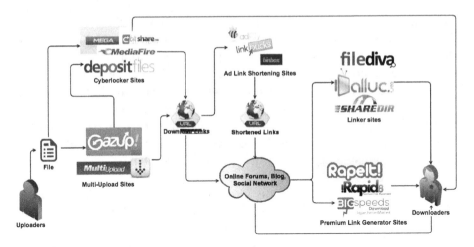

Figure 1. New cloud storage ecosystem.

cloud storage sites. In order to reap profits, premium link generator sites allow downloaders to enjoy premium services for free with no restrictions on downloading. The sites earn revenue from advertisers based on the number of premium users and/or their usage. The sites also provide resilient services to downloaders to enable them to operate after cloud storage sites are shut down by law enforcement.

The observations above indicate that the types of contributors in the cloud storage ecosystem have increased from two to five after the Megaupload case. The three new contributors to the ecosystem are: (i) ad-link shortening sites; (ii) multi-upload sites; and (iii) premium link generator sites. The entry of these new contributors appears to be a direct result of the Megaupload case.

Figure 1 presents the new cloud storage ecosystem. The major components of the ecosystem are:

- **Leader/Central Contributor:** The leader serves as a "hub" without which other ecosystem members would not be able to survive in the ecosystem [9].

    - **Cloud Storage Sites:** These sites provide free or premium file hosting services to uploaders.

- **Users:** Users are important entities in the ecosystem. There would be no business ecosystem without users. There are two types of users:

- **Uploaders:** These users actively provide content to cloud storage sites and publicize the content through various means.

- **Downloaders:** These users download content from cloud storage sites through various means.

- **Contributors:** These interdependent entities contribute to the growth of the business ecosystem and actively work on platforms provided by the ecosystem leader [9]. The contributor entities in a cloud storage ecosystem include:

  - **Linker Sites:** These sites provide indexing services for downloaders to search for files hosted on cloud storage sites.

  - **Ad-Link Shortening Sites:** These sites provide URL shortening and redirect services to convert cloud storage links before uploaders post them in public forums and blogs.

  - **Multi-Upload Sites:** These sites provide services for uploaders to upload a given file to multiple cloud storage sites.

  - **Premium Link Generator Sites:** These sites provide services for downloaders who do not wish to subscribe to premium accounts, but wish to download files without any restrictions.

3.   Related Work

In September 2014, the Digital Citizens Alliance commissioned Net-Names to study the revenue model of cloud storage providers. The study [4] estimated that the top-30 cloud storage sites had annual revenue amounting to $96.2 million. Similarly, another report commissioned by Digital Citizens Alliance in February 2014 [3] noted that a huge amount of advertising income was generated by BitTorrent sites, linker sites, cloud storage sites and streaming sites. However, these reports only estimated the advertising income and subscription income generated by cloud storage sites and linker sites; they did not consider the multiplicative effect of the other contributors in the cloud storage ecosystem mentioned above.

Discussions of cloud storage revenue models usually focus on the advertising income and subscription income generated by cloud storage sites and linker sites [7]. However, the studies largely overlook the revenue generated by the entire cloud storage ecosystem. This chapter describes the revenue models of the five contributors described in the previous section.

4.   Cloud Storage Ecosystem Revenue Model

This section describes the dataset used in the study and the cloud storage ecosystem revenue model and its components.

4.1   Dataset

This study has drawn on data from a number of public sources. The selection of sites corresponding to the different contributors in the cloud storage ecosystem was based on the research team's knowledge and decade-long experience in digital forensics and Internet piracy.

- **Web Traffic Data:**
    - **Unique Page Views:** This data was collected from Alexa Internet, a web traffic data analysis company owned by Amazon, that collects data on browsing behavior. The Alexa ranking is one of the most important indices of the browsing behavior of Internet users.
    - **Number of Unique Visitors:** This data was collected from SiteWorthTraffic, an online web service that estimates website value. SiteWorthTraffic provides the unique page views of websites drawn from web traffic analysis sources.

- **Coud Storage Ecosystem Sites:**
    - **Leader/Central Contributor Sites:** The top-ten cloud storage sites were selected based on the experience of frequent users of cloud storage sites.
    - **Contributor Sites:**
        * **Linker Sites:** The top-ten sites were selected based on results provided by search engines.
        * **Ad-Link Shortening Sites:** The top-five sites were selected based on user input.
        * **Multi-Upload Sites:** The top-ten sites were selected based on results provided by search engines.
        * **Premium Link Generator Sites:** The top-ten sites were selected based on information in web forums and results provided by search engines.

4.2   Leader/Central Contributor Revenue Model

In general, cloud storage sites operate using the "freemium" business model [6], the most common Internet service business model. In this model, a service provider offers limited services free-of-charge and provides extra features and capacity for a fee. Numerous Internet services utilize cloud storage and provide a number of features to generate revenue. The current cloud storage ecosystem presented in Figure 1 shows that users share cloud storage files using various online services. This section provides details of the cloud storage business model and how services leverage cloud storage to generate revenue.

The two main mechanisms for generating revenue are advertisements and premium services:

- **Advertisements:** Advertisements are a major source of revenue for cloud storage sites. When a user browses a file to be downloaded, the website typically displays a number of advertisements on the screen. If the user does not have a premium account, the cloud storage site may require the user to wait for a few minutes (to check out the advertisements) before clicking the download button. Users are also encouraged to upload and share files; the greater the number of download URLs generated and published, the greater the likelihood that users will visit the download pages. Advertising companies place ads on cloud storage download pages frequented by large numbers of users. The Alexa ranking provides useful web traffic data that can be used to estimate advertising revenue. Based on the web traffic and daily page view information, it is possible to estimate the popularity of cloud storage sites and the average advertisement revenue, and to compute the monthly advertisement revenue generated by cloud storage sites. The current value of the cost per 1,000 impressions (CPM) is around $3 [12]. In estimating the advertising revenue, a cloud storage site is assumed to join one advertisement service and one advertisement banner is displayed on each download page. Thus, the advertising service will pay the site $3 per 1,000 (= 0.003) unique page views:

$$Monthly\ Ad\ Revenue = 0.003 \times Unique\ Page\ Views\ per\ Month \tag{1}$$

- **Premium Accounts:** Premium accounts are also a major source of revenue for cloud storage sites. Like Dropbox, Google Drive and Apple iCloud, cloud storage sites provide massive amounts of storage to users who register for premium accounts. Premium users also receive much more benefits and functionality than non-paying users. These include more online storage, uploads of files of unlimited size and downloads of multiple files simultaneously, without speed limits and with the download links being preserved forever. Since advertising revenue depends on the popularity of a site and user activity, the revenue is unpredictable. Therefore, it is important for cloud storage sites to encourage users to sign up for premium services. This provides stable income while incentivizing premium users to keep using the services. According to SiteWorth-Traffic, MEGA had 1,647,489 unique visitors per month and, as of July 2014, had one million registered users. Based on these statistics, the estimated number of registered users at a cloud storage site can be assumed to be 60.69% (= 1,000,000 ÷ 1,647,489) of the unique visitors:

$$Registered\ Users = 0.6069 \times Unique\ Visitors \qquad (2)$$

In a news article [10], MEGA's Founder Kim Dotcom said that, in a freemium model, conversion rates of free users to paid users are in the range of 1% to 5%. A cloud storage site provides free storage to registered users and provides more storage and faster download speeds if they pay a fee. Using the average free-to-paid user conversion rate of 3% (= 0.03), the number of premium users is given by:

$$Premium\ Users = 0.03 \times Registered\ Users \qquad (3)$$

MEGA claimed to have one million registered users as of July 2014. Therefore, according to Equation (3), it had 30,000 paid users at that time. Based on MEGA's price schedule, these users would have paid MEGA between \$352,393 to \$1,165,800 per month.

4.3   Contributor Revenue Models

As mentioned above, there are four major contributors in a cloud storage ecosystem: (i) linker site; (ii) ad-link shortening site; (iii) multi-upload site; and (iv) premium link generator site. The following are the revenue models of the four major contributors:

- **Linker Sites:** Typical cloud storage sites do not provide a file search feature. This new business opportunity is exploited by cloud storage indexing sites, also known as linker sites. Like web search engines, these sites index cloud storage links collected from web forums, blogs and social networks. They enable users to search for files, access file links and download the files without having to obtain the links from the file uploaders.

  One of the largest linker sites is FileTube (`www.filestube.com`). It indexes files maintained at more than 60 cloud storage sites and encourages users to report new links to increase the size of the file link database. A "meta linker" site, Filediva (`www.filediva.com`), enables users to search for and retrieve files from multiple linker sites. Clearly, linker sites have significantly increased the popularity of cloud storage sites.

- **Ad-Link Shortening Sites:** Many file uploaders do not share their cloud storage links directly. Instead, they use an ad-link shortening service to convert (i.e., help hide) their actual cloud storage links before they post them on public forums and blogs. A file downloader needs to access a shortened link before accessing the real cloud storage download link. This enables the uploader to earn additional advertising income by sharing the shortened link. A popular URL shortening service is AdFly (`adf.ly`), which enables uploaders to earn $4 per 1,000 clicks.

  A similar service is provided by URL sharing sites that share files like cloud storage sites, but allow users to input any text content and generate links for sharing the content. Binbox (`binbox.io`) is a popular link sharing service, which enables registered users to earn $5 per 1,000 clicks and to password-protect the links that are shared in web forums and social networks. URL sharing sites are becoming increasingly popular; they protect the content to be shared and can be used to disseminate secret messages. In many data leakage cases, hackers share passwords or email addresses using these services. Hence, uploaders not only earn income from pay-per-downloads provided by cloud storage sites, but also earn income from pay-per-clicks provided by ad-link shortening sites. Even if a user does not download a file completely, an uploader still earns revenue from the shortened link.

- **Multi-Upload Sites:** Multi-upload sites provide all-in-one uploading services. A file that is uploaded to a multi-upload site is automatically sent to multiple cloud storage sites. The download links from the various cloud storage sites are provided to the user to share the file. The multi-loading functionality enables file persistence – until all the file download links are removed, it is possible for users to access and download the file. An example is MultiUpload (`multiupload.biz`), which uploads a file to 21 cloud storage sites with just one click. As in the case of a linker site, a multi-upload site increases the content on a cloud storage site and increases the web traffic as well.

- **Premium Link Generator Sites:** Premium link generator sites provide special services for users who do not wish to subscribe to premium accounts, but still desire to download files without any restrictions. These sites operate by purchasing and then using a number of premium accounts at many cloud storage sites. A user who wishes to download a file, copies and pastes the cloud storage file link at the premium link generator site. The premium link generator site downloads the file using its premium account and forwards the downloaded file to the user. As in the case of a proxy server, the speed of forwarding a file is faster than a free download from a cloud storage site.

Another approach is for a user to register a premium account with a premium link generator site. The user can then download files without speed restrictions from multiple cloud storage sites; the user saves money because it is not necessary to set up premium accounts at any of the cloud storage sites. Rapid8 (`rapid8.com`) is a popular premium link generator site, which enables users to obtain premium access to more than 45 cloud storage sites. Premium link generator sites earn revenue by displaying advisements and asking users to donate their premium accounts to provide better services.

5.   Results and Analysis

This section summarizes the results based on traffic data collected in September 2014.

5.1   Leader/Central Contributor Revenue

In a 2012 press release [5], the U.S. Department of Justice asserted that Megaupload had about 150 million registered users and generated more than \$175 million in criminal proceeds. Approximately \$150 million came from premium users while the remaining \$25 million was online advertising revenue.

The fundamental question is how a cloud storage site can earn so much revenue. To answer this question, this research attempts to estimate the revenue earned by a cloud storage site based on web traffic popularity, advertisements and number of premium users. The number of premium users is estimated based on the number of unique visitors and the advertisement revenue is estimated from the number of unique page views. Finally, the monthly and annual revenue estimates of a cloud storage site are computed.

Table 1. Ranks and unique page views/month for cloud storage sites.

Cloud Storage	Rank	Unique Page Views
Mediafire	201	149,945,280
Rapidgator	580	52,434,480
MEGA	624	49,424,670
Turbobit	968	31,417,350
Bitshare	1,402	21,691,860
Sendspace	1,858	16,368,150
Freakshare	2,152	14,131,980
Depositfiles	2,541	12,137,340
Uploadable	2,564	11,754,690
Rapidshare	3,081	9,782,220

Page Views. Traffic data for the study was collected from Alexa and SiteWorthTraffic. A unique page view is defined as a single user viewing a webpage one or more times. A unique visitor is a single user who visits a website one or more times. Unique page views and unique visitors are important measures of website popularity. Cloud storage sites provide this statistical information to advertising companies to encourage them to place ads on their webpages.

Data provided by Alexa and SiteWorthTraffic (as of September 2014) was used to estimate the popularity of cloud storage sites and the number of cloud storage site users. Table 1 presents the estimated unique page views per month for ten major cloud storage sites. The results indicate that Mediafire is the most popular cloud storage site based on Alexa data. Although Mediafire is popular in the United States, the result is unexpected. Upon reflection, it appears that Mediafire's popularity may stem from the fact that it does not remove a download URL unless the associated file is reported as infringing a copyright. As a result, numerous users trust Mediafire and prefer to use it to share normal files; this generates more web traffic at Mediafire than at other cloud storage sites.

Premium Account Revenue. The numbers of registered users and premium account users estimated using Equations (2) and (3), respectively, were used to compute the revenue from premium accounts. Specifically, the equations stipulate that 60.69% of the unique visitors are registered users and 3% are premium users. Based on these approximate percentages, the numbers of unique visitors to the targeted cloud storage sites were used to estimate the numbers of registered users and premium users. Table 2 presents the results. In the case of Mediafire,

Table 2.   Estimates of cloud storage site users.

Cloud Storage	Unique Visitors	Registered Users	Premium Users
Mediafire	1,666,059	1,666,059	30,333
MEGA	1,647,489	1,647,489	29,995
Rapidgator	582,606	353,583	10,607
Turbobit	349,082	211,857	6,355
Bitshare	241,021	146,275	4,388
Sendspace	181,868	110,375	3,311
Freakshare	157,022	95,296	2,858
Depositfiles	134,859	81,845	2,455
Uploadable	130,608	79,266	2,377
Rapidshare	108,691	65,964	1,978

the estimates are 1,666,059 registered users, 30,333 of them premium users.

Table 3.   Estimates of monthly revenue from premium users.

Cloud Storage	Premium Users	Fee	Revenue
MEGA	29,995	$38.86	$1,165,605.70
Mediafire	30,333	$24.99	$758,021.67
Rapidshare	1,978	$129.58	$256,309.24
Rapidgator	10,607	$12.99	$137,784.93
Sendspace	3,311	$19.99	$66,186.89
Bitshare	4,388	$9.99	$43,836.12
Turbobit	6,355	$6.66	$42,324.30
Uploadable	2,377	$12.99	$30,877.23
Depositfiles	2,455	$11.95	$29,337.25
Freakshare	2,858	$9.99	$28,551.42

Table 3 shows the monthly premium user revenue estimates for ten major cloud storage sites. The monthly subscription fee of each site was used to estimate its monthly revenue. The results indicate that, although only 3% of the registered users are premium users, significant amounts of revenue are drawn from the users' desire to maintain cloud storage services.

On average, cloud storage sites earn $255,883.48 in revenue each month. Because the system architectures of the cloud storage sites are not known, the costs of maintaining their large-scale content distribution networks are not known and it is not clear whether or not their monthly revenues cover their operational costs. Regardless, cloud storage sites cannot rely on premium account subscriptions to maintain sol-

Table 4. Monthly advertisement revenue estimates.

Cloud Storage	Unique Page Views	Ad Revenue
Mediafire	149,945,280	$449,835.84
Rapidgator	52,434,480	$157,303.44
MEGA	49,424,670	$148,274.01
Turbobit	31,417,350	$94,252.05
Bitshare	21,691,860	$65,075.58
Sendspace	16,368,150	$49,104.45
Freakshare	14,131,980	$42,395.94
Depositfiles	12,137,340	$36,412.02
Uploadable	11,754,690	$35,264.07
Rapidshare	9,782,220	$29,346.66

vency. Clearly, they need other revenue sources to continue to operate, let alone thrive.

Advertisement Revenue Estimates. This section estimates the revenue that a cloud storage site can earn based on unique page views. The advertisement revenue of each cloud storage site is estimated using Equation (1).

Table 4 shows the advertisement revenue estimates of ten major cloud storage sites based on the unique page view data provided by SiteWorth-Traffic. Clearly, large numbers of unique page views are important to cloud storage sites. Sites that encourage more user to access their download pages can earn more ad revenue. Additionally, cloud storage sites can cooperate with online advertising companies to collect and analyze user behavior and produce targeted ads. For example, music ads could be displayed when a user accesses an MP3 file download page. In fact, cloud storage sites also monetize the data collected about user behavior by selling it to marketing companies; this can be a substantial and stable source of income. To increase this type of revenue, some cloud storage sites entice users by offering substantial storage space and attractive pay-per-download and premium referral schemes.

Cloud Storage Site Revenue Estimates. Table 5 presents the estimated monthly premium user revenue and monthly advertisement revenue. MEGA earned $1,313,879.71 per month or $15,766,556.52 annually. MEGA's predecessor, Megaupload, earned about $175 million in net income over seven years; in contrast, MEGA's revenue is estimated to be around $110,383,560 over seven years. Obviously, MEGA could

Table 5. Total monthly revenue estimates.

Cloud Storage	Premium Revenue	Ad Revenue	Revenue	Ratio
MEGA	$1,165,605.70	$148,274.01	$1,313,879.71	89%
Mediafire	$758,021.67	$449,835.84	$1,207,857.51	63%
Rapidgator	$137,784.93	$157,303.44	$295,088.37	47%
Rapidshare	$256,309.24	$29,346.66	$285,655.90	90%
Turbobit	$42,324.30	$94,252.05	$136,576.35	31%
Sendspace	$66,186.89	$49,104.45	$115,291.34	57%
Bitshare	$43,836.12	$65,075.58	$108,911.70	40%
Freakshare	$28,551.42	$42,395.94	$70,947.36	40%
Uploadable	$30,877.23	$35,264.07	$66,141.30	47%
Depositfiles	$29,337.25	$36,412.02	$65,749.27	45%

earn much more than Megaupload because it will likely have more users and provide more sophisticated storage services in the near future.

On average, cloud storage sites earn $366,609.88 in monthly revenue. Cloud storage sites that cooperate with advertising and marketing companies earn substantially more revenue.

In general, cloud storage sites earn revenue via two methods. The first is by displaying advertisements and selling user behavior data. The second is from free subscriptions. Cloud storage sites encourage frequent visitors to create accounts for additional features, which means more user behavior data can be collected and sold. Also, attractive pay-per-download schemes encourage uploaders to share files to attract more visitors and potential subscribers. More visitors increases the web traffic and popularity of cloud storage sites, which enable them to earn more ad income and data sales revenue.

As seen in Table 5, most of the revenue comes from premium account subscriptions, with some cloud storage sites (e.g., MEGA and Rapidshare) having more than 89% of their revenue coming from premium accounts. Premium users generally want much larger storage space, faster download speeds and/or higher pay-per-download rates. Some cloud storage sites also implement referral schemes that provide incentives to premium users when they get other users to sign on to premium accounts. A referral can earn as much as 20% of the initial subscription fee for the premium service [2]. In summary, this business model makes cloud storage sites one of the most successful and financially-rewarding Internet services.

Table 6. Monthly revenue estimates for linker sites.

Linker Site	Rank	Unique Page Views	Revenue
4shared	296	101,820,960	$305,462.88
Alluc	9,739	3,094,680	$9,284.04
Filediva	31,651	974,400	$2,923.20
Filesloop	39,037	900,810	$2,702.43
Keep2Share	37,508	822,240	$2,466.72
Filetram	43,574	697,950	$2,093.85
mega-search.me	47,763	636,720	$1,910.16
Sharedir	67,156	448,800	$1,346.40
Filesdeck	86,259	439,380	$1,318.14
rapid-search-engine	101,050	298,260	$894.78

5.2   Contributor Revenue

This section presents the monthly revenue estimates of the contributors in the cloud storage ecosystem.

Linker Site Revenue. Table 6 presents the monthly revenue estimates for ten major linker sites. Note that FilesTube, one of the largest linker sites, recently shut down its search engine; for this reason, FilesTube is not included in the table. The table reveals that 4shared has the largest monthly advertisement revenue, primarily because 4shared is a linker site that also provides traditional cloud storage services. When 4share's revenue is excluded, linker sites have an average monthly advertisement revenue of around $2,771.08. The average revenue is considerable because linker sites do not have to implement large file storage systems. All they require is a search engine that collects and provides download links for cloud storage files.

Table 7. Monthly revenue estimates for ad-link shortening sites.

Ad-Link Shortening Site	Rank	Unique Page Views	Revenue
AdFly	164	189,208,590	$567,625.77
Linkbucks	1,035	29,798,070	$89,394.21
Adfoc	6,661	4,565,670	$13,697.01
Binbox	7,285	4,137,120	$12,411.36
Shorte.st	8,593	3,589,080	$10,767.24

Ad-Link Shortening Site Revenue. Table 7 presents the monthly revenue estimates for five major ad-link shortening sites. The data re-

Table 8.   Monthly revenue estimates for multi-upload sites.

Multi-Upload Site	Rank	Unique Page Views	Revenue
mirrorcreator	2,381	12,952,950	$38,858.85
embedupload	9,280	3,277,170	$9,831.51
go4up	21,247	1,431,360	$4,294.08
mirrorupload	38,431	791,340	$2,374.02
uploadseeds	48,184	625,500	$1,876.50
multfile	65,647	469,800	$1,409.40
uploadmirrors	66,519	457,200	$1,371.60
multiupfile	82,031	361,620	$1,084.86
exoshare	99,959	308,550	$925.65
multiupload.biz	216,555	146,460	$439.38

veals remarkable numbers of unique page views per month. Of particular interest is AdFly. AdFly draws its revenue entirely from advertisements. Still, it earns around $567,625 a month, which is more than the revenue that most cloud storage sites earn from premium users.

Multi-Upload Site Revenue.   Table 8 presents the monthly revenue estimates for ten major multi-upload sites. The average monthly revenue for the multi-update sites is $6,246.59. Compared with the other types of contributors, multi-upload sites have the lowest maintenance costs because they only need to make available the uploading APIs provided by cloud storage sites.

Table 9.   Monthly revenue estimates for premium link generator sites.

Premium Link Generator	Rank	Unique Page Views	Revenue
premiumleech	48,332	629,220	$1,887.66
simply-debrid	54,750	555,480	$1,666.44
generatorlinkpremium	83,095	366,000	$1,098.00
hyperspeeds	92,910	349,650	$1,048.95
Rapid8	106,937	288,390	$865.17
hungryleech	116,439	261,180	$783.54
premium4.us	136,060	223,170	$669.51
leecher.us	136,398	220,950	$662.85
speedyspeeds	181,917	181,917	$545.75
premium-leechers	374,287	97,470	$292.41

Premium Link Generator Site Revenue.   Table 9 presents the monthly revenue estimates for ten major premium link generator sites. The average monthly advertisement revenue for premium link generator sites is around \$952.03, which is even lower than that for multi-upload sites. Premium link generator sites also gain revenue by using ad-link shortening site services and by encouraging users to provide their cloud storage site premium accounts and subscribe to their paid services. Therefore, the actual monthly revenues for the listed premium link generator sites should be larger than the current estimates.

6. Discussion

Increasing numbers of individuals are using cloud storage sites and the cloud storage ecosystem continues to grow. It is common knowledge that most copyright-infringing files are shared via cloud storage sites. This research has shown that cloud storage sites and other entities in the cloud storage ecosystem earn substantial revenue. Criminal entities utilize the ecosystem to make available copyright-infringing files as well as files containing child pornography, or recruiting, planning and coordination information for criminal and terrorist entities. The estimation methods used in this research are useful in web service investigations to assess the revenue earned by the targeted entities based on their web traffic and domain information.

7. Conclusions

This chapter has focused on the cloud storage ecosystem and the revenue models of entities in the ecosystem. New contributors, namely ad-link shortening sites, multi-upload sites and premium link generator sites, have joined the ecosystem and share the profits. This chapter has also presented a methodology for estimating the monthly revenues of cloud storage ecosystem entities based on page view traffic and the numbers of unique users. The methodology is especially useful in web service investigations to assess the revenue earned by the targeted entities. The results indicate that cloud storage sites primarily rely on premium account subscriptions and advertising for revenue. The results also suggest that key contributors earn significant revenue even when they merely provide services to support cloud storage.

Future research will examine the relationship between ad-link shortening sites and cloud storage sites. One finding of this study is that ad-link shortening sites earn more revenue that many cloud storage sites and increasing numbers of users are leveraging ad-link shortening sites to share files. Future research will also analyze ad-link shortening links to determine whether or not their popularity stems from the fact that most of the actual links point to cloud storage.

References

[1] D. Antoniades, E. Markatos and C. Dovrolis, One-click hosting services: A file-sharing hideout, *Proceedings of the Ninth ACM SIG-COMM Conference on Internet Measurement*, pp. 223–234, 2009.

[2] S. Arooj, Top 15 websites to earn money by uploading files, Anzaq (www.anzaq.com/2013/07/top-15-websites-to-earn-money-by.html), 2014.

[3] Digital Citizens Alliance, Good Money Gone Bad: Digital Thieves and the Hijacking of the Online Ad Business, Washington, DC (digitalcontentnext.org/wp-content/uploads/2014/09/goodmon.pdf), 2014.

[4] Digital Citizens Alliance, Behind the Cyberlocker Door: Cyberlockers Make Millions on Others' Creations, Washington, DC (www.digitalcitizensalliance.org/cac/alliance/content.aspx?page=cyberlockers), 2016.

[5] Federal Bureau of Investigation, Justice Department charges leaders of Megaupload with widespread online copyright infringement, Press Release, Washington, DC, January 19, 2012.

[6] L. Gannes, Case studies in Freemium: Pandora, Dropbox, Evernote, Automattic and MailChimp, Gigaom, Austin, Texas (gigaom.com/2010/03/26/case-studies-in-freemium-pandora-dropbox-evernote-automattic-and-mailchimp), 2010.

[7] Z. Jelveh and K. Ross, Profiting from filesharing: A measurement study of economic incentives in cyberlockers, *Proceedings of the Twelfth IEEE International Conference on Peer-to-Peer Computing*, pp. 57–62, 2012.

[8] A. Mahanti, C. Williamson, N. Carlsson, M. Arlitt and A. Mahanti, Characterizing the file hosting ecosystem: A view from the edge, *Performance Evaluation*, vol. 68(11), pp. 1085–1102, 2011.

[9] J. Moore, Predators and prey: A new ecology of competition, *Harvard Business Review*, vol. 71(3), pp. 75–83, 1993.

[10] R. O'Neill, Mega outlines 2014 development plans, *ZDNet*, January 16, 2014.

[11] D. Price, Sizing the Piracy Universe, NetNames, London, United Kingdom (copyrightalliance.org/sites/default/files/2013-netnames-piracy.pdf), 2013.

[12] S. Saha, Top 20 highest paying CPM advertising networks 2014, Digital Guide Technology Blog (`www.techgyd.com/top-20-high est-paying-cpm-advertising-networks-2014/7405`), February 27, 2014.

[13] U.S. Attorney's Office, Eastern District of Virginia, Release for Victim Notification, United States v. Kim Dotcom, et al., Crim. No. 1:12CR3 (E.D. Va. O'Grady, J.), Alexandria, Virginia (`www.justice.gov/usao-edva/release-victim-notification`), April 22, 2015.

[14] E. Van de Sar, Top 10 largest file-sharing sites, TorrentFreak (`torrentfreak.com/top-10-largest-file-sharing-sites-110 828`), August 27, 2011.

V

SOCIAL MEDIA FORENSICS

Chapter 13

WINDOWS 8.x FACEBOOK AND TWITTER METRO APP ARTIFACTS

Swasti Bhushan Deb

Abstract   The release of Windows 8.x for personal computers has increased user appetite for metro apps. Many social media metro apps are available in the Windows Store, the installation of which integrates social media platforms directly into the operating system. Metro applications enable social media platforms to be accessed without an Internet browser. The increased demand for metro apps has turned out to be a gold mine in digital forensic investigations. This is because, whenever an app is executed within an operating system, evidentiary traces of activities are left behind. Hence, it is important to locate and analyze evidentiary traces in Windows 8.x personal computer environments.

This chapter focuses on the forensic analysis of two widely-used personal computer based, social media metro apps – Facebook and Twitter. Experiments were performed to determine if the activities piloted via these metro apps could be identified and reconstructed. The results reveal that, in the case of Facebook and Twitter metro apps, potential evidence and valuable data exist and can be located and analyzed by digital forensic investigators.

Keywords: Metro apps, Windows 8.x, social media, Facebook, Twitter, artifacts

1.   Introduction

Social media are driving a variety of forms of social interaction, discussion, exchange and collaboration. This makes social media the playground for cyber criminals. As enterprise networks become more secure, cyber criminals focus on exploiting social media platforms and preying on their subscribers. Social media metro apps for Windows 8.x personal computers enable users to exchange information without having to use web browsers, just like the apps on smartphones and tablets. Cy-

© IFIP International Federation for Information Processing 2016
Published by Springer International Publishing AG 2016. All Rights Reserved
G. Peterson and S. Shenoi (Eds.): Advances in Digital Forensics XII, IFIP AICT 484, pp. 259–279, 2016.
DOI: 10.1007/978-3-319-46279-0_13

ber criminals can leverage metro apps to perpetrate activities such as defamation, stalking, malware distribution and catphishing.

Web browsers on personal computers have been the primary instrument for committing online fraud and criminal activities; this makes them a gold mine for digital forensic investigators. The traditional approach of accessing social media sites using a browser leaves traces such as the browsing history, cookies, caches, downloads and bookmarks, enabling forensic investigators to reconstruct user activities. As metro apps replace browsers for social media access via Windows 8.x personal computers, they will have important forensic implications. The metro environment in Windows 8.x features a tile-based start screen, where each tile represents a metro application and displays relevant information. For example, a Twitter metro app may show the latest tweets, a Facebook metro app may display the latest posts and news items and a weather app may show the current temperature and forecast. Clearly, metro apps on Windows 8.x personal computers can provide a wealth of information of use in forensic investigations.

Windows 8.x features a metro-styled interface designed for touchscreen, mouse, keyboard and pen inputs. Communications apps enable users to interact with each other via email, calendars and social networks, and other means. The Microsoft account integration feature also facilitates synchronization of user data and integration with other Microsoft services such as SkyDrive, Skype, Xbox Live, Xbox Music and Xbox Video. The immersive environment of Windows 8.x leads to each app leaving a unique set of forensic artifacts.

The Facebook metro app provides a user interface with a sidebar on the left-hand side that features messages, news feeds, events, friends, photos, groups and settings. Friend requests, the inbox and notification counters are presented at the top-right-hand corner of the app.

The Twitter metro app, which may be downloaded from the Windows Store, requires a user to login during its first use. The second launch of the app prompts the user to run it in the background. This enables the user to view quick status notifications on the lock screen. The distinctive features provided by Windows 8.x are Search and Share charms. The Search charm (keyboard shortcut WIN+Q) enables users to search Twitter for hash tags or accounts from any app. The Share charm (keyboard shortcut WIN+H) enables users to tweet from any app at any time and to share content from any app to Twitter [11].

Despite the popularity of the Facebook and Twitter metro apps in Windows 8.x personal computers, very little research has focused on evaluating their evidentiary importance. Investigating a criminal case involving social media platforms is a two-step approach: (i) obtain evidence such as login IP addresses with timestamps, registered email address and phone numbers of a suspected social media user at the service provider's end; and (ii) conduct a forensic analysis of the traces left behind by the use of browsers and apps at the user's end. This research focuses on the user's end and attempts to identify the nature and locations of the forensic artifacts that are created and retained when metro apps are utilized to access and operate Facebook and Twitter accounts.

2.   Related Work

The forensic analysis of Facebook and Twitter metro apps on personal computers running Windows 8.x has largely been ignored in the literature. On the other hand, considerable research has focused on social media app forensics on Android and iOS platforms.

2.1   Windows 8.x Artifacts

Thomson [18] has researched the forensic aspects of Windows 8.x systems; in particular, the forensic artifacts specific to metro apps in the Consumer Preview 32-bit edition of Windows 8.x. Brewer et al. [3] have compared the Windows 7 and Windows 8 registries with regard to various forensic considerations; their work showed that the registry has not changed significantly from Windows 7 to Windows 8. Stormo [17] has also analyzed the Windows 8 registry and Goh [8] has discussed the challenges involved in forensic investigations of personal computers running Windows 8. Khatri's forensic blog [10] discusses the forensic importance of search histories in Windows 8.x systems. Despite these research efforts, Murphy et al. [15] state that there is a significant need to better understand the storage mechanisms and forensic artifacts related to Windows Phone 8 systems.

Iqbal et al. [9] have investigated the forensic aspects of Windows RT systems, which have some similarities with Windows 8 systems. In particular, Iqbal et al. describe the filesystem structure and potential forensic artifacts, and proceed to specify a forensically-sound acquisition method for Windows RT tablets. Lee and Chung [12] have identified and analyzed artifacts of Viber and Line in Windows 8 systems; their work is important because of the wide use of instant messaging apps.

Researchers have investigated the traces of social media activities left on computer systems. Zellers [20] has discussed keyword searches for MySpace artifacts and evidence reconstruction from a Windows personal computer. Al Mutawa et al. [1] have examined the forensic artifacts created by Facebook's instant messaging service, and describe a process for recovering and reconstructing the artifacts left on a computer hard drive. Dickson [4, 5] has developed forensic techniques for recovering artifacts from AOL Instant Messenger and Yahoo Messenger.

2.2   Social Media Artifacts

Large numbers of users connect to social media sites via mobile device apps. As a result, the forensic analysis of social media apps for mobile devices is a hot topic for research in the digital forensics community.

Al Mutawa et al. [2] have investigated the artifacts related to the use of social media apps on a variety of smartphones and operating systems. Their research has identified the locations where artifacts corresponding to Facebook, Twitter and MySpace apps are stored and how they can be recovered from the internal memory of Android and iOS smartphones. Meanwhile, Parsons [16] has developed a forensic analysis methodology for Windows 10 metro apps.

Despite the body of research related to social medial apps on mobile devices, there is limited, if any, published work on the forensic analysis of Facebook and Twitter metro apps. The goal of this research is to determine if activities piloted through these metro apps can be identified and reconstructed. The focus is on performing experimental tests and analyses of Facebook and Twitter metro app data to identify data sources of interest in forensic examinations.

3.   Proposed Methodology

In a criminal investigation involving social media, the evidentiary records obtained from the Facebook Law Enforcement Portal [6] include the IP addresses corresponding to account creation, login and logout actions, along with the registered mobile number, email id, etc. corresponding to the Facebook profile/page of a probable suspect. Twitter [19] provides similar evidentiary records. However, these records are insufficient for determining whether or not a crime may have been committed using a Windows 8.x personal computer. This is because it is necessary to also seize the Windows 8.x computer allegedly used by the suspect and conduct a forensic analysis of the computer, including the metro apps. This section presents a detailed description of the forensic analysis methodology for extracting artifacts associated with Facebook and Twitter metro apps on Windows 8.x computers.

Table 1 presents the hardware and software used in the experimental methodology. Snapshots of the computer drive before and after user activities were taken using Regshot. These snapshots were used to analyze the system files and folders for changes that took place during the user activities. Regshot is an open-source registry comparison utility

Table 1. Details of tools used.

Tools	Use	Version	License
Laptop	Create virtual environments	Windows 8.x	Single Language
VMware Workstation	Simulate a Windows 8.x personal computer environment	11.0.0 Build-2305329	Commercial
Regshot	Monitor changes to the files and registry	1.9.0	Open Source
FTK Imager	View and analyze the virtual disks of VM1 and VM2	3.2.0.0	Free
SQLite Manager	View and analyze SQLite files	0.8.3.1	Free
WinPrefetch-View	Analyze Prefetch files	1.15	Free

that takes snapshots of the registry and system drive, compares the two snapshots and identifies the differences.

The experimental methodology involved three phases, which are described in the following sections.

3.1   Phase 1

A Windows 8.x Single Language operating system was used as the base operating system on which the test environments were installed. VMware version 11.0.0 was installed on the base operating system prior to conducting the experiments. Two Windows 8 Single Language 64-bit virtual machines (VMs) were created to simulate the test environment, one each for testing the traces of Facebook and Twitter Metro app activities. FTK Imager and SQLite Manager were also installed on the base operating systems and configured during this phase.

3.2   Phase 2

The second phase focused on preparing the test environments, VM1 and VM2. Each virtual machine was configured with two partitions – the C and D drives with 30 GB storage, 3 GB RAM, a bridge network connection and one processor (with one core). VM1 was used to conduct tests of the Facebook metro app while VM2 was used to conduct tests of the Twitter metro app. A Microsoft account was created using fictitious information on each virtual machine. The Microsoft accounts were created in order to install the metro apps.

To confirm the validity of forensic data identified during Phases 2 and 3, the two virtual machines were fresh with only the built-in metro apps; no third-party metro apps were installed prior to conducting the experiments. Regshot was the only additional software installed on the two virtual machines.

3.3 Phase 3

The following activities were performed on VM1 in chronological order:

- A snapshot of the VM1 system drive was taken using Regshot (Snapshot 1).

- The Facebook metro app was installed in VM1 from the Windows Store.

- A test subject logged into a fictitious Facebook account via the installed Facebook metro app and performed common user activities.

- A snapshot of the VM1 system drive was taken using Regshot (Snapshot 2).

- Snapshots 1 and 2 were compared using Regshot.

- The results were saved in a text file and VM1 was shut down.

The following activities were performed on VM2 in chronological order:

- A snapshot of the VM2 system drive was taken using Regshot (Snapshot 3).

- The Twitter metro app was installed in VM2 from the Windows Store.

- A test subject logged into a fictitious Twitter account via the installed Twitter metro app and performed common user activities.

- A snapshot of the VM2 system drive was taken using Regshot (Snapshot 4).

- Snapshots 3 and 4 were compared using Regshot.

- The results were saved in a text file and VM2 was shut down.

In an effort to ascertain the locations of potential forensic artifacts associated with the metro apps, Regshot was used to monitor the states of the virtual machines during every step in the experiments and the changes in the system directories were documented in detail.

Table 2. Activities performed via the Facebook and Twitter metro apps.

Metro App	User Activities
Facebook	The app was installed from the Windows Store and an account was created for the test subject
	Text messages and images were sent and received
	Posts were shared and tagged as like; status was updated; photos were uploaded; friends were tagged, etc.
Twitter	The app was installed from the Windows Store and an account was created for the test subject
	Tweets were posted; photos were uploaded along with captions
	Users were followed; followers were messaged
	Searches were made of users and hashtags from within the app

This phase also documented the system files that were created, modified or deleted by the user activities listed Table 2, as well as the locations of potential evidence left behind by user interactions with the metro apps. For each of the activities performed, a baseline snapshot of the system drive was taken using Regshot. The text file output for each comparison of snapshots was found to contain the list of system files, registry, etc., reflecting the changes that had occurred to each virtual machine as a result of user interactions. The text file outputs from Regshot were used to determine the types of files that were created, changed or deleted during the experiments as well as the locations of the potential evidence left behind.

4.   Results

Windows 8.x metro apps have altered the field of digital forensics, leading to new sources of evidence while requiring forensic examiners to keep abreast of the latest app developments in order to interpret and reconstruct data of evidentiary value. From a forensic perspective, the metro user interface retains many of the key artifacts present in earlier versions of Windows, but there are several new artifacts and some previous artifacts are missing or changed. This section provides a brief overview of the app data and user data storage in Windows 8.x, followed by the experimental results.

4.1   App Data Storage and User Data Storage

According to Microsoft, app data is mutable data that is specific to an app. It includes the runtime state, user preferences and other settings. Windows 8.x manages the data store of an app, ensuring that it is isolated from other apps and other users. The contents of the data store are also preserved when a user installs an update to an app and the contents of the data store are removed cleanly when an app is uninstalled [14].

Apps manage or interact with two types of data: (i) app data, which is created and managed by an app, is specific to the internal functions and configurations of the app; (ii) user data, which is created and managed by a user when using an app, includes user-selected preferences, app configuration options, document and media files, email and communication transcripts, and database records that hold content created by the user [13].

4.2   Artifacts and Their Locations

Regshot identifies the changes that have occurred to a particular Windows system and categorizes them according to:

- **Registry Keys and Values:** Added, modified and deleted.

- **Files and Folders:** Added and deleted.

- **File Attributes:** Modified.

Analyses of the changes listed above revealed the locations and the data structures of the artifacts.

Tables 3 and 4 summarize the relevant artifacts that were created, changed or deleted, along with their locations. The text file outputs of Regshot were used to identify the locations of the relevant artifacts. All the system files, folders, registry key/values and file attributes in the Regshot outputs were explored. The metro app installation and user activities listed in Table 2 played a major role in performing this task. In order to identify the artifacts and their locations, the virtual disk of each virtual machine was imported into FTK imager as an image file and analyzed.

The `AppData\Local` directory contains data specific to each metro app and does not roam with the user. User-specific data files for the Facebook and Twitter metro apps are stored in `C:\Users\{UserName}\AppData\Local\Packages\{packageid}` where `UserName` corresponds to the Windows user name and `packageid` corresponds to the Windows Store application package identifier.

Facebook and Twitter user data reside in the packages `Facebook.Facebook_8xx8rvfyw5nnt` and `9E2F88E3.Twitter_wgeqdkkx372wm`, respectively. Figures 1 and 2 present the data structures of the Facebook and Twitter app packages located at `C:\Users\{UserName}\AppData\Local\Packages`.

Table 3. Facebook metro app artifacts.

Location	Significance
`C:\ProgramFiles\WindowsApps\Facebook.` `Facebook_1.4.0.9_x64__8xx8rvfyw5nnt`	Facebook app installation path
`C:\Users\{UserName}\AppData\` `Local\Packages\Facebook.Facebook_` `8xx8rvfyw5nnt\`	Path to Facebook user data, the most important artifact location
`C:\Windows\Prefetch\FACEBOOK.` `EXE-C042A127.pf`	Facebook app prefetch file
`C:\Users\{username}\AppData\` `Local\Packages\Facebook.Facebook_` `8xx8rvfyw5nnt\TempState`	Path to uploaded photos

Table 4. Twitter metro app artifacts.

Location	Significance
`C:\ProgramFiles\WindowsApps\9E2F88E3.` `Twitter_1.1.13.8_x64__wgeqdkkx372wm`	Twitter app installation path
`C:\Users\{UserName}\AppData\Local\` `Packages\9E2F88E3.Twitter_wgeqdkkx372wm`	Path to Twitter user data, the most important artifact location
`C:\Windows\Prefetch\TWITTER-WIN8.` `EXE-9C6C7EE3.pf`	Twitter app prefetch file
`C:\Users\{UserName}\AppData\Local\` `Packages\9E2F88E3.Twitter_wgeqdkkx372wm\` `TempState`	Path to uploaded photos

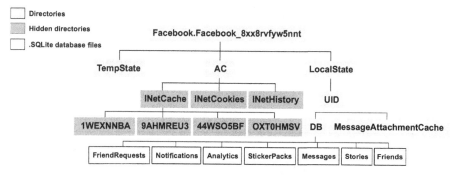

Figure 1. Data structure of the Facebook metro app package.

5.   Analysis of Results

This section discusses the results of forensic analyses of the artifacts listed in Tables 3 and 4. Descriptions of the analyses and the related findings are also provided.

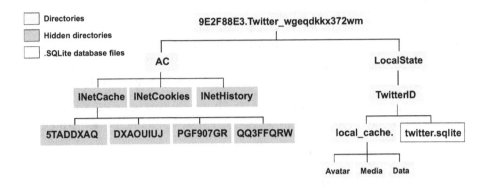

Figure 2. Data structure of the Twitter metro app package.

Table 5. Structure and forensic relevance of Facebook metro app artifacts.

Directory		Forensic Relevance
AC	INetCache	Contained four randomly-numbered hidden folders; each folder had files with the display pictures of Facebook friends, search results, etc.; each profile picture correlated with a Facebook friend (Figure 3)
	INetCoookies	No cookie files were found
	INetHistory	Found to be empty
LocalState	UID/DB	The UID corresponded to the Facebook profile id of the test subject; the directory contained database files associated with text messages, notifications, stories, friends list, etc.; this is the most important directory from the forensic perspective
	UID/MessageAttachmentCache	Contained randomly-numbered folders (e.g., bef9de3f1acaaa4d34273d597809f77e.jpg); these folders were named using the MD5 hashes of the files/pictures sent to friends via chat; the folders also contained the picture/file attachments sent to friends via chat

5.1   Analysis of Facebook Metro App Artifacts

The Facebook app identifier `Facebook.Facebook_8xx8rvfyw5nnt` located at `C:\Users\{UserName}\AppData\Local\Packages` was used to reconstruct user data, including the friends list and text messages. Table 5 shows the structure and forensic relevance of the `AC` and `LocalState` directories. Figure 3 shows the data in the "friends" table of the `Friends.sqlite` database.

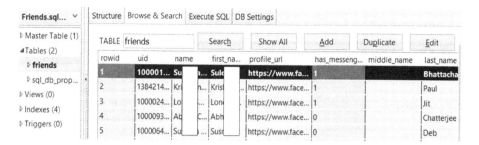

Figure 3. Table viewed and examined using SQLite Manager.

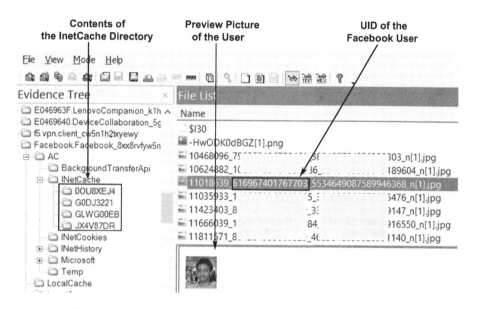

Figure 4. Correlation of display pictures with Facebook UIDs.

The `InetCache` directory contained four randomly-numbered hidden folders. These folders contained the display pictures (`.jpg` files) of the friends/profiles of the users whose notifications appeared in news feeds, search queries, personal chats/messages, etc. The display pictures were found to correlate with the Facebook users as shown in Figure 4. FTK imager was used to view and examine the display pictures and their related information.

5.2   Analysis of Database Files

Analysis of the database files (see Figure 1 for the database files and their locations) revealed that they store a substantial amount of valuable user data. SQLite Manager was used to analyze the database files and

Table 6.   Important databases and tables.

Database (.SQLite)	Table	Remarks
Friends	"friends"	Friends list of the Facebook test subject
FriendRequests	"friend_requests"	Friend requests sent to the test subject by Facebook users
Messages	"messages" "threads" "users"	Messages sent and received
Stories	"places"	Geographical locations in stories, updates, etc.
	"stories"	Stories in news feeds
Notifications	"notifications"	Notifications in a news feed when other Facebook users comment, like or share something

reconstruct the chat logs, friends list, notifications etc. Table 6 lists the important tables associated with the databases.

Figure 5.   JSON-formatted "sender" column value.

Analysis of Facebook Chat Artifacts.   Chat and message histories are threaded together [7]. Table 7 presents the tables in the Messages database and their forensic artifacts. As detailed in Figure 5 and Tables 6 and 7, the "messages" table of the Messages.sqlite database was found to contain forensically-important user data. The "content" column contains the textual content of chat communications and, along with the "sender" column data, can be used to determine who sent the messages.

The data in the "sender" column is in the JavaScript object notation (JSON) format. Figure 5 shows a typical "sender" column value.

The files in C:\Users\{UserName}\AppData\Local\Packages\Face book.Facebook_8xx8rvfyw5nnt\LocalState\UID\MessageAttachmen tCache contain the files and photos sent as attachments during a chat. These attachments are located in individual folders named after the MD5 hash values of the uploaded files with the same extensions as the files

Table 7. Recovered artifacts.

Table	Recovered Artifacts
"friends"	Facebook UID, registered email id, mobile numbers, names of friends Friends who used the Facebook Messenger app Communication ranks indicating the frequencies of interactions between the test subject and friends (likes, share, comments); close friends have communication ranks close to 1 (e.g., 0.75)
"friend_requests"	Names and UIDs of Facebook users who sent friend requests Local times when the friend requests were sent by Facebook users
"messages"	Attributes of messages communicated with friends such as individual/group chat sessions in plaintext, attachments in chat/message sessions, etc. Timestamps in the Unix epoch format when messages were sent or received by the test subject
"threads"	Unique thread id generated for each chat session; chats with unique users have unique thread ids Names, participants of chat groups, timestamp of the last chat communication in a message thread
"stories"	Public URLs of stories in news feeds; attachments available with stories along with their timestamps Status updates, tagged geolocations, friends and the privacy scope of posts; comments/likes and posts shared
"places"	Geolocations, if any, tagged in stories, along with the names of the geographical locations in plaintext Public URLs of pages located near the geographical locations
"notifications"	Facebook notifications in a news feed at a particular instant when other Facebook users comment, like or share Public URL of the notification, local time when the notification was created and whether or not the particular notification was read by the test subject

and photos. Deleting the attachments from a chat thread removes the files and images, but the parent folders are retained.

Analysis of Facebook Posts/Status Update Artifacts. A status/story update in the news feed of a user is reflected in the "stories" table of the `Stories.sqlite` database (Table 8). Traces of the test subject's post/comment on a friend's timeline are not directly recorded in a database. However, if a friend likes/comments/shares the post, they

Table 8.   Important columns in the `Stories.sqlite` database.

Column Name	Forensic Significance
"creation_time"	Post/status update timestamp in the Unix epoch format
"url"	URL of the post/status update
"edit_history"	Number of times the post/status update was edited
"privacy_scope"	Privacy settings of a post/status update
"can_viewer_edit"	Value of one indicates post/status update by the test subject that cannot be edited by friends; value of zero indicates post/status update by a friend
"can_viewer_delete"	Value of one indicates post/status update by the test subject that cannot be deleted by friends; value of zero indicates post/status update by a friend
"message"	Indicates the comments, status update, etc.

are reflected in the "notifications" table of the `Notifications.sqlite` database. The "title_text" column values indicate the notifications that appear in the news feed.

Status updates by the test subject are stored as "can_viewer_delete" and "can_viewer_edit" column values in the "stories" table. A value of one indicates a status update by the test subject. A value of zero indicates an update by a Facebook friend.

The "edit_history" column values indicate changes/edits to posts. A value of zero indicates no changes, a value of one indicates that the post was edited once, and so on.

The "privacy_scope" column values detail the privacy settings of the account. The "privacy_scope" values may be queried by a forensic investigator who is interested in the status of the posts.

Analysis of Photo Upload Artifacts. An uploaded photo may include a caption. A photo may be uploaded from the locally-available photos or via the camera app interface. Photos uploaded in a post/photo album are located at `C:\Users\{UserName}\AppData\Local\Packages \Facebook.Facebook_8xx8rvfyw5nnt\TempState`. The date of creation of a photo (`.jpg file`) in this location corresponds to the time at which it was uploaded. Table 9 presents the naming conventions of the files found in the `TempState` directory. Intentionally deleting files in the directory does not delete their entries in the `Messages.sqlite` database.

Table 10 shows the registry keys that hold information about the most recently uploaded photos from different sources.

Analysis revealed that the "stories" table of the `Stories.sqlite` database records only the caption accompanying a photo. The "mes-

Table 9. Photo upload artifacts in the `TempState` directory.

Photos	Naming Convention	Artifacts Found
Locally-available photos	`x.jpg`, where x is the MD5 hash value of an uploaded photo	The actual uploaded photos with timestamps and the `.jpg` files named after the MD5 hash values of the photos
Facebook app camera photos	`picture00x.jpg`, where x is incremented for every new photo uploaded using the built-in camera interface	The actual uploaded photos with timestamps

Table 10. Registry keys with information about uploaded photos.

Registry Subkey	Significance
`KEY_USERS\SID\Software\Classes\LocalSettings\` `Software\Microsoft\Windows\CurrentVersion\` `AppModel\SystemAppData\Facebook.Facebook_` `8xx8rvfyw5nnt\PersistedStorageItemTable\System\` `688c235d-95bf-4ee0-af07-6b1058b568e9.Request.0`	Last uploaded photos; uploaded from the locally-available photos
`HKEY_USERS\SID\Software\Classes\LocalSettings\` `Software\Microsoft\Windows\CurrentVersion\` `AppModel\SystemAppData\Facebook.Facebook_` `8xx8rvfyw5nnt\PersistedStorageItemTable\System\` `c19f7613-f825-47a9-b5b9-5f44847eabc8.Request.0`	Last uploaded photos; uploaded via the camera interface of the app

sage" column reveals the caption if the "can_viewer_delete" and "can_viewer_edit" column values are one. The contents of the `TempState` directory and the "message" column of the `Stories.sqlite` database reveal correlations between the textual content and the uploaded photos. The creation dates of the `.jpg` files in the `TempState` directory are equivalent to the "creation_time" values that are adequate for reconstructing photo posts.

5.3   Analysis of Twitter Metro App Artifacts

This section presents information about Twitter metro app artifacts and their locations. Table 11 presents the contents of the `AC` directory and their forensic significance. Table 12 presents the contents of the `LocalState\TwitterID` directory and their forensic significance.

Twitter.sqlite Database.   This database, which is located at `C:\Use` `rs\{Username}\AppData\Local\Microsoft\Windows\9E2F88E3.Twit`

Table 11.   Forensic relevance of files in AC.

Directory/Files	Forensic Relevance
INetCache	Contains four randomly-numbered hidden folders; each folder contains files that encompass the default display pictures of Twitter followers
INetCoookies	Cookie information related to Facebook profiles
INetHistory	Empty

Table 12.   Forensic relevance of files in LocalState.

Directory/Files	Forensic Relevance
.local_cache/Avatar	Contains randomly-numbered files corresponding to the avatar or header photos of the profiles of users followed by the test subject on Twitter
Media	Contains randomly-numbered files corresponding to the photos included in the tweets of users followed by the test subject
Twitter.sqlite	Contains information about latest tweets, private messages sent to followers, favorite lists, etc.

Table 13.   Artifacts found in the Twitter.sqlite database.

Table	Artifacts Found
"activities2"	Information about actions such as follow and favorite, and the related timestamps
	Information about the users on whom the actions were performed
"messages"	Message content in plaintext, sender screen names and Twitter UIDs
"search_queries"	Search queries issued by the test subject
"statuses"	Contents of tweets made by the test subject and tweets of users followed by the test subject
	Tweet timestamps in the Unix epoch format, public URLs of tweets and geolocations
	Twitter UIDs of the authors of tweets, retweets, counts of retweets for each tweet
"users"	Screen names, locations, follower and friend counts; short URLs leading to tweets

ter_wgeqdkkx372wm, contains forensically-interesting information about the test subject. Table 13 lists the important tables in the database.

Figure 6. The "activities2" table viewed using SQLite Manager.

Tweet Artifacts. The contents of a tweet may include captions, photos, etc. Photos may be uploaded from existing photos residing on the hard drive or via the built-in camera interface of the app. For each tweet, user-specific artifacts are found in the "statuses" table. Tweet captions are stored as "content" column values and tweet timestamps as "created_at" column values. The "entities" column values provide the contents of tweets posted by the test subject.

Figure 6 shows the forensically-important data that resides in the columns of the "activities2" in the **Twitter.sqlite** database. Note that the "activities2" table is viewed using SQLite Manager.

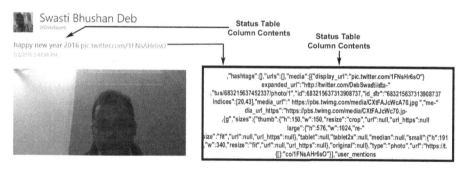

Figure 7. Reconstruction of a tweet using information from the "statuses" table.

For tweets involving photos, the photos taken via the camera interface are stored in the **TempState** directory, with the naming convention: **picture00x.jpg**, where **x** is incremented for every new photo uploaded using the camera interface. The creation timestamps of the **.jpg** files in the directory are the same as the corresponding "created" column values in the "statuses" table. Figure 7 shows the reconstruction of a tweet based on the "content" and "entities" columns of the "statuses" table.

Table 14.   Summary of Facebook metro app artifacts.

Facebook User Activity	Artifacts Found
Private Messages	Messages in plaintext, file attachments, photo attachments (existing and those taken by the camera), sender UIDs, names, coordinates, timestamps when messages were sent/received
Notifications	Text included in notifications, URLs of posts, likes and shares by friends, read/unread status
Friends List	Names, UIDs, contact emails, phone numbers of friends, friends using messenger, communication rank, friend requests by other friends
Status Updates	Captions, privacy scope of posts, status update timestamps, coordinates, edit histories, photos uploaded, last photos uploaded, photos uploaded from locally-available photos or captured via the camera interface, status updates from friends
Friend/Page Searches	Tentative indications leading to searches, dates and times of the searches
Photo Albums	Names of albums, photos in albums, uploaded times, types of photos uploaded (locally available or taken via the camera interface), URLs in the albums, privacy scopes

Table 15.   Summary of Twitter metro app artifacts.

Twitter User Activity	Artifacts Found
Private Messages	Messages in plaintext, sent/received timestamps, sender/receiver screen names and Twitter UIDs
Tweets	Posted tweets, captions and photos, timestamps, tweets by followers, favorite tweets, retweets
Search Queries	Search queries in plaintext

6.   Discussion

The results presented in the preceding sections demonstrate that a wide range of artifacts related to Facebook and Twitter metro apps can be located and analyzed in digital forensic investigations. This section summarizes the results and discusses the main findings.

Tables 14 and 15 summarize the Facebook and Twitter metro app artifacts that were found in the experiments. The artifacts closely model the activities performed by the test subject.

A user who desires to hide his/her activities would typically edit posts or delete posts and messages. As discussed in Section 5, the majority of artifacts were found in SQLite databases. Thus, the modified and deleted activities can be reconstructed by recovering the corresponding SQLite records from the associated databases. The recovery of records and their reconstruction are facilitated by forensic tools such as Oxygen Forensics SQLite Viewer and Sanderson Forensics SQLite Recovery.

From a forensic standpoint, the volume shadow service (VSS) plays a significant role in reconstructing modified or deleted user activities because it creates and maintains multiple historical snapshots of the volumes on a disk. This service is advantageous when important files have been modified, rolled over or intentionally removed or deleted. Forensic examiners can cross-check shadow copies to (at the very least) determine if information was removed. The volume shadow service maintains a record of every block of data that has changed and only backs up a block if it is about to be modified; this enables it to store considerable data in a small amount of space.

The volume shadow service is available in Windows 8.x, but it is not accessible via Windows Explorer. The volume shadow copy service administrative command-line tool `vssadmin` may be used to display the list of volume shadow copy backups and all the installed shadow copy writers and providers in the command window. GUI-based tools such as ShadowExplorer may be used to access and display shadow copies.

7.   Conclusions

Metro apps in Windows 8.x personal computer environments enable social media platforms to be accessed without an Internet browser. Since these apps leave valuable evidentiary traces of user activity, it is important to locate, analyze and reconstruct the traces in digital forensic investigations.

Unfortunately, little digital forensic research has focused on locating and analyzing Facebook and Twitter metro app artifacts in Windows 8.x personal computer environments. Indeed, the vast majority of studies have been limited to the analysis of social media apps on smartphones. The research described in this chapter involved an exhaustive analysis of the artifacts that remain after Facebook and Twitter metro apps are used. Digital forensic professionals should be aware that metro apps are a gold mine in investigations and, as the experimental results presented in this chapter reveal, activities piloted via metro apps can be located, identified and reconstructed, even if attempts have been made to modify or delete posts and tweets.

References

[1] N. Al Mutawa, I. Al Awadhi, I. Baggili and A. Marrington, Forensic artifacts of Facebook's instant messaging service, *Proceedings of the International Conference on Internet Technology and Secured Transactions*, pp. 771–776, 2011.

[2] N. Al Mutawa, I. Baggili and A. Marrington, Forensic analysis of social networking applications on mobile devices, *Digital Investigation*, vol. 9(S), pp. S24–S33, 2012.

[3] M. Brewer, T. Fenger, R. Boggs and C. Vance, A Comparison Between the Windows 8 and Windows 7 Registries, Forensic Science Center, Marshall University, Huntington, West Virginia (`www.marshall.edu/forensics/files/Matts-Paper.pdf`), 2014.

[4] M. Dickson, An examination into AOL Instant Messenger 5.5 contact identification, *Digital Investigation*, vol. 3(4), pp. 227–237, 2006.

[5] M. Dickson, An examination into Yahoo Messenger 7.0 contact identification, *Digital Investigation*, vol. 3(3), pp. 159–165, 2006.

[6] Facebook, Law Enforcement Online Requests, Menlo Park, California (`www.facebook.com/records/x/login`), 2016.

[7] Facebook Help Center, How does chat work with messages? Facebook, Menlo Park, California (`www.facebook.com/help/124629310950859`), 2016.

[8] T. Goh, Challenges in Windows 8 Operating System for Digital Forensic Investigations, M.F.I.T. Thesis, School of Computing and Mathematical Sciences, Auckland University of Technology, Auckland, New Zealand, 2014.

[9] A. Iqbal, H. Al Obaidli, A. Marrington and A. Jones, Windows Surface RT tablet forensics, *Digital Investigation*, vol. 11(S1), pp. S87–S93, 2014.

[10] Y. Khatri, Search History on Windows 8 and 8.1, Yogesh Khatri's Forensic Blog, Swift Forensics (`www.swiftforensics.com/2014/04/search-history-on-windows-8-and-81.html`), April 1, 2014.

[11] M. Kruzeniski, Welcome Twitter for Windows 8, Twitter, San Francisco, California (`blog.twitter.com/2013/welcome-twitter-for-windows-8`), March 14, 2013.

[12] C. Lee and M. Chung, Digital forensic analysis on Windows 8 style UI instant messenger applications, in *Computer Science and its Applications: Ubiquitous Information Technologies*, J. Park, I. Stojmenovic, H. Jeong and G. Yi (Eds.), Springer, Berlin Heidelberg, Germany, pp. 1037–1042, 2015.

[13] Microsoft Windows Dev Center, App and User Data, Microsoft, Redmond, Washington (msdn.microsoft.com/en-us/library/windows/apps/jj553522.aspx), 2016.

[14] Microsoft Windows Dev Center, App Data Storage, Microsoft, Redmond, Washington (msdn.microsoft.com/en-us/library/windows/apps/hh464917.aspx), 2016.

[15] C. Murphy, A. Leong, M. Gaffney, S. Punja, J. Gibb and B. McGarry, Windows Phone 8 Forensic Artifacts, InfoSec Reading Room, SANS Institute, Bethesda, Maryland, 2015.

[16] A. Parsons, Windows 10 Forensics Part 2: Facebook App Forensics, Computer and Digital Forensics Blog, Senator Patrick Leahy Center for Digital Investigation, Champlain College, Burlington, Vermont (computerforensicsblog.champlain.edu/2015/04/01/windows-10-facebook-forensics), April 1, 2015.

[17] J. Stormo, Analysis of Windows 8 Registry Artifacts, M.S. Thesis, Department of Computer Science, University of New Orleans, New Orleans, Louisiana, 2013.

[18] A. Thomson, Windows 8 Forensic Guide, M.F.S. Thesis, Department of Forensic Sciences, George Washington University, Washington, DC (www.propellerheadforensics.files.wordpress.com/2012/05/thomson_windows-8-forensic-guide2.pdf), 2012.

[19] Twitter, Law Enforcement Request, San Francisco, California (support.twitter.com/forms/lawenforcement), 2016.

[20] F. Zellers, MySpace.com Forensic Artifacts Keyword Searches (www.inlanddirect.com/CEIC-2008.pdf), 2008.

Chapter 14

PROFILING FLASH MOB ORGANIZERS IN WEB DISCUSSION FORUMS

Vivien Chan, Kam-Pui Chow and Raymond Chan

Abstract   The flash mob phenomenon has been well studied in sociology and other disciplines, but not in the area of digital forensics. Flash mobs sometimes become violent, perpetrate criminal acts and pose threats to public safely. For these reasons, understanding flash mob activities and identifying flash mob organizers are important tasks for law enforcement. This chapter presents a technique for extracting key online behavioral attributes from a popular Hong Kong discussion forum to identify topic authors – potential flash mob organizers – who belong to a vocal minority, but have the motivation and the ability to exert significant social influence in the discussion forum. The results suggest that, when attempting to interpret flash mob phenomena, it is important to consider the online behavioral attributes of different types of forum users, instead of merely using aggregated or mean behavioral data.

Keywords: Criminal profiling, discussion forums, flash mob organizers

1.   Introduction

A flash mob is a sudden public gathering at which people perform unusual or seemingly random acts and then quickly disperse; it is typically organized by leveraging the Internet and/or social media [9]. Although some researchers believe that it is inappropriate to use the term to describe political protests or criminal acts organized via the Internet or social media, it is clear that the organization of flash mobs for political protests and criminal purposes is an increasing trend [6].

The Umbrella Movement in Hong Kong, which was launched in late September 2014, leveraged several social media platforms to create popular support and motivate citizens to participate in many street demonstrations against the Hong Kong Government [10, 17]. After the Umbrella Movement ended in December 2014, the street demonstrations

© IFIP International Federation for Information Processing 2016
Published by Springer International Publishing AG 2016. All Rights Reserved
G. Peterson and S. Shenoi (Eds.): Advances in Digital Forensics XII, IFIP AICT 484, pp. 281–293, 2016.
DOI: 10.1007/978-3-319-46279-0_14

in Hong Kong persisted, but in a very different form. Specifically, a number of flash-mob-like invocations were posted by organizers on popular social media platforms under innocuous topics such as "shopping," "recover a district" and "anti-traders." The term "shopping" actually refers to protests against government policies, "recover a district" refers to protests against mainland Chinese tourists and "anti-traders" refers to protests against Mainland Chinese citizens who take advantage of multiple entry visas to import goods from Hong Kong to Mainland China. These flash-mob-like activities are very different from traditional street protests. In many instances, flash mobs suddenly emerged in and around tourist shopping areas to disrupt business and traffic, and then dispersed. Clearly, such flash mobs could become aggressive and pose threats to social order [14].

This research focuses on understanding flash mob activities with the goal of identifying potential flash mob organizers in web forums before the mobs manifest themselves. Specific questions are: What are the key online behavioral attributes of flash mob organizers? How can these attributes be used to identify flash mob organizers at an early stage? How can the social influence of flash mob organizers be measured?

2.   Related Work

Studies of flash mob phenomena have primarily been conducted by researchers in the areas of sociology and public health. Many of these studies report that the increasing use of social media enhance the potential that flash mobs will be created for criminal purposes and may therefore pose threats to public safety [6, 12, 13]. In the cyber domain, Al-Khateeb and Agarwal [1] have proposed a conceptual framework that uses hypergraphs to model the complex relations observed in deviant cyber flash mob social networks.

A search of the literature reveals that there are no studies related to classifying web discussion forum users based on their social influence. The classification of users in online discussion forums is important because it can help identify individuals who are influential at instigating flash-mob-like activities at an early stage. Having classified web discussion users into groups, it is useful to borrow the concept of social influence as used in other fields to compare the influencing power of the different groups.

The concept of social influence has been studied extensively in sociology, marketing and political science. In recent years, several researchers have focused on social influence in social media platforms such as Facebook and Twitter. The approaches for analyzing social influence are broadly categorized as graph-based approaches and attribute-based approaches. Graph-based approaches model social networks as graphs and make use the HITS algorithm [7] or the Brin-Page PageRank algorithm [2] or their variants to measure social influence. Attribute-based approaches make use of attributes derived from social media networks, such as the number of followers, number of retweets, number of tweets per user, tweeting rate, etc., to measure social influence [3, 8]. However, at this time, no consensus approach exists for measuring the social influence of social network and discussion forum users.

3.   Profiling Flash Mob Organizers

The most commonly used social media by flash-mob-like protest organizers in Hong Kong are Facebook and online discussion forums. According to the U.S. Census Bureau, there were four million active Hong Kong Facebook users in December 2014, corresponding to a penetration rate of 56.7%. Meanwhile, Hong Kong Golden is one of the most popular web discussion forums in Hong Kong. According to the Hong Kong Golden website [4], it had more than 170,000 registered users as of June 2015. The political discussions on Facebook and Hong Kong Golden are often very heated. Unfortunately, many of the conversations on Facebook take place in private pages or groups and are difficult to access for research purposes. However, the discussions on Hong Kong Golden (and other similar web forums) are mostly public. As a result, it was possible to tap into this public pool of data for the research effort.

3.1   Discussion Forum Dataset

This research collected data from the "Current Affairs" sub-category of the Hong Kong Golden discussion forum from January to April 2015. It important to note that flash-mob-like protest activities took place nearly every weekend during this four-month period. The sub-category was selected because it was the most popular venue for Hong Kong users who wished to discuss political issues and most of the flash-mob-like protest announcements were posted on this sub-category. The following characteristics were observed in the Hong Kong Golden dataset:

- **User Characteristics:** Different users play different roles in the discussion forum. In general, a discussion forum user belongs to one of four groups:

    - **Post Author:** A post author only posts responses to other users and does not create topics. Most forum users are expected to be of this type.

- **Topic Author Only:** A topic author only creates topics and does not post responses to other users.
- **Topic Author Self-Responder:** A topic author self-responder only posts responses to self-created topics and does not post responses to topics created by other users.
- **Topic-Post Author:** A topic-post author creates new topics and posts responses to topics created by others. This group of individuals is of most interest in the study.

Note that a topic author refer to all types of topic authors, including, topic author only, topic author self-responder and topic-post author. The objective is to study topic authors who might initiate flash-mob-like protest activities in a discussion forum.

- **Topic Characteristics:** The Hong Kong Golden discussion forum employs a topic ranking scheme that places topics with higher ranks on the first page of a sub-category. The ranking of a topic is based on the number of new posts to the topic on a given day. A topic with a higher ranking has a higher chance of being read and a higher chance of having responses posted by forum users.

- **Post Characteristics:** Some topic authors exploit the topic ranking scheme by posting many empty posts or spam posts to topics created by themselves to enhance the rankings of the topics. Other post authors in the forum may also help push topics to higher rankings.

3.2 Key Behavioral Attributes

The primary online attributes of topic authors with regard to their influencing power in discussion forums are: (i) motivation; and (ii) ability. Table 1 defines the online attributes of topic authors. A flash mob organizer would be more motivated than other users in posting new topics and pushing the topics to higher rankings. In a study on well-being and civic engagement in offline settings for online discussion forums, Pendry and Salvatore [11] conclude that the strong identification of users with other forum users is a predictor of the offline engagement of users in the forum cause. Thus, it is important for a topic author to also have the ability to engage other users in discussions of the created topics.

3.3 Social Influence

As discussed in the previous section, graph-based and attribute-based approaches have been employed to measure social influence in social me-

Table 1. Attributes of topic authors extracted from a discussion forum.

Attribute	Definition	Description
Motivation 1	Number of topics created by a topic author	This shows that the topic author is engaging the community frequently
Motivation 2	Number of empty/spam posts created by a topic author	This shows that the topic author is attempting to increase the ranking of the topic
Ability 1	Number of non-empty/non-spam posts created by a topic author	This shows that the topic author is engaging in conversations with other post authors
Ability 2	Number of posts created by a topic author that are responded to by other post authors (including both empty/spam posts and non-empty/non-spam posts)	This shows that the topic author is attracting other forum users to discuss the topic

dia platforms. However, there is no consensus on an approach for measuring social influence. This research uses a simple, intuitive measure of social influence based on attributes extracted from the Hong Kong Golden online discussion forum.

While a large number of posts to topics created by a topic author implies the popularity of the topics, it does not imply greater social influence of the topic author because some of the posts could be self-created responses or empty or spam posts designed to enhance the ranking of the topics. On the other hand, if the topics created by a topic author receive many non-empty/non-spam posts from other post authors, then it is likely that the topics were well received or generated a lot of discussion in the online forum. Thus, the standard z-score, which is used as a measure, considers empty/spam posts as well as non-empty/non-spam posts by other post authors.

Assume that a topic author receives $n = r + s$ posts in response to his/her topics, where r is the number of non-empty/non-spam posts by other post authors and s is the number of empty/spam posts by other post authors. Assume that a random post author responds with non-empty/non-spam posts with probability $p = 0.5$ and empty/spam posts with probability $1 - p = 0.5$. Then, a random post author would post $n * p = n/2$ non-empty/non-spam posts with a standard deviation of:

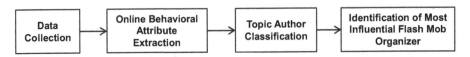

Figure 1. Profiling influential users.

$$\sqrt{n * p * (1 - p)} = \frac{\sqrt{n}}{2} \tag{1}$$

Thus, the z-score is given by:

$$z\text{-}score = \frac{r - \frac{n}{2}}{\frac{\sqrt{n}}{2}} = \frac{r - s}{\sqrt{r + s}} \tag{2}$$

Since it is common practice to use exponential rate parameterization, the logarithm of the z-score is used as the final social influence measure:

$$Social \ Influence \ Index = log(z\text{-}score) \tag{3}$$

Note that the higher the social influence index value, the greater the influence of the topic author in the discussion forum.

3.4   Profiling Flash Mob Organizers

Empirical observations of discussion forum activities revealed that potential flash mob organizers usually work in groups as opposed to just one or two individuals. This makes it possible to identify a group of topic authors with similar online attributes. Thus, cluster analysis was applied to the dataset and the social influence index values of the clusters were compared.

Figure 1 presents the methodology for profiling potential flash mob organizers. Four steps are involved: (i) collection of data from the discussion forum; (ii) extraction of key online behavioral attributes from the dataset; (iii) classification of topic authors based on the behavioral attributes; and (iv) identification of the group of most influential users based on the social influence index.

4.   Description of Experiments

A discussion forum has two main components: (i) topic variables; and (ii) post variables. Usually, a topic author creates a new topic and other forum users (called post authors) respond by replying to the topic through posts. However, unlike other social media platforms (e.g., Facebook and Twitter), friendship relations and/or follower information are not available. Therefore, the raw dataset was used for analysis.

Table 2. Data collected from January 2015 to April 2015.

Attribute	Jan	Feb	Mar	Apr
Number of topics	3,273	3,896	5,912	4,174
Number of posts	130,400	135,806	199,118	164,333
Number of topic authors	1,026	1,154	1,506	1,161
Number of post authors	13,484	13,221	14,694	14,343

Table 2 and Figure 2 provide details about the raw dataset, which was constructed from January 2015 through April 2015. During the four-month period, a total of 17,255 topics and 629,657 posts were collected. These topics were created by 3,040 distinct topic authors.

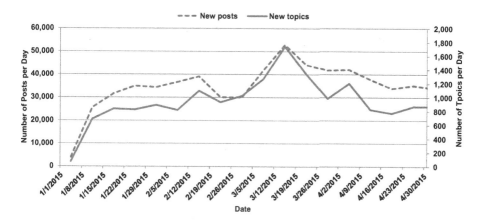

Figure 2. New topics and posts per week (January through April 2015).

In Figure 2, the drop in the number of posts on February 22, 2015 is probably due to the Lunar New Year holiday in Hong Kong while the spike on March 15, 2015 coincided with the most aggressive street protests that occurred during the four-month period. Of the 3,040 unique topic authors, 65% were active topic authors for just one month, 19% were active for two months, 9% were active for three months and only 7% were active during the entire four-month data collection period. The majority of the topic authors (87%) were also post authors who responded to topics created by other topic authors. A minority of topic authors (5%) only created topics and did not respond to topics created by other users. The remaining topic authors (8%) only responded to their own topics.

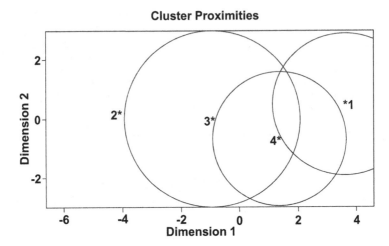

Figure 3. Cluster analysis results.

4.1   Classification of Topic Authors

In order to identify the most influential individuals in the discussion forum, an attempt was made to classify the topic authors into different groups. The cluster analysis involved two stages. First, initial groupings were derived by performing hierarchical agglomerative clustering using Ward's method. Next, the optimum number of clusters was selected based on a cubic clustering criterion value, which was set to a threshold of 3.

The analysis yielded the four clusters shown in Figure 3. Table 3 shows the differences in the mean online behavioral characteristics for the four clusters.

The four clusters correspond to the following topic author types:

- **Type 1: Topic Author (Inactive-Silent-Majority):** This cluster contains the largest number of topic authors ($n = 1,552$; 51.1%) from the sample population. These individuals are the least motivated and have the lowest ability of the four types of topic authors. The majority of individuals in this group ($n = 1,391$; 90%) posted topics during just one month. Also, this was the group with the highest percentage of topic authors ($n = 290$; 17%) who never responded to topics created by others. In terms of the number of topics created, the individuals in this group created an average of one to two topics during the four-month period, indicating that they were relatively silent in the discussion forum.

Table 3.   Cluster differences of online behavioral characteristics.

	Univariate F	Cluster Means (Raw Scores)[a]			
		Type 1 (n=1,552)	Type 2 (n=155)	Type 3 (n=457)	Type 4 (n=876)
Cluster-Defining Attributes					
Motivation 1	533.53*	1.26[b]	58.19	8.42	2.75[b]
Motivation 2	140.51*	0.71[b]	141.24	16.58	1.22[b]
Ability 1	479.02*	1.17	162.37	33.74	10.25
Ability 2	417.85*	16.85	1,853.03	286.78	115.32
Variables External to Cluster Solution					
Influence Index	809.78*	3.07	3.75	3.34	3.24
Mean No. Months	967.44*	1.11	3.52	2.47	1.63
Mean Time New Topics	22.76*	144h25[b]	57h44	123h53[b]	150h20[b]

* $p < .001$

[a] Higher mean value corresponds to higher motivation, ability or social influence

[b] Tukey HSD comparisons indicate mean scores are not significantly different at $p < .05$

- **Type 2: Topic Author (Active-Vocal-Minority):** This cluster contains the smallest number of topic authors ($n = 155$; 5.1%) from the sample population. These individuals, who are the most motivated topic authors with the highest ability, received an average of around 1,853 posts per topic created and self-responded with an average of 162 non-empty posts per topic. The majority of individuals in this group ($n = 106$; 68%) posted an average of 71 new topics continuously during the four-month period. The mean time between the creation of new topics was the shortest among the four groups (less than 58 hours); these individuals created a new topic every 2.5 days.

- **Type 3: Topic Author (Moderate-Active:)** This cluster ($n = 457$; 15.0%) is fairly similar to the Type 2 cluster and the individuals are ranked second in terms of motivation and ability as topic authors. The majority of individuals in this group ($n = 278$; 61%) were active as topic authors for two to three months.

- **Type 4: Topic Author (Moderate-Inactive):** This cluster contains the second largest number of topic authors ($n = 876$; 28.8%), after the Type 1 topic authors. No significant difference was observed between the motivation scores of the Type 4 and Type 1 topic authors. The only difference between the individuals in the two clusters is their ability to engage other post authors, with Type 4 individuals showing a better ability to engage other post authors than Type 1 individuals.

Table 4. Cluster differences of flash-mob-like topics.

	Type 1 (n=1,552)	Type 2 (n=155)	Type 3 (n=457)	Type 4 (n=876)
Number of flash-mob-like topics	199	1,076	408	211
Number of reply posts	29,477	334,279	154,705	111,196

4.2   Cluster Comparison

A one-way between-subjects ANOVA test was conducted to compare the means of two sets of variables, namely, the cluster-defining attributes and variables external to the cluster solution, for the four clusters. Note that a significant effect exists for all the attributes at the p <.001 level for the four clusters in Table 3.

Post hoc comparisons using the Tukey HSD indicate that the mean scores of all the cluster-defining attributes for the four clusters are significantly different. The mean scores of Motivation 1 (M = 58.19; SD = 74.99), Motivation 2 (M = 141.24; SD = 364.10), Ability 1 (M = 162.37; SD = 218.21) and Ability 2 (M = 1,853.03; SD = 2,712.46) for Type 2 topic authors (active-vocal-minority) are significantly higher than those in the other three clusters. The results suggest that the four clusters have significantly different mean scores for the key behavioral attributes.

For the set of variables external to cluster solution, an analysis of variance revealed that the social influence index is significantly different (F(3, 3,036) = 809.78; p = .000). Once again, the Type 2 topic authors (active-vocal-minority) have the highest mean social influence index (M = 3.75; SD = 0.34) while Type 1 topic authors (inactive-silent-majority) have the lowest mean social influence index (M = 3.07; SD = 0.09).

The final question is whether or not Type 2 topic authors are potentially organizers of flash-mob-like activities. To answer this question, a bag of words containing phrases related to calling for flash-mob-like demonstrations and the corresponding location names was created. The bag of words was used to identify flash-mob-like topics. Table 4 summarizes the results. Type 2 topic authors created the largest number of flash-mob-like topics (1,076), which accounted for 57% of the total. In addition, Type 2 topic authors received the largest number of responses (334,279), corresponding to 53% of the total.

5.   Discussion

The results demonstrate that it is feasible to classify topic authors into four groups using the online behavioral attributes of motivation and ability. The minority Type 2 group of topic authors (active-vocal-minority; n=155; 5.1%) is actually the most vocal and influential group in the online discussion forum. This group of just 5.1% of topic authors produced the largest number of new topics in a short duration of time and were highly motivated in pushing their topics to higher rankings. Moreover, the topics created by the group were mostly related to flash-mob-like activities. At the same time, these topic authors received the largest number of responses among all the topic authors and were also actively involved in discussions with other forum users. In addition, this group has the highest social influence index, meaning that this minority group is not just vocal, but also influential in the online discussion forum. Based on their high social influence and creation of the largest number of flash-mob-like topics, it is highly likely that Type 2 topic authors (active-vocal-minority) are potential flash mob organizers.

This finding echoes the research results of Mustafaraj et al. [8] related to Twitter, according to which the behaviors of the vocal minority (users who tweet very often) and the silent majority (users who tweeted only once) were significantly different. They also pointed out that, "when the size of the minority opinion holding group increases more than 10% of the network size, then the minority opinion takes hold and becomes the opinion of the majority."

6.   Conclusions

Flash mobs have the potential to become violent, perpetrate criminal acts and pose threats to public safely. As a result, understanding flash mob activities and identifying flash mob organizers are important tasks for law enforcement. The technique for the early identification of potential flash mob organizers in discussion forums discerned four types of topic authors who have significantly different online behavioral attributes ranging from being part of a vocal minority to a being members of the silent majority. Based on the online behavioral attributes and an intuitive social influence index, potential flash mob organizers belong to a vocal minority, but have the motivation and the ability to exert significant social influence in a web discussion forum.

Future research will attempt to characterize the followers of potential flash mob organizers. Additionally, it will develop measures for discerning flash-mob-like activities based on web discussion forum topics.

References

[1] S. Al-Khateeb and N. Agarwal, Developing a conceptual framework for modeling a deviant cyber flash mob: A socio-computational approach leveraging hypergraph constructs, *Journal of Digital Forensics, Security and Law*, vol. 9(2), pp. 113–128, 2014.

[2] S. Brin and L. Page, The anatomy of a large-scale hypertextual web search engine, *Proceedings of the Seventh International Conference on the World Wide Web*, pp. 107–117, 1998.

[3] M. Cha, H. Haddadi, F. Benevenuto and K. Gummadi, Measuring user influence in Twitter: The million follower fallacy, *Proceedings of the Fourth International AAAI Conference on Weblogs and Social Media*, pp. 10–17, 2010.

[4] HKGolden.com, Hong Kong Golden, Hong Kong, China (`www.hkgolden.com`), 2016.

[5] A. Java, P. Kolari, T. Finin and T. Oates, Modeling the spread of influence in the blogosphere, *Proceedings of the Fifteenth International World Wide Web Conference*, pp. 407–416, 2006.

[6] L. Kiltz, Flash mobs: The newest threat to local governments, *Public Management*, vol. 93(11), pp. 6–10, 2011.

[7] J. Kleinberg, Authoritative sources in a hyperlinked environment, *Journal of the ACM*, vol. 46(5), pp. 604–632, 1999.

[8] E. Mustafaraj, S. Finn, C. Whitlock and P. Metaxas, Vocal minority versus silent majority: Discovering the opinions of the long tail, *Proceedings of the Third IEEE International Conference on Social Computing*, pp. 103–110, 2011.

[9] Oxford Dictionaries, Flash mob (`www.oxforddictionaries.com/definition/english/flash-mob`), 2016.

[10] E. Parker, Social media and the Hong Kong protests, *The New Yorker*, October 1, 2014.

[11] L. Pendry and J. Salvatore, Individual and social benefits of online discussion forums, *Computers in Human Behavior*, vol. 50, pp. 211–220, 2015.

[12] G. Seivold (Ed.), The less amusing side of flash mobs, *Security Director's Report*, pp. 2–4, November 2011.

[13] S. Solecki and K. Goldschmidt, Adolescents texting and twittering: The flash mob phenomena, *Journal of Pediatric Nursing*, vol. 26(2), pp. 167–169, 2011.

[14] South China Morning Post, Parallel trading (`www.scmp.com/topics/parallel-trading`), 2016.

[15] J. Tang, J. Sun, C. Wang and Z. Yang, Social influence analysis in large-scale networks, *Proceedings of the Fifteenth ACM SIGKDD International Conference on Knowledge Discovery and Data Mining*, pp. 807–816, 2009.

[16] M. Trusov, A. Bodapati and R. Bucklin, Determining influential users in Internet social networks, *Journal of Marketing Research*, vol. 47(4), pp. 643–658, 2010.

[17] Wikipedia, 2014 Hong Kong protests (`en.wikipedia.org/wiki/2014HongKongprotests`), 2016.

VI

IMAGE FORENSICS

Chapter 15

ENHANCING IMAGE FORGERY DETECTION USING 2-D CROSS PRODUCTS

Songpon Teerakanok and Tetsutaro Uehara

Abstract   The availability of sophisticated, easy-to-use image editing tools means that the authenticity of digital images can no longer be guaranteed. This chapter proposes a new method for enhancing image forgery detection by combining two detection techniques using a 2-dimensional cross product. Compared with traditional approaches, the method yields better detection results in which the tampered regions are clearly identified. Another advantage is that the method can be applied to enhance a variety of detection algorithms. The method was tested on the CASIA TIDE v2.0 public dataset of color images and the results compared against those obtained using the re-interpolation, JPEG noise quantization and noise estimation techniques. The experimental results indicate that the proposed method is efficient and has superior detection characteristics.

Keywords: Image tampering, forgery detection, cross product

1.   Introduction

The proliferation of low-cost, high-quality digital cameras and sophisticated image processing software make it very easy to manipulate or forge digital images without any obvious traces. Due to the dramatic increase in doctored images [1], the authenticity and trustworthiness of digital images are always in question. This situation can pose serious problems in criminal investigations, judicial proceedings, journalism, medical imaging and even insurance claim processing, where the authenticity of every digital image must be guaranteed.

A digital image may be tampered with via image retouching, splicing and/or copy-move forging. Retouching, cloning and healing are meth-

© IFIP International Federation for Information Processing 2016
Published by Springer International Publishing AG 2016. All Rights Reserved
G. Peterson and S. Shenoi (Eds.): Advances in Digital Forensics XII, IFIP AICT 484, pp. 297–310, 2016.
DOI: 10.1007/978-3-319-46279-0_15

Figure 1. Original and forged images [1, 3].

ods of image manipulation in which some elements are removed, altered, blurred or emphasized using parts or properties of the same image; this type of manipulation also involves the adjustment of some image properties (e.g., color, white balance and contrast). Splicing [14] is a common image tampering technique; the technique combines image fragments from the same or different images to create a new image. Another popular technique for manipulating images is copy-move forgery [2]; this technique duplicates certain parts of a target image and places them elsewhere in the same image, the objective being to hide or emphasize parts of the target image. Figure 1 shows an original image (left) and its forged counterpart (right) [1, 3].

A number of researchers have studied the problem of image forgery detection. Zhao et al. [15] have leveraged JPEG compression characteristics to detect image inpainting in JPEG images. Kaur and Jyoti [7] have developed an image tampering detection method based on the inconsistency of JPEG grids in a suspect image. Cao et al. [2] have proposed an algorithm for detecting copy-move forgery using discrete cosine transforms and feature extraction. Talmale and Jasutkar [12] have evaluated a number of forgery detection methods. Birajdar and Mankar [1] have published a comprehensive survey of state-of-the-art passive techniques for detecting digital image forgeries.

In general, the image forgery detection techniques in the literature yield good results. However, in many cases, there is still a need for a human expert to make a final judgment about the detection results. The automation of this process can significantly reduce human effort in image forgery investigations.

This chapter proposes a new method for enhancing image forgery detection by combining two detection techniques using a 2-dimensional cross product. Compared with traditional approaches, the method yields better detection results in which the tampered regions are clearly iden-

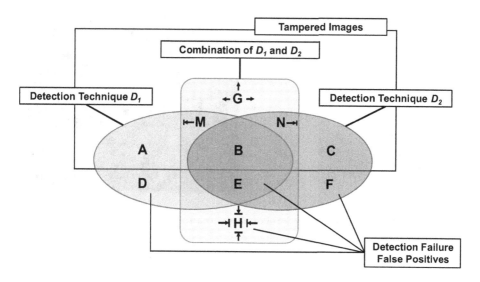

Figure 2. Proposed image forgery detection method.

tified. Another advantage is that the method can be applied to a wide variety of image forgery detection algorithms.

Figure 2 shows the conceptual idea underlying the proposed image forgery detection method. Specifically, two existing image forgery detection techniques D_1 and D_2 are combined. Regions A and C in the figure contain the tampered images that can be detected by techniques D_1 and D_2, respectively. Region B comprises the tampered images that both D_1 and D_2 can detect. In the case of detection failures, the false-positive results lie in the regions D, E and F.

When the proposed method is employed, tampered images that are detectable lie in regions B, M, N and G. The images in region G are the new tampered images that can be detected by combining techniques D_1 and D_2.

Due to the combination of techniques, the results are expected to be better than or at least equal to those contained in regions A, B and C. Hence, given regions M, N and G, the detection goal is to expand M and N to cover the A and C regions, and to expand G to cover additional tampered images.

A detection algorithm yields false-positive results when it determines that some authentic images have been tampered with. Thus, another important goal is to minimize the false-positive region H, ideally reduce it to null (empty). Unfortunately, the false-positive error problem is as yet unsolved and is the subject of ongoing research.

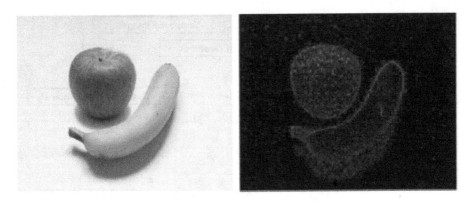

Figure 3. Applying error level analysis to a tampered JPEG image [3].

2.   Related Work

A number of techniques have been proposed for detecting image tampering. The detection techniques can be divided into two categories: (i) active techniques; and (ii) passive techniques [1, 9]. Active detection techniques require additional information to be inserted into the target media at the time of creation (e.g., tags or watermarks); this information can be used to detect tampering in a suspect image. This research focuses on passive or blind techniques for detecting image tampering.

A passive detection technique requires no prior knowledge of the target image. One of the most popular passive forgery detection techniques leverages image noise inconsistency [8, 10]. The technique examines the level or variance of noise in a target image and searches for inconsistencies in the noise levels in different regions of the image.

Due to the quantization process, a JPEG image has the same level of information loss throughout the image. However, a tampered image may contain different levels of information loss. The error level analysis technique [4] attempts to identify image forgeries based on this idea. It determines image altering by re-saving a JPEG image and then subtracting the original image from the re-saved image. When the target image is re-saved, the quantization process is invoked once again on the target image. Thus, the image constructed by subtracting the original image from the re-saved image reveals the difference in compression (noise quantization) in the tampered regions. Figure 3 shows an example of applying an error level analysis technique to a tampered JPEG image (original tampered image (left) and detection image (right)).

However, in some cases, the image created by subtracting the original image from the re-saved image may not clearly distinguish the tampered regions. Such a situation requires a human expert to make the final de-

Figure 4. Failure of error level analysis on a tampered JPEG image [3].

cision regarding image forgery. Figure 4 shows an unsuccessful example of using an error level analysis technique on a tampered image (left). The detection image obtained by subtraction (right) is noisy and it is difficult to identify the tampered regions.

Image transformation and re-sampling are the most common techniques for altering images. These methods usually involve an interpolation process. Fortunately, the characteristics of an interpolated image can be leveraged to detect forgery.

A number of researchers have studied the use of interpolation characteristics to detect image tampering [5, 11, 13]. For example, Gallagher [5] has proposed a method to detect interpolation (i.e., linear and cubic interpolation) in compressed JPEG images using statistical analyses of digitally-enlarged images.

Hwang and Har [6] have proposed a novel technique for detecting forged images using a re-interpolation algorithm. They use characteristics obtained from a discrete Fourier transform conversion of a target image to determine the rate of interpolation. Normally, a higher interpolation rate in an image leads to a lower number of high frequency elements in the discrete Fourier transform conversion results. Using image scaling and a discrete Fourier transform, a detection map is created that enables the identification of the tampered regions. Figure 5 shows an example of applying the re-interpolation technique to a tampered JPEG image (original tampered image (left) and detection image (right)).

3. Proposed Method

This section describes the method for enhancing image forgery detection by combining two detection techniques. The method first applies the two image forgery detection techniques to a target image. Next,

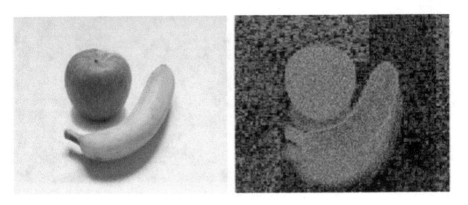

Figure 5. Applying a re-interpolation technique to a tampered JPEG image [3].

it combines the detection results obtained by each technique using a 2-dimensional cross product.

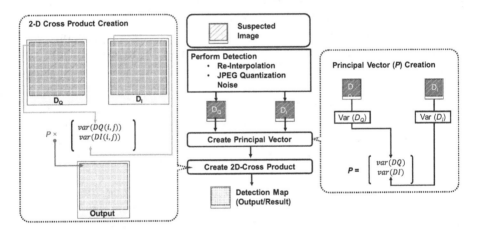

Figure 6. Overview of the proposed method.

Figure 6 presents an overview of the method. The goal is to combine two forgery detection techniques A and B on a target image I to obtain better results.

The proposed method involves the following steps:

- Techniques A and B are applied to the target image I to yield results R_A and R_B, respectively.

- The detection results R_A and R_B are used to create the principal vector $\vec{P}$.

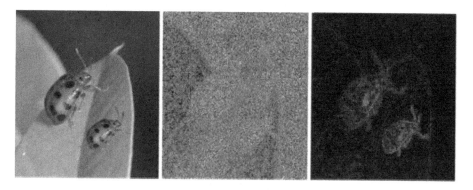

Figure 7. Detection using re-interpolation and JPEG noise quantization.

- The detection results R_A and R_B are divided into $m \times n$ fixed-size sub-blocks denoted by $R_A(i,j)$ and $R_B(i,j)$, where $1 \leq i \leq m$ and $1 \leq j \leq n$, respectively.

- A 2-dimensional cross product is performed of the principal vector $\vec{P}$ and every regional vector $V(i,j)$ created from the sub-blocks $R_A(i,j)$ and $R_B(i,j)$, where $1 \leq i \leq m$ and $1 \leq j \leq n$, respectively. This yields the enhanced detection result $D_E(i,j)$.

- $D_E(i,j)$ indicates the tampered regions in the target image I.

The image tampering detection method is implemented as a four-step procedure:

- **Step 1:** As shown in Figure 6, image forgery detection is enhanced by applying two detection techniques A and B in combination. First, image tampering detection is performed individually using techniques A and B:

$$R_{A,I} = D_A(I) \tag{1}$$

$$R_{B,I} = D_B(I) \tag{2}$$

where $D_A(I)$ and $D_B(I)$ correspond to performing image tampering detection on the target image I using techniques A and B, respectively. The detection results are $R_{A,I}$ and $R_{B,I}$.

Assume that detection technique A uses re-interpolation [6] while technique B uses JPEG noise quantization [4]. Figure 7 shows the corresponding detection results (original tampered image (left); re-interpolation detection image (center); and JPEG noise quantization detection image (right)).

- **Step 2:** The detection result images specified by Equations (1) and (2) are divided into $m \times n$ fixed-size rectangular sub-blocks. Let i and j be the row and column indices of the two result images. The sub-blocks of the two result images are expressed as $R_{A,I}(i,j)$ and $R_{B,I}(i,j)$, where $0 \leq i < m$ and $0 \leq j < n$.

- **Step 3:** A 2-dimensional cross product is performed on the result images $R_{A,I}$ and $R_{B,I}$. First, a principal vector $\vec{P}$ is created from $R_{A,I}$ and $R_{B,I}$ by computing the variance of each image:

$$\vec{P} = \begin{bmatrix} var(R_{A,I}) \\ var(R_{B,I}) \end{bmatrix} \tag{3}$$

- **Step 4:** Having created the principal vector, regional vectors $\vec{V}(i,j)$ are created for each sub-block of $R_{A,I}$ and $R_{B,I}$:

$$\vec{V}(i,j) = \begin{bmatrix} var(R_{A,I}(i,j)) \\ var(R_{B,I}(i,j)) \end{bmatrix} \tag{4}$$

- **Step 5:** The 2-dimensional cross product is performed of the principal vector $\vec{P}$ and every regional vector $\vec{V}(i,j)$ to yield the result matrix $M(i,j)$:

$$M(i,j) = \vec{P} \times \vec{V}(i,j) \tag{5}$$

- **Step 6:** The result matrix $M(i,j)$ is plotted to view the enhanced detection results.

Figure 8 compares the results obtained using the original techniques and those obtained using the proposed method (original tampered image (top left); re-interpolation detection image (top right); JPEG noise quantization detection image (bottom left); and proposed method detection image (bottom right)). The results show that the proposed method accurately extracts the tampered regions (i.e., two lady bugs) from the non-tampered regions compared with the original techniques (i.e., re-interpolation and JPEG noise quantization). The improvement in image tampering detection is beneficial to security and forensic practitioners as well to non-expert personnel who conduct image forgery investigations.

4.   Experimental Results

The experiments used the CASIA TIDE v2.0 [3] public dataset consisting of 7,491 authentic and 5,123 tampered color images. The authentic and tampered image sizes varied from small (240×160 pixels) to

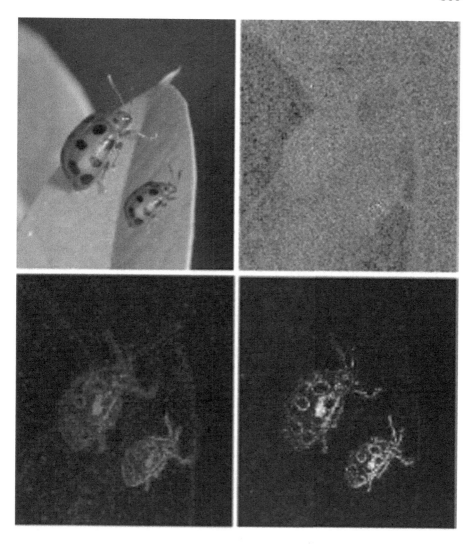

Figure 8. Comparison of detection results.

large (900 × 600 pixels). The sizes of the tampered regions within each forged image varied considerably.

The experiments focused on JPEG images. The proposed method was applied to three image tampering techniques: (i) re-interpolation; (ii) JPEG noise quantization; and (iii) noise estimation. Thus, three combinations of two techniques were employed: (i) re-interpolation with JPEG noise quantization; (ii) re-interpolation with noise estimation; and (iii) JPEG noise quantization with noise estimation.

Re-interpolation usually produces pattern mismatches between the forged and non-forged regions of a target image. However, it can be extremely difficult to precisely locate the tampered regions in the target image.

JPEG noise quantization can efficiently locate the tampered regions in a target image. However, this technique usually produces some irrelevant noise that can hinder the identification of forged images.

Noise estimation gives a result image that indicates the noise levels across a target image. Using the result image, it is possible to locate the tampered regions by considering the differences in the noise levels. However, in situations where the noise levels in the tampered and non-tampered regions are close to each other, it is difficult to detect forgeries and/or erroneous results may be obtained. Even human experts may have difficulty in precisely locating the tampered regions in a target image.

Figure 9 compares the results obtained by applying the three image tampering detection techniques individually with those obtained by applying them in combination using the proposed method. Specifically, Figure 9 shows the results obtained for four tampered images (larger images on the extreme left of the four rows). The smaller images to the right of each original image correspond to: top row (left to right) – re-interpolation detection image, JPEG noise quantization detection image and noise estimation detection image; and bottom row (left to right) – re-interpolation with JPEG noise quantization detection image, re-interpolation with noise estimation detection image and JPEG noise quantization with noise estimation detection image. The results show that the proposed method produces much better results than the individual techniques. Indeed, the proposed method yields improved clarity, enabling the tampered regions to be explicitly differentiated from other parts of the images.

Figure 10 shows an unsuccessful result obtained using the proposed method. The results indicate that only one tampered region exists – the yellow ribbon in the upper portion of the target image. JPEG noise quantization (top row) and noise estimation (bottom row) both produce false-positive results, incorrectly identifying non-tampered regions as tampered regions. The re-interpolation technique results show pattern inconsistencies in the yellow ribbon region as well as in the remainder of the target image. Indeed, the result is very noisy and cannot be used to accurately locate the tampered region (i.e., yellow ribbon). The reason is that the conventional detection techniques yield incorrect results. As a result, the proposed method, which combines the two

Figure 9. Comparison of detection results.

conventional techniques using a 2-dimensional cross product, also yields incorrect results.

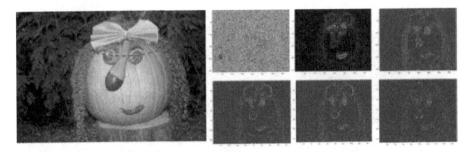

Figure 10.   Unsuccessful result.

5.   Discussion

The experimental results demonstrate that the combination of two passive detection methods can enhance image tampering detection. In particular, the clarity of a detection image is improved and the tampered regions are more easily distinguished from the non-tampered regions. The proposed method can be applied to any passive detection techniques that find inconsistencies in image properties (e.g., noise, color temperature and compression noise).

The proposed method suffers from some drawbacks. The main drawback is that, if the two tampering detection techniques that are combined produce noisy results or false-positive errors, then the results produced by the proposed method are affected negatively. Another challenge is to find the appropriate principal vector and regional vectors. The principal vector expresses the combination of the result images produced by the two tampering detection techniques. Regional vectors represent blocks of the two result images. Thus, performing 2-dimensional cross products of the principal and regional vectors essentially yields the differences between the principal vector and each regional vector. Creating principal and regional vectors based on simple variance calculations may not accurately represent the entire result images (in the case of the principal vector) and each portion of the result images (in the case of the regional vectors).

6.   Conclusions

The proposed method for image forgery detection combines two conventional passive detection techniques using a 2-dimensional cross product. The method can employ any passive detection techniques that find inconsistencies in target image properties (e.g., noise, color temperature and compression noise). Experimental results indicate that the method is efficient and has superior detection characteristics than when each passive detection technique is used individually. In particular, the clarity of the detection images are improved, enabling the tampered regions to be distinguished from the non-tampered regions more easily. The improvement in tampered image detection is beneficial to security and forensic practitioners as well to non-expert personnel who conduct image forgery investigations. Another advantage is that the proposed method is readily automated, potentially reducing the human effort involved in image forgery investigations.

The principal drawback of the method is that its results are dependent on the results produced by the individual detection techniques. Another problem is posed by creating the principal vector and regional vectors using simple variance calculations; this potentially affects the fidelity of image representations and, consequently, the detection results. Future research will attempt to enhance the proposed image forgery detection method by addressing these two limitations.

References

[1] G. Birajdar and V. Mankar, Digital image forgery detection using passive techniques: A survey, *Digital Investigation*, vol. 10(3), pp. 226–245, 2013.

[2] Y. Cao, T. Gao, L. Fan and Q. Yang, A robust detection algorithm for copy-move forgery in digital images, *Forensic Science International*, vol. 214(1-3), pp. 33–43, 2012.

[3] Chinese Academy of Sciences Institute of Automation (CAS-IA), CASIA v2.0, Beijing, China (`forensics.idealtest.org/casiav2`), 2016.

[4] H. Farid, Exposing digital forgeries from JPEG ghosts, *IEEE Transactions on Information Forensics and Security*, vol. 4(1), pp. 154–160, 2009.

[5] A. Gallagher, Detection of linear and cubic interpolation in JPEG compressed images, *Proceedings of the Second Canadian Conference on Computer and Robot Vision*, pp. 65–72, 2005.

[6] M. Hwang and D. Har, A novel forged image detection method using the characteristics of interpolation, *Journal of Forensic Sciences*, vol. 58(1), pp. 151–162, 2013.

[7] M. Kaur and Jyoti, Image tamper detection using non alignment of JPEG grids, *International Journal of Emerging Technologies in Computational and Applied Sciences*, vol. 6(4), pp. 331–333, 2013.

[8] B. Mahdian and S. Saic, Using noise inconsistencies for blind image forensics, *Image and Vision Computing*, vol. 27(10), pp. 1497–1503, 2009.

[9] B. Mahdian and S. Saic, A bibliography on blind methods for identifying image forgery, *Signal Processing: Image Communication*, vol. 25(6), pp. 389–399, 2010.

[10] X. Pan, X. Zhang and S. Lyu, Exposing image forgery with blind noise estimation, *Proceedings of the Thirteenth ACM Workshop on Multimedia and Security*, pp. 15–20, 2011.

[11] A. Popescu and H. Farid, Exposing digital forgeries in color filter array interpolated images, *IEEE Transactions on Signal Processing*, vol. 53(10), pp. 3948–3959, 2005.

[12] G. Talmale and R. Jasutkar, Analysis of different techniques of image forgery detection, *IJCA Proceedings on National Conference on Recent Trends in Computing*, vol. 2012(3), pp. 13–18, 2012.

[13] Y. Yun, J. Lee, D. Jung, D. Har and J. Choi, Detection of digital forgeries using an image interpolation from digital images, *Proceedings of the IEEE International Symposium on Consumer Electronics*, 2008.

[14] Z. Zhang, Y. Zhou, J. Kang and Y. Ren, Study of image splicing detection, *Proceedings of the Fourth International Conference on Intelligent Computing*, pp. 1103–1110, 2008.

[15] Y. Zhao, M. Liao, F. Shih and Y. Shi, Tampered region detection of inpainted JPEG images, *Optik – International Journal for Light and Electron Optics*, vol. 124(16), pp. 2487–2492, 2013.

Chapter 16

FORENSIC AUTHENTICATION OF BANK CHECKS

Rajesh Kumar and Gaurav Gupta

Abstract   This chapter describes an automated methodology for the forensic authentication of bank checks. The problem of check authentication is modeled as a two-class pattern recognition problem. Color and texture features are extracted from images of genuine and counterfeit checks. A support vector machine is utilized to determine check authenticity. Classification experiments involving a dataset of 50 bank checks yielded a detection accuracy of 99.0%. The automated methodology can be used by non-specialist personnel to detect check counterfeiting in a banking environment where large numbers of checks are handled on a daily basis.

Keywords: Bank checks, authenticity, pattern recognition, color, texture

1.   Introduction

The counterfeiting of currency notes, bank checks and certificates (e.g., birth, death and degree certificates) is a major problem in developing countries such as India. Even developed countries are encountering serious threats from counterfeiting. Technological advances, such as advanced scanning, color printing and color copying, have opened new avenues for criminals to run their counterfeiting businesses. The counterfeit materials look real to the naked eye. In fact, the quality of counterfeits is so good that even experts are often unable to distinguish them from the originals.

Counterfeit bank checks and currency notes directly affect a national economy. In recent years, the counterfeiting of checks, bank drafts and money orders has increased dramatically – this is evident from the number of alerts issued by the U.S. Federal Deposit Insurance Corporation. The number of alerts was 50 in 2003, 75 in 2004, 168 in 2005, 318 in

© IFIP International Federation for Information Processing 2016
Published by Springer International Publishing AG 2016. All Rights Reserved
G. Peterson and S. Shenoi (Eds.): Advances in Digital Forensics XII, IFIP AICT 484, pp. 311–322, 2016.
DOI: 10.1007/978-3-319-46279-0_16

2006 and 300 in 2007, a 500% increase in just four years. In 2007 alone, the United States, Canada and other countries jointly intercepted more than 590,000 counterfeit checks with a total face value of approximately $2.3 billion [12]. Clearly, the counterfeiting of checks and other financial documents is a serious concern.

The examination of counterfeit documents, in general, and counterfeit checks, in particular, relies on manual observations of certain built-in security features. In a forensic laboratory environment, counterfeit checks are examined microscopically and under different lighting conditions to identify discrepancies. Unfortunately, such examinations are cumbersome and infeasible in a banking environment where large numbers of checks are processed daily. Automated approaches that can be performed rapidly by non-specialist personnel are required to address the check counterfeiting problem.

Research in the area of automated authentication of security documents is relatively new. Several researchers have studied the problem of determining the authenticity of documents using pattern recognition [3, 9, 11]. Moreover, some researchers [2, 4, 6, 7] have examined printers, scanners and other devices that could indirectly help identify fraudulent documents.

This chapter describes an automated methodology for authenticating bank checks using pattern recognition. The objective was to implement a reliable system for determining the authenticity of large numbers of bank checks in real time. The problem was framed as a two-class classification problem involving pairs of checks: (i) Class I, when the reference and questioned checks are both genuine; and (ii) Class II, when one of the two checks (i.e., the questioned check) is fake. Since bank checks and other important documents incorporate security features based on the printing technology and printed designs, suitable features based on color and texture attributes were extracted and used for classification. A support vector machine (SVM) was trained and subsequently used for classification. The input vector to the support machine was a (dis)similarity index obtained by taking the absolute difference of corresponding elements in the feature vectors of a pair of genuine and fake checks. Classification experiments involving a dataset of 50 bank checks yielded a detection accuracy of 99.0%.

2.   Security Features in Bank Checks

Before designing an automated system for authenticating bank checks, it is important to understand the characteristics of checks and their security features. Knowledge of these characteristics and features is central to modeling bank check authentication as a pattern recognition problem.

Most important documents, including bank checks, have certain features that are considered to be difficult to copy and are, therefore, used for authentication purposes. These features are referred to in the forensic literature as security features. The more valuable or sensitive a document, the more complex are its security features. For example, passports, visas and currency notes have several complex security features; bank checks, official stamp paper and certificates have simpler (and relatively easy to copy) features due to their variations and lesser importance.

Security features are typically embedded in a document during paper manufacture and/or during printing. The features incorporated at the time of paper manufacture include paper type, thickness, surface roughness and watermarks. The features embedded during printing are the artistic design, printing patterns, micro features and the printing technology itself. Bank checks, like other security documents, have security features embedded in them during both phases.

2.1 Features Embedded During Manufacture

Paper plays an important role in the embedding of security features. Special types of paper are used for security documents because these types of paper are only available to official entities. The type of paper – made from cotton, grass or bamboo – is also a security feature. Different types of paper have unique physical and chemical properties that facilitate authentication. The thickness of the paper used for bank checks is also a distinguishing feature.

Other security features embedded during paper manufacture include watermarks and fluorescent optical fibers. Watermarks are designed into security documents to enhance identification and security. The watermark is actually a thinner area than the rest of the paper. The "dandy roll" used in the paper manufacturing process incorporates a metal representation of the watermark, which pushes paper fibers aside and leaves an imprint on the paper [8]. The imprint or watermark produced in this manner is more transparent than the rest of the paper and is readily visible.

Fluorescent optical fibers are also embedded as a security feature. The fibers are generally visible under ultra-violet light.

Watermarks and optical fibers are difficult to duplicate using scanners and copiers. However, as a result of cost considerations (especially with regard to embedding optical fibers), the vast majority of bank checks do not have these security features. Therefore, these features are not considered in the proposed methodology for detecting counterfeit bank checks.

2.2   Features Incorporated During Printing

Security features incorporated during the printing process include the type of printing ink, specially-designed fonts and artwork. The printing process varies from conventional offset printing to modern laser printing. Each printing process produces documents of a different quality; thus, the printing process itself incorporates security features in a document. Specialized technology such as intaglio printing is also used to print bank checks. This type of printing produces raised surfaces that can be felt by touching certain areas of a bank check. The security of the bank check is enhanced because the raised surfaces cannot be duplicated using a document reproduction device.

Using inks of different colors helps individualize bank checks. The inks range from conventional dye- or oil-based inks to special magnetic inks. Some inks are thermochromic – they change color when exposed to heat and return to their original color upon cooling; other inks are resistant to solvents. Thermochromic inks are resistant to color-copying and scanning while inks that are resistant to solvents are difficult to erase. Each of these inks can make a bank check distinctive. In addition to printing inks, a magnetic ink or toner is used in bank checks to print the magnetic ink character recognition (MICR) characters used to automate check processing and clearing [10].

Aside from printing processes and printing inks, special artwork is often printed on bank checks to provide additional security features. These may include micro-printing, crisscross lines, MICR characters and the bank logo, among others. Micro-printings are periodically-repeated characters, words or patterns that are distributed throughout a check. Scanning or copying these features may result in the deformation of their shapes [3]. Crisscross lines are intricate lines that are an essential part of security documents; these lines are also resistant to scanning and copying. The MICR characters and bank logo are typically printed in a distinctive manner to enhance the individuality of a bank check.

This work focuses on micro-printings on the backgrounds of bank checks to detect counterfeiting via the application of image processing and pattern recognition methodologies. Counterfeit detection primarily relies on color and texture features extracted from regions of interest that are confined to the backgrounds of bank checks.

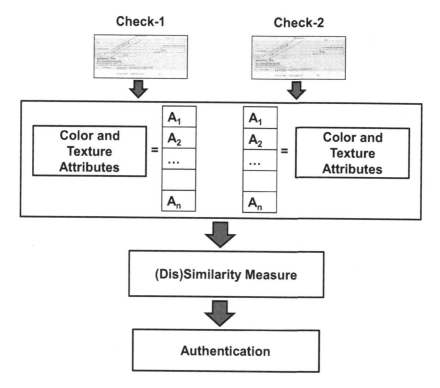

Figure 1. Bank check authentication methodology.

3. Bank Check Authentication Methodology

The authentication of a bank check can be framed as two-class classification problem. The two classes are: (i) Class I, when the questioned check and the reference check are both genuine; and (ii) Class II, when the questioned check is fake and the reference check is genuine.

Figure 1 presents the proposed bank check authentication methodology. To model the problem in a pattern recognition framework, images of the reference and questioned checks are first captured using a flatbed scanner. Some of the areas in the scanned checks with background designs are selected as the regions of interest. From the regions of interest on both types of checks, 2D histograms of the hue and saturation as color features and the gray level co-occurrence matrix of the intensity component as texture features are extracted. The feature vectors of the two checks are then combined to create a single feature vector.

After pairing the feature vectors, the resulting vector is submitted to a support vector machine classifier for authentication. Prior to the testing phase, the support vector machine is trained using a sufficient

Figure 2. Original check.

Figure 3. Counterfeit check created from the original check.

number of genuine-genuine and genuine-fake check pairs from a bank check image dataset.

3.1   Bank Check Image Dataset

The dataset used in the experiments comprised images of 25 genuine checks (five checks from five different banks) and 25 counterfeit checks. The counterfeit checks were created by scanning the 25 genuine checks using a flatbed scanner. The 25 scanned images were then reproduced using a high quality color printer on 100 GSM paper so that the printed checks looked like their original counterparts. After the counterfeited checks were printed, color images of all 50 checks (25 genuine and 25 fake) were captured at 300 dpi using a flatbed scanner. Figure 2 shows an original check and Figure 3 shows the counterfeit check created from the original check.

In a real scenario, a used check is sent for forensic analysis when its authenticity is suspected. A used check usually contains handwritten or printed information and a signature. Extracting features from an entire check introduces some bias. Keeping these facts in mind, regions containing background patterns (i.e., micro-printing) were selected for feature extraction purposes. Since a reasonable number of security features were embedded in the check backgrounds, the goal was to detect the discrepancies in the security features that resulted from the scanning and printing processes used to create the counterfeit checks.

3.2   Color and Texture Feature Extraction

The color and texture of the bank checks were assumed to be the principal features for the pattern recognition problem underlying check authentication. The reason is that, although the genuine and fake checks look similar, the changes in color and texture due to scanning and/or printing can be used to distinguish between the two types of checks. Specifically, color scanning and color printing are different tasks that involve different proprietary technologies.

To capture color information, the RGB color components of the check images were converted to the HSI (hue, saturation and intensity) color space as follows:

$$H = \frac{\sqrt{3}(G - B)}{2R - G - B} \tag{1}$$

$$S = 1 - \frac{min(R, G, B)}{255} \tag{2}$$

$$I = \frac{(R + G + B)}{3} \tag{3}$$

The HSI color space has been shown to be close to human perception and has been used in a number of computer vision problems, including face recognition [1]. Since color information in the HSI space is only contained in the hue and saturation components, color attributes were extracted as 2D hue-saturation histograms. The hue provides chromaticity (color spectrum) information while saturation expresses the purity of the color. Thus, a 2D histogram of hue and saturation gives the relative distributions of a particular hue (color) and its purity (saturation). To obtain a hue-saturation histogram, the hue was considered to range from $0°$ to $359°$ with a bin size of $30°$ while saturation ranged from 0 to 1 in a linear scale with a bin size of 0.2. This approach yielded a total of 60 features capturing color information.

To capture texture information, the gray level co-occurrence matrix (GLCM) of the intensity component was computed. The gray level co-occurrence matrix [5] is a matrix of relative frequencies with which gray values of two pixels, separated by a distance d and at an angle θ with the horizontal axis, occur on an image. To compute the features, for a given distance d, a joint probability matrix was determined by summing the gray level co-occurrence matrices for different values of θ and then normalizing the result.

Let $p_{\alpha\beta}$ be the joint probability of co-occurrence of two pixels with intensities α and β separated by (d, θ) in polar coordinates. Some commonly-used features based on a gray level co-occurrence matrix (of size $S \times S$) are defined as follows [5]:

$$Contrast = \sum_{\alpha,\beta=0}^{S-1} p_{\alpha\beta}(\alpha - \beta)^2 \tag{4}$$

$$Homogeneity = \sum_{\alpha,\beta=0}^{S-1} \frac{p_{\alpha\beta}}{1 + (\alpha - \beta)^2} \tag{5}$$

$$Energy = \sum_{\alpha,\beta=0}^{S-1} p_{\alpha\beta}^2 \tag{6}$$

$$Correlation = \sum_{\alpha,\beta=0}^{S-1} p_{\alpha\beta}[\frac{(\alpha - \mu_\alpha)(\beta - \mu_\beta)}{\sigma_\alpha \sigma_\beta}] \tag{7}$$

where:

$$\mu_\alpha = \sum_{\alpha,\beta=0}^{S-1} \alpha p_{\alpha\beta} \tag{8}$$

$$\mu_\beta = \sum_{\alpha,\beta=0}^{S-1} \beta p_{\alpha\beta} \tag{9}$$

$$\sigma_\alpha^2 = \sum_{\alpha,\beta=0}^{S-1} (1 - \mu_\alpha^2) p_{\alpha\beta} \tag{10}$$

$$\sigma_\beta^2 = \sum_{\alpha,\beta=0}^{S-1} (1 - \mu_\beta^2) p_{\alpha\beta} \tag{11}$$

The four features (contrast, homogeneity, energy and correlation) were extracted for three distances ($d = 5$, 10 and 15). This yielded a total of 12 ($= 4 \times 3$) texture features extracted from the gray level co-occurrence matrix. Upon combining the color and texture features, a feature vector of dimension 72 was created to represent a bank check.

3.3   Authentication

The authentication of a bank check was formulated as a two-class pattern recognition problem. Thus, for a given pair of bank checks, one of them known to be genuine (reference check), it is necessary to determine whether or not the two checks are similar; in other words, whether or not the second check (questioned check) is genuine.

A support vector machine classifier was used to solve the two-class pattern recognition problem. The input to the support vector machine classifier must be a vector that represents both the checks. Thus, a (dis)similarity index obtained by taking the absolute difference of the corresponding elements in the feature vector of the two checks was used as the input vector.

Let $v_r = (v_{r_1}, v_{r_2}, \cdots, v_{r_n})$ and $v_q = (v_{q_1}, v_{q_2}, \cdots, v_{q_n})$ be the feature vectors of the reference and questioned checks, respectively, where $n = 72$. Then, the combined vector obtained by pairing the two vectors is given by:

$$v = (|v_{r_1} - v_{q_1}|), (|v_{r_2} - v_{q_2}|), \cdots, (|v_{r_n} - v_{q_n}|) \qquad (12)$$

Following the usual leave-one-out pattern recognition strategy, the dataset was divided into two parts, one for training and the other for testing. A four-fold cross-validation over the training data was used to select the parameters of a support vector machine with a radial basis function (RBF) kernel. The optimal parameter, which were selected via cross-validation, were utilized for classifier design. The support vector machine was trained using the selected parameters and evaluated using the testing set. The classifier was designed to output 1 or -1 corresponding to both checks being genuine or one of the checks being counterfeit, respectively.

4.   Results and Discussion

The experimental evaluation was conducted using a dataset of 50 checks (25 genuine and 25 fake). The 25 genuine checks came from five different banks, five checks per bank. Each genuine check was used to create one counterfeit check, yielding the 50 checks in the dataset. Following the leave-one-out strategy, all the checks from four of the banks (i.e., 20 genuine and 20 fake checks) were kept for training. The checks from the remaining (fifth) bank (five genuine and five fake) were used for testing.

Consider the checks from a particular bank (five genuine and five fake checks). Although they were taken from different sources, the five genuine checks from the bank are similar (contemporary checks) and have similar security features. A pair of two genuine checks is formed in $^5C_2 = 10$ different ways. Similarly, a pair of genuine and fake checks from the ten checks is formed in $5 \times 5 = 25$ ways. Thus, for all the checks corresponding to a bank, there are ten input vectors for Class I (i.e., genuine-genuine) pairs and 25 input vectors for Class II (genuine-fake) pairs. To avoid bias towards any class, ten pairs were randomly selected out of the 25 vectors for Class II.

A total of 80 input vectors from four banks were designated for training and 20 input vectors from one bank were designated for testing. Of the 80 training vectors, 75% were randomly chosen for inner-level training and the remaining 25% for validation. This method was repeated five times so that the checks from each of the five banks could be utilized for testing purposes. The overall performance was computed as the mean of the five repetitions.

Experiments involving the trained support vector machine classifier yielded 99% overall accuracy for bank check authentication. The high accuracy may be due to several factors. One is that the counterfeit checks were created by scanning genuine checks and printing counterfeits in a pristine laboratory environment. This does not capture the security features of the genuine checks adequately and reliably. Moreover, in a real scenario, criminals would be likely to use more sophisticated techniques and equipment to create fake checks. The second reason is the small dataset. The third reason is the potential for the extracted features to capture color and texture information in very precise manner; gray level co-occurrence matrix features have been demonstrated to produce good results in a number of applications.

5. Conclusions

The proposed automated methodology for the forensic authentication of bank checks is implemented as a two-class pattern recognition problem involving pairs of checks: (i) Class I, when the reference and questioned checks are both genuine; and (ii) Class II, when one of the two checks (i.e., the questioned check) is fake. Color (2D hue-saturation histograms) and texture (gray level co-occurrence matrix of the intensity component) features were extracted from images of genuine and counterfeit checks. A trained support vector machine was utilized to determine check authenticity. Classification experiments involving a dataset of 50 bank checks yielded a detection accuracy of 99.0%. The automated methodology can be used by non-specialist personnel to detect check counterfeiting in a banking environment where large numbers of checks are handled on a daily basis.

References

[1] B. Chanda and D. Majumdar *Digital Image Processing and Analysis*, Prentice Hall of India, New Delhi, India, 2005.

[2] C. Chen and C. Chiu, A fuzzy neural approach to design of a Wiener printer model incorporated into model-based digital halftoning, *Applied Soft Computing*, vol. 12(4), pp. 1288–1302, 2012.

[3] U. Garain and B. Halder, On automatic authenticity verification of printed security documents, *Proceedings of the Sixth Indian Conference on Computer Vision, Graphics and Image Processing*, pp. 706–713, 2008.

[4] G. Gupta, S. Saha, S. Chakraborty and C. Mazumdar, Document frauds: Identification and linking fake documents to scanners and printers, *Proceedings of the International Conference on Computing: Theory and Applications*, pp. 497–501, 2007.

[5] R. Haralick, K. Shanmugam and I. Dinstein, Texture features for image classification, *IEEE Transactions on Systems, Man and Cybernetics*, vol. SMC-3(6), pp. 610–621, 1973.

[6] E. Kee and H. Farid, Printer profiling for forensics and ballistics, *Proceedings of the Tenth ACM Workshop on Multimedia and Security*, pp. 3–10, 2008.

[7] N. Khanna, A. Mikkilineni and E. Delp, Scanner identification using feature-based processing and analysis, *IEEE Transactions on Information Forensics and Security*, vol. 4(1), pp. 123–139, 2009.

[8] K. Koppenhaver, *Forensic Document Examination: Principles and Practice*, Humana Press, Totowa, New Jersey, 2007.

[9] C. Lampert, L. Mei and T. Breuel, Printing technique classification for document counterfeit detection, *Proceedings of the International Conference on Computational Intelligence and Security*, vol. 1, pp. 639–644, 2006.

[10] Reserved Bank of India, Mechanized Cheque Processing Using MICR Technology – Procedural Guidelines, Mumbai, India (www. rbi. org.in/scripts/PublicationsView.aspx?id=4551), 2014.

[11] A. Roy, B. Halder and U. Garain, Authentication of currency notes through printing technique verification, *Proceedings of the Seventh Indian Conference on Computer Vision, Graphics and Image Processing*, pp. 383–390, 2010.

[12] U.S. Department of Justice and Public Safety Canada, Public Advisory: Special Report on Counterfeit Checks and Money Orders, Washington, DC and Ottawa, Canada (www.justice.gov/opa/documents/08public-advisory-counterfeit.pdf), 2008.

VII

FORENSIC TECHNIQUES

Chapter 17

DATA TYPE CLASSIFICATION: HIERARCHICAL CLASS-TO-TYPE MODELING

Nicole Beebe, Lishu Liu and Minghe Sun

Abstract   Data and file type classification research conducted over the past ten to fifteen years has been dominated by competing experiments that only vary the number of classes, types of classes, machine learning technique and input vector. There has been surprisingly little innovation on fundamental approaches to data and file type classification. This chapter focuses on the empirical testing of a hypothesized, two-level hierarchical classification model and the empirical derivation and testing of several alternative classification models. Comparative evaluations are conducted on ten classification models to identify a final winning, two-level classification model consisting of five classes and 52 lower-level data and file types. Experimental results demonstrate that the approach leads to very good class-level classification performance, improved classification performance for data and file types without high entropy (e.g., compressed and encrypted data) and reasonably-equivalent classification performance for high-entropy data and file types.

Keywords: Statistical classification, data types, file types, hierarchical model

1.   Introduction

Statistical data type classification has many important applications in cyber security and digital forensics. Cyber security applications include intrusion detection, content-based firewall blocking, malware detection and analysis, and steganalysis. Data type classification can defend against many common signature obfuscation techniques and enhance the detection and blocking of undesired network traffic. It can also help map binary objects [12], which is useful in malware analysis and, possibly, steganalysis. In digital forensics, data type classification aids

© IFIP International Federation for Information Processing 2016
Published by Springer International Publishing AG 2016. All Rights Reserved
G. Peterson and S. Shenoi (Eds.): Advances in Digital Forensics XII, IFIP AICT 484, pp. 325–343, 2016.
DOI: 10.1007/978-3-319-46279-0_17

fragment identification, isolation, recovery and file reassembly. Commercial and open-source tools such as `file` and TrID are reliant on file signatures and other magic numbers, rendering them ineffective when file headers and/or other blocks containing key magic numbers are missing or corrupted, or when their locations in the files are unknown [16]. Data type classification can also aid forensic triage efforts and improve investigative efficiency by targeting or prioritizing investigative efforts and search results [8].

This research focuses on data type classification absent reliable file signatures, filename extensions and other filesystem data that may identify the data type, either based on the file type that the data fragment used to be a part of in the case of files and composite objects, or based on the data type or primitive data type as defined by Erbacher and Mulholland [13]. It is important to note that, when reliable file signatures, filename extensions or filesystem data exist pertaining to a data fragment, traditional file signature based methods should be used over statistical or specialized [24] data type classification methods, including the hierarchical modeling approaches explored in this chapter. However, in instances where such reliable metadata and/or magic numbers do not exist, alternative data type classification methods are needed.

A fair amount of data type classification research has been conducted in the past decade, especially in the digital forensics domain. Researchers have explored a wide variety of data and file types, classification algorithms and feature sets. Several researchers have limited their multi-class size to ten or less [1–4, 6, 10, 11, 13, 18–21, 23, 26]. Fewer researchers have investigated data type classification methodologies for scenarios involving more than ten classes [9, 12, 14, 16, 17, 22, 25]. Overall, support vector machines (SVMs) have prevailed, achieving the best balance between prediction accuracy and scalability [9, 14, 16, 20]. Research has also demonstrated the great discriminatory value of n-grams across a wide range of data and file types [9].

An evaluation of the extant research reveals that one of the most negative influences on prediction accuracy is the number of classes in a multi-class problem. As the number of classes increases, prediction accuracy tends to decrease, as shown in Figure 1, which records empirical prediction accuracy relative to the number of classes reported in sixteen data type classification publications [1, 2, 4–6, 10–12, 14, 18, 19, 21–23, 25, 26]. Reducing the number of classes is highly advantageous. However, many data type classification use cases require the ability to classify blocks among a large number of classes. Therefore, this research empirically examines a hierarchical modeling approach proposed by Conti et al. [12]. The approach classifies data and file types first into classes and

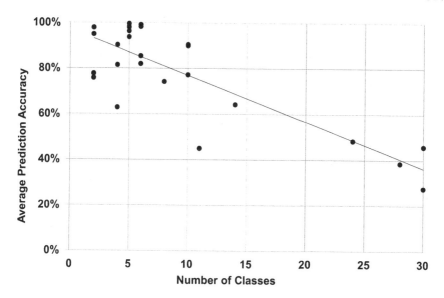

Figure 1. Average prediction accuracy vs. number of classes.

further classifies them into class-based types. This approach is expected to increase the overall prediction accuracy because each sequential classification problem becomes smaller in terms of the number of classes in each individual multi-class problem.

2. Methodology

This research employed a traditional empirical approach (hypothesis testing) as well as an exploratory approach. First, the six-class, two-level hierarchy shown in Table 1 was hypothesized based on knowledge of the internal data structures and encodings within each data and file type. Next, an exploratory data analysis was conducted to derive alternative hierarchical models from the data. Finally, a comparative evaluation was performed on the prediction accuracy at the class level and the type level. To accomplish this, two clustering algorithms, k-means and expectation maximization, were employed. The k-means algorithm was used to set the number of classes (clusters) *a priori* equal to the number of hypothesized classes; the model was considered to be validated if the resulting type-to-class cluster distribution matched the hypothesized hierarchical model. Expectation maximization clustering was used to derive alternative hierarchical models from the data. The precision, recall and overall classification accuracy levels were measured at the class level and file/data type level to determine the winning hierarchy. Two sample sizes ($n = 20$ and $n = 50$ samples) were employed per type and

Table 1. Hypothesized six-class, two-level hierarchy.

TEXT	**PSEUDO-RANDOM**
Delimited (.csv)	Encrypted (AES256)
JSON (.json)	Random
Base64 (N/A)	
Base85 (N/A)	
URL Encoding (N/A)	**COMPRESSED-LOSSY**
Postscript (.ps)	MP3 (.mp3)
Cascading Style Sheet (.css)	AAC (.m4a)
Log File (.log)	JPEG (.jpg)
Plain Text (.txt)	H264 (.mp4)
JavaScript (.js)	AVI (.avi)
Java Source Code (.java)	Windows Media Video (.wmv)
XML (.xml)	Flash Video (.flv)
HTML (.html)	Shockwave Flash (.swf)
Active Server Page (.asp)	Waveform Audio (.wav)
Rich Text Language (.rtf)	Windows Media Audio (.wma)
Thunderbird (.msf/none)	
	COMPRESSED-LOSSLESS
	Bi-Tonal Image (.tif/.tiff)
BINARY	GIF (.gif)
Bitmap (.bmp)	Portable Network Graphic (.png)
Windows Executable (.exe)	Bzip2 (.bz2)
Windows Library (.dll)	Gzip (.gz)
Linux Executable (.elf)	ZIP (.zip)
	Java Archive (.jar)
BINARY/TEXT	RPM Package Manger (.rpm)
MS Excel 97-2003 (.xls)	PDF (.pdf)
MS Word 97-2003 (.doc)	MS Word 2007+ (.docx)
MS PowerPoint 97-2003 (.ppt)	MS Excel 2007+ (.xlsx)
File System – EXT3/4	MS PowerPoint 2007+ (.pptx)
File System – NTFS	JBIG2 (.jb2)
File System – FAT	Outlook PST (.pst)

experiments were conducted with two different file-to-class assignment methods.

All the samples were 512 B fragments extracted from full files, beginning at file offset 512. The header block was excluded to ensure that the file classifications were not biased by file signatures. File signatures remain the most reliable means to type classify files (when they are present and reliable), but this work focuses on data and file type classification absent traditional, reliable file signatures, file extensions and filesystem data. File fragments used in the experiments were randomly selected from a large corpus of files created by the authors of this chapter for their prior work [9] and augmented with additional types from [7].

Table 2. Data and file types in the dataset.

Data Types				
JPG[1]	BZIP2[2]	WMV[2]	HTML[1]	TXT[1,2]
GIF[1]	GZIP[1]	MP3[2]	XML[1]	BASE64[2]
BMP[1]	DOC[1]	MP4[2]	JSON[2]	BASE85[2]
PNG[1]	DOCX[1]	AVI[2]	CSV[1]	URLENCODED[2]
TIF[2]	XLS[1]	FLV[2]	CSS[2]	FAT FS DATA[2]
PDF[1]	XLSX[1,2]	M4A[2]	LOG[1]	NTFS FS DATA[2]
PS[1]	PPT[1]	JAVA[1]	ASP[2]	EXT3 FS DATA[2]
ZIP[2]	PPTX[1]	JS[2]	DLL[2]	AES256[2]
RTF[2]	PST[2]	JAR[2]	ELF[2]	RANDOM[2]
SWF[2]	RPM[2]	JB2[2]	EXE[2]	
TBIRD[2]	WAV[2]	WMA[2]		

[1] Data Source: GovDocs [15]
[2] Data Source: Other [7]
"FS DATA" = File System Data ($MFT, inode tables, etc.)

The feature set included unigrams, bigrams, entropy, Kolmogorov complexity, mean byte value, Hamming weight, average contiguity between bytes and longest byte streak. Interested readers are referred to [9] for details and equations. The dataset included samples across 52 data and file types. Table 2 lists the data and file types in the dataset.

3. Experimentation

The experimental procedure involved several rounds of experiments to empirically test the hypothesized model, following which new models were derived empirically and evaluated comparatively. Each successive experimental round is discussed separately.

3.1 Hypothesized Model Testing

The first experimental round involved empirical testing of the hypothesized model. The k-means clustering algorithm was applied to 20 randomly-selected samples from each of the 52 data and file types. The value of k was set to six ($k = 6$) to see if the resulting six clusters aligned with the hypothesized file type classes. A simple voting method was used to assign types to classes such that the cluster with the most members of a single type was the winning class for the type. For example, if the cluster distribution for the $n = 20$ JPG samples was $[0, 1, 10, 3, 4, 2]$, then the type JPG was assigned to the third class because the majority of the samples were assigned to the third cluster.

Table 3. k-means ($k = 6$) clustering solution.

Class	Data and File Types
0	B85, AVI, B64, DLL, EXE, MOV, TBIRD
1	CSS, CSV, DOC, HTML, JAVA, JS, JSON, LOG, PST, RTF, URL, XML
2	AES, BMP, BZ2, DOCX, ELF, FLV, GIF, GZ, JAR, JB2, JPG, M4A, MP3, MP4, PDF, PNG, PPT, PPTX, RAND, RPM, SWF, WAV, WMV, XLSX, ZIP
3	EXT3
4	NTFS, TIF
5	B16, FAT, PS, TEXT, XLS

The type-to-class distribution for the k-means ($k = 6$) solution did not align with the hypothesized type-to-class model. This can be seen when comparing Table 3 with Table 1. In particular, the classifier was unable to separately classify lossy compressed files vs. lossless compressed files vs. random and encrypted files, which is where the majority of the deviations from the hypothesized model occurred.

3.2   Exploratory Cluster Analysis

The second experimental round applied expectation maximization (EM) clustering to empirically derive the classes from the data, including the number of classes. Unlike the previous round, the number of classes was not set *a priori*. Once again, 20 randomly-selected samples from each type were employed.

Table 4. Expectation maximization clustering solution.

Class	Data and File Types
0	AES, AVI, BMP, BZ2, DLL, DOCX, ELF, EXE, FLV, GIF, GZ, JAR, JB2, JPG, M4A, MOV, MP3, MP4, PDF, PNG, PPT, PPTX, RAND, RPM, SWF, WAV, WMV, XLSX, ZIP
1	[EMPTY]
2	B85, B64, FAT, PST
3	B16, CSS, CSV, DOC, EXT3, NTFS, HTML, JAVA, JS, JSON, LOG, PS, RTF, TBIRD, TIF, TEXT, URL, XLS, XML

The expectation maximization results in Table 4 provide intuitive classes; however, Classes 0 and 3 are disproportionately large. Also, Class 1 did not receive any members upon model convergence. Since the

Table 5. Sample output supporting the advanced type-to-class assignment method.

Data Type	Type-to-Cluster Distribution (n=50)	Class Assignment
EXT	[0, 0, 0, 0, 0, 37, 0, 0, 13, 0]	6
FAT	[0, 0, 0, 0, 0, 30, 0, 1, 19, 0]	6
NTFS	[0, 0, 0, 0, 0, 22, 0, 0, 28, 0]	9

primary motivation of hierarchical classification is to significantly reduce the multi-class size at all levels of the hierarchical classification process, large and empty hierarchical classes are undesirable.

In a *post hoc* treatment, Class 0 was further clustered using the k-means algorithm ($k = 3$). When selecting 20 instances per data and file type, only the AVI file type separated from the class, leaving two clusters (one with AVI and the other with the remaining 28 types). When selecting 50 instances per data and file type, only ELF and PDF separated out and AVI remained with the remaining 26 types.

Class 3 was clustered similarly with the k-means algorithm ($k = 3$). When selecting 20 instances per data and file type, only NTFS and TIF separated out, leaving the other 17 types in a single cluster. When selecting 50 instances per type, EXT3, NTFS and TIF separated out, still leaving the other 16 types in a single cluster. These findings underscore the challenge of statistically distinguishing between (classifying) lossy compressed objects, lossless compressed objects and random and encrypted data.

Advanced Type-to-Class Assignment Procedure. In the third experimental round, the number of randomly-selected samples per type was increased from $n = 20$ to $n = 50$ per type, and an advanced method was employed for type-to-class assignment. Instead of using a simple "maximum cluster assignment takes all" voting method, the type-to-cluster distribution matrix was clustered for the final class assignment.

To demonstrate and explain the advanced type-to-class assignment method, a partial type-to-cluster distribution matrix is shown in Table 5; this is taken from a 10-class model that resulted from expectation maximization clustering of 50 samples per type. The simple voting method classified NTFS data as Class 9 and EXT and FAT filesystem data as Class 6, despite the obvious similarity in class membership distributions. This suggests that they might be better classified as a singular class. This is just one example of several other similar situations.

Table 6.   Expectation maximization clustered matrix approach.

Class	Data and File Types
0	CSS, EXT3, FAT, NTFS, TIF, URL, XLS
1	B85, B16, B64, DOC, HTML, JAR, JAVA, PDF, PPT, PS, RPM
2	AES, AVI, BMP, BZ2, DLL, DOCX, ELF, EXE, FLV, GIF, GZ, JB2, JPG, M4A, MOV, MP3, MP4, PNG, PPTX, PST, RAND, SWF, WAV, WMV, XLSX, ZIP
3	CSV, JS, JSON, LOG, RTF, TBIRD, TEXT, XML

Table 7. k-means ($k = 6$) clustered matrix approach.

Class	Data and File Types
0	B85, AVI, DOC, ELF, EXE, PDF, PPT, PST, WAV
1	AES, BMP, BZ2, DLL, DOCX, FLV, GIF, GZ, JAR, JB2, JPG, M4A, MOV, MP3, MP4, PNG, PPTX, RAND, RPM, SWF, WMV, XLSX, ZIP
2	URL
3	CSV, JSON, LOG, RTF, TBIRD, TEXT
4	EXT3, FAT, NTFS, TIF
5	B16, B64, CSS, HTML, JAVA, JS, PS, XLS, XML

Table 8. k-means ($k = 4$) clustered matrix approach.

Class	Data and File Types
0	B16, CSS, EXT3, FAT, NTFS, PS, TIF, URL, XLS
1	B85, AVI, DOC, ELF, EXE, PDF, PPT, PST, WAV
2	B64, CSV, HTML, JAVA, JS, JSON, LOG, RTF, TBIRD, TEXT, XML
3	AES, BMP, BZ2, DLL, DOCX, FLV, GIF, GZ, JAR, JB2, JPG, M4A, MOV, MP3, MP4, PNG, PPTX, RAND, RPM, SWF, WMV, XLSX, ZIP

Using the advanced type-to-class membership assignment procedure, the type-to-cluster distribution matrix (comprising 50 samples of each of the 52 types) was clustered. This procedure resulted in the hierarchical models shown in Tables 6 through 9 using various clustering approaches.

Examination of the hierarchical models from a face validity perspective as well as a class balance perspective reveals that the advanced type-to-class assignment method outperforms the simple voting method. Also, meta-classes from across the various experiments can be qualitatively inferred by observing common type-to-cluster classification trends

Table 9. k-means ($k = 3$) clustered matrix approach.

Class	Data and File Types
0	B64, CSV, HTML, JAVA, JS, JSON, LOG, RTF, TBIRD, TEXT, XML
1	B16, CSS, ELF, EXT3, FAT, NTFS, PDF, PS, TIF, URL, XLS
2	B85, AES, AVI, BMP, BZ2, DLL, DOC, DOCX, EXE, FLV, GIF, GZ, JAR, JB2, JPG, M4A, MOV, MP3, MP4, PNG, PPT, PPTX, PST, RAND, RPM, SWF, WAV, WMV, XLSX, ZIP

Table 10. Meta-classes from hierarchical models.

Meta-Class	Data and File Types
Compressed	PPTX, RAND, AES, JB2, ZIP, XLSX, JPG, DLL, BMP, GZ, SWF, DOCX, GIF, MP4, MOV, MP3, PNG, M4A, FLV, WMV, BZ2
Text	TBIRD, XML, RTF, LOG, TEXT, JS, JSON, CSV
Binary-Text	NTFS, EXT3, URL, FAT, TIF, XLS, CSS

(see Table 10). However, the 16 types fail to consistently cluster into a stable hierarchy: B64, HTML, JAVA, LOG, B16, TIF, URL, XLS, B85, AVI, DOC, EXE, GIF, GZ, JB2 and WAV. Hence, while the meta-classes shown might be useful for a two-level hierarchical model limited to its constituent 36 file and data types, further exploratory analysis is needed to derive a more appropriate hierarchical model for all 52 file and data types considered in this work.

3.3 Identifying the Winning Model

The purpose of the final experimental round was to run repeated experiments for more robust results, from which a winning model would be selected. Three repeated experiments were conducted and quantitative measures of model quality were evaluated comparatively. Expectation maximization clustering was performed on the same input three times. Then, the simple voting method and the advanced assignment method described previously were applied to each set of expectation maximization clustered outputs. The prediction accuracy, precision and recall were then computed and evaluated.

Table 11. Repeated experiments (Round 1; simple voting method).

Class	Types Clustered into Class
0	HTML, JAVA, JS
1	JSON
2	B85, B16, B64, TBIRD, URL
3	TIF
4	EXT3, FAT
5	CSV, LOG, PS, RTF, TEXT, XML
6	CSS, DOC, ELF, NTFS, XLS
7	AVI, BMP, DLL, EXE, JAR, MOV, WAV
8	AES, BZ2, DOCX, FLV, GIF, GZ, JB2, JPG, M4A, MP3, MP4, PDF, PNG, PPT, PPTX, PST, RAND, RPM, SWF, WMV, XLSX, ZIP

Table 12. Repeated experiments (Round 1; advanced assignment method).

Class	Types Clustered into Class
0	CSS, ELF, EXT3, FAT, NTFS, XLS
1	AES, BZ2, FLV, GIF, GZ, JB2, JPG, M4A, MP3, MP4, PDF, PNG, PPT, PPTX, RAND, RPM, SWF, WMV, XLSX, ZIP
2	B85, B16, B64, TBIRD, URL
3	CSV, HTML, JAVA, JS, JSON, LOG, PS, RTF, TEXT, XML
4	AVI, BMP, DLL, DOC, DOCX, EXE, JAR, MOV, PST, TIF, WAV

Table 13. Repeated experiments (Round 2; simple voting method).

Class	Types Clustered into Class
0	CSS, NTFS, XLS
1	B85, ELF, MOV, WAV
2	AES, AVI, BMP, BZ2, DLL, DOC, DOCX, EXE, FLV, GIF, GZ, JAR, JB2, JPG, M4A, MP3, MP4, PDF, PNG, PPT, PPTX, PST, RAND, RPM, SWF, WMV, XLSX, ZIP
3	CSV, JSON, LOG
4	EXT3, FAT
5	URL
6	TIF
7	B16, B64, HTML, JAVA, JS, PS, RTF, TBIRD, TEXT, XML

Tables 11 through 16 present the results of the repeated experiments. The results of each experiment were evaluated considering face validity

Table 14. Repeated experiments (Round 2; advanced assignment method).

Class	Types Clustered into Class
0	B16, B64, CSV, HTML, JAVA, JS, JSON, LOG, PS, RTF, TBIRD, TEXT, XML
1	B85, AVI, BMP, CSS, DLL, DOC, ELF, EXE, EXT3, FAT, NTFS, MOV, PDF, TIF, URL, WAV, XLS
2	AES, BZ2, DOCX, FLV, GIF, GZ, JAR, JB2, JPG, M4A, MP3, MP4, PNG, PPT, PPTX, PST, RAND, RPM, SWF, WMV, XLSX, ZIP

Table 15. Repeated experiments (Round 3; simple voting method).

Class	Types Clustered into Class
0	CSS, ELF, NTFS, XLS
1	B85, B16, B64, CSV, HTML, JAVA, JS, JSON, LOG, PS, RTF, TBIRD, TEXT, URL, XML
2	AES, AVI, BMP, BZ2, DLL, DOC, DOCX, EXE, FLV, GIF, GZ, JAR, JB2, JPG, M4A, MOV, MP3, MP4, PDF, PNG, PPT, PPTX, PST, RAND, RPM, SWF, WAV, WMV, XLSX, ZIP
3	EXT3, FAT, TIF

Table 16. Repeated experiments (Round 3; advanced assignment method).

Class	Types Clustered into Class
0	B85, B16, B64, CSV, HTML, JAVA, JS, JSON, LOG, PS, RTF, TBIRD, TEXT, URL, XML
1	BMP, CSS, DLL, DOC, ELF, EXE, EXT3, FAT, NTFS, PDF, TIF, XLS
2	AES, AVI, BZ2, DOCX, FLV, GIF, GZ, JAR, JB2, JPG, M4A, MOV, MP3, MP4, PNG, PPT, PPTX, PST, RAND, RPM, SWF, WAV, WMV, XLSX, ZIP

and quantitative measures (overall model classification accuracy as well as type-level precision and recall). This validated the interim conclusion that the advanced type-to-class distribution matrix clustering approach outperforms the simple voting method for type-to-class assignment.

Upon comparing the quantitative measures across the three experiments for the type-to-class distribution matrix clustering method, it

Table 17. Winning hierarchical model.

Class: Title	File and Data Types Assigned to Class
0: Binary-Text	CSS, ELF, EXT3, FAT, NTFS, XLS
1: Compressed-Random	AES, BZ2, FLV, GIF, GZ, JB2, JPG, M4A, MP3, MP4, PDF, PNG, PPT, PPTX, RAND, RPM, SWF, WMV, XLSX, ZIP
2: Encoded Text	B85, B16, B64, TBIRD, URL
3: Unencoded Text	CSV, HTML, JAVA, JS, JSON, LOG, PS, RTF, TEXT, XML
4: Binary-Compressed	AVI, BMP, DLL, DOC, DOCX, EXE, JAR, MOV, PST, TIF, WAV

can be concluded that the hierarchy shown in Table 12 is the winning hierarchy. Table 17 redisplays the winning hierarchy with rough class descriptive titles. Note that the titles should be used with caution because they do not describe all the constituent file types in an ideal manner.

Table 18. Performance measures – Class-level classification.

Model	Train Time	Predict Time	Accuracy (No. Obs.)	C
Hypothesized	3m30.570s	0m08.705s	76.51% (62,426)	64
Table 12	2m22.398s	0m12.317s	88.88% (62,322)	512
Table 16	1m13.641s	0m11.018s	94.40% (62,081)	1,024

Table 18 presents the comparative sample-to-class classification predication accuracy and train/test run times for the hypothesized model and the two top-performing empirically-derived models, the Table 12 model and the Table 16 model. Tables 19 through 21 provide similar data for the two models; however, the values pertain to type-level, within-class classification.

4.   Winning Model Discussion

The hierarchical model shown in Table 16 exhibits superior performance when prediction accuracy is considered only at the class level. The class-level classification accuracy of the theoretical model is 76.51%. The classification accuracy for the model shown in Table 12 (i.e., the model selected as the winning hierarchy) is 88.88%. The accuracy improves to 94.40% for the model shown in Table 16.

Table 19. Performance measures – Type-level classification (Hypothesized model).

Class	Train Time	Predict Time	Accuracy (No. Obs.)	C
1	0m34.001s	0m2.471s	95.21% (19,638)	512
2	0m07.526s	0m0.047s	0.00% (9)	1,024
3	0m13.168s	0m0.414s	65.54% (5,613)	64
4	0m48.827s	0m1.853s	75.60% (5,291)	32
5	0m08.798s	0m0.732s	85.85% (3,902)	128
6	1m25.891s	0m5.594s	23.17% (27,973)	32

Table 20. Performance measures – Type-level classification (Table 12 model).

Model	Train Time	Predict Time	Accuracy (No. Obs.)	C
0	0m05.469s	0m00.661s	71.10% (7,453)	32
1	2m12.123s	0m10.278s	24.81% (28,081)	512
2	0m05.003s	0m00.982s	97.96% (5,918)	512
3	0m11.236s	0m00.752s	90.88% (12,609)	512
4	1m13.674s	0m01.882s	85.64% (8,261)	512

Table 21. Performance measures – Type-level classification (Table 16 model).

Model	Train Time	Predict Time	Accuracy (No. Obs.)	C
0	0m31.645s	0m02.387s	94.25% (18,509)	1,024
1	1m18.770s	0m01.267s	77.71% (11,855)	64
2	4m29.957s	0m11.186s	35.59% (31,717)	32

While the class-level classification accuracy of the model selected as the winning model (Table 12) is not maximal (it is less than that of the model shown in Table 16), its average within-class, type-level classification accuracy values exceed those of the other candidate models. The average type-level classification accuracy values are: theoretical model – 57.56%; winning model (Table 12) – 74.08%; and the model shown in Table 16 – 69.18%. These differing results are presented because some use cases may prefer to sacrifice type-level classification accuracy for class-level classification accuracy, while others may prefer the converse.

In selecting the model reflected by Table 12 as the winning model, the fact that 25 high-entropy file types classified in the most poorly-performing class in the Table 16 model was considered. Since this is one of only three classes in the model, having such a large, poorly-performing class is problematic. In contrast, the Table 12 model contains five classes and the most poorly-performing class (also characterized by high-entropy file types) only contains 20 file types. This is important because a hierarchical classification system that contains a singular, large, poorly-performing, high-entropy class among very few classes is only effective at the class level; its utility for type-level classification would be very limited. Therefore, it is important to minimize the number of file types in such a class. Hence, the Table 12 hierarchy is preferred to the Table 16 hierarchy – it contains more classes and fewer constituent file types in the characteristically poorly-performing, high-entropy class.

Hierarchical models with more classes are also favored because they provide greater analytical granularity at the class level than models with more types in fewer classes. For example, a possible application of class-level classification is network-based data triage and prioritization of limited deep packet inspection resources. Inbound packet payloads could be classified and marked for deep packet inspection consideration if the packet payload is classified at the class level in a particular category. Accordingly, the Table 12 model is favored over the Table 16 model.

Specific file types classified in the poorly-performing, high-entropy class for the Table 12 model were also examined. The only file type that may be better served by being in a different class is PDF. In contrast, in the Table 16 model, six file types may be better served by being in a different class: AVI, WAV, DOCX, JAR, MOV and PST.

Finally, the file-level recall and precision were comparatively evaluated for the experiments involving the top-two candidate hierarchical models – the Table 12 and Table 16 models (see Tables 22 and 23). The results are not compelling for one model over the other, but it is clear that the Table 12 model slightly outperforms the Table 16 model on average. Considering both recall and precision as equally important, the Table 12 model yields better results than the Table 16 model in a slight majority of cases (where there is a difference at all).

5.   Limitations and Future Research

Given the alternative findings on the impact of feature vector selection [9], it is unknown if feature vector selection will impact hierarchical modeling. Future research should explore the impact of varying feature vectors, either to reliably converge on a winning hierarchy or to determine if different hierarchical models require different input feature vectors or whether different features are better predictors for different classes. Future research should also explore the impact of reduced di-

Table 22. Comparative type-level recall and precision.

Type	Table 12 Recall	Table 12 Precision	Table 16 Recall	Table 16 Precision
TXT	0.979	0.793	0.968	0.830
CSV	0.988	0.979	0.986	0.962
LOG	0.985	0.933	0.990	0.933
HTML	0.897	0.749	0.901	0.874
XML	0.943	0.970	0.945	0.974
JSON	0.984	0.993	0.974	0.998
JS	0.935	0.904	0.940	0.908
JAVA	0.961	0.890	0.972	0.918
CSS	1.000	0.979	1.000	0.978
B64	1.000	0.983	1.000	0.987
B85	1.000	0.975	1.000	0.961
B16	1.000	0.975	0.999	0.976
URL	1.000	0.999	1.000	0.998
PS	0.986	0.944	0.983	0.942
RTF	0.998	0.979	0.974	0.978
TBIRD	1.000	0.950	0.976	0.924
PST	0.934	0.971	0.456	0.473
PNG	0.007	0.105	0.001	0.500
GIF	0.876	0.326	0.873	0.338
TIF	0.964	0.837	0.982	0.826
JB2	0.318	0.134	0.006	0.167
GZ	0.047	0.206	0.001	0.048
ZIP	0.003	0.500	0.001	1.000
JAR	0.963	0.736	0.380	0.385
RPM	0.527	0.148	0.330	0.188
BZ2	0.304	0.236	0.751	0.196
PDF	0.438	0.333	0.995	0.977
DOCX	0.975	0.757	0.560	0.613
XLSX	0.499	0.639	0.525	0.474
PPTX	0.000	0.000	0.003	0.250
JPG	0.507	0.242	0.649	0.236
MP3	0.910	0.324	0.679	0.438
M4A	0.544	0.182	0.084	0.221
MP4	0.403	0.387	0.598	0.240
AVI	0.931	0.863	0.828	0.614
WMV	0.020	0.571	0.614	0.199
FLV	0.479	0.223	0.313	0.406

mension feature vectors [2, 3] on hierarchical classification modeling, considering the trade-off between computational costs and classification accuracy. Finally, research should consider replicating the findings pre-

Table 23. Comparative type-level recall and precision (cont'd.).

Type	Table 12 Recall	Table 12 Precision	Table 16 Recall	Table 16 Precision
WAV	0.981	0.896	0.947	0.780
MOV	0.997	0.963	0.971	0.961
DOC	0.774	0.599	0.747	0.662
XLS	0.943	0.893	0.875	0.962
PPT	0.001	0.023	0.003	0.094
FAT	0.308	0.773	0.285	0.819
NTFS	0.735	0.854	0.713	0.948
EXT3	0.975	0.449	0.958	0.458
EXE	0.766	0.764	0.703	0.678
DLL	0.857	0.806	0.827	0.842
ELF	0.927	0.723	0.877	0.856
BMP	0.882	0.929	0.870	0.904
AES	0.038	0.109	0.000	0.000
RAND	0.000	0.000	0.002	0.063

sented in this work with alternate samples and/or more files per type during experimentation. This work would likely have to be facilitated by distributed computing given the computational costs associated with high-dimension vectors (65,500+ dimensions) and a large number of (2,600) observations (50 types × 52 files per type).

6.   Conclusions

This research demonstrates the utility of a multi-step approach for improving data and file type classification performance. The approach provides a means to classify inputs at the class level, which is faster than type-level classification (when the number of total types is held constant), and class-level classification may be adequate in some applications. It can also improve type-level classification by simply reducing the multi-class size of the sub-classification problems (once again, when the number of total types is held constant). In other applications, class-level classification may serve as a useful triage step to direct limited deep packet inspection resources or when applying specialized classification techniques, such as those advocated in [24]. In fact, one might contend that the optimal classification approach is a hybrid approach (combining statistical and specialized approaches) selected during the multi-level class-to-type hierarchical classification process. For example, a quick n-gram-based statistical classification for detecting an input as compressed (class-level) followed by specialized techniques for distinguishing between a PDF fragment from a PPTX fragment (type-level) may be the optimal approach, despite the body of research that takes a "one-size-fits-all," non-hierarchical, type-level classification approach.

This research has empirically tested and invalidated the hypothesized six-class, two-level hierarchy and has used exploratory analysis to empirically derive a winning two-level, five-class hierarchical model. A total of 52 file and data types were considered and file header blocks were excluded from the procedure to ensure that the file signatures did not bias the classification results. File header blocks were also excluded because the research focused on classifying file fragments absent reliable file signatures, file extensions or other filesystem data. The experimental results demonstrate that a two-level (class and type) classification hierarchical model is both feasible and advantageous. Moreover, the approach leads to very good class-level classification performance, improved classification performance for data and file types not exhibiting high entropy (e.g., compressed and encrypted data) and reasonably equivalent classification performance for high-entropy data and file types.

Note that the views expressed in this chapter do not necessarily reflect the official policies of the Naval Postgraduate School nor does the mention of trade names, commercial practices or organizations imply an endorsement by the U.S. Government.

Acknowledgement

This research was supported by the Naval Postgraduate School Assistance Grant/Agreement No. N00244-13-1-0027 awarded by the NAVSUP Fleet Logistics Center San Diego (NAVSUP FLC San Diego).

References

[1] I. Ahmed, K. Lhee, H. Shin and M. Hong, On improving the accuracy and performance of content-based file type identification, *Proceedings of the Fourteenth Australasian Conference on Information Security and Privacy*, pp. 44–59, 2009.

[2] I. Ahmed, K. Lhee, H. Shin and M. Hong, Fast file type identification, *Proceedings of the ACM Symposium on Applied Computing*, pp. 1601–1602, 2010.

[3] I. Ahmed, K. Lhee, H. Shin and M. Hong, Fast content-based file type identification, in *Advances in Digital Forensics VII*, G. Peterson and S. Shenoi (Eds.), Springer, Heidelberg, Germany, pp. 65–75, 2011.

[4] M. Amirani, M. Toorani and A. Beheshti, A new approach to content-based file type detection, *Proceedings of the IEEE Symposium on Computers and Communications*, pp. 1103–1108, 2008.

[5] M. Amirani, M. Toorani and S. Mihandoost, Feature-based type identification of file fragments, *Security and Communication Networks*, vol. 6(1), pp. 115–128, 2013.

[6] S. Axelsson, Using normalized compression distance for classifying file fragments, *Proceedings of the International Conference on Availability, Reliability and Security*, pp. 641–646, 2010.

[7] N. Beebe, UTSA Filetypes 1 Data Set, Department of Information Systems and Cyber Security, University of Texas at San Antonio, San Antonio, Texas (`digitalcorpora.org/corp/files/filetypes1`), 2016.

[8] N. Beebe and L. Liu, Ranking algorithms for digital forensic string search hits, *Digital Investigation*, vol. 11(S2), pp. S124–S132, 2014.

[9] N. Beebe, L. Maddox, L. Liu and M. Sun, Sceadan: Using concatenated n-gram vectors for improved file and data type classification, *IEEE Transactions on Information Forensics and Security*, vol. 8(9), pp. 1519–1530, 2013.

[10] W. Calhoun and D. Coles, Predicting the types of file fragments, *Digital Investigation*, vol. 5(S), pp. S14–S20, 2008.

[11] D. Cao, J. Luo, M. Yin and H. Yang, Feature-selection-based file type identification algorithm, *Proceedings of the IEEE International Conference on Intelligent Computing and Intelligent Systems*, vol. 3, pp. 58–62, 2010.

[12] G. Conti, S. Bratus, A. Shubina, B. Sangster, R. Ragsdale, M. Supan, A. Lichtenberg and R. Perez-Alemany, Automated mapping of large binary objects using primitive fragment type classification, *Digital Investigation*, vol. 7(S), pp. S3–S12, 2010.

[13] R. Erbacher and J. Mulholland, Identification and localization of data types within large-scale filesystems, *Proceedings of the Second International Workshop on Systematic Approaches to Digital Forensic Engineering*, pp. 55–70, 2007.

[14] S. Fitzgerald, G. Mathews, C. Morris and O. Zhulyn, Using NLP techniques for file fragment classification, *Digital Investigation*, vol. 9(S), pp. S44–S49, 2012.

[15] S. Garfinkel, P. Farrell, V. Roussev and G. Dinolt, Bringing science to digital forensics with standardized forensic corpora, *Digital Investigation*, vol. 6(S), pp. S2–S11, 2009.

[16] S. Gopal, Y. Yang, K. Salomatin and J. Carbonell, Statistical learning for file type identification, *Proceedings of the Tenth International Conference on Machine Learning and Applications*, vol. 1, pp. 68–73, 2011.

[17] G. Hall and W. Davis, Sliding Window Measurement for File Type Identification, Technical Report, Department of Computer Science, Texas State University-San Marcos, San Marcos, Texas, 2006.

[18] M. Karresand and N. Shahmehri, File type identification of data fragments by their binary structure, *Proceedings of the IEEE Information Assurance Workshop*, pp. 140–147, 2006.

[19] M. Karresand and N. Shahmehri, Oscar – File type identification of binary data in disk clusters and RAM pages, *Proceedings of the Twenty-First IFIP TC-11 International Conference on Information Security*, pp. 413–424, 2006.

[20] Q. Li, A. Ong, P. Suganthan and V. Thing, A novel support vector machine approach to high-entropy data fragment classification, *Proceedings of the South African Information Security Multi-Conference*, 2011.

[21] W. Li, K. Wang, S. Stolfo and B. Herzog, Fileprints: Identifying file types by *n*-gram analysis, *Proceedings of the Sixth Annual IEEE SMC Information Assurance Workshop*, pp. 64–71, 2005.

[22] M. McDaniel and M. Heydari, Content-based file type detection algorithms, *Proceedings of the Thirty-Sixth Annual Hawaii International Conference on System Sciences*, 2003.

[23] S. Moody and R. Erbacher, SADI – Statistical analysis for data type identification, *Proceedings of the Third International Workshop on Systematic Approaches to Digital Forensic Engineering*, pp. 41–54, 2008.

[24] V. Roussev and S. Garfinkel, File fragment classification – The case for specialized approaches, *Proceedings of the Fourth IEEE International Workshop on Systematic Approaches to Digital Forensic Engineering*, pp. 3–14, 2009.

[25] C. Veenman, Statistical disk cluster classification for file carving, *Proceedings of the Third International Symposium on Information Assurance and Security*, pp. 393–398, 2007.

[26] L. Zhang and G. White, An approach to detect executable content for anomaly-based network intrusion detection, *Proceedings of the IEEE International Symposium on Parallel and Distributed Processing*, 2007.

Chapter 18

SECURE FILE DELETION FOR SOLID STATE DRIVES

Bhupendra Singh, Ravi Saharan, Gaurav Somani and Gaurav Gupta

Abstract   Solid state drives are becoming more popular for data storage because of their reliability, performance and low power consumption. As the amount of sensitive data stored on these drives increases, the need to securely erase the sensitive information becomes more important. However, this is problematic because the tools and techniques used on traditional hard drives do not always work on solid state drives as a result of differences in the internal architectures. Single file sanitization is highly unreliable and difficult to accomplish on a solid state drive due to wear-leveling and related features. This chapter presents a reliable method for individual file sanitization on solid state drives. The method, called FTLSec, integrates a page-based encryption system in the generic flash translation layer. The efficacy of FTLSec is measured using a Flash-Sim solid state drive simulator. The results are compared with the well-known FAST flash translation layer scheme and an idealized page-mapped flash translation layer.

Keywords: Solid state drives, flash translation layer, secure file deletion

1.   Introduction

Large amounts of sensitive data are stored in digital storage media. The disposal of this sensitive data becomes important when it is no longer needed or when the individuals or organizations desire to replace their outdated computing equipment. Secure data deletion is also a critical component of the disposal policy of government and commercial enterprises.

Secure deletion is the process of deleting data so that it becomes non-recoverable [14]. Secure deletion is also referred to as purging, sanitization and erasing. A number of tools, techniques and standards are available for secure deletion from traditional storage devices such as hard

G. Peterson and S. Shenoi (Eds.): Advances in Digital Forensics XII, IFIP AICT 484, pp. 345–362, 2016.
DOI: 10.1007/978-3-319-46279-0_18

disk drives. However, since solid state drives (SSDs) are relatively new, fewer standards and techniques exist for this type of media.

Solid state drives have some advantages over mechanical spinning hard drives, but the flash memory they use has some inherent limitations such as finite erasure cycles [3] and erase-before-write [14]. Solid state drives store data in NAND flash memory, which is compartmented into blocks and pages. Each page contains multiple blocks. Pages are the units of read and write operations while erasures are performed on blocks. A page write must be preceded by an erasure. Because of the differences in atomicity, an erasure is a more costly operation than a read or write. Erasure also significantly degrades the overall write performance of flash memory – each block can be erased only a finite number of times (typically 10,000 to 100,000 times [3]) before it becomes unreliable.

To reduce the number of erasures, modern flash solid state drives include a flash translation layer (FTL). A flash translation layer uses a table that maps a logical address to a physical address to replace the erase-before-write by an out-of-place update method. When writing a new page, the flash translation layer selects an already free or erased page, writes to it, invalidates the previous version of the page and updates the mapping table. To implement this method, the flash translation layer employs a garbage collector (GC) [5, 7] to reclaim the invalid pages of a block by copying its valid pages (if any) to a new erased block and then erasing the entire original block. To lengthen the lifespan of a solid state drive, a flash translation layer implements a wear-leveling algorithm to distribute writes evenly across all the blocks in the flash solid state drive. Wear-leveling prevents data from being written continually to the same locations.

Solid state drives and hard disk drives have different internal architectures and storage mechanisms. As a result, the techniques applied to a hard disk drive for entire drive sanitization or single file sanitization may not work on a solid state drive. Secure deletion of a single file on a solid state drive is a relatively challenging task due to garbage collection and wear-leveling. The data that is left behind on invalid pages after an out-of-place update also complicates the secure deletion task.

To enable the secure deletion of a single file on a solid state drive, certain modifications to the generic flash translation layer are needed. This chapter describes a modification of the demand-based flash translation layer (DFTL) [5], which includes a page-based encryption system (PES). The modified flash translation layer technique is called FTLSec (flash translation layer with secure erase), which provides a means to securely delete a single file from a solid state drive. Experiments are conducted to demonstrate the utility of FTLSec and its superior performance compared with other flash translation layer schemes.

2.   Background

Presenting an array of logical block addresses (LBAs) makes sense for a hard disk drive because its sectors can be overwritten. However, the approach is not suited to flash memory. For this reason, an additional component, namely the flash translation layer, is required to hide the inner characteristics of NAND flash memory and expose only an array of logical block addresses to the operating system. The flash translation layer resides in the solid state drive controller. The main function of the flash translation layer is address translation, in which the logical addresses that are seen by the operating system are converted to the physical addresses of NAND flash memory. The mapping table and the other data structures used by the flash translation layer are stored in a small, fast, on-flash static RAM (SRAM) based cache. The limited size of SRAM prevents the flash translation layer from achieving high performance. Furthermore, more data in a solid state drive, means that there is more data in the SRAM, which is undesirable because the price per byte of SRAM is higher than that of a solid state drive.

In addition to address translation, the flash translation layer implements garbage collection and wear-leveling. Garbage collection runs in the background to create free pages from invalid pages. Because a solid state drive has a limited number of erase cycles, wear-leveling is employed to increase the lifespan of the drive by attempting to distribute data so that every block has the same level of wear.

Flash translation layer schemes are classified into three types based on their mapping granularity: (i) page-level mapping; (ii) block-level mapping; and (iii) hybrid mapping. The three schemes are ordered roughly by their level of complexity. Each flash translation layer scheme offers trade-offs in terms of performance, memory overhead and life expectancy.

The page-level mapping scheme is a naive approach in which every logical page is mapped to a corresponding physical page. Therefore, if n logical pages are mapped to physical pages, the size of the mapping table is n. This scheme offers considerable flexibility, but it needs a large mapping table and, consequently, large SRAM, which can significantly increase manufacturing costs. For example, a 1 GB flash memory chip with a page size of 2 KB requires 2 MB of SRAM to store the mapping table [5].

The block-level mapping scheme divides logical addresses into logical blocks and offsets, and only the logical block addresses are mapped to the physical block addresses (PBAs). Block-level mapping can handle larger SRAMs than are feasible with page-level mapping. The logical block offset in a logical block is the same as the physical block offset in a physical block. This mapping requires 64 (number of pages/block) times less SRAM memory than the page-level mapping scheme.

A hybrid mapping scheme [10, 13] is a combination of the page-level and block-level mapping schemes. All hybrid flash translation layer schemes share a fundamental idea: log-block mapping, which uses an approach similar to log-structured filesystems. In this scheme, the physical blocks are divided into two groups: (i) data blocks; and (ii) log blocks. Data blocks constitute the major portion of a flash solid state drive and are mapped by a block-mapping scheme; a small fixed number of blocks are tagged as log blocks and are maintained with page granularity. When an update request to a page in the data block arrives, the hybrid log-block scheme writes new data to the log block allocated from the pool and invalidates the previous version of the data that was stored in the data block. Note that, for each write request, the logical address of the page is also stored in the out-of-band (OOB) area of each page.

3.   Related Work

This section discusses existing work related to secure deletion on NAND flash drives. A user interacts with the physical medium using an interface. The interface offers functions that transform the user's data objects to a form suitable for storage on the physical medium. This transformation can also include operations such as encryption, error-correction and redundancy. Several layers and interfaces exist between user applications and the physical medium that stores data. Figure 1 shows the layers and interfaces through which data on a physical medium is accessed.

3.1   Layers and Interfaces

The lowest layer is the physical medium, also called the storage-management layer. NAND memory drives are accessed via a controller, specifically, an embedded processor that executes firmware code [14].

NAND flash memory is accessed via a flash translation layer controller that maps logical addresses from the operating system to the physical block addresses on the flash memory chip. Unlike a hard disk drive controller, the flash translation layer controller does not support in-place

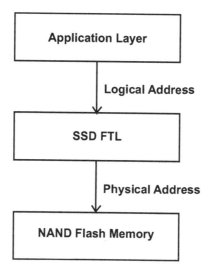

Figure 1. Interfaces involved in NAND flash memory data storage.

overwrites and remaps to new locations, leaving the stale data behind; this complicates secure deletion.

3.2 Choice of Layer for Secure Deletion

Secure deletion can be applied at any layer. Secure deletion at the lowest layer ensures that the data is securely deleted and is not recoverable; in contrast, secure deletion applied at the user layer allows the easy identification of data blocks. Secure deletion at the physical layer is preferable because the user does not know which data blocks to delete. Alternatively, a user layer approach allows for the easy identification of the data blocks to be deleted, but it has no information about the locations of the data blocks. A filesystem layer approach for secure deletion lies in between a physical layer approach and a user layer approach.

3.3 Controller Level Approaches

The flash translation layer manages the mapping between logical block addresses visible via standardized interfaces such as ATA and SCSI and physical pages of flash memory. These interfaces provide built-in erase commands that instruct on-board firmware to run a sanitization protocol on a flash drive. The commands are more reliable, but they are not supported by all flash drives. Moreover, the built-in commands are appropriate for entire drive sanitization, not for single file secure deletion.

The ATA interface specifications define the ERASE UNIT and ERASE UNIT ENH commands that securely erase all user-addressable areas [12]. The working draft ATA/ATAPI Command Set-3 (ACS-3) [18] incorporates a BLOCK ERASE EXT command that only succeeds if the sanitization feature set is supported by the device.

Wei et al. [19] have found that not all solid state drives support ATA commands. Some drives support ATA commands, but do not implement them correctly, leaving data intact on the drives. Other drives implement the ATA commands correctly. Thus, the support and implementations of ATA commands depend on the vendor. Swanson et al. [16] have proposed a reliable entire drive sanitization method that encrypts the data to be stored on a flash drive using a key, which is subsequently destroyed. In this case, every block is erased and written with a defined pattern, and erased again. Finally, the flash device is reinitialized by submitting a new (different) key to the flash controller.

3.4 Filesystem Level Approaches

Application level approaches are limited because they do not directly access the physical medium. Controller level approaches suffer from the inability to distinguish deleted data from valid data, because they cannot access the physical data locations and metadata. Filesystem level approaches lie in between these two approaches. The filesystem is generally unaware of the physical medium and accesses it via the device driver interface.

Data Compaction. Compaction balances the asymmetry between the write and erase granularities. It compacts a block (erase unit) containing the deleted data, copies the valid collocated data elsewhere and executes the erase operation. Copying data and then erasing an entire block is a costly operation that also adds wear to the NAND flash solid state drive. However, no immediate secure deletion approach based on erasure is available that can do better than one erase unit erasure per deletion. Immediate secure deletion requires a minimum of one erasure. Any improvement that further reduces the number of erase units erased per deletion must batch the deletions and perform intermittent secure deletion.

Single File Secure Deletion. Log-structured filesystems are commonly used as flash filesystems. Lee et al. [8] have proposed an efficient single file secure deletion approach for log-structured filesystems. In this approach, file data is encrypted and the keys are stored in the same block. To securely delete file data and metadata, the keys corresponding to the file on the block are simply erased. This approach was adapted to the YAFFS implementation [11].

Reardon et al. [14] have implemented a secure deletion approach for the UBIFS flash filesystem [6]. Each filesystem data node is encrypted when data on the data node is written and is decrypted when it is read from a flash memory device. Secure deletion is achieved by purging the keys from the logical key storage area, which houses all the keys.

Wei et al. [19] have proposed an immediate secure deletion approach for flash memory called scrubbing. Scrubbing re-programs individual pages to turn all the remaining ones into zeroes. The approach can remove data remnants by scrubbing pages that contain invalid data in a flash array, or it can prevent their creation by scrubbing the page containing the previous version when writing a new version. Erasing a flash memory erase unit is the only way to restore the charge to a cell, but cells can be drained when the write operation is used. These cells cannot be used to store new data, but their sensitive data is voided immediately. Fortunately, collocated data on the erase unit remains available. A concern with scrubbing is that it exhibits undefined behavior. Wei et al. have investigated the error rates for different types of memory and show that the rates vary widely. Scrubbing causes frequent errors in some devices and no errors in other devices.

3.5   Application Level Approaches

At the application layer, secure deletion approaches are carried out by user applications that interact with POSIX-compliant filesystems. The main approaches are: (i) overwriting the contents of a file before normal deletion (unlinking); (ii) unlinking a file and filling the free space on the drive; and (iii) overwriting the entire partition or drive by calling the secure deletion routine in the controller of the drive.

Overwriting makes multiple write passes with different bit patterns to sanitize a file [2]. Since a NAND flash drive does not allow in-place overwrites, the overwriting utilities do not necessarily work for securely deleting a single file.

Free space filling tools overwrite the free space on a drive and ensure that the sensitive data is securely deleted from the drive. Obviously, the cost of filling free space is proportional to the available free space. If the available free space is large, it will take a longer time to fill; this can result in high wear in flash memory devices.

Application level filling of free space is the only user level means of securely deleting data in YAFFS [14]. Reardon et al. [14] has introduced two methods that work on the YAFFS filesystem: (i) purging; and (ii) ballooning. Purging erases free space immediately while ballooning performs frequent secure deletions by keeping the filesystem full of junk data, causing more frequent YAFFS garbage collection.

Erasing the entire drive securely deletes data stored in NAND flash memory, including metadata and directory structures. The time required for this process depends on the size of the drive; erasure can take a long time for a large-capacity drive.

3.6   Cross Layer Approaches

As discussed above, secure deletion at the lowest layer has no information about the locations of deleted data objects. Thus, the higher layers can be used to pass information about the deleted data to the lowest layer, permitting the secure deletion of deleted data objects. TRIM [1] and TrueErase [4] use this type of approach.

A TRIM command [1] enables the operating system to wipe the pages that contain invalid data due to deletions by the user or the operating system. Trimming allows the solid state drive to handle garbage collection overhead that would otherwise significantly slow down future write operations on the involved blocks. TRIM wipes out the invalid pages on demand, so it ensures the secure deletion of data. TRIM commands were not designed for secure erasure, but instead to accelerate write operations on flash media. However, it is not possible to restrict TRIM commands only to sensitive blocks, which means that the underlying mechanism that securely deletes data must be efficient. TRIM commands are only effective when they are supported by the operating system and by the solid state drive.

TrueErase [4] irrevocably erases data and metadata on hard disk drives and solid state drives. TrueErase is a per-file, encryption-free secure deletion approach that keeps track of the sensitive data throughout the storage path. Information about the deleted blocks is forwarded to the lowest layer of the new communications channel added between the device driver and filesystem. To ensure secure deletion, the device driver is modified to implement immediate secure deletion using its lower layer interface. TrueErase is more effective than TRIM commands because it deletes data at a smaller granularity without any delayed deletions.

4.   Proposed Secure Deletion Approach

The proposed secure deletion approach uses a page-based encryption system (PES) to securely erase files. The approach also incorporates some modifications to the generic flash translation layer. The approach involves three steps: (i) encrypt each page before writing it to the NAND

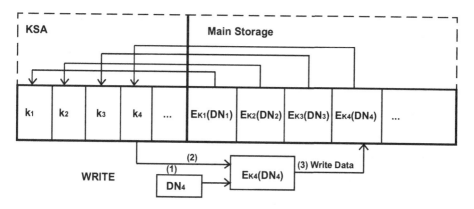

Figure 2. Writing to a new page.

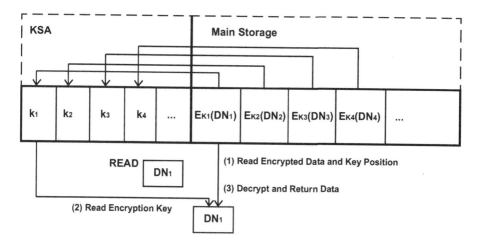

Figure 3. Reading from Page DN$_1$.

flash and decrypt each page before reading the data; (ii) store the keys in a fixed area called the key storage area (KSA); and (iii) when a specific file is to be deleted, erase the block where the file encryption keys are stored. Figure 2 shows data being written to a new page while Figure 3 shows data being read from a page.

Key Storage Area. The key storage area is reserved. Migrating blocks of the NAND flash solid state drive are used to store the encryption/decryption keys of all the pages. The locations of the encryption/decryption keys of a page are stored in the page header. The locations correspond to the logical key storage area number and offset. In order to delete a key (which decrypts deleted data), the blocks in the key storage area must be erased regularly. When a page becomes invalid upon removal or updating, the encryption/decryption keys of the page that are maintained in the key storage area are marked as deleted. This approach is different from file deletion – whenever a page is discarded, its corresponding encryption/decryption keys are marked as deleted. A deleted key remains tagged as deleted until it is purged and a fresh random key takes its place; this fresh key is tagged as unused.

Purging.   Purging is a regular process that erases keys from the key storage area. Purging is done on each block of the key storage area. In this process, a new block of key storage area is selected to copy the used keys that reside in the same locations, and the deleted or unused keys are replaced with new unused random data. This random data, which is inexpensive and easy to generate, is assigned to the new keys when needed.

Keys that are tagged as unused are logically-fixed in the key storage area because their corresponding pages are already stored on the NAND flash solid state drive until erase operations are performed at the key locations. All the blocks containing invalid data are erased, thus purging the unused and deleted keys along with the pages they encrypt.

Key State Map.   The key state map maps key positions to key states. Keys can be in one of three states – unused, used or deleted. Unused keys are keys that can be assigned and then tagged as used. Used keys are used to encrypt/decrypt valid pages; these keys ensure the availability of user data. Deleted keys are keys that are used to encrypt/decrypt deleted data, specifically, pages that are no longer needed by the filesystem and should be securely erased by the filesystem to achieve the goal of secure deletion. A purging operation replaces unused and deleted keys with new values; the used keys remain on the storage medium.

Figures 4 and 5 show representations of key state maps before aand after keys are purged.

Flash Translation Layer Modifications.   In order to enable the secure deletion of a single file, the generic flash translation layer is modified and a page-based encryption system is integrated in it. All the incoming data is encrypted before writing to NAND flash memory and decrypted for each read operation. The keys are stored in the reserved key storage area and key locations are assigned to the data of each page. The page-level mapping table of the modified flash translation layer also stores a reference to the encryption/decryption key positions so that the

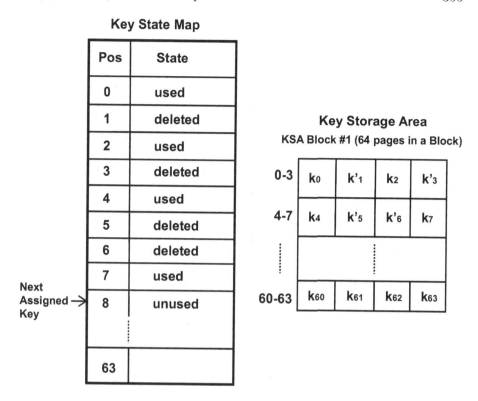

Figure 4. Key state map before purging keys.

algorithm that builds its logical pages to physical pages, also builds the corresponding encryption/decryption key positions.

A key position has two parts: (i) logical key storage area block number; and (ii) offset within the key storage area block. The metadata relating to each key storage area block, comprising the logical key storage area block number and epoch number, are stored in the last page of each logical key storage area block.

5. Experimental Results

No publicly-available flash solid state drive prototype exists for testing flash translation layer schemes. Therefore, experiments were performed using an open-source, validated flash solid state drive simulator named FlashSim [7]. The simulator was used to evaluate various flash translation layer schemes proposed in the literature. FlashSim uses a modular architecture and facilitates the integration of new flash translation layer schemes. In the experiments, FlashSim was used to evaluate the performance of the proposed flash translation layer (FTLSec) along with two

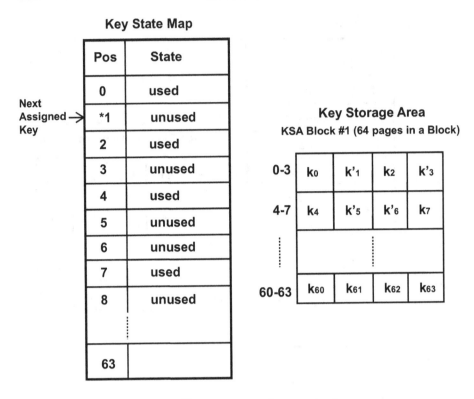

Figure 5. Key state map after purging keys.

traditional flash translation layer schemes: (i) a hybrid flash translation layer scheme (FAST) [9]; and (ii) an ideal page-mapped flash translation layer scheme [5].

5.1   Experimental Setup

The experiments simulated 16 GB of NAND flash memory. Table 1 presents the simulation parameters. The number of extra blocks was varied from 5% to 9% of the total blocks. The extra blocks were used as log blocks by the FAST hybrid flash translation layer scheme.

Experimental Workloads. Real-world traces were used as workloads to measure the performance of FTLSec against the hybrid flash translation layer scheme FAST and the idealized page-mapped flash translation layer scheme. Different types of traces that have been used to evaluate the performance of storage systems were selected.

Table 2 lists the characteristics of each type of trace. Financial1 was taken from OLTP applications running at two large financial in-

Table 1. Simulation parameters.

Parameter	Value
SSD Capacity	16 GB
Page Size	2 KB
Page OOB	64 B
Pages per Block	64 pages
Percentage of Extra Blocks	5% to 9%
Page Read Delay	0.1309 ms
Page Write Delay	0.4059 ms
Block Erase Delay	2 ms

Table 2. Experimental workloads.

Workload	Average Request Size (KB)	Read (%)	Write (%)
Financial1	3.00	9.0	76.8
WebSearch	14.86	97.3	2.70
Exchange	12.00	46.4	53.6

stitutions (OLTP Application I/O) [17]. The Financial1 trace is write-dominant. The WebSearch trace is a read-dominant I/O trace (Search Engine I/O) [17]. The Exchange trace was collected from a Microsoft Exchange mail server [15].

Performance Metrics.   Two metrics were used in the simulations: (i) number of erased blocks (indicator of garbage collection efficacy); and (ii) average response time (device service time plus the time spent in the driver queue).

5.2   Garbage Collection Overhead

Garbage collection may involve various types of merge operations (e.g., switch, partial and full) at the time of servicing update requests. These merge operations create overhead in the form of block erases and when copying valid pages in the blocks (victim blocks) to other (free) blocks.

Figure 6 shows the impact of the garbage collection overhead. The results demonstrate that FTLSec has fewer garbage collection operations than FAST for all the workloads. Also, when the number of extra blocks used for log blocks increases, the number of garbage collection operations decreases. Figure 6 also shows that the number of block erasures is the

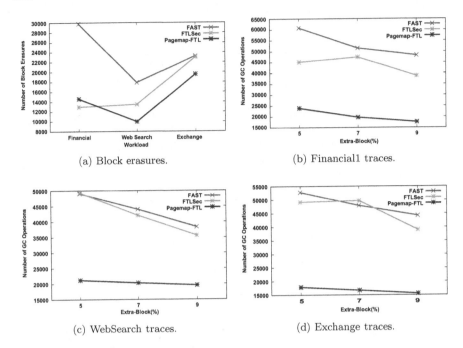

(a) Block erasures.

(b) Financial1 traces.

(c) WebSearch traces.

(d) Exchange traces.

Figure 6. Garbage collection overhead.

lowest for the WebSearch workload. This is because WebSearch is highly
read-dominant and issues a small number of write requests. As a result,
WebSearch has a lower garbage collection overhead than the Financial1
and Exchange traces.

5.3   Impact of Extra Blocks

As discussed above, extra blocks are used to support merge operations
during garbage collection. The number of extra blocks in the experiments was varied from 5% to 9% of the total blocks while the solid state
drive capacity was kept constant throughout the experiments.

6.   Countering Secure Deletion

To counter anti-forensic approaches such as secure deletion on solid
state drives, a digital forensic investigator must have a good understanding of the tools and techniques used to securely delete drive content.
This section highlights some anti-anti-forensic techniques to counter secure deletion when one or more files are securely deleted and when an
entire drive is sanitized.

6.1 Countering Single File Sanitization

The targets of the most privacy protection tools are messenger chats, pictures, documents and video files. Secure removal of these artifacts with overwriting techniques does not guarantee their complete removal and leaves some traces. The traces include:

- **Recent Events:** Recent events such as browser histories, Skype and Hangout chats, documents and downloads can still be found in the *Pagefile.sys* and *Hiberfil.sys* files.

- **Multiple Copies:** Windows often creates multiple copies of some types of files. These copies are generated when copying or moving files, temporarily saving copies of working documents, and compressing and decompressing files. Performing a secure deletion only on the target file leaves the other copies intact, which means that they could be located and extracted by digital forensic investigators.

- **File Fragments:** If a file on a solid state drive is erased by overwriting, fragments of the file may still reside on the drive because most operating systems have filesystem fragmentation. It is possible to partially carve a file if the fragments left before defragmentation have not been overwritten.

- **Volatile Evidence:** A computer or laptop that was running when it was seized may still have artifacts in RAM.

- **Volume Shadow Copy:** Older versions of a file may exist in the volume shadow copy.

6.2 Countering Entire Drive Sanitization

The sanitization of an entire solid state drive is performed with vendor-defined commands that, in turn, invoke TRIM. Modern solid state drives are compliant with DRAT (definite read after trim) or DZAT (definite zero after trim) [1]. This makes the solid state drive controller return all zeroes or garbage data, even if the drive contains actual data. In this case, the recovery of solid state drive data is a difficult and time-consuming task. However, if the solid state drive firmware is not updated or is buggy, the data may still be found on the disk.

7. Conclusions

Solid state drives with NAND flash memory are becoming increasingly common for storing sensitive data. This makes the sanitization of solid state drives a critical component of data management. The FTLSec (file translation layer with secure erase) method presented in this chapter reliably sanitizes individual files on a solid state drive. FTLSec achieves its functionality by integrating a page-based encryption system in the generic flash translation layer. Experiments demonstrate the FTLSec has fewer block erasures and garbage collection operations compared with the well-known FAST flash translation layer scheme and an idealized page-mapped flash translation layer scheme.

References

[1] O. Afonin, D. Nikolaev and Y. Gubanov, Countering anti-forensic efforts – Part 2, *Forensic Magazine*, September 16, 2015.

[2] Australian Signals Directorate, Information Security Manual, Kingston, Australia (`www.asd.gov.au/infosec/ism/index.htm`), 2015.

[3] T. Chung, D. Park, S. Park, D. Lee, S. Lee and H. Song, A survey of the flash translation layer, *Journal of Systems Architecture*, vol. 55(5-6), pp. 332–343, 2009.

[4] S. Diesburg, C. Meyers, M. Stanovich, M. Mitchell, J. Marshall, J. Gould, A. Wang and G. Kuenning, TrueErase: Per-file secure deletion for the storage data path, *Proceedings of the Twenty-Eighth Annual Computer Security Applications Conference*, pp. 439–448, 2012.

[5] A. Gupta, Y. Kim and B. Urgaonkar, DFTL: A flash translation layer employing demand-based selective caching of page-level address mappings, *ACM SIGPLAN Notices*, vol. 44(3), pp. 229–240, 2009.

[6] A. Hunter, A Brief Introduction to the Design of UBIFS, Version 0.1 (`www.linux-mtd.infradead.org/doc/ubifs_whitepaper.pdf`), 2008.

[7] Y. Kim, B. Tauras, A. Gupta and B. Urgaonkar, FlashSim: A simulator for NAND-flash-based solid-state drives, *Proceedings of the First Conference on Advances in System Simulation*, pp. 125–131, 2009.

[8] J. Lee, S. Yi, J. Heo, H. Park, S. Shin and Y. Cho, An efficient secure deletion scheme for flash filesystems, *Journal of Information Science and Engineering*, vol. 26(1), pp. 27–38, 2010.

[9] S. Lee, D. Park, T. Chung, D. Lee, S. Park and H. Song, A log-buffer-based flash translation layer using fully-associative sector translation, *ACM Transactions on Embedded Computing Systems*, vol. 6(3), article no. 18, 2007.

[10] S. Lee, D. Shin, Y. Kim and J. Kim, Last: Locality-aware sector translation for NAND flash memory based storage systems, *ACM SIGOPS Operating Systems Review*, vol. 42(6), pp. 36–42, 2008.

[11] C. Manning, How YAFFS Works (`www.yaffs.net/sites/yaffs.net/files/HowYaffsWorks.pdf`), 2012.

[12] P. McLean (Ed.), Information Technology – AT Attachment-3 Interface (ATA-3), X3T13 2008D Revision 7b, X3T13 Technical Committee, American National Standard of Accredited Standards Committee X3, Washington, DC (`www.scs.stanford.edu/11wi-cs140/pintos/specs/ata-3-std.pdf`), 1997.

[13] C. Park, W. Cheon, J. Kang, K. Roh, W. Cho and J. Kim, A reconfigurable FTL (flash translation layer) architecture for NAND flash based applications, *ACM Transactions on Embedded Computing Systems*, vol. 7(4), article no. 38, 2008.

[14] J. Reardon, D. Basin and S. Capkun, SoK: Secure data deletion, *Proceedings of the IEEE Symposium on Security and Privacy*, pp. 301–315, 2013.

[15] Storage Networking Industry Association, SNIA IOTTA Repository, Microsoft Enterprise Traces, Colorado Springs, Colorado (`iotta.snia.org/traces/130`), 2011.

[16] S. Swanson and M. Wei, SAFE: Fast, Verifiable Sanitization for SSDs, Non-Volatile Systems Laboratory, Department of Computer Science and Engineering, University of California – San Diego, San Diego, California (`cseweb.ucsd.edu/~swanson/papers/TR-cs2011-0963-Safe.pdf`), 2010.

[17] UMass Trace Repository, Storage, Laboratory for Advanced Software Systems, University of Massachusetts, Amherst, Massachusetts (`traces.cs.umass.edu/index.php/Storage/Storage`), 2007.

[18] R. Weber (Ed.), Information Technology – ATA/ATAPI Command Set-3 (ACS-3), T13/2161-D Revision 5, T13 Technical Committee, American National Standard of Accredited Standards Committee INCITS, Washington, DC (`www.t13.org/Documents/UploadedDocuments/docs2013/d2161r5-ATAATAPI_Command_Set_-_3.pdf`), 2013.

[19] M. Wei, L. Grupp, F. Spada and S. Swanson, Reliably erasing data from flash-based solid state drives, *Proceedings of the Ninth USENIX Conference on File and Storage Technologies*, 2011.

VIII

FORENSIC TOOLS

Chapter 19

A TOOL FOR VOLATILE MEMORY ACQUISITION FROM ANDROID DEVICES

Haiyu Yang, Jianwei Zhuge, Huiming Liu and Wei Liu

Abstract   Memory forensic tools provide a thorough way to detect malware and investigate cyber crimes. However, existing memory forensic tools must be compiled against the exact version of the kernel source code and the exact kernel configuration. This poses a problem for Android devices because there are more than 1,000 manufacturers and each manufacturer maintains its own kernel. Moreover, new security enhancements introduced in Android Lollipop prevent most memory acquisition tools from executing.

This chapter describes AMExtractor, a tool for acquiring volatile physical memory from a wide range of Android devices with high integrity. AMExtractor uses /dev/kmem to execute code in kernel mode, which is supported by most Android devices. Device-specific information is extracted at runtime without any assumptions about the target kernel source code and configuration. AMExtractor has been successfully tested on several devices shipped with different versions of the Android operating system, including the latest Android Lollipop. Memory images dumped by AMExtractor can be exported to other forensic frameworks for deep analysis. A rootkit was successfully detected using the Volatility Framework on memory images retrieved by AMExtractor.

Keywords: Mobile device forensics, memory forensics, Android, rootkit detection

1.   Introduction

The Android operating system is the most popular smartphone platform with a market share of 82.8% in Q2 2015 [7]. The popularity of the operating system makes it vital for digital forensic investigators to acquire and analyze evidence from Android devices. Most digital forensic

© IFIP International Federation for Information Processing 2016
Published by Springer International Publishing AG 2016. All Rights Reserved
G. Peterson and S. Shenoi (Eds.): Advances in Digital Forensics XII, IFIP AICT 484, pp. 365–378, 2016.
DOI: 10.1007/978-3-319-46279-0_19

tools and frameworks focus on extracting user data and metadata from the Android filesystem instead of volatile memory. However, new security enhancements, such as full-disk encryption introduced in Android Ice Cream (version 4.0), make it extremely difficult to recover evidence via filesystem forensics [2].

Volatile memory is valuable because it contains a wealth of information that is otherwise unrecoverable. The evidence in volatile memory includes objects related to running and terminated processes, open files, network activity, memory mappings and more [1]. This evidence could be extracted directly if a full physical memory dump were to be obtained. Often, a full copy of volatile memory is the first, but essential, step in advanced Android forensics and threat analysis.

Volatile memory acquisition from Android devices is challenging. A major challenge is the fragmentation of Android devices – there are more than 24,000 distinct Android devices and 1,294 manufacturers [13]. This fragmentation introduces flaws in Android memory acquisition tools:

- **Availability:** Memory acquisition tools do not work on several devices because they lack certain functionality. LiME, the most popular tool in the Android community, relies on loadable kernel module (LKM) support by target devices. However, many Android devices do not provide this functionality. For example, Google Nexus smartphones do not support loadable kernel modules – attempting to load a kernel module using the `insmod` command produces a "function not implemented" error. Loadable kernel module support is a compile-time option and enabling it requires the kernel to be compiled and the boot partition flashed. Some manufacturers incorporate security enhancement mechanisms that prevent unofficial kernel modules from running. For example, Samsung Galaxy has KNOX that only allows kernel modules with Samsung signatures to be loaded.

- **Compatibility:** It is very difficult to port some memory acquisition tools to new devices. For example, LiME must be compiled against the exact version of the target kernel source code and the exact kernel configuration. However, these conditions are not always met because most mobile phone manufacturers do not release their source code.

- **Accuracy:** Some memory acquisition tools have large forensic impacts on target devices, producing evidence that may not be admissible in court. For example, the `fmem` memory acquisition tool for Linux systems can be used to copy data from kernel mode to user mode. However, it involves frequent copying that may override memory content and contaminate the memory. Other tools that work in user mode only have access to the memory of particular processes; thus, they are incapable of detecting rootkits.

This chapter describes AMExtractor (Android Memory Extractor), a widely applicable tool for acquiring volatile memory from Android devices. AMExtractor has three advantages compared with existing tools. First, AMExtractor uses the /dev/kmem device to execute code in kernel space; this bypasses the loadable kernel module restriction and works well on the latest stock ROMs without any modifications. Second, AMExtractor does not need the source code of the target device and it is compatible with most Android operating system versions, including the latest Lollipop. Third, AMExtractor runs in kernel mode. This makes the tool forensically sound – it has minimal impact on target devices because it reads and transmits memory content only in kernel mode and minimizes data copying. Unlike tools that run in user mode, AMExtractor can find information hidden from user mode and it is not affected by rootkits.

AMExtractor was tested on four mobile phone models: (i) Samsung Galaxy Nexus; (ii) LG Nexus 4; (iii) LG Nexus 5; and (iv) Samsung Galaxy S4. Different versions of stock and third-party ROMs as well as the latest stock firmware were tested without any failures. AMExtractor was evaluated by comparing it against LiME and fmem. The results demonstrate that the dumped memory is nearly the same as that obtained with LiME. The AMExtractor output was also exported to the Volatility Framework to detect the presence of rootkits. Evidence of malware invisible to traditional security tools was discovered.

2.   Related Work

Traditional memory acquisition methods can be classified as: (i) hardware methods; and (ii) software methods [5].

2.1   Hardware Methods

JTAG test pins can be used to retrieve the internal memory of a device. This method was verified on the Nokia 5110 model by Willassen, [20]. However, over and above the difficulty of directly programming JTAG to acquire live memory dumps, not all Android devices have JTAG test pins. Muller developed the FROST framework [12] to retrieve sensitive information, including disk encryption keys from memory using a cold attack. Specifically, FROST is able to read the remaining memory content after a mobile phone maintained at a low temperature is powered off. The limitation of FROST is that it is necessary to unlock the phone and flash the recovery image; this causes the phone to be reset to the factory settings with the loss of all user data. Moreover, FROST relies on the data remanence property to read memory; thus, the memory retrieved may not be an exact copy of the live memory.

2.2   Software Methods

Traditionally, memory content can be acquired from /dev/mem devices. However, this approach does not work for mobile phones with RAM in excess of 896 MB [17]. Kollar [8] has developed fmem, a loadable kernel module that creates a /dev/fmem device supporting memory acquisition. Unfortunately, fmem does not work on Android devices by default [17]. Additionally, reading memory from such devices in user space involves too many interactions between user space and kernel space, which can modify the original content.

Sun et al. [16] have implemented a reliable memory acquisition tool called TrustDump. TrustDump is a TrustZone-based memory acquisition tool that can extract the RAM memory and CPU register values of a mobile device even when the operating system has crashed or has been compromised. However, TrustDump is only supported on Freescale i.MX53 QSB, an embedded development board, making it an impractical tool for evidence acquisition from Android devices.

LiME [17] is another popular forensic tool. It is a loadable kernel module that parses the memory mapping structure in a kernel and dumps the memory content to an SD card or transmits it over a TCP connection. By using a direct I/O or kernel socket technique, LiME minimizes its interactions with user and kernel space, thereby providing a more forensically-sound memory dump. LiME uses a custom format to reduce the size of memory images, a feature supported by other memory analysis tools.

However, LiME has some shortcomings. Its portability across a range of smartphone models poses problems with regard to memory forensics [17]. When attempting to load a kernel module, if module verification is enabled (true for every kernel tested in this work), the kernel performs several checks to ensure that the module was compiled for the specific version of the running kernel. LiME needs the kernel source code of the target phone. This constraint cannot always be satisfied because manufacturers tend to delay the publication of source code or never publish their code. However, even if the source code is available, the kernel configuration and toolchains must be exactly the same as for the stock firmware running on the phone. Any change prevents the module from being loaded due to a CRC checksum mismatch. Recompiling

Table 1. Volatile memory acquisition support by commercial tools.

Products	Status
Cellebrite	No support, but support is planned
XRY	No support
Oxygen Forensic	No support
Magnet IEF	No support

the kernel and flashing it to a phone appears to be the best approach, but changing the original system is not always acceptable, especially in forensic research. Even worse, recently released phones such as the Google Nexus and Samsung Galaxy series, by default, turn off the loadable kernel module compiling option in their Linux kernels.

Stuttgen and Cohen [15] have proposed a method for loading a module into a Linux kernel without kernel source code by developing a truly version-independent kernel module and modifying it prior to loading. Using the checksum and kernel information retrieved from another existing kernel module, they were able to dynamically modify the module to perform a robust memory acquisition. However, their method is not widely applicable due to the lack of existing kernel modules in Android devices.

With regard to code injection techniques, `devik` and `sd` [4] have proposed a method that dynamically patches a Linux kernel without using a loadable kernel module. Lineberry [9] has presented a similar method. The methods focus on hooking the `syscall` table instead of reading memory content. AMExtractor follows this approach, but modifies it to hook device drivers.

2.3 Commercial Memory Forensics Tools

At this time, the major commercial digital forensic tools do not support volatile memory acquisition from mobile phones. Table 1 shows the status of memory acquisition support by popular commercial tools.

3. AMExtractor Design

Figure 1 presents the AMExtractor architecture. AMExtractor is an ELF file that runs in user space, but requires root privileges to execute code at the kernel level.

Root privileges are indispensable to using AMExtractor. An existing root manager or kernel bug exploit may be used to root Android devices. This prerequisite is relatively easy to satisfy because many users root

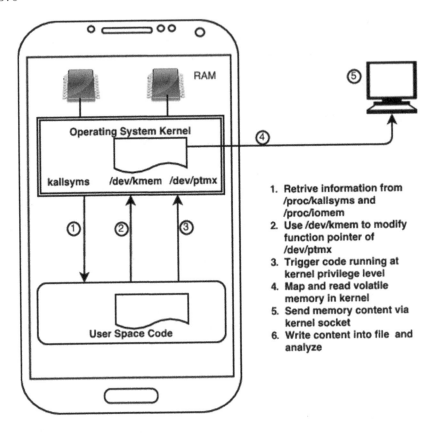

Figure 1. AMExtractor architecture.

their devices [10]. Moreover, many root solutions have been published; at least two universal solutions were presented recently [21, 22] In any case, methods for obtaining root privileges are outside the scope of this research.

The AMExtractor memory dump process involves the following steps:

- **Step 1: Retrieve Information:** AMExtractor reuses some kernel facilities for robustness and compatibility. Information about the running system, including physical memory offset and kernel symbols, is retrieved at runtime. The kernel function address and physical memory layout are retrieved using /proc/kallsyms and /proc/iomem. Disassembly of the vm_normal_page function is also required.

- **Step 2: Modify the Function Pointer:** Having gathered enough system information, AMExtractor needs to modify only one byte of the target kernel. The function pointer points to custom code developed by the authors of this chapter and this function is invoked by a device operation such as `fsync` on `/dev/ptmx`. Note that `/dev/kmem` was chosen to modify the kernel because it is supported by all Android and Linux versions. The impact on the target system caused by the modification is small because only one byte of the target kernel is modified.

- **Step 3: Trigger Code Running at the Kernel Privilege Level:** With the function pointer pointing to the custom code, calling the particular method on a modified device leads to the custom code executing at the kernel privilege level. Unused file operators exposed by the kernel are chosen for minimal changes to the kernel (e.g., operators of `/dev/ptmx`, `/dev/zero` and `/dev/null`). Experiments revealed that the `fsync` operator of `/dev/ptmx` could be used in most cases.

- **Step 4: Map and Read Volatile Kernel Memory:** When the custom code executes at the kernel privilege level, it enumerates pages using the memory management facilities provided by the kernel. Upon enumerating the managed resource in `iomem_resource`, all the system RAM can be found with the starting and ending addresses. For each page in the address range of system RAM, AMExtractor translates the page frame number into the virtual address. The virtual address can be used by a socket read/write function. The extraction process is practically the same as that of LiME. The only difference is that AMExtractor does not rely on the source code of the target device kernel while LiME must be compiled against it.

- **Step 5: Transmit Memory Content via a Kernel Socket:** A kernel socket is used to transmit memory content instead of copying data to user mode. This method minimizes interactions between user space and kernel space, and, thus, has a minimal impact on the target system. The link to a personal computer for memory content transmission can be created by an ADB bridge or Wi-Fi connection and the content sent out via TCP/IP.

- **Step 6: Write Memory Content to a File and Analyze the Content:** The memory content can be received by and written to a file on a separate personal computer for further analysis. The output format of AMExtractor is compatible with many memory analysis toolkits, including Volatility [19].

4.   Implementation

This section presents details about the AMExtractor implementation. Using /dev/kmem instead of a loadable kernel module strengthens the tool, but introduces some challenges. This section describes these challenges and the methods used to solve them.

4.1   Gathering Information

The first step is to dynamically read the kernel symbols. This is not required for tools using loadable kernel modules because they have already been compiled against the source code. However, AMExtractor needs to know the function addresses before it can use /dev/kmem. Fortunately, the Android kernel has a symbol table exported in /proc/kallsyms that provides enough information.

The content of /proc/kallsyms is a simple plaintext file that is easy to parse:

```
c4508000 T stext
c4508000 T _sinittext
c4508000 T _stext
c4508000 T __init_begin
c450805c t __create_page_tables
c4508060 t __enable_mmu_loc
. . .
. . .
```

However, the kernels of most phones restrict the kernel pointer addresses from being printed. Fortunately, /proc/sys/kernel/kptr_restrict can be used to turn off this restriction.

4.2   Using /dev/kmem to Deploy the Trigger

While each loadable kernel module has a well-defined entry, tools based on /dev/kmem do not. Therefore, a technique for triggering code in kernel space is needed. AMExtractor deploys the trigger by modifying one function pointer to the custom code. The triggering process proceeds as follows:

- Find a device created by a Linux kernel for which **struct file_operations** is writable.

- Modify the function pointer of the structure to the custom code.

- Trigger the custom code by calling the corresponding device function.

AMExtractor uses the `/dev/ptmx` device. This device has an operation structure that is always writable because the method of the device is assigned during booting. For certain versions of the Android kernel, `/dev/zero` and `/dev/null` are suitable alternatives.

4.3   Running Code at the Kernel Privilege Level

Triggering the custom code at the kernel privilege level is straightforward. All that is needed is to open the modified device in the previous step and perform the operation, i.e., call `fsync()` on `/dev/ptmx`.

4.4   Mappping and Reading Kernel Memory

This process is nearly the same as that of LiME. When enumerating pages, the `iomem_resource` structure is traversed, the page frame number is translated to the page pointer and the page is mapped to a virtual address. The difference between AMExtractor and LiME lies in the translation method. Tools based on loadable kernel modules can perform the translation using `pfn_to_page`. However, `pfn_to_page` is a macro that is compiled (inline) into other functions. Therefore, it is impossible to reuse `pfn_to_page` in the target kernel and it is necessary to re-implement the logic of the macro. A hard coded implementation of the macro is also infeasible because there are three different memory models in a Android kernel, corresponding to the different implementations of `pfn_to_page`. It is infeasible to enumerate the three implementations and identify the correct one because a wrong choice causes kernel panic. The problem is solved as follows:

- Find a function that contains the `pfn_to_page` macro.

- Reverse-engineer the binary code of the function.

- Re-implement the logic of the macro.

The following code snippet is the disassembled output of the `pfn_to_page` macro in IDA Pro:

```
C024F344 loc_out
C024F344      LDR     R3, =0xC122AFC0
              ; load address of memory_map into r0
C024F348      LDR     R0, [R3]
C024F34C      ADD     R0, R0, R4, LSL #5
              ; r4 contains page frame number
              ; sizeof(struct page) == 32
C024F350      LDMFD   SP, {R4,R5, R11, SP, PC}; return
C024F354
```

Table 2. Tests of forensic soundness.

Device	ROM	Version	LKM	LiME	AMExtractor
Galaxy Nexus	Stock ROM	4.3	No	Failed	Successful
Galaxy Nexus	Paranoid	4.4.4	Yes	Success	Successful
Nexus 4	Stock ROM	4.2.2	No	Failed	Successful
Nexus 4	Stock ROM	5.1.1	No	Failed	Successful
Nexus 5	Stock ROM	4.4.4	No	Failed	Successful
Nexus 5	Stock ROM	5.1.1	No	Failed	Successful
Nexus 5	Self-compiled	5.0	Yes	Successful	Successful
Galaxy S4	Stock ROM	5.0	Yes	Failed	Successful

Obviously, the device uses a flat memory model and the size of the structure page is 32.

4.5 Transmitting Memory Content

Using the page pointer provided by `pfn_to_page`, calling `kmap` maps the page with a virtual address that is useful in the kernel socket. Functions `sock_create_kern` and `kernel_sendmsg` can then be used in the kernel without copying data to user space.

5. Experimental Evaluation

Experiments were conducted using AMExtractor on various devices and the extracted memory was analyzed. The experimental results demonstrate that AMExtractor has wide applicability on the latest firmware versions. Also, the extracted memory was successfully analyzed to detect rootkit activities; this is not possible using traditional user space tools.

5.1 Applicability Evaluation

AMExtractor was tested on four phone models: Galaxy Nexus, Nexus 4, Nexus 5 and Samsung Galaxy S4. Various versions of stock ROMs and third-party ROMs were included in the experiments. Also, a custom kernel with a loadable kernel module option was compiled to test LiME.

As shown in Table 2, AMExtractor successfully dumped the memory contents of all the phones shipped with latest ROMs. The Samsung Galaxy S4 with KNOX enabled was also tested. LiME only succeeded on the self-compiled ROM of Nexus 5 and one third-party ROM of Galaxy Nexus. Although the Galaxy S4 enabled a loadable kernel module in stock ROM, the security enhancements provided by KNOX prevented

Table 3. Tests of forensic soundness.

Acquisition Tool	Number of Pages	Identical Percentage
AMExtractor	484,096	99.06%
LiME	484,096	99.46%
fmem	484,096	80.17%

an unofficial kernel module from being loaded. In contrast, AMExtractor worked well even when KNOX was operational.

5.2 Integrity Evaluation

Forensic soundness is a critical criterion for evaluating a memory forensic tool. Comparisons of the memory dumped by different tools serves as a good proof of soundness. In the evaluation, the dumped memory contents were compared against the memory of the Android emulator to demonstrate integrity. In order to make LiME and fmem work properly, a self-compiled kernel was flashed to Nexus 5. Table 3 presents the results.

Although the memory contents may change during the long dumping process, the memory contents dumped by AMExtractor and LiME were nearly the same. This is not surprising because the same approaches are used to enumerate pages and transmit the memory contents.

6. In-Depth Analysis of Extracted Memory

Volatile memory is valuable in forensic investigations. Efforts have been made to extract information and evidence from volatile memory dumps. A promising application is rootkit detection. Modern malware often uses kernel-level techniques to hide their activities. Kernel rootkits run with the highest operating system privileges. These rootkits can modify the interactions between user mode and kernel mode to cloak themselves. The following code snippet shows a typical Android rootkit that hides its file and process:

```
shell@hammerhead:/ # ps | grep wmr
1|root@hammerhead:/ #
```

Rootkit detection is difficult because a rootkit may be able to subvert the software intended to find it. The sample rootkit above can hide itself when a user issues the **ps** command to list suspicious processes. However, analysis of the full memory dump provided by AMExtractor can reveal evidence of malware activities. Specifically, in the rootkit example above, the package name of the rootkit cannot be found in the `ps` output. However, the rootkit is revealed when the memory extracted by AMExtractor is analyzed:

```
user@PC:~$ vol.py --profile=LinuxGNARM -f ./dump_memory
linux_pslist | grep wmr
Volatility Foundation Volatility Framework 2.4
0xc61d1a40 com.mwr.dz          1657    10064      10064
      0x85170000 2015-09-01 07:24:01
0xc510f840 m.mwr.dz:remote     1670    10064      10064
      0x85dc4000 2015-09-01 07:24:01
```

Note that no processes with the string "wmr" in their names are listed because the rootkit has hidden them. However, when Volatility is used to analyze the AMExtractor memory dump, the processes become visible:

```
user@PC:~$ vol.py --profile=LinuxGNARM -f ./dump_memory
linux_check_syscall_arm
Volatility Foundation Volatility Framework 2.4
/*--------------omitted---------------*/
  0xd7 0xc00cdfd0 sys_setfsuid
  0xd8 0xc00ce0ac sys_setfsgid
  0xd9 0xbf004000 HOOKED
  0xda 0xc0188024 sys_pivot_root
  0xdb 0xc0150e44 sys_mincore
  0xdc 0xc014cb38 sys_madvise

/*--------------omitted---------------*/
```

Furthermore, `sys_call_table` can be analyzed using the memory dump provided by AMExtractor. As seen in the output above, `sys_getdents64` was compromised by malware.

Although AMExtractor can be applied to a wide variety of Android devices, the tool has some limitations. The code executed in the kernel is located in user space. The control flow of the kernel may be redirected to custom code by modifying a function pointer. ARM CPUs provide the *Privileged Execute Never* (PXN) permission to prevent such activities. If a target kernel were to fully utilize PXN functionality, AMExtractor would fail. Moreover, AMExtractor relies on `/proc/kallsyms` and `/dev/kmem`. Fortunately, most Android devices, including all the devices tested, do not use PXN [6].

7.   Conclusions

The AMExtractor tool is designed to acquire volatile physical memory from Android devices with the latest ROMs and firmware. The tool utilizes `/dev/kmem` to perform memory extractions with high integrity and better applicability than existing tools. Memory images dumped by AMExtractor may be exported to other forensic frameworks for deep analysis. Additionally, AMExtractor supports rootkit detection. In an experiment, a rootkit was successfully detected using the Volatility Framework on volatile memory retrieved by AMExtractor.

Acknowledgement

This research was supported by the National Natural Science Foundation of China under Grant No. 61472209 and by the Tsinghua University Initiative Scientific Research Program (20151080436).

References

[1] D. Apostolopoulos, G. Marinakis, C. Ntantogian and C. Xenakis, Discovering authentication credentials in volatile memory of Android mobile devices, *Proceedings of the Twelfth IFIP WG 6.11 Conference on e-Business, e-Services and e-Society*, pp. 178–185, 2013.

[2] K. Barmpatsalou, D. Damopoulos, G. Kambourakis and V. Katos, A critical review of seven years of mobile device forensics, *Digital Investigation*, vol. 10(4), pp. 323–349, 2013.

[3] T. Cannon and S. Bradford, Into the droid: Gaining access to Android user data, presented at the *Defcon Hacking Conference*, 2012.

[4] devik and sd, Linux on-the-fly kernel patching without LKM, *Phrack*, vol. 11(58), 2001.

[5] G. Garcia, Forensic physical memory analysis: An overview of tools and techniques, presented at the *TKK T-110.5290 Seminar on Network Security*, 2007.

[6] X. Ge, H. Vijayakumar and T. Jaeger, Sprobes: Enforcing kernel code integrity in the TrustZone architecture, presented at the *Third Workshop on Mobile Security Technologies*, 2014.

[7] International Data Corporation, Smartphone OS market share, 2015 Q2, Framington, Massachusetts (`www.idc.com/prodserv/smartphone-os-market-share.jsp`), 2015.

[8] I. Kollar, Forensic RAM Dump Image Analyzer, Master's Thesis, Department of Software Engineering, Charles University in Prague, Prague, Czech Republic, 2009.

[9] A. Lineberry, Malicious code injection via `/dev/mem`, presented at the *Black Hat Europe Conference*, 2009.

[10] K. Lucic, Over 27.44% users root their phone(s) in order to remove built-in apps, *Android Headlines*, Valencia, California, November 13, 2014.

[11] H. Macht, Live Memory Forensics on Android with Volatility, Diploma Thesis in Computer Science, Department of Computer Science, Friedrich-Alexander University Erlangen-Nuremberg, Erlangen, Germany, 2013.

[12] T. Muller and M. Spreitzenbarth, FROST – Forensic recovery of scrambled telephones, *Proceedings of the Eleventh International Conference on Applied Cryptography and Network Security*, pp. 373–388, 2013.

[13] OpenSignal, Android fragmentation visualized, London, United Kingdom (`opensignal.com/reports/2015/08/android-fragmen tation`), 2015.

[14] J. Park and S. Choi, Studying security weaknesses of Android systems, *International Journal of Security and its Applications*, vol. 9(3), pp. 7–12, 2015.

[15] J. Stuttgen and M. Cohen, Robust Linux memory acquisition with minimal target impact, *Digital Investigation*, vol. 11(S1), pp. S112–S119, 2014.

[16] H. Sun, K. Sun, Y. Wang, J. Jing and S. Jajodia, TrustDump: Reliable memory acquisition from smartphones, *Proceedings of the Nineteenth European Symposium on Research in Computer Security*, pp. 202–218, 2014.

[17] J. Sylve, A. Case, L. Marziale and G. Richard, Acquisition and analysis of volatile memory from Android devices, *Digital Investigation*, vol. 8(3-4), pp. 175–184, 2012.

[18] V. Thing, K. Ng and E. Chang, Live memory forensics of mobile phones, *Digital Investigation*, vol. 7(S), pp. S74–S82, 2010.

[19] Volatility Foundation, Volatility Framework (`www.volatilityfoun dation.org`), 2016.

[20] S. Willassen, Forensic analysis of mobile phone internal memory, in *Advances in Digital Forensics*, M. Pollitt and S. Shenoi, Springer, Boston, Massachusetts, pp. 191–204, 2005.

[21] W. Xu, Ah! Universal Android rooting is back, presented at the *Black Hat USA Conference*, 2015.

[22] W. Xu and Y. Fu, Own your Android! Yet another universal root, presented at the *Ninth USENIX Workshop on Offensive Technologies*, 2015.

Chapter 20

ADVANCED AUTOMATED DISK
INVESTIGATION TOOLKIT

Umit Karabiyik and Sudhir Aggarwal

Abstract   Open source software tools designed for disk analysis play a critical
role in digital forensic investigations. The tools typically are onerous
to use and rely on expertise in investigative techniques and disk structures. Previous research presented the design and initial development
of a toolkit that can be used as an automated assistant in forensic investigations. This chapter builds on the previous work and presents an
advanced automated disk investigation toolkit (AUDIT) that leverages
a dynamic knowledge base and database. AUDIT has new reporting and
inference functionality. It facilitates the investigative process by handling core information technology expertise, including the choice and
operational sequence of tools and their configurations. The ability of
AUDIT to serve as an intelligent digital assistant is evaluated using a
series of tests that compare it against standard benchmark disk images
and examine the support it provides to human investigators.

Keywords: Digital forensics, disk investigation toolkit, expert systems

1.   Introduction

Forensic investigations of disks are challenging because of the wide variety of available tools. Existing commercial and open source tools must
be considered and new tools are constantly being released. Investigators
are expected to know how to use and configure these tools and they
are required to have a fair degree of information technology expertise.
They must also have considerable knowledge about the technical details
of each new disk type, filesystem and the locations on the disk where
information could be hidden.

This chapter builds on previous work on tool development [10] and
presents an advanced automated disk investigation toolkit (AUDIT) that
has been substantially improved and that leverages a dynamic knowl-

© IFIP International Federation for Information Processing 2016
Published by Springer International Publishing AG 2016. All Rights Reserved
G. Peterson and S. Shenoi (Eds.): Advances in Digital Forensics XII, IFIP AICT 484, pp. 379–396, 2016.
DOI: 10.1007/978-3-319-46279-0_20

edge base and database. AUDIT is designed to support the integration of open source digital forensic tools within the Java Expert System Shell (Jess) [4] in order to enhance disk forensic investigations. The most important internal design change is the ability of AUDIT to dynamically update the knowledge base and database components with information from the expert system component. This substantially extends system functionality. Another important addition is the reporting mechanism that describes the activities of the system, including the inferences involved in decision making, which are useful when explaining how and why certain forensic tools were invoked automatically by AUDIT.

The long-term goal of this research is to create an intelligent assistant that supports forensic investigations. The assumption is that an investigator may not have adequate technical knowledge about the tools that could be used and/or the disk images to be examined. The current version of AUDIT is designed to speed up and enhance disk examinations regardless of the investigator's knowledge and skill levels. AUDIT currently supports the examinations of disks for graphic files, documents, email files and addresses, and also more specialized examinations involving credit card information and social security numbers. AUDIT is designed to be extensible so that new functionality is easily integrated in the existing system.

Researchers caution that the automation of the digital forensic process should not be "dumbed down" by encouraging expert investigators to rely more heavily on automation than their own knowledge [9, 12]. An important goal for AUDIT is to ensure that this does not occur. Although AUDIT incorporates knowledge of tools and disk structures, the assumption is that the investigator is, in fact, skilled in the art of investigations. AUDIT speeds up the technical aspects of the investigative process as suggested in [9]. Experimental evidence obtained from the analysis of several test disk images is used to demonstrate AUDIT's ability to significantly support human investigators.

2.   Related Work

Stallard and Levitt [15] proposed one of the earliest applications of expert systems in the area of digital forensics. They used an expert system with a decision tree to detect network anomalies when attackers attempt to clear traces in log files. Liao et al. [11] also used an expert system to analyze log files; however, their approach leveraged fuzzy logic.

The Open Computer Forensics Architecture (OCFA) [16] is an early example of automating the digital forensic process. OCFA modules work independently on specific file types to extract file content, but the architecture is not designed to search and recover files from a given device.

The Digital Forensics Framework (DFF) is an open source digital investigation tool and development platform [2]. It is a good example of tool integration and collaboration that reduces the burden on investigators when they use task-specific tools. However, the framework still requires knowledge and skills related to integrated tools and disk structures.

Fiwalk [5] is the closest work to that described in this chapter. Fiwalk automates the processing of forensic data to assist users who desire to develop programs that can automatically process disk images. The main differences between Fiwalk and this work is that Fiwalk specifically works on filesystem data and does not incorporate any artificial intelligence techniques. Fiwalk does simplify the task of filesystem analysis, but it requires knowledge about the filesystem and its structure.

Hoelz et al. [8] have developed the MultiAgent Digital Investigation Toolkit (MADIK) to assist forensics experts. They use an artificial intelligence approach where each agent specializes in a different task such as hashing and keyword search. However, the work does not leverage knowledge about forensic tools to assist non-expert users.

Fizaine and Clarke [3] have proposed a crime-dependent automated search engine for digital forensics. This tool focuses on the early stage of an investigation and collects information about specific crimes by assuming that most crimes have similar patterns. However, their approach does not support automated tool integration and configuration.

Commercial tools such as FTK [1] and EnCase [7] also automate examination tasks in order to assist investigators. The tools expect users to be technically skilled and to take training courses in order to use the tools effectively. Furthermore, the tools do not explain the decision making process, leaving this to expert investigators. Additionally, the tools are closed source and are not extensible by users.

At this time, no researchers have specifically addressed the problem of assisting human examiners during the analysis phase of investigations using an expert system. Additionally, existing systems do not support a general open source tool integration process; instead, they only integrate task-specific modules to automate certain activities.

3. AUDIT

Figure 1 presents the architecture of the advanced automated disk investigation toolkit (AUDIT). AUDIT has three components: (i) database (of tasks and tools); (ii) knowledge base; and (iii) core engine (which

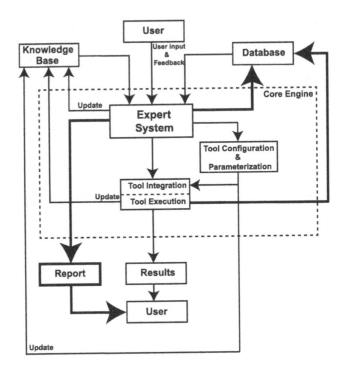

Figure 1.   AUDIT architecture.

includes an expert system, tool integration component and configuration component). The elements in bold indicate major changes from the previous version of AUDIT. Bold boxes show new or substantially changed components. Bold connections show new update capabilities.

The new version of AUDIT can dynamically update its knowledge base (designed using Jess [4]) and its database. These are used by the expert system to configure and integrate the open source tools as needed. The dynamic knowledge base enables AUDIT to evolve during its execution by collecting more information about the target disk and investigation. For example, the database was initially designed to work on single partition disk images. However, this database is now modified based on the expertise in the knowledge base to enable AUDIT to analyze multi-partitioned disks.

3.1   Database

The AUDIT database maintains information about the tools that can be used with AUDIT and the investigative tasks that a typical investigator would perform (Figure 2). The database is designed using the MySQL relational database management system. The database main-

ident	toolname	task	para	p_in	input	p_o	output	p_conf	config	p1	p2	p3	S	F	R
☐ blklsUnalloc	blkls	recovering_unallo...	-A	N/A	?imageP...	>	?outputPath	N/A	N/A	N/A	N/A	N/A	0	0	0
☐ tskRecAlloc	tsk_recover	allocated_space_r...	-a	N/A	?imageP...	N/A	?outputPath	N/A	N/A	N/A	N/A	N/A	0	0	0
☐ tskRecBoth	tsk_recover	alloc/unalloc spac...	-e	N/A	?imageP...	N/A	?outputPath	N/A	N/A	N/A	N/A	N/A	0	0	0
☐ blklsSlack	blkls	recovering_slack_...	-s	N/A	?imageP...	>	?outputPath	N/A	N/A	N/A	N/A	N/A	0	0	0
☐ fileSystemType	fsstat	getting_filesystem...	-t -o	?imgO...	?imageP...	N/A	N/A	N/A	N/A	N/A	N/A	N/A	0	0	0
☐ documentFilesFree...	photorec	document_files_se...	N/A	N/A	?imageP...	/d	?outputPath	/cmd	fileopt.	ever...	doc.e...	freesp...	0	0	0
☐ documentFilesPR	photorec	document_files_se...	N/A	N/A	?imageP...	/d	?outputPath	/cmd	fileopt.	ever...	doc.e...	whole...	0	0	0
☐ emailFilesPR	photorec	email_files_search	N/A	N/A	?imageP...	/d	?outputPath	/cmd	fileopt.	ever...	pst.e...	whole...	0	0	0
☐ emailsBulkExt	bulk_extra...	email_address_sea...	N/A	N/A	?imageP...	-o	?outputPath	-x	all	-e	email	N/A	0	0	0

Figure 2. Sample entries in the Tools table in the AUDIT database.

tains an entry for each tool that specifies configurations, input parameters and outputs for various tasks. Some of the configuration/parameter values are fixed whereas others are variable and can be defined during execution and, thus, changed dynamically.

For example, the **emailsBulkExt** entry specifies that the forensic tool **bulk_extractor** needs parameter -x. The **bulk_extractor** tool can use different scanners for different types of information such as email addresses and credit card numbers. Parameters -x in column **p_conf** and **all** in column **config** disable all scanners. Parameters -e in column **p1** and **email** in column **p2** enable a scanner for email address search.

In the previous version of AUDIT, the database table was static and could not be updated with knowledge collected during an investigation. In the new version, the database table is initially read by the expert system. The fields filled with keywords such as **?imagePath** are recognized by the expert system and changed as needed with the related values collected during the investigation. Note that empty fields are filled with **N/A** values to enable the expert system to recognize the empty fields correctly.

3.2 Knowledge Base

The AUDIT knowledge base is created using the rule-based programming functionality provided by the Java Expert System Shell (Jess). The knowledge base contains facts and rules, some of which are predefined and embedded in the system; others are created during an investigation. Most of the knowledge base is designed for forward chaining, which means that the rules are in the form of IF-THEN statements. However, backward chaining is used when creating inference reports that are discussed later in this chapter. Facts and rules can be added, deleted and modified as needed. In expert systems, facts can be quite simple such as "(John is male)" or more complex such as "(?person (gender ?gen)(age 25)(weight 180))."

```
(defrule update-knowledge-base-rule
(disk-image-path is ?imagePath)
(output-path is ?outputPath)
?toolInfo <- (tools (toolname ?tName)(input ?in)(output ?out))
=>
(if (eq ?in "?imagePath") then (modify ?toolInfo (input ?imagePath))
else (if (eq ?in "?outputPath")
then (modify ?toolInfo (input ?outputPath))))
(if (eq ?out "?outputPath")
then (modify ?toolInfo (output ?outputPath))))
```

Figure 3. Rule for updating the knowledge base.

The new version of AUDIT uses complex facts that were implemented in the previous version. These facts are typically modified frequently via update rules as shown in Figure 3.

```
(MAIN::tools (ident "emailsBulkExt")
(toolname "bulk_extractor")(task "email_address_search")
(input "?imagePath")(p_out "-o")(output "?outputPath")(p_conf "-x")
(config "all")(p1 "-e")(p2 "email"))

(MAIN::tools (ident "emailsBulkExt")
(toolname "bulk_extractor")(task "email_address_search")
(input "/home/utk/part5.img")(p_out "-o")(output "/home/utk/t2")
(p_conf "-x")(config "all")(p1 "-e")(p2 "email"))
```

Figure 4. Original fact before and after an update.

When a user enters a case, all the input and output values of the tool are changed. Figure 4 shows the facts present in the knowledge base before and after an update.

3.3   Core Engine

The core engine controls the execution of the system using the database, knowledge base and user input. The engine reads the tool specifications and investigative tasks from the database and creates new rules and facts as needed. It also links the investigative tasks and tools to the knowledge base and user input and feedback.

In the new version of AUDIT, the database is updated dynamically when new information is gathered by the expert system and after the tools are executed. The update process is performed by the core engine via updating rules. For example, Figure 5 shows the rule that updates the database when the input and output paths are entered by a user.

```
(defrule update-database-rule "updating database"
(disk-image-path is ?imagePath)
(output-path is ?outputPath)
(tools (toolname ?tName)(input ?in)(output ?out))
=>
(updateDatabase ?imagePath "?imagePath"
    "UPDATE TOOLS SET input = ? WHERE input = ?")
(updateDatabase ?outputPath "?outputPath"
    "UPDATE TOOLS SET output = ? WHERE output = ?"))
```

Figure 5. Rule for updating the database.

By doing so, previously-loaded incomplete data in the database (i.e., variables used with the `?<variableName>` structure) become complete and are ready to be used by other rules. In the case of an update after a tool has terminated execution, AUDIT asks the user if the tool performed successfully or if it failed. Based on the feedback received from the user, related fields (S, F and R) for the tool are updated in the database. This information can be used to compare tools against each other; however, this feature is outside the scope of the research and is not discussed in this chapter.

3.4   Expert System

One of the important changes from the previous version of AUDIT is the migration of the expert system shell from CLIPS [14] to Jess [4]. Jess is written in Java and can access all Java APIs. The reasons for the migration were:

- **GUI User Interface:** CLIPS does not have a mechanism to allow users to create a GUI interface for expert system applications. Although extensions to CLIPS exist for this purpose, they are not maintained well, have limited access to CLIPS functionality and are infrequently used by the community.

- **External User Functions:** CLIPS and Jess support users in creating custom external functions. However, CLIPS requires recompilation to integrate functions whereas Jess provides direct access to an external function from a file that contains Jess constructs without recompilation.

- **Database support:** CLIPS does not have direct support for relational database management systems. However, Jess provides full support for most common relational database management systems, many of which are available in Java libraries.

```
(defrule find-email-addresses-BE
(search type is 4) ; email address search
(output-path is ?outputPath)
(disk-image-path is ?imagePath)
(tools (ident "emailsBulkExt")(toolname ?tName)
(task "emails_address_search")(params ?params)(p_in ?par_in)
(input ?input)(p_out ?par_out)(output ?output)(p_conf ?par_conf)
(config ?config)(p1 ?p1)(p2 ?p2)(p3 ?p3))
=>
(my-system-bulk-ex ?tName ?params ?par_in ?input ?par_out
(str-cat ?outputPath "/bulk_ext") ?par_conf ?config ?p1 ?p2 ?p3)
(assert (bulk-extractor is called))
)
```

Figure 6. Rule for email adddress searches.

AUDIT begins its execution by connecting to the database and reading all the data from it. The data is entered into a Jess template called tools. When a specific input, output and task are selected by a user, AUDIT starts running to collect certain information about the input disk (e.g., disk partitioning, disk volume type and disk physical sector size). All this information is also entered into two templates named disk_layout and diskInfo located in the knowledge base. The Jess templates maintain knowledge about tool usage and input disk information in the knowledge base.

AUDIT uses the data from the task column in Figure 2 to activate rules when a specific task needs to be performed using a particular tool. For instance, Figure 6 shows a rule that obtains relevant information from the database to use the bulk_extractor tool for email address searches. The line that begins with (tools (ident ...) represents the pattern in the tools template that is populated with information from the database and knowledge base. Note that (toolname ?tName) is a slot declared in the tools template and ?tName is a variable name declared for this slot in order to store the tool name.

In Figure 6, it is specifically mentioned that the selected task is email address search. This is done by making the (task "emails_address_search") slot part of the pattern. In the event that multiple tools are available for the same type of task, another slot (ident "emailsBulkExt") is added to enable the rule to run only for a specific tool. The same rule can be used for other tools that perform the same task by specifying the ident slot (e.g., (ident "emailsMultigrep")). In fact, the rule can be extended by changing the object of ident to a variable, thus allowing multiple tools to run or choosing a specific

```
bulk_extractor /home/utk/part5.img -o /home/utk/t2/bulk_ext -x all -e email
```

Figure 7. Using **bulk_extractor** for email address search.

tool based on other knowledge. Figure 7 shows the Linux command that AUDIT executes for the selected tool after the rule in Figure 6 is activated.

The new capabilities of AUDIT are illustrated by its ability to implement examinations of multi-partition disks. In these scenarios, the knowledge base has to be changed dynamically because each partition in a disk has to be treated as an individual disk image. The new dynamic database and knowledge base capabilities enable this task to be performed in an efficient manner.

4. Reporting in AUDIT

Popular digital forensics tools (e.g., FTK and EnCase) generate investigation reports help explain the investigative findings using technical details. The reporting mechanism in AUDIT currently does not generate a full technical report; instead, it identifies all the procedures and tools used in the investigation. However, it also describes how and why the tools were used; this feature is not provided by other forensic tools.

AUDIT reports include detailed information about the input disk, the tools invoked and their usage, inference information about what caused a tool to run, and the disk layout in the case of multiple partitions. A report is created automatically and user feedback is added to the report after user interactions. Figure 8 shows a portion of the examination report generated after the analysis of a single partition disk.

Figure 9 shows the report related to one of the rules (slack-space-extraction-rule) that fired during the analysis. The firing facts (facts start with **fact-id**) explain the actions that were previously taken and why. Note that the **fact-id** number is actually the time the fact was (and, thus, the order in which facts were) added to the knowledge base.

The inference report informs the user that AUDIT has learned input, output and task information from facts **f-36**, **f-37** and **f-48**, respectively. The user can see that slack space carving starts only if the expert system knows that allocated space and unallocated space were previously analyzed as evidenced by facts **f-54** and **f-56**. The rule is fired when all the facts are true, including fact **f-10**. Note that this complex fact indicates that the tool **blkls** has been invoked. The execution order is seen clearly in Figure 8. Furthermore, **f-48** is added when the user

```
Single partition disk!
.
.
.
Volume Type = Unknown
Sector Size = 512
Disk (Physical) Block  Size = unknown
Path to the input file - >> /home/utk/ecitTest-3.raw
Path to the output directory - >> /home/utk/t1
Document file search will be performed!
*************************************************************
tsk_recover is running on the input disk image to extract
user created/deleted files! Command line below is used:
tsk_recover -a /home/utk/ecitTest-3.raw
/home/utk/t1/tsk_recover/allocated -o 0
*************************************************************
tsk_recover is running on the input disk image to extract
user created/deleted files! Command line below is used:
tsk_recover /home/utk/ecitTest-3.raw
/home/utk/t1/tsk_recover/unallocated -o 0
*************************************************************
blkls is running on the input disk image to extract
unconventional spaces! Command line below is used:
blkls -s /home/utk/ecitTest-3.raw -o 0 >
/home/utk/t1/slackSpace/slack.dd
*************************************************************
.
.
.
Feedback: Interesting data is not found so far.
```

Figure 8.   Partial examination report for a single partition disk image.

```
Fired Rule Name : MAIN::slack-space-extraction-rule
Firing Facts : [Token: size=7;sortcode=14478322;negcnt=0
f-49 (MAIN::start slack space carving);
f-56 (MAIN::unallocated space analyzed);
f-54 (MAIN::allocated space analyzed);
f-36 (MAIN::disk-image-path is "/home/utk/part5.img");
f-37 (MAIN::output-path is "/home/utk/t1");
f-48 (MAIN::search type is 1);
f-10 (MAIN::tools (ident "blklsSlack") (toolname "blkls")
(task "recovering_slack_space") (params "-s") (p_in "N/A")
(input "/home/utk/part5.img") (p_out ">")
(output "/home/utk/t1") (p_conf "N/A") (config "N/A")
(p1 "N/A") (p2 "N/A") (p3 "N/A"));]
```

Figure 9.   Partial inference report for slack space extraction.

selects "document search" and f-49 is added because a document search analysis rule adds fact f-49 to the knowledge base when it is fired.

Examination and inference reports are useful to expert and non-expert users. For example, expert users could use the inference order to discern the order in which the tools were invoked and parts of the disk were analyzed. They could then redo certain analyses (using information in the command lines reported by AUDIT) with other tools for purposes of verification. From the initial disk analysis by AUDIT, they would already have obtained substantial information about the disk with considerable time savings. On the other hand, non-expert users could, for example, obtain information about the use of a standard carving tool that could accelerate their learning.

5. Testing AUDIT

This section presents the results of tests conducted on AUDIT to explore and evaluate its capabilities. Note that even testing the data hiding process is non-trivial because few, if any, tools are available that support the hiding process.

The experiments involved two groups of tests. The first group of tests ran AUDIT on widely-used tool testing disk images from NIST [13] and the Digital Corpora [6]. The second group of tests compared AUDIT's performance against that of a fairly knowledgeable non-expert human investigator. Specifically, the investigator had moderate technical knowledge and some experience related to forensic investigations. He had good knowledge about open source tools and disk structures. The goal of the tests was to evaluate how AUDIT can support human investigators.

5.1 Experimental Setup

Disk images were created using ForGe [17], a forensics disk image generator. The first step involved setting up a "case," which involved generating a 1 GB disk image with a sector size of 512 bytes and a cluster size of eight sectors or 4 KB. The NTFS filesystem was used for the disk image because it is the only filesystem that is fully supported by ForGe. Note that ForGe does not allow the creation of multi-partition disk images.

The next step was to create a "trivial strategy" representing a directory tree containing files normally found in a filesystem. The directory tree included 31 directories named and structured to mimic a Windows operating system folder hierarchy. All the directories contained ten files, except for the root directory, which contained no files. Thus, each generated disk image had 300 "trivial" files that were not hidden.

Table 1. File extensions and numbers of files in the dataset.

Ext	Qty	Ext	Qty	Ext	Qty	Ext	Qty	Ext	Qty
pdf	257	xls	60	csv	17	log	5	sys	1
html	227	ppt	54	pst	9	png	3	tmp	1
jpg	104	xml	31	unk	7	text	3	dbase3	1
txt	84	gif	27	gz	7	kmz	2	rtf	1
doc	67	ps	22	swf	7	pps	2	kml	1

An initial dataset of 1,000 random unique files was obtained from the Govdocs1 digital corpus [6]. Table 1 lists the file extensions and numbers of corresponding files in the initial dataset.

Table 2. Sizes, types and numbers of horse images.

Size	Ext	Qty	Ext	Qty	Ext	Qty
> 4 KB	jpg	14	jpg	16	png	0
< 4 KB	jpg	11	jpg	5	png	4

Fifty horse images representing illegal images were added to the initial dataset. Table 2 lists the sizes, types and numbers of the horse images. The 300 trivial files were chosen randomly from the resulting set of 1,050 files.

The final step in generating a disk image using ForGe was to create a "secret strategy" representing files that were hidden in forensically-interesting ways. Three hiding methods were used in the tests: (i) placing a file in file slack space; (ii) placing a file in disk unallocated space; and (iii) deleting a file from the filesystem. The files to be hidden were chosen randomly from the set of 1,050 files. The original set of 1,050 files was divided into three subsets: (i) graphic files of horse images less than 4 KB (Type 1); (ii) Outlook email archive (pst) files (Type 2); and (iii) all the remaining files (Type 3). Files less than 4 KB were hidden in the file slack because larger files would not fit due to the fixed cluster size. The possibility of hiding a pst file in each disk image was considered in order to test AUDIT's new email search functionality.

ForGe imposes limitations on how files can be hidden. Specifically, it only allows a maximum of one file to be hidden on disk for each hiding method. Therefore, a file was chosen at random from each of the three subsets and was assigned a hiding method. A Type 1 file was assigned to the file slack hiding method only. Files chosen from the other two subsets were randomly assigned to the unallocated and deleted hiding methods.

Table 3. Number of files in each area on the disks.

	Allocated Space	Deleted Space	Slack Space	Unallocated Space
Disk 1	16	2	1	0
Disk 2	15	3	0	1
Disk 3	16	3	1	2
Disk 4	22	4	0	1
Disk 5	26	1	1	0

Next, it was determined randomly whether or not a hiding method would be used in a test. Thus, a minimum of zero and maximum of three hiding methods were present in each test.

A disk image contained very few hidden files. Since it was unlikely that files would contain credit card or social security numbers, some document files that included such numbers, email addresses and user names were manually hidden in deleted space or unallocated space. Table 3 shows the final numbers of forensically-interesting files contained in the five test cases (disks). Note that the human investigator was unaware of the numbers, types and locations of the hidden files.

5.2   Testing Regiment 1

The first testing regimen conducted experiments in two phases to evaluate AUDIT's performance on the five test disks. In the first phase, the investigator (expert) was asked to use his own skills and open source tools (e.g., SleuthKit and photorec), but not to use AUDIT. In the second phase, the investigator was asked to exclusively use AUDIT. The investigator analyzed the disks in order and was given instructions for each disk that are discussed below. Due to space limitations, only a subset of the results are presented.

For all the disks, the investigator was asked to find graphic and email files on the disks and report the locations of the files. For Disk 1, the exact numbers of graphic and email files were provided.

Table 4 shows the results related to finding graphic and email files. In general, the performance of the investigator was almost as good as that of the investigator using AUDIT. However, better performance was observed when the investigator used AUDIT on Disks 1 and 2. In the case of Disk 1, the investigator (without AUDIT) was unable to report the location of one horse image (located in slack space) because he found the image using a file carver that only handles sector-level information. When analyzing the remaining disks, the investigator (without AUDIT)

Table 4. Finding graphic and email files.

Disk		Graphic Files	Email Files	File Locations
1	Expert	17/17	2/2	×
	AUDIT	17/17	2/2	✓
2	Expert	15/17	2/2	✓
	AUDIT	17/17	2/2	✓
3	Expert	13/13	5/5	✓
	AUDIT	13/13	5/5	✓
4	Expert	21/21	3/3	✓
	AUDIT	21/21	3/3	✓
5	Expert	24/24	2/2	✓
	AUDIT	24/24	2/2	✓

correctly reported the locations because by then he had learned how slack space is analyzed using AUDIT.

In the case of Disk 2, the investigator missed two graphic (png) files because he did not extend his search to all graphic file types. In contrast, when the investigator used AUDIT, he found all the files and their locations.

The investigator was told that Disks 3 and 4 contained hidden document files. His task was to recover the files from the hidden locations and report the file types, numbers of files and their locations. In the case of Disk 3, the investigator was also asked to find files containing credit card numbers, social security numbers and email addresses to test AUDIT's search capabilities. In the case of Disk 4, the investigator was asked to find files containing email addresses. In the case of Disk 5, the investigator was asked to find social security numbers and email addresses.

Table 5. Hidden document files and their locations.

Disk		Qty	Type	Location	Qty	Type	Location
3	Expert	2	pdf	unallocated	2	doc and xls	deleted
	AUDIT	2	pdf	unallocated	2	doc and xls	deleted
4	Expert	1	xls	unallocated	1	pdf	deleted
	AUDIT	1	xls	unallocated	1	pdf	deleted

Table 5 shows that all the hidden files were found regardless of whether or not the investigator used AUDIT.

Table 6 compares the time required by the investigator to analyze each disk without and with AUDIT. Better results were obtained when the

Table 6.   Analysis times with and without AUDIT.

	Disk 1	Disk 2	Disk 3	Disk 4	Disk 5
Expert	9m 26s	13m 45s	25m 10s	18m 45s	26m 13s
AUDIT	7m 55s	5m 33s	12m 8s	10m 16s	20m 51s

investigator used AUDIT. In the case of Disk 1 the investigator was not yet familiar with AUDIT's output, so the times were similar. However, for Disks 2, 3 and 4, the investigator generally took about half as much time when AUDIT was used. The time required when AUDIT was used on Disk 5 was surprising until it was determined that the investigator did not scan the AUDIT output of allocated files until very late.

Table 7.   Sample benchmark disk images.

Disk Name	Category	Target	Source
dfr-04-fat	Deleted file recovery	36	NIST
dfr-05-ntfs	Deleted/fragmented file recovery	7	NIST
L0_Documents	Non-fragmented carving	7	NIST
L0_Graphics	Non-fragmented carving	6	NIST
L1_Documents	Fragmented file carving	7	NIST
L1_Graphics	Fragmented file carving	6	NIST
nps-2010-emails	Email address recovery	30	Digital Corpora

5.3   Testing Regimen 2

The second testing regimen evaluated the performance of AUDIT on benchmark disk images as well as on multi-partition disk images. Table 7 lists the sample benchmark disk images. AUDIT was applied to the first two disk images to recover several non-fragmented files with non-ASCII file names from dfr-04-fat and to recover several fragmented and deleted files from dfr-05-ntfs. All 36 deleted files, which were located across multiple partitions, were recovered from Disk 1. AUDIT also recovered all seven files from Disk 2. Although fragmented file recovery is typically a difficult task, it was not the case in this situation.

The file carving functionality of AUDIT was also tested. AUDIT was applied to the disk images L0_Documents and L0_Graphics in order to carve non-fragmented documents and graphic files, respectively. The filesystems in both disk images were corrupted, so no metadata information was available. Nevertheless, AUDIT was used to successfully carve all the files at the correct locations as in the disk creation reports [13].

The next two test cases evaluated the use of AUDIT when carving sequentially-fragmented documents and graphic files from the disk images, L1_Documents and L1_Graphics, respectively. AUDIT was used to successfully carve all the sequentially-fragmented files (seven documents and six graphic files). All the contents of the carved files were complete when compared against the disk image reports [13].

The last test case evaluated the email address search functionality of AUDIT. The test disk image nps-2010-emails contained 30 email addresses located in several file types, including documents and compressed files.

AUDIT invoked the bulk_extractor tool to find the email addresses. It retrieved all the email addresses in the narrative file nps-2010-emails, except for one email address (plain_utf16@textedit.com) with non-ASCII content. AUDIT also automatically recovered email addresses from documents; a visual check showed one of the addresses was in a txt file. This demonstrates the power of AUDIT's tool integration functionality.

6.   Conclusions

AUDIT is a unique extensible tool that is designed to configure, integrate and use open source tools for disk investigations while leveraging expert system capabilities. The principal contribution of this research is the enhanced design and a new implementation of the AUDIT toolkit. AUDIT is the first tool to use an expert system to automate the technical aspects of disk investigations at an expert investigator level. The new implementation better automates several tasks using open source tools for general and specific search tasks. These include the determination of the level of knowledge of the investigator and the use of this information to make further choices during a disk investigation; use of domain-specific knowledge embedded in the knowledge base and database to configure and parameterize the appropriate digital forensic tools for execution; execution of the appropriate tools at the correct times; and execution of tools based on the dynamic knowledge obtained from previous executions. Thus, AUDIT supports the integrated use of digital forensic tools.

The second contribution of this research is that AUDIT now creates two reports for an investigator, an inference report and an examination report. The inference report specifies the logic of how and why certain tools were automatically used; none of the existing tools provides such information. The examination report details the findings related to the analysis.

The third contribution of this research is the significant testing that shows how AUDIT can support the investigative process by handling core information technology expertise, including the choice and operational sequence of tools and their proper configurations.

AUDIT is already a very effective digital forensic assistant. As the scope and functionality of AUDIT are extended and refined, it may well become an indispensable tool for digital forensic investigations. The latest version of AUDIT is available at `sourceforge.net/projects/audit-toolkit`.

Acknowledgement

The authors wish to thank Clayton Butler for his help with this research.

References

[1] AccessData, Forensic Toolkit (FTK), Lindon, Utah (`www.access data.com/solutions/digital-forensics/forensic-toolkit-f tk`), 2016.

[2] ArxSys, Digital Forensics Framework, Le Kremlin-Bicetre, France (`www.digital-forensic.org`), 2016.

[3] J. Fizaine and N. Clarke, A crime-dependent automated search engine for digital forensics, *Advances in Communications, Computing, Networks and Security*, vol. 10, pp. 73–87, 2013.

[4] E. Friedman-Hill, Jess, the Rule Engine for the Java Platform, Sandia National Laboratories, Livermore, California (`www.jessrules.com`), 2016.

[5] S. Garfinkel, Automating disk forensic processing with SleuthKit, XML and Python, *Proceedings of the Fourth IEEE International Workshop on Systematic Approaches to Digital Forensic Engineering*, pp. 73–84, 2009.

[6] S. Garfinkel, P. Farrell, V. Roussev and G. Dinolt, Bringing science to digital forensics with standardized forensic corpora, *Digital Investigation*, vol. 6(S), pp. S2–S11, 2009.

[7] Guidance Software, EnCase Forensic, Pasadena, California (`www.guidancesoftware.com/encase-forensic.htm`), 2016.

[8] B. Hoelz, C. Ralha and R. Geeverghese, Artificial intelligence applied to computer forensics, *Proceedings of the ACM Symposium on Applied Computing*, pp. 883–888, 2009.

[9] J. James and P. Gladyshev, Challenges with Automation in Digital Forensic Investigations, Digital Forensic Investigation Research Group, University College Dublin, Dublin, Ireland, 2013.

[10] U. Karabiyik and S. Aggarwal, AUDIT: Automated disk investigation toolkit, *Journal of Digital Forensics, Security and Law*, vol. 9(2), pp. 129–144, 2014.

[11] N. Liao, S. Tian and T. Wang, Network forensics based on fuzzy logic and expert system, *Computer Communications*, vol. 32(17), pp. 1881–1892, 2009.

[12] M. Meyers and M. Rogers, Computer forensics: The need for standardization and certification, *International Journal of Digital Evidence*, vol. 32(2), 2004.

[13] National Institute of Standards and Technology, The CFReDS Project, Gaithersburg, Maryland (www.cfreds.nist.gov), 2016.

[14] SourceForge, CLIPS: A Tool for Building Expert Systems (www.clipsrules.sourceforge.net), 2016.

[15] T. Stallard and K. Levitt, Automated analysis for digital forensic science: Semantic integrity checking, *Proceedings of the Nineteenth Annual Computer Security Applications Conference*, pp. 160–167, 2003.

[16] O. Vermaas, J. Simons and R. Meijer, Open computer forensic architecture a way to process terabytes of forensic disk images, in *Open Source Software for Digital Forensics*, E. Huebner and S. Zanero (Eds.), Springer, New York, pp. 45–67, 2010.

[17] H. Visti, ForGe: Forensic test image generator (www.github.com/hannuvisti/forge), 2015.

Printed in the United States
By Bookmasters